"African politics is often reduced to primordial ethnic affiliations tempered by electoral patronage. This book effectively challenges this conventional wisdom by adopting and refining an approach to political affiliations first developed to understand European and US politics as involving socioeconomic cleavages (including ethnic ones) refracted through regional and local lenses. Africa turns out to be less distinctive after all."

John Agnew, co-author of *Mapping Populism: Taking Politics to the People*

"Catherine Boone convincingly shows that spatial inequalities structure political competition in Africa, much as they do in other parts of the world. This is a must-read for all scholars of comparative politics."

Melissa Rogers, Claremont Graduate University

"This kind of focus on the territoriality of political and economic administration is rare in political science but Boone shows just how powerful it can be. If you buy the argument – and I do – this understanding either displaces or profoundly changes how we think about ethnicity and its supposedly defining political and economic role on the continent."

Antoinette Handley, University of Toronto

"This is a big book that promises to have a major impact. The book seems well positioned to shake up – disrupt, in tech speak – the political science literature on Africa. Among other remarkable strengths, the book offers exciting new data on regional voting patterns; broad and deep coverage of colonial period and the inequalities it created; and a convincing critique of micro, clientelist, ethnic approaches."

Ben Schneider, Massachusetts Institute of Technology

Inequality and Political Cleavage in Africa

This pathbreaking work integrates African countries into broader comparative theories of how spatial inequality shapes political competition over the construction of markets, states, and nations. Existing literature on African countries has found economic cleavages, institutions, and policy choices to be of low salience in national politics. This book inverts these arguments. Boone trains our analytic focus on the spatial inequalities and territorial institutions that structure national politics in Africa, showing that regional cleavages find expression in both electoral competition and policy struggles over redistribution, sectoral investment, market integration, and state design. Leveraging comparative politics theory, Boone argues that African countries' regional and core–periphery tensions are similar to those that have shaped national economic integration in other parts of the world. Bringing together electoral and economic geography, the book offers a new and powerful map of political competition on the African continent.

Catherine Boone is Professor of Comparative Politics at the London School of Economics and Political Science. Her works include *Property and Political Order in Africa: Land Rights and the Structure of Politics* (2014), *Political Topographies of the African State* (2003), and *Merchant Capital and the Roots of State Power in Senegal* (1993).

Cambridge Studies in Comparative Politics

General Editor

Kathleen Thelen, *Massachusetts Institute of Technology*

Associate Editors

Lisa Blaydes, *Stanford University*
Catherine Boone, *London School of Economics*
Thad Dunning, *University of California, Berkeley*
Anna Grzymala-Busse, *Stanford University*
Torben Iversen, *Harvard University*
Stathis Kalyvas, *University of Oxford*
Melanie Manion, *Duke University*
Prerna Singh, *Brown University*
Dan Slater, *University of Michigan*
Susan Stokes, *Yale University*
Tariq Thachil, *University of Pennsylvania*
Erik Wibbels, *University of Pennsylvania*

Series Founder

Peter Lange, *Duke University*

Editor Emeritus

Margaret Levi, *Stanford University*

Other Books in the Series

Christopher Adolph, *Bankers, Bureaucrats, and Central Bank Politics: The Myth of Neutrality*
Michael Albertus, *Autocracy and Redistribution: The Politics of Land Reform*
Michael Albertus, *Property without Rights: Origins and Consequences of the Property Rights Gap*
Santiago Anria, *When Movements Become Parties: The Bolivian MAS in Comparative Perspective*
Ben W. Ansell, *From the Ballot to the Blackboard: The Redistributive Political Economy of Education*
Ben W. Ansell and Johannes Lindvall, *Inward Conquest: The Political Origins of Modern Public Services*
Ben W. Ansell and David J. Samuels, *Inequality and Democratization: An Elite-Competition Approach*
Ana Arjona, *Rebelocracy: Social Order in the Colombian Civil War*
Leonardo R. Arriola, *Multi-Ethnic Coalitions in Africa: Business Financing of Opposition Election Campaigns*

Continued after the index

Inequality and Political Cleavage in Africa

Regionalism by Design

CATHERINE BOONE
London School of Economics and Political Science

Shaftesbury Road, Cambridge CB2 8EA, United Kingdom

One Liberty Plaza, 20th Floor, New York, NY 10006, USA

477 Williamstown Road, Port Melbourne, VIC 3207, Australia

314–321, 3rd Floor, Plot 3, Splendor Forum, Jasola District Centre, New Delhi – 110025, India

103 Penang Road, #05–06/07, Visioncrest Commercial, Singapore 238467

Cambridge University Press is part of Cambridge University Press & Assessment, a department of the University of Cambridge.

We share the University's mission to contribute to society through the pursuit of education, learning and research at the highest international levels of excellence.

www.cambridge.org
Information on this title: www.cambridge.org/9781009441636
DOI: 10.1017/9781009441667

© Catherine Boone 2024

This publication is in copyright. Subject to statutory exception and to the provisions of relevant collective licensing agreements, no reproduction of any part may take place without the written permission of Cambridge University Press & Assessment.

First published 2024

A catalogue record for this publication is available from the British Library

A Cataloging-in-Publication data record for this book is available from the Library of Congress

ISBN 978-1-009-44163-6 Hardback
ISBN 978-1-009-44161-2 Paperback

Cambridge University Press & Assessment has no responsibility for the persistence or accuracy of URLs for external or third-party internet websites referred to in this publication and does not guarantee that any content on such websites is, or will remain, accurate or appropriate.

Why countries have the political cleavages they do and why those cleavages change [or not] are among the enduring mysteries of comparative politics.

Ronald Rogowski 1987: 1121

One of the biggest things that this country has to live with, if it does not address it at this point in time, is the gross inequality between regions, zones and parts of this country. That is a matter that has to be addressed at this particular time. We should not leave that problem to future generations.

Abdul Bahari Ali Jillo, MP for Isiolo South
Kenya Hansard, June 20, 2020, p. 1455

Contents

List of Figures	*page* xi
List of Tables	xiii
Preface and Acknowledgments	xv
1 Economic Inequalities and Territorial Oppositions in African Politics	1
2 Region and Regionalism in African Politics	25
3 Endowment, Institutions, and Spatial Inequality: Regions by Design	48
4 Regional Blocs and Bloc Voting in National Elections *with Juliette Crespin-Boucaud, PhD*	90
5 Regional Hierarchies and Winning Coalitions	149
6 Territorial Oppositions in African Politics	168
7 Regionalism and the National Agenda	195
8 Conclusion: Inequality and Political Cleavage in African Politics	223
Appendices	243
References	281
Index	321

Figures

1.1 Interpersonal and spatial inequality in African countries, 2012 (with comparison to some other high inequality countries)	*page* 5
1.2 Territorially divided states: Theoretical expectations and African exemplars	9
1.3 Regional cleavages and national politics: Causes and effects	20
2.1 Spatial inequality in African countries compared to other countries, by world region	33
3.1 Uneven development and territorial institutions bring spatial inequalities to the fore in politics	52
3.2 Tiered institutional structure and regional economic differentiation in an African colony	65
3.3 Persistence of Native Authority (NA) borders in 2012 Admin2 units: Ghana and Nigeria	73
4.1 Ghana, Kenya, Malawi, and Zambia: Persistent electoral blocs	101
4.2 Côte d'Ivoire, South Africa, Uganda, and Zimbabwe: Persistent electoral blocs and oppositional zones	102
4.3 Nigeria: Persistent electoral blocs	103
4.4 Tanzania, Cameroon, and Mali: Persistent electoral blocs and oppositional zones	105
4.5 (a–c) Bloc advantage and disadvantage (composite 1990s through 2010s)	114
4.6 (a–b) Colonial producer regions and electoral bloc overlay (panels a and b)	125
4.7 Ethnic profile of the electoral blocs (2010s)	134
5.1 Bloc political dominance: Bloc types I–IV	153
6.1 Kenya electoral blocs, disparities in regional GDP proxy and education	171

xi

List of Figures

6.2 Zambia electoral blocs, disparities in regional GDP proxy and education — 177

6.3 Malawi electoral blocs, disparities in regional GDP proxy and education — 182

6.4 Uganda electoral blocs, disparities in regional GDP proxy and education — 187

7.1 Regional preferences over state design — 218

A.1 Interpersonal and spatial inequality in African countries using population-weighted CoV — 243

A.2 Spatial inequality in African countries (unweighted by population) — 244

E.1 Overlap of electoral blocs and colonial-era producer zones: Cameroon, Ghana, Kenya, and Malawi — 274

E.2 Overlap of electoral blocs and colonial-era producer zones: Mali, Nigeria, South Africa, and Tanzania — 275

E.3 Overlap of electoral blocs and colonial-era producer zones: Zambia and Zimbabwe — 276

Tables

3.1	Constituencies (2000) nested within Admin2 units (2000)	*page* 75
4.1	Advantage of electoral blocs (including oppositional zones) over non-blocs in the same country	111
4.2	Colonial-era producer regions: Percentage of colonial producer region in a persistent electoral bloc or oppositional zone today, and continuing sectoral specializations	118
4.3	Producer profile of electoral blocs in 2010	122
4.4	Electoral bloc overlap with colonial-era Admin1s	130
4.5	Ethnic profile of units comprising the persistent electoral blocs (2010s)	135
5.1	National winning coalitions: Winner bloc plus non-blocs	159
A.1	Spatial inequality averages by world region, 2010	245
B.1	Overview of twelve countries	247
B.2	Electoral data and bloc boundaries overview	249
B.3	Demographic and health surveys	252
C.1	"Colonial Admin1" corresponding units	260
C.2	Global Moran's I (vote shares)	262
C.3	Area of all blocs, combined, as percentage of national area (sq. km)	264
C.4	Bloc population density in 1990, 2000, and 2015, compared to national averages (w/o capital city)	264
C.5	Summary of electoral bloc characteristics, with stability of regional inequalities over time and consistency across indicators	267
D.1	Producer profiles of the non-bloc regions: Export and traded food crops	271
F.1	Bloc political dominance	277
F.2	Gap magnitude: Relative luminosity gap between the bloc ranked first and the bloc ranked second in 1992, 2000, and 2013	278

Preface and Acknowledgments

This book argues that *regionalism* – defined as political competition along the lines of subnational regions defined roughly at the provincial level – animates national politics in African countries. This happens just as it does in territorially-divided countries in other parts of the world, and for largely the same reasons. Economic inequality among regions gives rise to rival preferences over redistribution, growth strategies, market integration, and state design. These fuel regional cleavages, producing political dynamics that go far in defining development trajectories of national systems as a whole. Challenges of national integration and social cleavage that have often been attributed to ethnic politics, or to politicians' opportunistic manipulation of ethnicity are, in this account, traceable to spatial inequalities and the territorial institutions that bring these to the fore.

It emerges from a research project I led at the London School of Economics, "Spatial Inequalities in African Political Economy" (2019–2022) (ESRC ES/R005753/1), which drew together the contributions of many persons. Professor Michael Wahman (Political Science, Michigan State University), a co-principal investigator (PI), contributed to the conceptualization, identification, and write-up of the original regional voting blocs analysis, which was published in *Political Geography* (Boone, Wahman, Kyburz, & Linke 2022). That coauthored paper is a precursor to the work on these countries that appears in Chapters 4 and 6. Stephan Kyburz (Ph.D., Economics, University of Bern) did the first version of the electoral bloc analysis in 2020, with essential contributions from co-PI Andrew Linke (Geography, University of Utah), who led us in our first efforts to use spatial analysis to make sense of the African electoral data. At the LSE, co-PI Leigh Gardner contributed to the historical boundary analysis (Chapter 3), along with her coauthor Jutta Bolt (University of Groningen) and LSE Ph.D. student in Economic History, Jennifer Kohler. Field work included research on land politics in Tanzania in 2011 and 2012,

xv

xvi *Preface and Acknowledgments*

on the land sector in Côte d'Ivoire from 2015 to 2020, in Kenya from 2017 to 2022 on devolution and the land settlement schemes. The Kenya settlement scheme mapping project was made possible by a collaboration with Dr. Fibian Lukalo at the National Land Commission of Kenya and Professor Sandra Joireman, University of Richmond.

Juliette Crespin-Boucaud (Ph.D., Paris School of Economics) was a doctoral researcher on the Spatial Inequalities project in 2021 and 2022. Juliette played a key role in the conceptualization, analysis, and interpretation of the spatial inequality measures that feature here, and is coauthor of Chapter 4. Rebecca Simson (Ph.D., Economic History, LSE) collaborated on an early working paper on spatial inequality in African countries (Boone & Simson 2019). Johan Iddawela (Ph.D., Geography, LSE) did the first version of the boundary analysis in 2019. Cristin Fergus (Ph.D., International Development, LSE) prepared electoral data and file structures in 2018 and organized and prepared the final versions of many of the tables and figures. Linchuan Xu (Economics, LSE) made the final version of the maps in QGIS. Yuezhou Yang (Ph.D., International Development, LSE) collected data on Tanzania and produced the overview of country indicators that appears in Appendix Table B.1. Michaela Collord (Ph.D., Oxford, Politics, now at the University of Nottingham) worked as a postdoc on the Tanzania and Uganda cases for this project in 2020 and 2021. The assistance of LSE undergraduate and M.Sc. students Eva Richter, Jonathan Karl, and Victor Selanius was invaluable. My coauthors in Boone, Bado, Dion, and Zigbo (2021) and Boone, Lukalo, and Joireman (2021) contributed to the analyses of land politics that feature in Chapter 7.

Dann Naseemullah, Alexandra Hartman, William Hurst, Omar McDoom, and Elliott Green offered welcome feedback at a book workshop hosted at the LSE in February 2022. LSE undergraduates in GV334, "Comparative Politics of Inequality," have read several sections of this work. David Soskice, Clark Gibson, Shaheen Mozaffar, Melissa Rogers, Sebastian Elischer, Joan Ricart-Huguet, Camilo Acero-Vargas, Jorich Loubser, Nic Cheeseman, Michaela Collord, Franz Borge Weitze, Faustin Maganga, Alexander Trubowitz, Peter Trubowitz, and four anonymous reviewers also provided feedback on earlier versions of all or parts of this work. I also incurred many debts in giving talks on this project in the political science departments of Yale, University of Michigan, University of California at Berkeley, University of California, San Diego, University of Gothenburg, University of Geneva, Oxford, LSE, and the Institut Barcelona d'Estudis Internacionals; at the Harvard Academy for International and Area Studies, the African Studies Centre at Leiden University, and the British Institute in Eastern Africa in Nairobi; as well as at annual meetings of the American Political Science Association, the African Studies Association, and the Society for the Advancement of Socioeconomics. Pablo Beramendi offered valuable feedback as the manuscript was going to press. At CUP, Rachel Blaifeder has been the ideal editor.

My greatest thanks go to Peter Trubowitz, who always believed that this work would come together as a book, and to my sons, Joshua and Alexander.

1

Economic Inequalities and Territorial Oppositions in African Politics

> Geography has been a blind spot for political scientists.
>
> Rodden 2010: 322

> Poor countries are not uniformly poor.
>
> Azam 2006: 213

INTRODUCTION

Socioeconomic inequality is very high in African countries, but very little systematic scholarly attention has been given to the political effects of this. Many attributes of African economies predict high inequality, including natural resource dependence, trade openness, and low levels of economic development. Economic theory long held that, under these conditions, development itself would *increase* socioeconomic inequality (Kuznets 1963; Williamson 1965). Because so much social science research takes inequality as an indicator of latent social conflict, simple deduction might lead one to expect rancor and division over economic policy and redistributive issues to structure national political life in African countries. Yet much of political science writing on African countries argues that structural socioeconomic disparities are *not* politicized in any systematic way, except in some extreme cases of civil war, and has pointed a finger at *cultural* or communal differences to explain political division.[1] This presents a puzzle that has bedeviled several generations of research on African political economy. Do socioeconomic cleavages and

---

[1] Structural grievances are those derived from an individual or group's disadvantaged position in society. Thus, Boix (2003), Acemoglu and Robinson (2006), and Svolik (2012) argue that economic inequality can be taken as a proxy for the threat of mass opposition to authoritarian regimes (Thomson 2018: 1598).

economic interests structure national political life in African countries, as theory would predict? If so, how, and why?

Existing work in Africa-centered political science has attempted to solve the inequality puzzle by arguing that in African countries, political elites manipulate deep-rooted ethnic identities to channel politics along the lines of patron–client relationships, undercutting possibilities for the mobilization of class-based or issue-based politics. Ethnic clientelism focuses the political energies of individuals and communities on the micropolitics of retail-level provision of clinics and boreholes, sidelining policy issues of national consequence. Most scholarly work thus suggests that socioeconomic cleavages do not structure national political debate, or may do so only at the margins, *because of* the intense salience of ethnic politics. What scholars have read as the weakness of electoral pressures for development-oriented policies in African countries is taken as evidence in support of this view.

This book advances a different theory. I argue that while scholars have not found strongly politicized class cleavages in most African countries, they have missed the dominant form of inequality politics in African countries. At the national level, the most politically salient form of economic inequality is *spatial inequality*. I theorize that spatial inequalities between regions go far in structuring political competition in national elections, and that these same regional cleavages underpin the enduring salience of competition around territorially targeted economic policy and issues of constitutional design.

This theory is rooted in comparative political economy (CPE) literatures on why, how, and which geographic inequalities become salient in national politics. Most such work has been developed through research on European and Latin American countries. In this book, I show that this regional perspective on political economy resonates strongly in most African countries.

In most African countries, regional economic differentiation and inequality are strongly accentuated by territorial institutions that channel both political representation and state action. Strongly regionalized economies have developed within the framework of strongly territorial political institutions. Much theory in CPE predicts that, where spatial inequalities are high and territorial institutions are strong, regionalist interests and political strategies tend to predominate over programmatic, state-wide strategies across many policy and governance arenas (Beramendi 2012; Rogers 2016). I find that this is indeed the case in much of Africa. What classic works in social cleavage theory call the "spatial–territorial dimension of politics" is a critical but largely unobserved and undertheorized driver of political competition in African countries (Lipset & Rokkan 1967; Rokkan 1971; Caramani 2004). These regional dynamics transcend the spatial and temporal scale of individual patron–client ties and local ethnic identities that are observed in individual acts of voting or one-off clientelistic exchanges within electoral constituencies. By placing microlevel behavior in a wider context, this book brings the larger stakes and purposes of national politics into focus.

Introduction 3

Significant research programs in comparative politics associate stark regional inequalities with distinctive sets of political and economic challenges. In countries as diverse as Italy, Spain, Germany, Indonesia, and China, regionalized competition exerts a pull on the overall character of national politics, development trajectories, and patterns of policy competition. Around the world, economic inequality across subnational regions is strongly associated with core–periphery tensions, tensions between wealth-generating and lagging regions, problems of national integration (including the high political salience of ethnic and regional identities), and tensions arising from divergent regional policy preferences (Rogers 2016). In cross-national studies, underprovision of public goods, weak programmatic politics, the prevalence of accountability-eroding electoral clientelism, and civil conflict around questions of territorial dominance or autonomy are sociopolitical ills that have been attributed, at least in part, to high levels of spatial inequality. The relationship of "ethnicity" to these outcomes is variable and contingent, even within the context of one country.

In African countries, the lack of systematic and reliable empirical data at the subnational level has made it difficult to develop and test theories linking spatial inequalities and political outcomes. An earlier generation of qualitative political scientists and historians accorded considerable importance to the role of regional tensions in shaping politics in the 1950s through the 1970s, and these insights have fed into contemporary research that considers regional politics and questions of national integration.[2] So far, however, this type of analysis has not congealed into theories of structure and variation in national-level electoral geography, or of territorial dynamics in African politics.

From the 1990s onward, much scholarship on African politics has downplayed spatial inequalities and has seen politicized *cultural* heterogeneity as the cause of political division and of the prevalence of clientelism over substantive policy appeals in elections. Influential political sociologists and economists, such as Donald Horowitz (1985) and Easterly and Levine (1997), along with a generation of scholars focused on elections and individual voting behavior in the multiparty era, identified ethnicity as an overwhelmingly determinant force in African politics *and* an ideological force that is orthogonal to – that is, that cuts across and neutralizes – programmatic economic interests and socioeconomic cleavages. Many of these scholars would grant that ethnicity produces a territorial or regional effect when coethnics are spatially clustered, but the spatial clustering itself is often portrayed as an *effect* of ethnicity, a prepolitical expression of ideological or cultural preference rooted in the distant past, and exogenous to politics. Institutions and economic geography are usually taken to be invariant (or controlled for) within and across countries. Two key shapers of structure and variation in political competition within and across nations – institutions and economic geography – are thus left out of the analysis.

---

[2] See, for example, Englebert 2003, 2005; Forrest 2004; Albaugh 2011; Arriola 2013; Morse 2014; Bates 2017; Rabinowitz 2018; LeVan 2019.

Economic Inequalities and Territorial Oppositions in African Politics

This work leverages CPE theories of social cleavage, uneven development, and institutions to propose a theory of the sources and correlates of regional cleavage in national politics. I will argue that these give structure to electoral competition at the national level and shape the policy content of the national political agenda in many, perhaps most, African countries.

A theory of regional cleavages as the driver of national politics links the study of politics in Africa to classic works on social cleavage and political economy in other parts of the world. This opens the door to significant revisions of prevailing axioms in the study of African politics. Many inferences about national-level politics that are extrapolated directly from micro studies of electoral behavior ignore the ways in which factors that are unobserved in micro studies – including highly uneven patterns of economic development and strongly territorial political institutions – shape politics at the national level. I argue here that economic geography and political institutions play a significant role in shaping political interests and identities, producing cohesion and division in these over time, and in defining the mechanisms and dynamics by which local-level clientelism may (or may not) be subsumed within regional-level electoral cleavages. My analysis replaces common arguments about volatility and fluidity in national political alignments in Africa with theory and evidence of persistent cleavage structures over time. This more expansive theoretical framing sharpens our ability to draw political inferences from existing descriptions of ethnic and electoral politics and reveals the larger stakes in political and policy debates that have long been sidelined in political science studies of African countries.

In an influential study, Herbst (2000) pointed to political divisions along geographic lines in African countries when he wrote of the stark cleavage between capital cities and rural hinterlands. Herbst depicted hinterlands as largely resistant to incorporation into the national fold, and to the "rural areas" as constituting a largely undifferentiated and recalcitrant periphery in most countries. Here, I invert Herbst's model by locating dynamic drivers of politics *in the regions*. What Herbst refers to generically as the "hinterlands" are treated here as segmented and differentiated landscapes composed of regions marked by economic inequalities and power differentials, variable alignments vis-à-vis the center, distinctive production profiles and economic interests, and varying modes and degrees of integration into the national economy. Relations among such regions are potentially competitive, with tension arising from rival policy preferences and competing visions of state- and economy-building. National regimes are shown to be rooted to a very significant extent in regional strongholds, to achieve national predominance on the basis of predominantly rural electoral coalitions, and to be invested politically in the prosperity of regionally specific sectors of the economy (Rabinowitz 2018). In many African countries, the persistent lines of social cleavage that are visible at the national level are *regional* in nature, often taking forms that are familiar to scholars of regional competition and cleavage in other parts of the world.

1.1 INEQUALITY STRUCTURES IN AFRICAN COUNTRIES

This work focuses on territorial oppositions – the divergent interests and priorities of subnational regions in relation to, and in competition with, each other – that grow out of the process of building a national state and economy. It argues that institutions contribute to the structuring of these territorial differences and inequalities, and that institutions work to bring these inequalities to the fore in national political competition.

My point of departure is the dramatic extent of both interpersonal income inequality and regional economic disparities in most African countries. Not only are some of the world's highest levels of interpersonal income inequality found in sub-Saharan African countries, but levels of spatial inequality among regions (provinces) in most African countries are *also* extremely high. Economic disparities across subnational regions in most African countries are higher than they are in textbook cases of high spatial inequality featured in the CPE literature – including Spain, the United States, Mexico, and Argentina.

These strong inequality patterns are captured in the scatterplot in Figure 1.1, adapted from Rogers (2016). High inequality countries from around the world – including Brazil, Mexico, Malaysia, and the USA – are featured in orange, for comparison.

The vertical axis captures interpersonal income inequality. Measured by national Gini coefficients (as shown), Africa's levels of income inequality are among the highest in the world, even exceeding Latin America's stratospheric

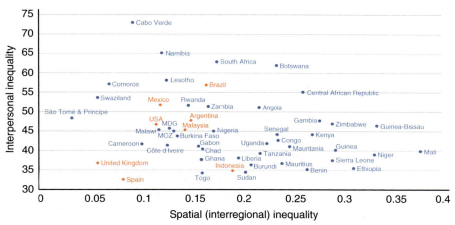

FIGURE 1.1 Interpersonal and spatial inequality in African countries, 2012 (with comparison to some other high inequality countries)
Notes and sources: The Y-axis is the coefficient of variation in adjusted nighttime luminosity across provinces (Admin1 regions), unweighted for population, in 2012 (Lessmann & Seidel 2015, 2017). The X-axis is Gini of interpersonal income inequality (Milanovic 2014). See Appendix Figure A1.1 for the population weighted data.

6   *Economic Inequalities and Territorial Oppositions in African Politics*

levels by some measures.[3] By the Gini index of household consumption expenditure for 2008, Africa was the world's most unequal macroregion, with a Gini of 67 compared to 50 for Latin America and the Caribbean.[4] These high levels of interpersonal inequality are a long-standing feature of economic structure in African countries and have been traced back to the 1950s, when the earliest data are available (Milanovic 2014: 11).

The income Gini captures the familiar picture of African societies as polarized between small, wealthy elites in urban, formal sector employment (i.e., positions in the higher echelons of the state, and in top private and multinational firms) on the one hand, and large majorities trapped in low-productivity rural livelihoods (agriculture, pastoralism, etc.) and the informal sector. As van de Walle explained (2009), the smallness and weakness of the middle class is a corollary of this bifurcation. National-level policy factors, including regressive taxation structure and very low levels of income redistribution, contribute to high levels of interpersonal inequality, but the main drivers lie on the production side. There is strong variation across African countries: Those with higher levels of economic development tend to score higher on the Gini index.[5] This is consistent with Kuznets' prediction that development itself would increase interpersonal income inequality.

The horizontal axis in Figure 1.1 measures spatial inequality. The figure captures variation in levels of economic development across provinces, proxied by nighttime luminosity, a commonly used if coarse measure of subnational GDP. By this measure, levels of spatial inequality, or inequality across provinces, in sub-Saharan Africa countries also rank among the highest in the world (Table A.1).[6] Most African countries rank higher on this measure than country exemplars of very high spatial inequality featured in the CPE literature, including the United Kingdom, Spain, Indonesia, Argentina, and Mexico.

---

[3] World Bank Povcalnet consumption data show seven of the world's ten most unequal countries are in Africa, with the regional average country consumption Gini of 0.43 the highest regional average in the world (Beegle et al. 2016: 127).

[4] Jirasevetakul and Langer 2016: 9. This figure includes North Africa. Shimeles and Nagassaga examine asset inequality data for forty-four African countries over two decades and report that average asset-based Ginis are in the 40–45% range, which "could easily imply that the top 1% owned 35–40% of household assets and amenities in Africa" (2017:17). See Jerven 2013 on data quality problems.

[5] This relationship holds even when Africa's ten most unequal countries are removed from the sample (Shimeles & Nagassaga 2017: 12 inter alia).

[6] Lessmann and Seidel (2017) report average coefficients of variation in predicted GDP per capita at the Admin1 level (based on adjusted nighttime luminosity data) for 1992–2012. In a study based on national accounts data from all world regions, Gennaioli et al. (2014) found that the ratio of GDP per capita across Admin1 regions in 2010, excluding the region of the capital city, differed by a factor of almost 3 for Kenya, Mozambique, and Benin, and by a factor of 2.0 for Tanzania. For the United Kingdom, it was 1.3 (1.8 with the capital city included). For similar conclusions about inequality for eleven African countries from an IMF team using individual-level consumption and birthplace data, see Brunori et al. 2016.

1.1 *Inequality Structures in African Countries* 7

Indeed, in a global sample of countries measuring spatial inequality, almost all African countries stand out with extreme scores on the spatial inequality dimension (along with a number of non-African countries, including Syria and Pakistan).

In African countries, national capitals do have stark advantages over the provinces in terms of levels of economic development, as the urban bias literature underscores. Yet these data and many alternative measures of spatial inequality show that *there are also sharp differences across predominantly rural regions.* In Tanzania in 2016, for example, average consumption per adult in Manyara region, the richest of the provinces, was almost three times that of Ruvuma and Kigoma regions.[7] Similarly, in Ghana, living standards in the central cocoa-producing regions are twice what they are in the poorest rural regions of the northern savanna, where livelihoods are centered on pastoralism and subsistence agriculture. In Kenya, early childhood mortality rates are almost *four times* higher in the western county of Homa Bay, lying on the lowland shores of Lake Victoria, than they are in Nyeri County in the agriculturally rich central highlands.[8] As Sahn and Stifel argued, in most countries, indicators of poverty "differ markedly *between rural regions* of almost every country" (2000: 593). Changes over time in rural well-being – net improvements and declines – also "differ dramatically across rural areas" and are often highly regionalized (Sahn & Stifel 2000: 593). When countries are growing, some rural regions benefit, while others fall behind.

The existence of two forms of extreme socioeconomic inequality – interpersonal income inequality *and* spatial inequality across regions – complicates the inequality puzzle in African countries. Melissa Rogers argued that "these indicators represent distinct potential distributional conflicts within a nation" (2016: 27). In Rogers' global sample of countries, interpersonal and spatial (interregional) inequality are weakly correlated. She found this to be the case for sub-Saharan Africa, as well. Some countries are indeed marked by levels of interpersonal *income* inequality that are far more extreme (by both world and African standards) than their levels of *spatial* inequality.[9] South Africa is the clearest example. Others exhibit the reverse combination, where *spatial*

---

[7] See Boone and Simson 2019: Appendix 1, Table E. Calculated from DHS consumption data.

[8] "Children born in Homa Bay county were 5 times as likely to die before age 5 as children born in Nyeri County in 1965 and reduced to 3.8 times by 2013. The Western part of the country was the worst place to be born [in 1965] and remained the most disadvantaged through to 2013" (Macharia et al. 2019).

[9] Using the unweighted CoV across Admin1 regions, we also observed a strong and highly significant negative correlation between the two inequality measures (Boone & Simson 2019). The correlation coefficient is –0.40 at the 0.01 level. Countries with higher interpersonal inequality (generally the more economically developed countries, such as South Africa and Namibia) register lower spatial inequality. In general, the poorer countries are marked by higher levels of spatial inequality (i.e., of dispersion in the nightlight-based proxy measure for regional GDP per capita).

8   *Economic Inequalities and Territorial Oppositions in African Politics*

inequality appears far more extreme than *income* inequality. Mali and Ethiopia
are exemplars of this pattern. Yet for most African countries, *both* income and
spatial inequality are very high by world standards. The presence of both high
income and high spatial inequality means that there are stark *potential* lines
of socioeconomic cleavage and distributional conflict in most African countries. Will structural economic inequalities find expression in politics, and if
so, which ones, and how?

So far, most studies of African electoral politics have discounted programmatic economic concerns as a driver of political competition, or argued explicitly that the ethnic cleavages visible at the national level are not systematically
related to structural socioeconomic cleavages. This is puzzling for comparative
political economists who expect inequalities rooted in the economy – be they
along class, sectional, or sectoral lines – to stoke systemic distributive conflict.

1.2 MAIN ARGUMENT

CPE scholars argue that *institutional structure* is critical in shaping inequality's political effects. A substantial line of theory predicts that, where strong
regional inequalities are overlaid by strongly territorial institutions, "distributional conflict will exist primarily among territorial groups" (Rogers 2016: 2).
Strongly territorial political institutions will work to *accentuate* the political
salience of spatial inequality and to channel the politics of inequality into "a
distribution game ... across and within geographic districts" (Rogers 2016: 2;
see also Rodden 2010; Beramendi 2012).

In this book, I deploy this insight to identify and unlock the puzzle of inequality politics in African countries. In most African countries, spatial inequality
is high, *and* structures of political representation, government administration,
and resource allocation are *strongly territorial.* As CPE theory would predict,
in most African countries, national competition can be described as "territorial
politics in regionally divided countries."

Figure 1.2 captures theoretical expectations about the relationship between
high spatial inequality and strongly territorial institutions (Rogers 2016),
and locates African countries on this conceptual map. My main argument is
that most African countries fall into Cell 1 of Figure 1.2, where high spatial inequality and strongly territorial institutions coincide, and that territorial
politics predominates. Yet there is cross-national variation in the relationship
between institutional and inequality structures in African countries, as noted
above, and this offers some additional analytic leverage.

Most African countries are located in Cell 1 in Figure 1.2. Rural populations predominate – in most countries, over 50% of the population is largely
dependent on land-based livelihoods. In most, natural endowment is highly
unevenly distributed across space, giving rise to strong sectoral–spatial differentiation. This unevenness is associated with spatial inequalities and different
modes of integration into the national polity and economy. Strongly territorial

1.2 *Main Argument*

Spatial (Regional) Inequality

		Higher	Lower
Territorial Institutions	Strongly territorial institutions promote segmentation, regionalization	1. regional politics predominates. e.g. Kenya	2. not expected
	Centralizing and nationalizing institutions mute or dilute territorial interests	3. regional competition is muted; regional tensions are not easily channeled directly into politics. e.g. ~ TZ	4. class- or rich-poor politics. e.g. South Africa

FIGURE 1.2 Territorially divided states: Theoretical expectations and African exemplars
Notes: Territorially divided states are characterized by high spatial inequality and strongly territorial institutions that align with geographical economic disparities, as typified in Cell 1. "TZ" is mainland Tanzania.

institutions of administration, political representation, and land tenure (property rights in land) overlay regionalized patterns of economic development and magnify their political salience. Rules of electoral competition, including multiparty competition organized around territorially defined electoral constituencies, contribute to the political salience of geographically specific interests. In these countries, regionalism is expected to trump class politics. Examples are Kenya, Zambia, and Côte d'Ivoire.

In Cell 4 of Figure 1.2, where strongly centralizing institutions coincide with lower spatial inequality, the political salience of interpersonal income and class differences is expected to be stronger. In more industrialized and urbanized countries, the political salience of spatial inequality falls relative to income inequality. With nationally integrated labor markets and high levels of proletarianization, the salience of rich–poor polarization increases in national politics. Universalizing institutions associated with the development of mass- and class-based society – such as national parties and trade unions – give voice to class-like demands and policy responses. Administrative divisions cut across, rather than overlay and reinforce, the most extreme spatial disparities. In the sub-Saharan Africa context, South Africa is the exemplar. In South Africa, a strongly integrated national bureaucracy and an electoral system based on proportional representation have also promoted what Caramani (2004) calls the "nationalization of politics."[10] Under these conditions, class politics dilutes

---

[10] There are indeed persistent regional electoral blocs in Western Cape and part of KwaZulu-Natal, respectively. These exist as exceptions to the predominant, nationalized voting pattern. See Chapters 4 and 7.

Economic Inequalities and Territorial Oppositions in African Politics

or trumps the politics of regionalism. In Botswana and Namibia, where levels of urbanization and of interpersonal income inequality are also very high, territorial cleavages also have lower political salience (see Baleyte et al. 2020). In these counterfactual cases, regional tensions do not predominate; they are overwhelmed by other social cleavages.[11]

The two cells on the opposite diagonal are theoretically generated types that are not associated with unambiguous empirical referents in the African context. Cell 2, where spatial inequality is low and national institutions are strongly territorial, is not expected in African countries. Under colonial rule, strongly territorial state institutions coevolved with highly uneven patterns of economic development and political control of African populations (see Chapter 3).

Cell 3 describes a configuration in which spatial inequality is high, but strongly nationalizing institutions mute or dilute the salience of territorial identities and interests, and provide few supports for regional interests to coalesce in the political arena. As suggested in Figure 1.2, Tanzania has features that pull it toward Cell 3, but it is not a pure type (as indicated by the tilde).[12] While there are clear patterns of regional inequality and Tanzania's electoral rules encourage the political expression of territorial interests, key features of institutional structure have been nationalizing: These include centralized ruling party and line-ministry control over regional, district, and local administration; direct administration of rural localities; nationalizing (rather than region- or district-specific) land tenure institutions; and one-party rule between 1965 and 1995.[13] Regional tensions have decisively shaped the national trajectory, but in mainland Tanzania these have been attenuated for much of the last sixty years of independence.

This book argues that in most sub-Saharan Africa countries from the 1950s to today, including the post-1990 era multiparty politics, the salience of territorial politics has been high. I show that national politics in many and perhaps most African countries is structured along regional lines in ways that are critical to understanding the stakes of economic modernization and bureaucratic consolidation. Cell 1 captures the predominant tendency, describing not only Kenya but also most of the countries in the twelve-country study (see Section 1.4) that provides empirical foundations for the main arguments advanced

---

[11] For Botswana, this could be conceptualized as an urban–rural cleavage, rather than a class-like cleavage. Cell 4 could also describe countries where levels of economic development are extremely low across *all* predominantly rural provinces. Pourtier (1980, 1989) writes that in Gabon under colonial rule, the regions were not territorially differentiated, either economically or politically. Economic development through the 1980s centered mostly on oil extraction in the capital city region and offshore.

[12] Rwanda since 1995 could also fit into Cell 3.

[13] These arguments pertain to mainland Tanzania. See Tordoff 1965; Morse 2014; Boone and Nyeme 2015; Mugizi and Pastory 2022. In Tanzania, economic policy has also played a role. See Chapters 3 and 4 and the conclusion to Chapter 6.

1.3 Theoretical Foundations

across Chapters 2 through 7.[14] Most of the analysis concentrates on identifying structure and variation within the predominant pattern captured in Cell 1, identifying the institutional and sectoral–spatial features of African political economies that account for this, and identifying the effects of regionalism in political and policy dynamics at the national level. South Africa serves as the main counterfactual in an argument that is developed in the first part of Chapter 7.

This book develops the theory that regional differences and spatial inequalities, in interaction with state institutional structure, shape politics and policy in African countries, as they do in countries with high spatial inequality and strongly territorial state institutions in other parts of the world. These effects are not reducible to ethnic effects. Indeed, the same institutional factors have shaped *both* economic geography and ethnic identities. Territorial institutions play a strong role in defining the content of ethnic and regional identities, *which identities* find expression in politics, and the spatial scale at which they find expression in the national arena. Cleavages that find expression in national politics in contemporary African countries tend to be associated with *regional* identities and interests. These *transcend* the ethnic identities that are linked to precolonial indigenous languages and ancestral property rights, and colonial native authority units.[15]

1.3 THEORETICAL FOUNDATIONS

Unfolding processes of state-building and national economic development have created regional winners and losers. Regional actors have coalesced with the framework of regional administrative and political institutions and mobilized over time in defense of their interests. Since the 1940s if not before, moves toward economic integration and political centralization have stirred center–periphery tensions and other territorial oppositions, as predicted by Lipset and Rokkan (1967) and other theorists of territorial politics. Forces of market expansion and agglomeration exert a pull in favor of already leading regions. These tend to be export-producing regions, as much trade theory

---

[14] I do not advance a general argument about the political effects of variation in levels of spatial inequality or in the intensity of regionalism across Cell 1 and 3 cases in Africa. In a global sample, almost all African countries stand out for high spatial inequality and are thus roughly similar in this regard. This book focuses on the political implications of high spatial inequality. Within the chapters, I do draw some comparisons of regional inequality levels across African countries and venture some inferences from this. South Africa is singled out as a case in Africa that manifests a categorically different inequality structure (Cell 4), and this provides some analytic leverage on the argument.

[15] This is consonant with Posner's (2005) argument that the institutional structure of the state determines the *scale* of electoral coalition-building. Yet in an analysis of Zambia, Posner offered an explanation for regional (provincial-level) electoral coalitions that differ from the one I advance here. He argued that they arise from ties of coethnicity based on a shared language.

12 *Economic Inequalities and Territorial Oppositions in African Politics*

would predict.[16] Postcolonial governments have both spurred on and regulated these processes. They have differentially allocated the costs and benefits of change over time, shaping and politicizing the pace and direction of national economic integration. Clientelism, pork barrelism, and low levels of redistributive spending are starkly visible in African countries, as is the case in other territorially divided countries around the world (Rogers 2016).

Theoretical tools from historical sociology, economics, and comparative political economy provide foundations for these arguments.

The "Territorial–Geographical Dimension" of Politics: Rokkan

A two-dimensional space describes alternative cleavage structures in classic studies of the political development of Europe, with the functional (income or class) axis of cleavage predominating over the territorial axis as the major source of differentiation in party system structure in Europe from the 1950s to the 2000s.[17] For the earlier period, however, a different configuration tended to prevail, and this is what interests us here.

Lipset and Rokkan (1967) studied the ways in which patterns of urban-rural, core–periphery, and church–state cleavage were activated in national politics in modernizing Europe by the accelerating forces of urbanization and early stages of industrialization. Development of national economies and the growth of modern national bureaucracies under centralizing rulers are drivers of tensions between core and periphery, and across regions within peripheries. Lipset and Rokkan emphasized what they depicted as "territorial oppositions," which they argued were linked to different regional economies, and the varying types of social organization (including but not reducible to cultural and social values) embedded in them. I adopt a similar theorization, emphasizing heterogeneity in regional economies and hierarchy among them, and arguing that tensions and competition arising from this find expression in political organization and economic interests, and ultimately, national politics.

Class politics and territorial politics are associated with very different forms of political competition and bargaining. Class politics revolves around social contracting to divide economic surpluses generated by growth (or the costs of decline), predominantly between two nonspatial but intrinsically interdependent

---

[16] The Ricardo–Viner and Heckscher–Ohlin–Samuelson models predict that trade will favor factors of production specific to the export sector.

[17] Stein Rokkan (1971, inter alia) theorized that the territorial dimensions of state authority would be gradually effaced as salient in national politics as "modernization" progressed, even if territorial cleavages in national electorates tended to persist, albeit unevenly across countries. Caramani (2004: 16) argued that formation of national electorates and party systems can best be interpreted starting from Rokkan's concept of the territorial–geographical dimension of politics.

1.3 Theoretical Foundations

parties: owners of capital and owners of labor power. Territorial politics by contrast focuses on relative advantage and disadvantage across geographic segments of the national polity. It is driven by concern not only with securing state spending "here" rather than "there," as scholars of the electoral logics of distributive politics at the micro level have argued, but also with the evolution of relations between leading and lagging regions, adverse incorporation into national political economy of lagging regions or those on the sidelines of power, and caution vis-à-vis growth strategies that may channel advantages to already dominant regions. Rather than a politics around division of an economic surplus generated within firms, sectors, or the national economy, as is the case in class politics, territorial politics revolves around winners and losers created by spatial expansion and/or segmentation of markets, spatially targeted policy, the commodification and decommodification of access to immobile natural resources, and the spatial limits, autonomy, and powers of the local state vis-à-vis the center.

In the African context, the spatial–territorial dimension of politics focuses on distributional tensions among regions. The politics of clinics and boreholes may be an instantiation of this at the neighborhood or micro level. Yet when analysis scales up to the national level, regional coalitions are primary contenders, especially those regions that are most deeply integrated into the national economy, and when larger, more programmatic issues and tensions are at stake in the formulation of national policy.

Particular types of collective action problems around growth strategy and redistribution emerge at this level. Programmatic policies, both social and economic-developmental, often have a strong spatial bias. Indeed, these often involve spatially targeted state spending and development policies. Market-expanding policies are likely to reinforce the advantage of leading regions and may compound the adverse incorporation of lagging regions. The bearers of such interests are not only the cabinet-level ethnic brokers featured in studies of autocratic rulers' "ethnic arithmetic," but also political party builders, local and regional elites, and multitudes of ordinary citizens who are linked to regional economies through their occupations, livelihoods, place-based associational lives, local citizenship responsibilities and rights, and property holding. This includes farmers organized into producer associations such as cooperatives in sectors that are deeply incorporated into the national economy. They are sensitive to regionally targeted sectoral development and regulatory policies.

The argument that politics in many African countries can be understood as driven by distributional tensions that cleave the national *body politic* along regional lines was a leitmotif in African studies from the 1960s. This study argues that such strains have persisted over many decades and are strongly visible today in patterns of coalition and cleavage in electoral politics at the national level, as well as in cleavages around political issues that tap into regional tensions and divides.

Spatial Inequality: Rokkan Meets Krugman

The New Economic Geography (NEG) as pioneered and popularized by Krugman (1991, 1998) helps explain where regional inequalities are likely to emerge, and how and why they are likely to deepen over time in the absence of profound change in technology or institutions. The Old Economic Geography assumed that, over time, regional growth rates and income levels would converge as capital chased lower labor costs, and as migrants moved to regions that offered the best wages for their skill-mix. The old school believed that regional economic disparities would erode over time. The New Economic Geography undercut this logic, demonstrating convincingly that economies of scale in production – theorized as a type of market imperfection – generated increasing returns for already dynamic regions. Density and agglomeration themselves have a positive effect on economic activity. Empirically, the New Economic Geography has won out, as regional convergence ended in most OECD countries around the 1970s, giving way to decades of growing regional inequality within the EU countries and the United States that would contribute to the political and social strains of the 2000s. "The great divergence" in regional growth patterns within the developed countries emerged as a new, politically urgent object of study in political economy and regional economics.

In Africa, too, the convergence process that 1950s and 1960s economists expected to see has failed to materialize. There is far less convergence not only between African countries and the West, but also across regions within African countries than was predicted in the heyday of mainstream development theory in the 1960s and 1970s. With a few notable exceptions, the relative rankings of regions within national economies in Africa over the last several decades (measured by regional GDP or standards of living) have proved to be remarkably stable. Analysts often describe uneven spatial distributions of income that were established in the first half of the twentieth century as *entrenched* (Moyo 2014: 11).[18] This reflects inter alia the limited structural transformation of African economies over the last several decades (limited industrialization in particular, and the persistence of large and growing rural populations). But even in other settings, agglomeration theory suggests that markets tend to concentrate growth in already leading regions, making the catch-up of lagging regions a very uncertain proposition (Scott & Storper 2003). Regional economic convergence was unlikely to happen automatically, or evenly in time and space. Poverty traps are real.

---

[18] Persistence in regional economic profiles and in growth disparities between lagging and leading regions is a phenomenon that is not specific to Africa. Even in the OECD, as Rickard argues, "patterns of economic geography remain relatively stable over the medium run" (2018: 31). Within the EU, cohesion policies aimed at supporting growth in lagging regions have not reversed preexisting regional inequalities or even mitigated them to the extent that proponents of these policies had hoped and expected (see Iammarino, Rodriguez-Pose, & Storper 2019; McCann 2020).

1.3 Theoretical Foundations

Venables (2010: 470) suggested that focusing on agglomeration forces can support a core–periphery view of the national economy. This is the line of reasoning followed here. This suggests an economic model of persistent spatial inequalities that is highly complementary to the Lipset–Rokkan model of political and economic development.

Drawing on earlier theorists of uneven economic development, my analysis foregrounds the role of national economic integration in producing centripetal (agglomeration) pressures that tend to exacerbate uneven development and spatial inequality. In African countries, regional growth rates and endowments differ, creating hierarchies of regions defined by differential growth rates (and levels), and geographies of relative winners and losers. Large literatures in economic geography lead us to *expect* such unevenness to give rise to demands from some peripheries for alternative models of incorporation and state-building. Demands may take the form of calls for more local autonomy (and less central state intervention), more redistribution, or sector-specific economic policies that reflect particular regional interests. Core–periphery tensions and region-specific needs and claims on the state create the *potential* for regional or territorial politics in African countries. These would be *expected* to trump class cleavages in structuring politics and policy debates where the potential for class cleavages to form as a strong axis of competition is low.

In African countries, evidence of the cumulative advantages of already favored regions is starkest in the rise of capital cities. Expansion of the state itself has been a major driver of primary (or primate) city growth and agglomeration of economic activity, including tertiary sector activity and wage/salaried employment, in capital cities. However, the rise of primate cities has generally not been accompanied by structural change in national economies along the agrarian-to-industrial pattern observed in America and Europe in earlier centuries. In the Lipset–Rokkan model, urbanization and industrialization drove the "nationalization of politics" by eroding preexisting, regionalized and regionally differentiated social structures, and promoting the rise of a new, nonterritorial [territory-wide] national economy and class structure. Africa's leading cities, by contrast, have been dubbed service or consumption cities. Their rise has not been driven by industrialization (although they tend to be sites in which national manufacturing industry is concentrated), or accompanied by absolute decline in rural population counts or, in most cases, the formation of social classes based on the capital–labor division associated with industrialization. (South Africa's leading cities provide a stark exception to this rule.) The phenomenon of urban economic advantage is well recognized in the political science literature in Africa, along with some of its political correlates and effects. Less recognized is the fact emphasized here – growth and forces of agglomeration have also tended to favor the *already leading predominantly rural regions*.

Predominance of natural resource-based sectors and industries means that levels and location of economic activities are strongly influenced by natural

16   *Economic Inequalities and Territorial Oppositions in African Politics*

endowment. Other factor-mobility-constraining "market imperfections" reinforce endowment-related disparities between leading and lagging regions. These are related most obviously to institutions and transport infrastructure (or connectivity more generally), but less visible impediments to population mobility are also important.[19] Uneven levels of incorporation into national markets mean that market-based "universalistic policies" are not actually space-neutral or spatially blind. Political dynamics, in turn, play a role in shaping economic structure over time.

Divergence of regional trajectories is a corollary of the above. When overall national growth rates are positive, different parts of a country will share very unequally in this prosperity. When times are bad, the burden is distributed unevenly. Divergence itself (relative gains/losses) as well as region-specific attributes shape the political preferences of region-based actors.

Institutions Matter: CPE Theorists

Theory in comparative political economy predicts distinctive political outcomes in countries that *combine* high levels of regional socioeconomic inequality with strongly territorial, or territorially fragmented, political systems (Beramendi 2012; Rogers 2016).[20] Such political systems are defined not only by strongly territorial systems of political representation, but also by structures of public administration and bureaucracy that divide the polity into internally cohesive "state segments" with low cross-unit bureaucratic interdependency. In these settings, the structure of the national political system is expected to bring territorial oppositions to the fore, to amplify the political salience of interregional distributive issues and of spatial inequalities in national politics, and to highlight tensions around the terms of incorporation of regions into the national political economy. Canonical cases are the United States, Canada, Spain, Germany, and Argentina, where concerns with disparities in interregional resources and distribution of power are central to the logics of national politics.

Focusing on institutional determinants, Melissa Rogers (2016) argues that in "territorially divided states" we should expect that (a) territorial institutions define collective actors in politics – including political identities and agendas; (b) institutional structure promotes and heightens the salience of distributive conflict across geographic units – "at the extreme, politics becomes conflict

---

[19] Impediments to cross-regional population mobility which are inherent in social, institutional, and political factors deepen regional inequalities and weaken the market and social forces that would presumably otherwise promote regional convergence. One of the most systemic and important of these institutional factors is neocustomary land tenure regimes, which provide access to the subsistence economy to large shares of the population. See Chapters 2 and 3.

[20] Beramendi writes of Spain, and Rogers' book is a comparative analysis of the United States, Germany, and Argentina. For country-level analyses, see also Bensel (1984) on the United States, Diaz-Cayeros (2006) on Mexico, and Gibson (2006, 2013) on Mexico and Argentina.

1.3 Theoretical Foundations

about distribution of resources among jurisdictions" (Beramendi 2012: 40); and (c) political competition produces centrifugal forces: Diverse regional economic profiles generate distinctive and often divergent political preferences, including divergent preferences arising from cross-regional economic inequality itself.

Juxtaposed to these are countries with strongly centralizing and homogenizing institutional structures. These include strong proportional representation (PR) and national list voting and parliamentary systems that dilute the salience of geography in electoral dynamics; resource allocation through corporatist (functional) structures, and state territorial administration through functionally defined authorities (e.g., national social security administration or national education ministry), rather than territorially defined authorities, to check spatial nonuniformity in the supply of government. A corollary of these is strong party systems and nationalized parties, and civil society organizations such as strong labor unions, producer peak associations, and religious organizations of national scope that pull together cross-local political coalitions. France is often cited as a paradigmatic case.

In this study, I argue that the predicted effects of strongly territorial political institutions and high spatial inequality feature prominently in the politics of most African countries. In many African countries, strongly territorial political institutions structure the integration of citizens into national political life. These work to aggregate political preferences around territory in general and around region or district in particular, apportion resource access among territorially defined population groups, and create territorially defined channels by which citizens access top-down resource flows from the central state.

The most important institutions are ethnically defined territorial constituencies (former Native Authorities) which prevail in many parts of most countries, single-member district (SMD) electoral systems, and territorial administrative units at the provincial (Admin1) and district (Admin2) levels that divide national space into state segments that often differ strongly from each other in their economic and governing structures. Territorial administration creates "containers" within which policy is tailored for local circumstance and implemented, and within which parties and political entrepreneurs may build coalitions and alliances across multiple levels of the administrative hierarchy, from the microlevel, to the constituency, district, and regional level. State institutions and institutional practices often define separate and unequal systems of property holding (in land) for territorially defined subgroups of citizens, foster regional economic segmentation, and supply regionally differentiated government services, resource flows, and policy.[21] Correlates of these state features

---

[21] There are nationalizing institutions, too. These include the national civil service, the military, national education systems, and presidentialism, although these may also work in ways that reinforce regional bias.

18 Economic Inequalities and Territorial Oppositions in African Politics

are weakly nationalized party systems (i.e., regionalized electoral mobilization) and the relative weakness of trans-local or cross-regional societal organizations and mechanisms of interest aggregation.

As Isham et al. (2005: 145, n. 5) note, a large class of models and theories in comparative political economy shows that political institutions are themselves conditioned by economic structure. Both factors shape the power and interests of different social groups and these, in turn, compete to shape and reshape political institutions. These endogeneities are strongly present in the case material examined here. The strong territoriality of governance structures in African countries coevolved with colonial economies that were dependent upon "enclaved" or regionally specific production of export commodities. In this study, I deal with this endogeneity head-on by showing how territorial institutional structures and uneven development coevolved in the British and French colonies of sub-Saharan Africa, producing a "regionalization by design" of both colonial economies and citizenries. The institutional structure of the postcolonial state itself is treated as an overtime effect of postcolonial politics, again conditioned by economic structure. As Rogers (2016) argues, struggles over constitutional order and state design in regionally divided states with high spatial inequality can be expected to unfold in particular ways: that is, over the distribution of political authority and prerogative between regions, and between regions and the central state.

1.4 MAIN ARGUMENTS AND CHAPTER OUTLINE

In many, perhaps most, African countries, governmental institutional structures (administrative, economic, and representative) *overlay* patterns of spatial inequality and uneven economic development across predominantly rural regions. The central argument of this book is that, where this is the case, regional cleavages go far in structuring national electorates, and regionalism is a salient force in national-level politics. As Stephanie Rickard (2018: 24) observed, "regional effects are strongest when institutions and socioeconomic inequalities align." Because these institutional structures and patterns of uneven development are traceable to state formation projects set in motion in the early twentieth century, I dub the dominant, overtime tendency *Regionalism by Design*. Counterfactual cases in Africa are countries where these forces are mitigated by more strongly nationalized economies (nationally integrated economies), administrative systems, and political systems.[22] These counterfactual conditions strongly mitigate or attenuate the political salience of regional inequality and economic differentiation. Class-like politics tends to trump territorial politics.

---

[22] Or, in theory, by absence of the pressures of national economic integration, as could be the case where all rural regions are marked by very low levels of economic development, and there is little inequality or economic differentiation across regions.

1.4 Main Arguments and Chapter Outline

Institutions play a critical role in producing and reproducing regionally uneven development, and shaping the political expression of regional inequalities and difference. State institutional structure has gone far in defining the political identities of subnational collectivities (via ethnicization of state-delimited "tribal" territories under colonial rule).[23] At the same time, state-led economic development within the template of colonial- and postcolonial territorial administration has *given rise to*, and/or entrenched, differences in levels of development and sectoral profiles of subnational regions. Factors related to endowment and location combine with active state promotion of regional economic specialization, accentuating the sectoral economic profiles (e.g., export crop production, labor-exporting systems, pastoral zones) of subnational units delimited, roughly, by the boundaries of administrative districts or provinces. Spatial inequalities across such units have tended to be persistent, indeed entrenched, over the last fifty years. Economically leading regions of the late 1950s and early 1960s are, in most cases, economically leading regions in the 2010s.

Such *persistence* of spatial inequality and hierarchy, combined with the *alignment* of socioeconomic differences with formal (institutional) territorial divisions, has contributed mightily to making regional inequalities politically salient in national politics in African countries. Alignment of economic inequality with institutional structures of representation has worked to promote regional bloc voting in national politics and to structure patterns of competition and coalition formation across regional units. Policy competition across regions arises around policies that have distributive implications and regionally uneven effects. Regional tensions also surround choices over constitutional arrangements that distribute powers across territorial subunits of the state.

These arguments about the causes and effects of regional political cleavages and regionalism in African politics are developed across Chapters 2–7 of the book, following the schema in Figure 1.3.

Operationally, Chapters 4–6 adopt an electoral geography definition of "cleavage" by taking spatially distinct clusterings and discontinuities in electoral patterns as indicative of political cleavages in the electorate.[24] Using electoral geography methods and logics, I identify patterns of persistent regional bloc voting in presidential elections in a diverse sample of twelve African countries since the 1990s and take this as evidence of *regional* structure and cleavage in political competition at the national level.[25] The persistent electoral bloc is taken as the expression of a type of political coalition

---

[23] See, for example, Iliffe 1979; Ranger 1983; Mamdani 1996; Lynch 2011; and Onoma 2013.

[24] West defines cleavages as "strongly structured lines of salient division among politically important actors" (2005: 501–502).

[25] As Caramani (2004) explains, in countries with few salient geographic cleavages or relatively low spatial inequality, we would expect to see little by way of persistent geographic clustering in voting in national elections.

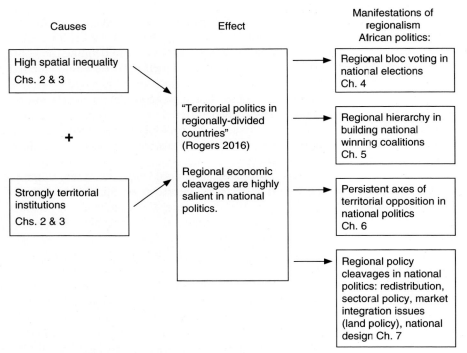

FIGURE 1.3 Regional cleavages and national politics: Causes and effects
Notes: Schematic outline of main arguments and chapter structure.

(or coalescence of interests) that developed since the late colonial period, generally at the provincial scale. Political competition between these blocs goes far in defining the structure of competition in national political arenas over time. This is a form of politics shaped in large part by the alignment of the territorial structure of the state with sectorally heterogeneous and economically unequal regions.

By leveraging analysis of economic inequality across these persistent electoral blocs in each of twelve countries, it is possible to address a series of questions about how spatial inequalities are manifest in national politics, and how they shape issues that are salient on the national political agenda. Why do persistent regional blocs emerge in some parts of a country, but not in others? What are the origins and bases of bloc cohesion and cleavage? How do these relate to ethnicity in politics? Are patterns stable over time? To what extent does economic hierarchy among blocs correspond to patterns of political dominance (and exclusion) in national politics? How do spatial inequalities and cleavages shape coalition-building strategies in national elections? Zooming out to encompass the secondary literature on a wider range of African countries, I ask: Is regionalism manifest in national policy agendas,

Chapter Outline and Summary 21

and if so, how? Answers to these questions are developed over the course of the chapters outlined below.

CHAPTER OUTLINE AND SUMMARY

Chapter 2 develops the conceptual and theoretical framework in five steps. The first situates this analytic and theoretical approach with respect to earlier work on ethnicity and region in African countries. Earlier work is marked by a strong tendency to look away from regional economic inequality as a political force in African countries, and has defaulted to theories centered on ethnicity, understood as a force orthogonal to programmatic economic policy interests and devoid of economic ideology. The second part of Chapter 2 grounds the concepts of "region" and regional inequality. In African countries, the sources of regional economic *difference* are found in the uneven distribution of natural endowments, regionally specific patterns of state intervention in the economy that date to the colonial period, strong spatial–sectoral differentiation, and institutional administrative structure. Regional *inequality* is a corollary of the sectoral heterogeneity of regions that make up the national economy, and of constraints on the mobility of factors of production that would, in a perfectly neoclassical world, lead to convergence in regional levels of economic development and incomes. Part three follows Lipset and Rokkan in theorizing the particular sources and nature of regional cleavages that arise in the course of state-building and national economic integration. Part four identifies institutions that contribute to the "regionalization" of national economies and politics in African countries. The last part lays out the main elements of an approach to the analysis of regionalism that is fit for African contexts.

Chapter 3 develops the spatial inequality and institutional arguments in historical context. I identify the colonial origins of the institutional structures and patterns of uneven economic development that create the template for political regionalism. The analysis shows how and why functional economic regions and administrative regions tended to align in the African colonies, defining patterns of regional difference and inequality in the early decades of the twentieth century that are often strongly visible today. This process also established the framework within which politically salient ethnic identities developed, and defined political (eventually, electoral) constituencies in strongly territorial terms. With the opening of political space for colony-wide politics in the 1940s, existing administrative and political structures worked to channel regional interests and ideologies of regional consciousness into the national political arena. A boundary persistence analysis underscores the large extent to which colonial territorial grids have been reproduced over time, defining the institutional playing field of politics in many African countries today. The final section of Chapter 3 (Section 3.6) argues for explaining institutional persistence (and changes) in terms of when and how African political leaders, social elites, farmers, landholders, and members of rural communities found

22   *Economic Inequalities and Territorial Oppositions in African Politics*

advantage (or the avoidance of bads) in territorial institutions forged under colonialism. Regional cleavages, and the territorial institutions that help frame and reproduce them, that were in place in the 1950s and 1960s have structured patterns of national-level political competition in many African countries for many decades.

Chapter 4 argues that regional interests and tensions are manifest in *regional bloc voting* in the contemporary era of multiparty politics (1990s–2010s). It is coauthored with Juliette Crespin-Boucaud and draws on earlier work with Michael Wahman and other collaborators (Boone, Wahman, Kyburz, & Linke 2022). We present an electoral geography analysis of constituency-level voting in presidential elections in twelve countries over the course of 1990–2015 (44 elections).[26] Regional bloc voting is visible in all twelve. Across the twelve countries, we identity a total of thirty-six distinct, persistent regional-level electoral blocs. Leveraging a variety of data sources, we describe the economic attributes of the persistent electoral blocs and how they differ from parts of each country in which persistent clustering of regional bloc voting does *not* occur. These data consist of forty rounds of DHS surveys for geocoded data on education and ethnicity, nighttime luminosity data, historical maps of producer regions, and raster data describing population densities and contemporary crop production profiles. The analysis in Chapter 4 underpins two critical planks of this book's argument. First, the prevalence of regionalized voting patterns across a diverse set of African countries supports the argument that regionalism is a distinct feature of political competition in many, perhaps most, African countries. Second, the economic profiles of the electoral blocs provide strong clues as to bloc etiology. We begin to see why persistent, multiethnic electoral blocs coalesce in some regions but not in others.

We find that most of the persistent electoral blocs arise in rural regions that are wealthier, better educated, more densely populated, and more deeply incorporated into the national economy than other rural areas. Most of the persistent blocs are specialized in high-value export crops (or traded food crops). Some have nonagricultural production profiles as labor-exporting or mining regions. Most coalesce within provincial-level or Admin1 regions that were defined in the colonial era, the boundaries of which have mostly been reproduced intact since then (sometimes with subdivisions). Rural regions in which persistent electoral blocs do not form (which we call the "non-bloc" regions), by contrast, tend to be characterized by lower levels of economic development, lower educational levels, lower population densities, and the lack of sectoral economic specialization. The evidence is consistent with the

---

[26] In some countries, the unit of analysis is the district, Admin3, or similar, rather than the electoral constituency. See Appendix B. Bensel (1984: 7) argued that roll-call voting within the legislature is the best way to track regional interests in national politics, but that electoral returns were a second best.

Chapter Outline and Summary 23

argument that state institutions work to channel politics arising from uneven economic development into the national political arena.

Section 4.7 of Chapter 4 identifies multiple micro- and mezo-level mechanisms that contribute to this outcome. They are related to interests, organizations, ideology, and the actions of political agents and coalition-builders. Cross-nationally, the observed regional bloc voting is not systematically related to the geographic distribution of ethnic identities. Blocs emerge in countries wherein ethnicity has low political salience (Mali, Tanzania), as well as in high ethnic salience countries like Kenya. Almost all persistent electoral blocs are multiethnic, even in Kenya where politics is highly ethnicized. Many of the blocs are nonethnic, and/or explicitly regional (e.g., Northern Nigeria). Conversely, the non-bloc areas of all countries are home to multi-constituency ethnic groups that do not present as persistent electoral blocs.

Chapter 5, "Bloc Hierarchies and National Winning Coalitions," argues that regional economic hierarchies are strongly reflected in the structure of electoral dominance in national political arenas. Using the twelve countries examined in the preceding chapter, I show that the within-country distribution of spatial inequality produces hierarchies of electoral blocs and non-blocs, structuring political dynamics at the national level. In most countries, economically dominant blocs tend to dominate politically and to forge national coalitions with constituencies in non-bloc areas to win presidential elections. I argue that these patterns are isomorphic to patterns of coalition-building between economically leading and lagging regions in other parts of the world, and that they tend to reproduce regionalism in national politics.

Chapter 6 identifies patterns of bloc polarization, or "territorial oppositions" in national politics. I argue that axes of territorial cleavage arising between predominantly rural regions tend to take canonical forms associated with core–periphery politics in countries that are undergoing national economic integration and the growth of the central state. This chapter argues that stable axes of sectional competition, whereby leading regions square off against each other or against the periphery, are indeed visible in the electoral data and in persistent policy cleavages in countries in this study. In broad outlines, these often conform to models of territorial oppositions in national politics advanced by earlier scholars (Lipset & Rokkan 1967; Gourevitch 1979; Bayart 2013). Four countries – Kenya, Zambia, Malawi, and Uganda – serve as archetypes to show this.

Chapter 7 argues that regional competition in African countries finds expression in tensions, debates, and competition over policy. I argue that regional economic tensions tend to find expression in four persistently salient issue areas: (a) redistributive social policy, (b) regionally specific [sectorally specific] investment and regulatory policy, (c) land policy, where we see redistributive tensions and conflicts that arise in the building of national land markets, and (d) issues around state structure (the territorial division of powers and prerogatives). In most countries, regional cleavages trump class-like or interpersonal income inequalities as a driver of national-level contestation over issues of policy and collective choice. South Africa, where regional inequality is lower and nationalizing institutions are stronger, is an outlier: Redistributive social policy is more developed than it is anywhere else in Africa, and the issue of national land market integration is far less salient than in many African countries.[27]

The conclusion argues that a theory of regional cleavages embeds the behavioral assumptions of microlevel, ethnicity-focused models in a broader spatial, institutional, and temporal frame. A national-level, theoretically grounded framework built on economic geography and institutions produces general findings about political dynamics in African countries that are close to what classical and mainstream treatments in the CP and CPE literatures would lead us to expect. Many debates within the literature on African politics can be refined or transcended by more systematic consideration of the dynamics of political scale, with the regional scale providing a theoretical and conceptual map that enables scholars to identify cleavage structures in national politics.

The challenges of territorial politics in regionally divided countries that confront most African countries today are increasingly prominent in non-African countries, including the postindustrial countries of the West. The United States and the United Kingdom are striking examples. This makes research on the politics of spatial inequality in African countries, including the present work, I hope, relevant to general understandings of how economic and spatial inequalities may evolve over time and heighten the challenges of national politics, and to calls for place-based economic development strategies in the name of national cohesion.

---

[27] This is also consistent with the fact that redistributive social policies are better developed in countries with higher GDP per capita. Since levels of spatial inequality across regions are inversely correlated with levels of overall economic development at the country level, this finding is not unexpected.

2

Region and Regionalism in African Politics

> Despite the political consequences of economic geography, many scholars fail to take geography seriously. Some scholars simply ignore the uneven distribution of economic activity.
>
> Rickard 2018: 28

> It should be noted that most ethnic groups are not culturally homogeneous.
>
> Kimenyi and Ngungu 2005: 151

Does regional inequality give rise to political cleavages in African countries? If so, why and how? At what scale of politics? In what ways would we expect regional difference and inequality to shape national politics and the policies of the central state? The theory of regional politics advanced here is drawn from CP and CPE theories of regional tensions that arise in the course of state-building and national economic integration. These are accentuated when socioeconomic inequality and territorial institutions align.

This book argues that regional economic differentiation and spatial inequalities, in interaction with strongly territorial state institutions, shape politics and policy in African countries as they do in countries in other parts of the world. National economic integration and processes of state-building activate subnational interests and fuel political tensions over the terms of integration of subnational regions into the national polity and the national market. Regional economic and political heterogeneity, and cross-regional inequalities, shape both preferences and the relative bargaining power of subnational (regional) collectivities. These forces combine to produce persistent regional cleavage structures in national politics.

This chapter builds theoretical foundations for this argument in five steps. Section 2.1 locates these arguments with respect to earlier work on ethnicity and region in the study of African politics. Section 2.2 links regional economic heterogeneity within African countries to regional economic *inequalities*. Section 2.3 revisits earlier theories of core–periphery and regional tensions that arise in the course of state-building and national economic integration. I use these to hone expectations about how, and along which issue dimensions, we should expect regional tensions to find expression at the national level in African countries. Section 2.4 factors institutions into the equation. Section 2.5 pulls together these elements to propose a theory of why regional cleavages are salient in African countries and how these are expressed in national politics.

2.1 ETHNICITY AND REGION IN AFRICAN POLITICS: EARLIER WORK

> Perhaps the "ethnic" approach to African history has most determinedly blocked the application of spatial analysis.
>
> Howard and Shain 2004:10

Africa's high Gini coefficients resonate with the long-standing understanding of African societies as characterized by an elite–mass cleavage, with a very small middle class (at best) sandwiched in between.[1] But does economic inequality drive politics? An earlier generation of scholars sought an answer by applying *class analytic* models to African politics. Their answer was "no." They encountered difficulty in gaining analytic traction outside the industrialized economies of North Africa and the mining sectors of southern Africa where labor unions and union mobilization were prominent features of politics.[2] The difficulty in applying class analytic models to most African countries did not lie in demonstrating huge gaps in income and living standards. Rather, it lay in making the argument that wealth or income cleavage represented an axis of political organization and mobilization (Bienen & Herbst 1996). Electoral alignments did not fall along class lines. Interests of the masses, or "the poor versus rich divide," seldom defined rival positions in national political debate. Poor people rallied behind ethnic elites who did not speak the language of class conflict. Ethnicity, rather than economic or economic–geography factors, was widely seen as the source of social cleavage in African politics.

When competitive elections returned in the 1990s after three decades of no elections or one-party rule in most African countries, political scientists explored voting patterns and electoral dynamics, but rarely tested theories about economic inequality and economic policy interests as factors shaping

---

[1] See van de Walle 2009.
[2] On unions, see, for example, Bergen 2007; Kraus 2007; LeBas 2011.

2.1 Ethnicity and Region in African Politics

electoral mobilization and voting. One reason for this is the absence or spotty coverage of subnational electoral data (often missing at the constituency or lower levels) and of spatially disaggregated data on income, socioeconomic status, and occupations. Much survey research on African voters in the late 1990s and early 2000s examined survey respondents in "single national constituencies."[3] Geographic segmentation of the electorate was either not taken into account or washed out of analyses through the use of regional fixed-effects models. Scholars defaulted back to the ethnicity paradigm of African politics, wherein ethnicity was taken as a wellspring of pre-political affinities that were assumed to vary by ethnic group. In some work, ethnic voting was simply as voting for "shared preferences" for local public goods that everyone wanted, with all communities simply preferring "us over them," or wanting state spending "here, rather than there."

Like political sociology theories of patrimonialism, the micro-strain of ethnic theory cut against theories of electorates as cleaved by structural socioeconomic divisions or policy interests. It suggested that voters in a given locality were more likely to opt for a politician offering an immediate handout than one proffering policy promises that he or she might not be able to honor. Indeed, an explicit argument in the ethnic clientelism literature has been that highly localized patronage politics keeps issues having to do with economic policy out of electoral politics, rendering most elections largely void of substantive policy or ideological content.

The term "ethno-regionalism" often appears in the framing of behavioral and party politics research on African voters and distributive politics, and in the Africa-focused parties and elections literature. Scholars recognize that, in Africa, ethnic groups are geographically clustered, and national-level voting patterns are often described as ethno-regional. Yet observations about geography were not incorporated systematically into studies of African party and electoral politics in the post-1990 era. Most academic writers have been agnostic about the substantive meaning of "region." Many scholars married the concept of region to prevailing theories of ethnic politics, generally eschewing the economic–geography connotations of the term region. Often the implicit suggestion is that ethno-regionalism is *caused by* ethnicity (birds of a feather flock together). By this reasoning, ethno-regions are the geographic by-product or expression of ethnic politics.[4]

---

[3] Afrobarometer (AB) surveys, a widely available source of cross-nationally comparative public opinion data for African countries, were not designed to be representative at subnational levels until the 2010s. Round 5 (2013) and Round 6 (2015) surveys included 19 sub-Saharan countries and had a median number of respondents per Admin1 region (province) of only 125 persons (Iddawela, Lee, and Rodriguez-Pose 2021: 46, n. 4). Questions survey citizens' attitudes on democracy, governance, and civil society, but do not solicit opinions on particular public policies or sectoral issues.

[4] Kasara (2007) wrote that many political scientists writing about Africa take "ethnic group" as a shorthand for "interest group."

Microlevel voting research often referred to general theories of ethnic politics to provide theoretical framing and an interpretive lens to draw macro-level inferences for *national politics*. In ethnic determinants models, ethnic brokers aggregate votes from local constituencies to the national level. At the regional and national levels, ethnic big men forge "coalitions of convenience" (Horowitz 1985) based on their own strategic political calculations. Such coalitions are said to rest on political opportunism and to have little by way of programmatic or policy content. By this logic, such coalitions will be unstable because they are not founded on shared interests in policy or ideology, or a preferred national growth model. This is what makes ethnic politics, in theory, so much more volatile and divisive than the everyday politics of policy bargaining and policy incrementalism. The specter of violent conflict imbues ethnicity studies in academic and policy work with particular urgency and import.

Some scholars, including Erdmann (2004, 2007) and Basedau (2019), have pointed out that the micro and macro literatures on ethnic politics fit together uncomfortably at best. Individual ethnic identities are more situationally dependent than theory allows, and national coalitions are more stable and substantively oriented than theories of ethnic clientelism predict. Behavioral models black-box the processes of interest formation and aggregation that link clientelistic or ethnic voting at the polling station or constituency level to national-level coalitional politics. Stable ethnic alliances and, indeed, the emergence of multiethnic "super-ethnicities" in the course of national political competition, go unexplained. Prominent examples of such alliances are the confederate groups of Kalenjin and Mijikenda in Kenya, the Group Akan coalition in Côte d'Ivoire, the super-ethnicity of Akan in Ghana, and the Bemba language group in Zambia. Work that does scale up to the level of parties and party systems (Elischer 2013) often takes note of regional voting patterns, but has remained mostly focused on the dynamics of electoral systems and electoral process, rather than on exploring the causes and consequences of the geographical patterning in the data (Elischer 2013, Wahman 2017). While most take the regional patterning as evidence of ethnic voting, others question this by noting that electoral regions are often actually multiethnic (Ferree & Horowitz 2010) and by pointing out that the observed patterns demonstrate the limits of ethnic census models of voting (Cheeseman & Hinfelaar 2009). Ishiyama (2012) and others have argued that, in fact, it is very difficult to disentangle ethnic effects from nonethnic effects that may be associated with administrative units.[5] Rachel Riedl (2014) argued that ethnic identity in most

---

[5] Inclusion of geographic factors and/or socioeconomic factors as controls in regression models often washes out the ethnicity variable or strongly attenuates its predictive power (Ejdemyr et al. 2018; Harris & Posner 2019). Inclusion of Admin1 regions as a control in models that predict partisan voting often dilutes or almost completely washes out the predictive power of ethnicity. Ethnicity's effect may be partly conditional on local ethnic concentrations (see, e.g., Ichino & Nathan 2013; Horowitz 2019), perhaps reflecting geographic concentration that gives rise to "patterns of shared interests" (Ishiyama 2012: 768; see also Mozaffar et al. 2003).

2.1 Ethnicity and Region in African Politics

African settings is too fragmented to be a source of "social cleavage," and that the cleavage concept does not carry well into African politics.

In the last decade, more dissonance has emerged around long-standing ways of conceptualizing the relationship between ethnicity and economic interests. Geocoded survey data show that ethnic maps and poverty maps often align. An emergent line of research on "ethnic inequality" raises questions about treating the two social facts in isolation from each other. Alesina et al. (2016) find that there are strong economic inequalities across ethnic groups, measured in terms of nighttime luminosity in districts dubbed "ethnic homelands." Higashijima and Houle (2018) find that "ethnic inequality" reinforces the strength of ethnic identity, but that this effect tapers off as within-group inequality rises. Using survey data, Lieberman and McClendon (2012) found that socioeconomic status and ethnic identity often align to such an extent that it can be difficult to disentangle the two. When geography is taken into account, it becomes very obvious that ethnic and economic dimensions of identity can overlap with income-determining and occupational aspects of identity, such as urban/rural residence and agricultural/pastoral livelihoods (see Fotini 2012: 47).[6] Some scholars have found that when ethnicity (or preferences more generally) and region coincide (Selway 2015; Rickard 2018), or when ethnicity and inequality overlap, the political effects are particularly strong.[7]

Conflict scholars have indeed documented the salience of severe spatial inequalities in explanations of state disintegration in Africa.[8] Yet civil war studies have developed largely independently of studies of electoral politics, or the politics-as-usual of coalition-building, institutional choice, and policy competition. This siloing-off makes it difficult to see regional and territorial politics in the context of national trajectories over time, especially given that some countries that have experienced wars of secession are also, unsurprisingly, homes to the continent's most prominent federal experiments in power and resource sharing across regions (Ethiopia, Nigeria, Cameroon). Distributive tensions and economic inequalities across and among regions are woven into

---

[6] Sociological theories of "horizontal inequalities" – where group identity and economic inequalities overlap – *do* draw the connection between group identities and group inequality. Yet they do not theorize the spatial dimensions of this in a systematic way. "Horizontal" has been generally taken to mean communal or ethnic (Stewart 2000), but it is used by some scholars, especially in quantitative work, as a synonym for "spatial" or regional (Mveyange 2015; Archibong 2018).

[7] This is, perhaps, the literal meaning of the term "ethno-regionalism," but this term combines two causal mechanisms – ethnicity and regionalism – that have long been taken in much political science literature as analytically distinct, and indeed, as rival accounts of political cause and effect.

[8] See Ostby, Nordhas, and Rod (2009) and de Vries, Englebert, and Schomerus (2019). Azam (2001) integrated civil war into a politics-as-usual model by arguing that the threat of secession may be a bargaining position (in pursuit of favorable regional policy) that can harden and escalate. See also Englebert (2005). For Lipset and Rokkan (1967), the regional politics of partisan and policy competition, and struggles over state design, is what is left after wars of secession have resolved the most intractable regional conflicts.

the everyday, year-on-year flow of politics in these countries, finding expression not only in war but also in electoral politics and policy competition.

In much work on African politics in the last two decades, voting and elections have been theorized as having everything to do with the retail politics of social service delivery or ethnic rent- and office-seeking, and very little to do with issues of regional economic interests and the territorial politics of state-building or state design. Conversely, territorial politics and state design have been cast as all about civil war and post-conflict deal-making when in fact, in most cases, these issues and forms of politics are concurrent, overlapping, and often iterated. They involve the same parties, same voters, and same geographically defined social groups. This book argues that in many, perhaps most, African countries, the imbrication of territorial politics and electoral politics is *politics as usual*.

2.2 REGIONS AND REGIONAL ECONOMIC DIVERSITY

The concept of region as it is used here is anchored in theories that seek to describe and explain spatially uneven processes of economic and political transformation within a single national unit. I use it here to marry economic and political geography to capture similarity, variation, and hierarchy in how subnational territories (state segments) are integrated to national political economies. Drawing on a historical analysis, comparative politics theory, and evidence from twelve African countries, I aim to demonstrate the large extent to which regional tensions arising from spatial inequalities and sectoral differences underlie overall cleavage structures in national polities, and, following Lipset and Rokkan (1967), condition the organization, goals, and policy options of national political systems as a whole.

It is rare to find the concept of region used in a theoretically motivated way in studies of African politics. Prominent work has distinguished between the political core and "rural hinterlands" of African countries, but has conceptualized the vast rural periphery of most African states as mostly undifferentiated. Herbst (2000) imagined the rural periphery as largely nonincorporated into the national polity or economy. The rural–urban divide featured in many influential studies pivots on the contrast between the two, rather than on efforts to describe and theorize the effects of differentiation across predominantly rural regions.[9]

---

[9] National capitals do indeed have stark advantages over the provinces in levels of prosperity and economic development. These are often so extreme that the urban bias literature plausibly suggested that the urban-versus-rural divide (understood as capital city versus everywhere else) was the main territorial cleavage in national politics. See Bates (1981), Bates and Block (2013), and Harding (2020). Yet scholars who have analyzed electoral populism in African cities have not argued that this is the case, although it might be possible to do so for Zambia. See Conroy-Krutz (2006), Resnick (2014), and Nathan (2019).

2.2 Regions and Regional Economic Diversity

In political science studies of African politics, the term region or ethno-region is often invoked informally, in a casual manner, as a synonym for "subnational." Sometimes ethnicity and region are used as synonyms, or packaged together agnostically as "ethno-region" (ethnicity and region? ethnicity or region?). At times, "ethno-region" refers to administrative units that contain two or more geographically proximate ethnic groups.[10] Some scholars do distinguish clearly between geographic or administrative units (region, province) and cultural or identitarian phenomena.[11] Bates (1989, 2017) and Boone (2003, 2014) take national political geographies as composed of economically and politically differentiated regions (which intersect with politically salient kinship and ethnicity in variable ways). Rabinowitz (2018) and Hassan (2020) also employ such a model. Other studies that tackle regionalism as a political phenomenon in the African context are Balans, Coulon, and Gastellu (1975), Bayart (1985), Pourtier (1989), Forrest (2004), Englebert (2005), and Markakis (2011).

Following convention in the regional economics literature, the term "region" as it is used here in a generic sense is anchored in the territorial structure of the state. It refers generally to subnational administrative and political units at the provincial or Admin1 level. These are subdivided into smaller units of administration and political representation, including districts (Admin2 units) and electoral constituencies.

In African countries, the administrative definition of "region" often *corresponds to* functional meanings of "region" in ways that are highly salient for politics. The functional economic meaning of subnational region points to a region's distinctive productive-sector profile, role or position in a national "division of labor," and in some cases, social cohesion produced by shared interdependencies, common pool assets, and jointness in policy interests.[12] Diversity of subnational regions in terms of their productive-sector profile is not only a strong correlate of economic inequality across them, but also a leading *cause* of such inequality. In Ghana, for example, farmers in southern districts that produce cocoa, a high-value crop, are much wealthier than those in the northern provinces who produce cotton, or rely on subsistence agriculture. Within the territorial grid of national states, the salience of these same regional units as units of "supply of government" and "political demand for government" is also high. Supply of government comes in the form of territorial administration, state investment, social service provision, market

---

[10] For Posner (2005), region (province) corresponded to identity group formation on the basis of language, as opposed to "tribe," which crystallized at the district level.

[11] These include Kaspin (1995), Scarritt and Mozaffar (1999), Mozaffar et al. (2003), Erdmann (2004), and Posner (2004b). Some explicitly distinguish between geographic units like "northern Malawi" or "Kenya Coast," on the one hand, and ethnic identities on the other.

[12] Scott and Storper (2003: 586) define economic "region" in terms of localized production systems sustained by informal conventions, untraded interdependencies, and relational assets.

regulation and services, and in some times and places, political repression. Units of demand for government (or demands *on* government) are the units of political representation that structure collective action in national politics. These factors combine to underpin the high political salience of regions in African countries.

Regions in African Countries: Different and Unequal

> In most of the countries of [West Africa], there is a sharp contrast between a relatively affluent south and a poorer north. For instance, ... in Côte d'Ivoire, the northerners produce cotton, but it is very much a poorer crop than the coffee and cocoa produced by southerners. In Nigeria, the giant country of Africa, the northerners rely on a typical Sahelian agriculture, growing cotton and millet, while oil [and services] dominate the southern economy. (Azam 2008: 225)

In almost all countries of the world, subnational regions vary in their economic profile. They differ in terms of their levels of economic development, industrial composition, extent of diversification, employment profile, contribution to national GDP, and growth and inequality profiles. Yet in OECD countries, with their densely networked market economies and welfare states, levels of interpersonal income inequality and of spatial inequality across regions are generally low by international standards. African countries lie at the other extreme. Generic structural features of national economies are strongly associated with high levels of subnational (regional) and interpersonal income inequality: Primary sector production represents a large share of total economic output, livelihoods of a large share of the population are natural-resource-dependent, population densities are lower, cross-regional population mobility is lower, states are weaker, and economies are more open to international trade.[13] All these factors predict high inequality. Most African countries thus present a "perfect storm" of factors that reinforce each other to predict high levels of both interpersonal and interregional inequality.

Milanovic argued in 2003 that disparities in regional per capita incomes in African countries were far more extreme than previously thought (2003: 13). His observation refers to the fact that much analysis has implicitly taken "rural Africa" to be uniformly poor. Low levels of economic development and the predominance of smallholder agriculture in most African countries were supposed to have leveling effects that flattened the socioeconomic landscape. The urban–rural divide was taken as the critical one, politically speaking.[14] Yet, as

---

[13] See UNRISD 2010: 70–72, 82–83. On a range of possible determinants, see Lessmann and Seidel (2015: 24–27).

[14] Rural poverty is indeed far greater than urban poverty. "Rural areas almost universally lag far behind urban areas" by all measures (Kakwani & Soares 2005: 28–29).

2.2 Regions and Regional Economic Diversity

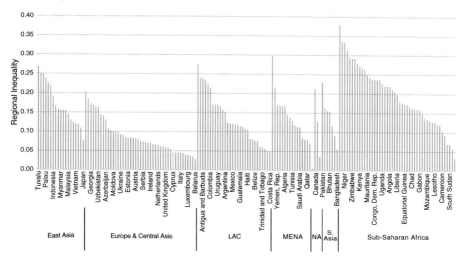

FIGURE 2.1 Spatial inequality in African countries compared to other countries, by world region
Notes and source: Data derived from nightlight density, unweighted coefficient of variation at Admin1, 2010. From Lessmann and Seidel, 2017. Figure adapted from Boone and Simson 2019. For the full SSA sample, see Figure A.2 in Appendix A.

it turns out, disparities across rural regions account for a very large share of overall inequality within African countries.[15] Comparing consumption survey data across subnational regions for Ghana and Côte d'Ivoire, for example, Brown and Langer (2009: 16–24) described regional economic disparities in both countries as "severe" and "huge." This holds for many African countries: Variations in levels of development *across regions* are very large.

Rough proxies for provincial-level GPD per capita convey a general sense of the stark magnitude of spatial inequalities in African countries compared to countries in other parts of the world.[16] Figure 2.1 captures cross-country variation in levels of regional inequality, as measured by provincial-level differences in nightlight (NL) intensity. The data were produced by Lessmann and Seidel (2015, 2017). African countries appear on the right side of the figure, with a sub-Saharan Africa (SSA) mean that is the highest of all world

---
[15] See Kanbur and Venables (2005: 11), Okojie and Shimeles (2006), Lessmann (2013), Mveyange (2015), Beegle et al. (2016), World Bank (2016: 4), Shimeles and Nabassaga (2017: 13; 2018). For a review, see Boone and Simson (2019).
[16] Lessmann and Seidel (2015: 20–21) report that by GDP per capita modeled from nightlight density data, the sub-Saharan Africa countries display, on average, the *highest* levels of subnational inequality, and that this finding is consistent across several different inequality measures. See also Lessmann and Seidel (2017), Chen and Nordhaus (2011).

34 *Region and Regionalism in African Politics*

regions. The SSA average is 50% higher than that of Latin America and the Caribbean, double that of Europe and Central Asia, and triple that of North America. While the United Kingdom struggled with Europe's highest level of regional inequality in 2020, regional inequality in Kenya was about *five times* higher.

Expectations of general convergence, where poor regions were expected to grow faster and catch up with richer ones as development progressed, have been deceptive. Analyzing data from the mid-1980s to 2000, Sahn and Stifel found that rural areas have not been converging around some average level of economic development or a higher standard. Rather, changes over time in rural well-being "differ dramatically across rural areas."[17] Patterns of growth and decline are often highly regionalized. Studies from other parts of the world also show high levels of heterogeneity in how different rural regions are affected by growth that is registered at the national level. When countries are growing, some rural regions may prosper while others stagnate or decline.

In both Tanzania and Kenya, for example, there are not only huge gaps in income and consumption between capital cities and the rest of each country, but also striking variations across provinces (Admin1 regions) in average nightlight and consumption (Boone & Simson 2019). Even excluding the regions containing capital cities, some rural provinces are, by average consumption scores, at least twice as wealthy as others. Huge gaps in living standards in these African countries are not only an urban–rural reality, but also a rural–rural reality.

Strong regional inequalities are related to variation in the profile of the primary sector activities – agriculture, pastoralism, and mining – that are the basis of most occupations and livelihoods, and to sectoral variations in how these are integrated into national economies.[18] About 65% of all Africans make their living in resource-dependent activities, a figure that can be compared to less than 1% in the United States in 2003 (Porter 2003: 559). Smallholder agriculture (centered on small family farms) is the dominant mode of production. Large-scale commercial agriculture exists in concentrated enclaves in many countries, but this is a strong exception to the predominant pattern continent-wide.

---

[17] Sahn and Stifel 2003: 593, and 593 n.25. Their study was based on twelve countries. The strong correlation between urban–rural inequality and regional inequality suggests that spatially uneven levels of urbanization are among the drivers of regional inequality (Beegle et al. 2016: 130).

[18] "Integration into the national economy" can refer both to "role" (e.g., as a pastoral region, a labor-exporting region, or an export-crop-producing region) and to level or extent. Low integration refers to a region in which most factors of production are untraded (i.e., not commodities) or only locally traded; most factors are embedded in untraded local interdependencies (i.e., nonmarket relations); and the region is largely self-sufficient – it does not depend on high levels of trade with other regions in the national economy. High integration would signal the opposite of these regional attributes.

2.2 Regions and Regional Economic Diversity

Distribution of the natural endowments that support these activities is highly uneven. The most basic of these are good soil and rainfall. Only about 25% of the land surface of the continent is arable, and there are "large differences in productivity and orientation of agriculture across space."[19] Within agriculture, sectoral differentiation is strongly spatialized: Patterns in the development of export crop production are often described as "regionalized" or enclaved. These export-producing zones are areas with high agro-ecological potential. They tend to be the most deeply integrated into national (and indeed the international) economy, and to support higher rural population densities. These factors contribute to agricultural intensification, the diversification of nonagricultural livelihood opportunities, and higher incomes.[20] Uneven integration into the national economy, access to markets, and distribution of national transport and communication systems all reflect and create regional inequality. The very narrow coverage of national social safety nets in most countries means that, for most, policy does not do much to mitigate the resulting high levels of cross-regional variation in levels of economic development.

Differences in the production profiles of regions and regional economic *inequalities* are strongly related in African countries.[21] In African countries, stark patterns of sectoral-spatial differentiation of the national economy align with regional patterns in the distribution of poverty. When subnational-level poverty data are projected onto maps, it is obvious that regions with poor soil quality and low rainfall are almost always very poor regions, measured by the poverty of the population compared to national averages. Remote regions, with poor connectivity to the rest of the national economy, are almost always poor. Regions of smallholder export crop production, by contrast, have traditionally been, and are now, among the best-off rural regions.[22] They generally have higher rural incomes, better access to social services and education, higher nightlight density, proximity to markets, and proximity to opportunities for wage-earning and other forms of

---

[19] Dercon and Gollin (2014: 484) inter alia. Rural populations are thus highly spatially clustered. Across all of SSA in the early 2000s, 90% of the population was concentrated in less than 21% of the land surface (Jayne et al. 2014: 4). See also Isham et al. 2005: 153, n. 15.

[20] Kopper and Jayne (2019: 4) distinguish agricultural regions in Africa by high or low agro-ecological potential, market access conditions (within 5 km of tarmac road, or not), and population density.

[21] In other words, interregional inequality is largely a function of regional differentiation.

[22] Levels of spatial connectivity, defined largely in terms of transport connectivity, are highly heterogeneous within most African countries, and are correlated with "large differences in productivity and in the orientation of agriculture across space" (Dercon & Gollin 2014: 484; see also Bloom et al. 1988). Judith Heyer wrote that "[i] is important to draw attention to the unevenness of sub-Saharan African rural areas' development ... What distinguishes different areas is both what is happening in the national and international economy and the internal characteristics of the areas themselves. Differences across regions are often as great as differences across countries" (1987: 549–550).

off-farm income.[23] Rural regions adjacent to main urban centers often benefit from the locational effects of proximity, density, and agglomeration, including access to markets, employment opportunities, and connectivity.

Spatial inequalities exhibit strong path dependencies in most countries of the world (Ottaviano 2003). This is also true of spatial inequalities established in African countries in the first decades of the twentieth century. These have been strongly persistent over time. As van de Walle (2009) pointed out, a large part of the explanation lies in entrenchment of the primary commodity-dependent, export-oriented structure of most national economies. Limited structural transformation of most national economies from the 1950s until today is a basic fact of African political economy.

Regional specializations in natural-resource-dependent activities geared to world markets (export agriculture, mining) correspond to patterns of advantage in national economies that have been strongly persistent over time.[24] Export-crop-producing regions were and largely remain (compared to other rural regions) leading "growth regions," measured in terms of investment in production and infrastructure, incomes, and other measures of well-being, connectivity, and density of economic activity.[25] Under colonial rule, spatially targeted public policy favored export-producing zones almost exclusively, especially before 1945. State action in other regions tended to be predatory – purely extractive – to greater or lesser degrees. Where control over land in export-crop-producing regions remained in the hands of African smallholders, control over the basic productive factors – land and labor – was widely distributed, and local populations were in a better position to capture the fruits of their labor, their own entrepreneurial energies and skills, and forms of social organization (such as the extended household as a production unit). In general, smallholder agriculture in cash crop sectors produced a wider distribution of

---

[23] Boone and Wahman (2015). See also Roessler et al. (2022). This resonates with Michalopoulos (2012) and Alesina, Michalopoulous, and Papaioannou's (2016) argument that "land inequality" across what they call ethnic homelands is the leading determinant of inequality across ethnic groups.

[24] Structure and variation in regional economic profiles can be described and measured in functional terms (sectoral), relational terms (as in a division of labor, or sectoral interdependencies), or relative terms, with reference to a single metric. Many studies use a mix of these analytic tools because each may have distinctive implications for income distribution across and within regions, collective action, policy preferences, growth profiles of regions, and positionality within the national economy. Where salient variables cluster, typologies are common. Beramendi et al. (2015: 60), for example, conceptualize "types" of subnational economy defined in terms of empirical clusters of attributes that appear historically – nature of endowment, industrial mix, and product mix (a.k.a. industrial composition), organization of production (factor intensity in production), population density and demographic attributes, location in the national economy.

[25] This is consistent with the predictions of trade theory. See Hiscox 2002. "Sector" in this trade literature refers to agriculture or manufacturing, and "industry" refers to subsectors, such as cocoa, or textiles. Here I use the term "sector" to refer to distinct economies within agriculture, such as the coffee sector, cotton sector, food crop sector, etc.

2.2 Regions and Regional Economic Diversity

economic rents from exporting than other types of extractive activities, and producer earnings were often a source of wealth accumulation and rising incomes (Isham et al., 2005). Where land was expropriated by foreign companies or white settlers and Africans were forced into laboring on the colonial farms and plantations on very disadvantageous terms, local populations sometimes suffered the erosion of preexisting forms of social cohesion. Many experienced immiseration as well. Food-producing and labor-sending regions received very little investment during the colonial era and were often hurt by import competition, peripheralization as colonial growth poles developed elsewhere, and seasonal out-migration of working-age adults. Regions made remote by how colonial boundaries and transportation networks reconfigured political and economic space and, by the colonial redirection of trade flows toward the coastal ports and Europe, were likely to be strongly disadvantaged. Subsistence agriculture and pastoralism are often the livelihoods of the poorest of the rural poor. These predominate in remote regions (Dercon & Gollin 2014: 485).

In African countries, noneconomic impediments to integration of capital, land, and labor markets are high, and this plays a critical role in reproducing cross-regional inequality. Capital markets are weak and poorly functioning, especially in the rural areas (Aker et al. 2010). Land suitable for agriculture – the most important productive asset – is nonmobile, and in most parts of most countries, it is untraded on formal markets. Labor mobility, especially rural-to-rural migration in land-based rural occupational categories (farming, pastoralism, fishing, etc.) is constrained by social and institutional factors. As Fessha and Kirby write, "the central assumption of population mobility simply does not hold" (2008: 251). Brown and Langer stress that these factors "may play an important role in maintaining or even exacerbating a country's regional inequalities" (2009: 3–4).

Rates of internal migration in most African countries – interjurisdictional migration – are low by international standards (World Bank 2009: 156). In a 2014 study of Uganda, Cali *assumed* that districts constitute separate labor markets, writing that this is a reasonable approximation based on Uganda's 1992 and 2000 household surveys: "Labor mobility between districts is limited ... The figures are very low by international standards" (Cali 2014: 1149, 1151). World Bank authors (2009) found internal migration rates (internal migrants as a percentage of working-age population) in Malawi to be extremely low: 2.7% in 2005, of which almost half (43%) were found to have migrated in the last five years. Comparison figures for Colombia, another country in which the majority of provinces are considered to be predominantly rural, are 20.1 and 26% (World Bank 2009; Ramírez & Manuel de Aguas 2017). African countries' low rates of rural-to-urban migration – compared to what rural–urban income differentials would predict – are a puzzle that migration scholarship has sought to explain (De Brauw et al. 2014). Rodden (2004: 495) and others have suggested that the hyper-growth of megacities like Lagos,

38   *Region and Regionalism in African Politics*

Abidjan, and Nairobi may be one indicator of strong impediments to more dispersed patterns of interjurisdictional mobility.[26]

Some of the major impediments to interregional labor mobility are institutional. J-P Azam wrote that "rules of land ownership inhibit migration" (2008: 226), and this is correct. Land tenure regimes work to decommodify land by restricting the development of land markets, and by reserving land access to territorially defined membership groups. As Muyanga and Jayne put it, there are "well known constraints to migration by members of one ethnic group to lands held by other ethnic groups" (2014: 99). Neocustomary land tenure regimes work in principle to reserve access to land ownership to "members only," or may provide use rights that are jeopardized if the family leaves the locale. Informal sales and informal markets exist, but the levels of land commodification and functioning land market institutions required for open land markets do not exist in most places. Strong discontinuities in population density across district borders in some parts of Kenya are testimony to these effects (Golaz & Médard 2016). Political institutional structure thus contributes to what are often glaring economic inequalities across regions and populations residing therein.

Government policy has at times aimed to mitigate regional inequalities through interregional transfers, but as in the developed world, this has rarely overturned existing regional economic hierarchies. In Africa, regional redistribution has taken the form of targeted state investment in infrastructure and productive sectors in lagging regions, and efforts to provide social services, especially primary education, more universally throughout the national territory. Some studies do indeed detect a fall in interregional inequality in the early postcolonial period (1965–1975) (UNRISD 2010), attributing this in part to regional compensation mechanisms and targeted investment in sectors in lagging regions. A subsequent rise in regional inequality in the 1980s and 1990s happened during a long period of economic downturn, coinciding with the deflationary and liberalizing reforms undertaken under World Bank and IMF-sponsored Structural Adjustment Programs (UNRISD 2010: 90, 93).[27] Some recent studies that measure cross-regional inequality in terms of nighttime luminosity describe spatial (subnational) inequality as peaking around 2000 and leveling off or falling thereafter.[28] Even

---

[26] On land liquidity and internal migration, see also Chernina et al. 2014. In African countries, social and economic issues are not the only factors. Nigeria offers an extreme case of regional governments (states) imposing "local preference restrictions" on access to jobs, education, and social services (Kraxberger 2005).

[27] Ostby et al. (2009), Mveyange (2015), and Lessmann and Seidel (2017) detected a rise in spatial inequality in the 1990s.

[28] Mveyange (2015) found that intra-regional income inequality, measured by nightlight density across subnational Admin2 units, peaked around 2005 and decreased slightly thereafter. A factor in this is electrification itself. According to the World Bank, more than 70 million people gained access to electricity in sub-Saharan Africa between 2014 and 2020. See Trotter (2016). Some studies showed that trade liberalization decreased income inequality in the urban areas but increased it in the rural areas over this period (Okoje & Shimeles, 2006: 20; Shimeles & Nabassaga, 2017: 13).

2.3 Regionalism that Arises in the Course of State-Building

so, African countries remain among the most regionally unequal in the world and appear to have been so for many decades.

2.3 REGIONALISM THAT ARISES IN THE COURSE OF STATE-BUILDING

In studies of political development in Europe, the United Kingdom, and the United States in the late nineteenth and early twentieth centuries, CPE theories foreground challenges of building political hegemony in regionally differentiated societies that were marked by tensions arising from the erosion of regional autonomies, commodification of land and labor, and political centralization.[29] A tradition of work on the late-developing countries expands on these themes, theorizing structure and variation in national politics in terms of regional hierarchies, oppositions, and alliances.[30] The comparative work offers a tool kit of concepts and hypotheses that can be used to build theory that works for African countries.

Lipset and Rokkan (1967) studied regional cleavages in the development of European party systems from the 1840s to the 1920s. They conceptualized regional economic structure not only in terms of the urban (industrial) and rural (agricultural) dimension, but also in terms of the distinctiveness of the predominantly rural regions. Regions differed by crop specialization and land ownership structure, with zones of large landholdings and agricultural tenancy at one end of the spectrum, and zones where smallholder agriculture (small independent producers) predominated at the other. Regional cleavages formed around divergent preferences over policy, partisan affiliation, and centralization of political prerogative in the national state. Strong affiliation with agrarian parties developed in some regions, but not in others. Regions were divided over competing policy preferences over stricter or looser market controls, or policies favoring particular product markets.[31] Divergent political preferences were overlaid by, and sometimes compounded by, regional identities and religious differences, especially the Catholic–Protestant divide. Cleavages expressed "deeper differences in conceptions of nationhood, domestic priorities, ... and

---

[29] A large literature analyzes the political effects of uneven development in the member states of the EU. Rovny (2015: 915) wrote "that the centre-periphery divide is a long-term structural cleavage in many societies ... permeat[ing] the structural fabric of politics, as claimed by Lipset and Rokkan." Scholars have applied this model to Britain (Hechter 2000), Spain (Beramendi 2012), Italy (Locke 1995; Agnew 1996, 1997), and Germany.

[30] See, for example, Rubin (1997), Eaton (2001), Sinha (2005), Diaz-Cayeros (2006), Eaton (2016), and Naseemullah (2022).

[31] Issues connected to regional economic integration itself are often politicized. This is not surprising. Historically, the development of national markets in land, labor, and agricultural commodities has required strong, positive regulatory commitment and enforcement on the part of the state. Trade liberalization and integration projects create uneven landscapes of winners and losers.

over the terms of incorporation of regional groups into the national political system" (Lipset & Rokkan 1967: 10, 20–21).

Bensel (1984) offered a complementary, sectorally driven theorization of regional cleavage in the course of state-building in the American case. In *Sectionalism in American Political Development, 1880–1980*, he modeled the US economy in terms of "geographical division of labor between the advanced northern core and the underdeveloped southern and western periphery" (1984: 6). These regional differences and inequalities were rooted largely in "the relationship of the separate regional economies to the national political economy and the world system" (1984: 6), and gave rise to interregional competition over economic policy, divergent political goals, and fights over the power of the federal government. What was at stake in regional competition, Bensel argues, was "control over the national political economy, regional welfare, and ... the preservation of the social and political institutions which sustain the regional economy" (1984: 4). He takes *consistency of the shape of sectional cleavage* as evidence that sectionalism, rooted in a geographic division of labor and economic hierarchy among the regions, was the encompassing driver of preference divergence and competition. The same cleavage defined competition around issues spanning multiple policy areas over many decades.[32]

Lipset and Rokkan saw territorial oppositions in the political development of Western Europe – cross-regional, core–periphery, and urban–rural tensions – as the predominant form of social cleavage in countries in the throes of transition from agrarian to industrialized societies, that is, to what they conceptualized as fully integrated and mobilized nation-states. In the US context, V. O. Key (1964), Bensel (1984), and others also emphasized the sectoral and especially the agrarian aspects of regionalism, arguing that sectional political demands, in their strongest form, arise out of resource-based, extraction-dependent economies. As V. O. Key put it, "economically-based sectionalism in its more extreme form tends to be agrarian and rural" (Key 1964: 243, cited by Bensel 1984: 13).

The regionalism that arises in the course of state-building takes shape around issues having to do with integration of regions into the national economy, regional groupings' struggle for hegemony or protection of status within the national unit, and the regionally differentiated effects of economic policy. CPE literatures converge in identifying generic domains of national collective choice in which regional politics are likely to emerge.[33] These are

---

[32] Agnew makes a related argument for mid-twentieth-century Italy, relating sectional to class cleavages. He wrote that "economic and cultural differences overlap to reinforce the geographical definition of interests and identities [and] to overwhelm [other] differences, such as those based on social class" (1997: 104–105).

[33] Massetti and Schakel (2015) and Rovyn (2015: 916) argue that, for regionalist parties in European countries, the primary dimensions of contestation arise from center–periphery tensions, and competing preferences over economic development strategies and, in many cases, state structure. The region's relative economic position often predicts its position on the

2.4 Institutions in Territorially Divided Countries

areas in which the distribution of costs and benefits of national-level policy choices – such as trade, sectoral, regulatory, labor, fiscal policies – are distributed unevenly across regions, or across regionally concentrated sectors of the economy. Regional actors also bargain over the rules of the game where the outcome of *future* bargaining rounds is at stake. Economic heterogeneity and inequality are likely to give rise to regionally specific and sometimes divergent preferences over (a) redistributive policy, (b) sectoral policy, including trade policy, (c) stricter or looser controls on national market integration, and (d) questions of state structure and national design (i.e., the territorial form of the state) (Beramendi 2012: 40; Rogers 2016). Regionalism in African countries presents in all of these substantive domains.

2.4 INSTITUTIONS IN TERRITORIALLY DIVIDED COUNTRIES

Institutions are constitutive of state structure, political representation, and markets. They segment territory and apportion powers between center and locality, core and periphery, and hierarchically ordered authorities. Administrative rules distribute prerogatives among functionally or territorially defined bureaucratic agencies of the state. Institutions also "structure the nature and political power of constituencies and construct identities for political purposes" (Rogers 2016: 2). Markets work within rules that define the scope of commodification of land, labor, and capital; terms of exchange and contract; and terms of market competition between individuals and across subnational units (Polanyi, 1944; Weingast 1995).

In the regionalism that arises in the course of state-building and national integration, state structure itself and "rules of the game" for everyday political competition are major bones of contention. An influential vein of historical institutionalist work on European countries emphasizes how territoriality-enhancing representative institutions (such as single-member district electoral constituencies and federalism) and territoriality-mitigating institutions (proportional representation electoral systems and strong centralized states) emerged as *outcomes* of historical processes of state formation that were conditioned by socioeconomic structure, and balances of power among competing interests (Luebbert 1991; Ziblatt 2006; Iversen & Soskice 2019). In a study of Latin American state-building, Kurtz writes that "administrative development itself becomes the terrain on which political conflict is fought" (2013: 178). To take state institutions and state formation in African countries seriously, then state structure must be considered in a similar way – that is, as an outcome of endogenous political processes that can constrain politics in potentially consequential ways.

---

left–right dimension of politics. See also Henderson et al.'s (2013) study of fourteen substate regions in contemporary Europe. Bolton and Roland (1997) and Beramendi (2012) model rival regional preferences and strategic bargaining among regions over fiscal and redistributive policy (and institutions), based on each province's relative wealth and inequality profile.

Work on African states in the last several decades has tended to downplay institutional structure and its effects on politics. As Lockwood and coauthors recently put it,

Indeed, for several decades [following the 1970s and 1980s], the continent was assumed to be effectively "institutionless," lacking effective political organizations such as parties, and entirely reliant on informal institutions such as patronage and traditional authority to shape political behavior ... With few exceptions, parties and other formal institutions were side-lined in academic research over this period, in favor of concepts such as neopatrimonialism and clientelism, and a focus on big men and regimes of personal rule. (Lockwood, Krönke, & Mattes 2022: 204)

Many theories of state structure in Africa – in both its colonial and postcolonial forms – emphasize the absence or weakness of state institutions, especially outside of the capital cities. Herbst (2000) suggested that African states actually lack territorial structure and reach. He presented the extreme weakness of territorial and administrative institutions for projecting state power across space as a defining feature of African polities. A related argument that is common in behavioral and experimental studies is that the internal administrative boundaries of states are the "natural" expression of precolonial social organization and state structure, and thus have no effects independent of those that emanate from innate features of African society. These positions reinforce biases against institutionalist explanations in studies of African politics (and in favor of culturalist explanation).

The argument about institutions advanced in this book focuses on those that define basic parameters of state, national economy, and national political space in African countries carved out by late nineteenth- and twentieth-century imperial conquest, and forged over decades of direct colonial rule. Territorial divisions and subdivisions were defined by colonizers for their own alien purposes, in competition and conflict with African resisters and collaborators, often in stark discontinuity with earlier state forms and state goals. In the wake of conquest, one such purpose was to create a new framework that would facilitate the restructuring of economic activity and political authority (now subordinated to colonial overrule) within each colony. Another involved defining the social and geographic boundaries of political collectivities, and assigning and codifying new political/social identities on the basis of residence in territorial units defined by the colonial state. Posner wrote that "the impact of Africa's colonial era boundary drawing ... may lie as much within states as at their borders" (2004: 543), and this is the line of argument developed here.[34]

The resulting political segmentation of territory, and the imposition of a scalar, hierarchical ordering of political and administrative units have been

---

[34] There is a growing literature on internal boundaries and borders. See Lentz (2013), Nugent (2019), Leonardi (2020), Wilfahrt (2021), and Müller-Crepon (2023). See also Young (2018) and Hassan (2020).

2.5 Regionalism in African Countries

consequential for the organization of the economy, the presence and action of the state, and the political organization and representation of the citizenry.[35] Institutions that divide territory into "state segments" delimit the field of action of territorially defined state agencies that work in ways that promote regional economic differentiation. Often, policy is delivered in very different ways across regionally defined population groups. At the same time, multiscalar institutional structures create possibilities for vertical coalition-building strategies that accommodate heterogeneity in the nature of politics at different scales of the polity (Gibson 2006, 2013; Boone 2014; Mares 2015). Communities that cohere around local solidarities or local mechanisms of political control can be drawn into interest-based coalitions that span many electoral constituencies or districts. Such segmenting and scalar effects are accentuated, and more visible, under multipartism, opening up the analytic possibilities that are leveraged across Chapters 4–7 of this book. The politics of federalism and decentralization in African countries – on both the demand and supply side – are classic forms of territorial politics that play out in territorially divided states.[36]

Some of the correlates of strongly territorial features of the state's administrative and representative structures (and practices) are observed in the literature on African electoral politics, but are often attributed to the innate, centrifugal forces of ethnic diversity. Ethnic diversity has often been seen as the cause of weakly nationalized party systems, the importance of clientelism at the retail level of politics, and indeed, the *political* salience of ethnicity. I argue that political institutions not only contribute strongly to these outcomes but can also be strong drivers in themselves. At the same time, institutions overlay strong spatial inequalities to promote electoral coalition-building at the regional level, persistent regional oppositions in national politics, and regionalism in policy debates in national political arenas.

2.5 REGIONALISM IN AFRICAN COUNTRIES: WHEN INSTITUTIONS AND INEQUALITIES ALIGN

My main argument is that tensions rooted in regional economic heterogeneity and inequality are fundamental and persistent drivers of cleavage in national politics and policy debates in most African countries. An important cause of this, I argue, lies in how divergent interests arising from regional economic inequalities are channeled into national politics by political institutions. The high salience of regionalism in national politics is a function of *both* the degree or intensity of regional economic heterogeneity and inequality, and the extent

---

[35] Geographic scale refers to the relations between the micro (individual, household), the local (village, municipal), "local" (district, in some accounts), regional (provincial; administrative region), national, and global. Scalar hierarchies are a way of imposing government.

[36] Work on subnational unit creation since the 1990s does take state structure as a "dependent variable" in political analysis. See Chapter 7.

to which (and how) institutions work to channel regional interests into the public sphere. In many, perhaps most, African countries, governmental institutional structures (administrative, economic, representative, and around property rights) *overlay* or align with patterns of spatial inequality, sectoral specialization, and uneven economic development across predominantly rural regions. Institutions and inequalities tend to align. Where this is the case, regional cleavages go far in structuring national electorates, and regionalism is a salient force in national-level politics.

Territorial institutions have shaped patterns of sectoral–spatial differentiation in national economies, and define collective actors in politics in place-based terms (Chapter 3). They thus play a role in shaping political collectivities, the economic and political interests of actors at various scales of multitiered political systems (from local to district, regional, and national levels), and political strategies. Provincial divisions (Admin1 divisions) are often associated with politically salient factors that are sources of convergence or divergence in political preferences at the regional level. Policy is often tailored for particular territorial subunits and has helped to define and promote sectoral specialization within these administrative units over time. Regions and districts are units of national resource allocation. A corollary is jointness on the demand side in interaction with government: in demanding protection, representation, and spatially targeted policy. Electoral constituencies are nested within province- and district-level administrative units that are differentially affected by the gathering of power at the center of the political system, state-wide and regional policy, and growth (or decline) of the national economy over time. Citizens seek to valorize, protect, or contest subnational citizenship rights and property rights that are pegged to particular subnational jurisdictions.

State institutional structure thus plays both an important role in structuring units and their interests, and in the aggregation of interests in the national political arena. In Africa's multilevel political systems, political parties or other organizations and entrepreneurs compete at the national level by building alliances at regional and district levels. Because these institutional structures and patterns of uneven development are traceable to state formation projects set in motion in the early twentieth century and have been largely reproduced in the postcolonial period, I dub the dominant, overtime tendency *"regionalism by design"* (Chapter 3).

Evidence of the politicization of regional differentiation and regional economic inequality in structuring national politics is found in regional bloc voting, patterns of regional economic and political dominance in national politics, persistent regional polarizations in some countries, and the types of policy issues and constitutional debates that animate national political agendas.

Regional bloc voting and the "persistent electoral blocs" observed in our sample of twelve African countries in the 1990s–2010s are expressions of,

2.5 Regionalism in African Countries

and evidence of, regionalism in national politics (Chapter 4).[37] In all twelve countries, regional cleavage structure is visible in electoral politics, finding expression in predominantly rural regional voting blocs that span many constituencies and multiple administrative districts that have stuck together in most presidential elections over at least the last two decades. All countries are marked by high spatial inequalities by global standards, and in eleven of the twelve, regionalism is the predominant form of political cleavage in national politics. The outlier in the sample is South Africa, the one country in the sample in which regionalism is *not* a striking feature of national politics.

Evidence of the role of regional inequalities in structuring national political competition is also found in long-standing hierarchies among electoral blocs in terms of their economic standing, and the coalescing of national winning electoral coalitions around "economically leading electoral blocs" in most countries (Chapter 5). Many countries are marked by a decades-long polarization or "territorial opposition" between two main regions (Lipset & Rokkan 1967), creating a single axis of competition that defines national politics for many decades (Chapter 6). Regionalism in African countries also finds expression in the types of redistributive struggles that are prominent on national political agendas (Chapter 7).

Mechanisms by which spatial inequalities and territorial institutions produce these political effects arise from economic interests, the agency of political actors, and ideologies that tap into consciousness of a shared position of regional advantage or disadvantage in the national arena. *Regional economic interests* derive from sectoral roles and regional position within the national economy. Voters in contiguous, geographically defined electoral constituencies are likely to have shared preferences that arise from features of the endowment, local economic conditions, regions' sectoral production profiles, and the political–economic organization of the district and region they inhabit. Because electoral constituencies are nested in district and provincial administrative institutions, clusters of neighboring constituencies often experience jointness in the supply of, and demand for, spatially targeted government policy.[38] Following

---

[37] We use a regional GDP proxy (nighttime luminosity), educational data, and sectoral profiles to measure and describe regional economic differences. Writing of the OECD countries, Rickard reports that "[f]ew empirical measures of economic geography exist. Measuring geographic patterns of economic activities, such as sectoral employment, is difficult because doing so requires large amounts of highly disaggregated data" (2018: 28). She points out that some of the leading theoretical work in the field of political economy relies on highly aggregated and grossly simplifying assumptions about the spatial distribution of economic activity in OECD countries, so the need to do so here should not dissuade us. Simplified measures capture much of the variance we are interested in.

[38] Scholars often equate the interests of voters with those of the firm or sector in which they are employed, and argue that in localities in which most livelihoods depend on a given industry or sector, voters' fortunes and interests are tied to those of that sector. We know that individuals' fortunes are tied to sectors prominent in their localities and districts, even when they themselves do not work in that sector (Scheve & Slaughter 2001).

large political economy literatures, I use the extent and nature of a region's sectoral economic specialization to draw inferences about the policy interests of residents (voters) who live in that region, as well as the policy orientations of politicians who depend on the political support of persons tied to that region.[39] Interests are inferred from context, rather than observed directly at the individual level.[40]

Political agency is necessary to the production of regional cleavages and regionalism. The persistence of electoral blocs is itself an effect of, and indeed evidence of, political agency on the part of politicians, political party builders, regional leaders, builders of national winning coalitions in presidential elections, and other political entrepreneurs. Regional leaders and partisan actors exercise political agency by appealing to regional interests and, in the case of leading producer regions, by offering regionally targeted policies that can respond to such interests. Political leaders and partisan actors also appeal to regional consciousness of advantage and disadvantage within the national economy.

Political actors' interests and strategies, and those of political parties, are shaped by the unequal distribution of power across units, heterogeneity of regional interests, and aggregation rules. Members of Parliament have reelection-seeking strategies targeted at the constituency level, and this has been the focus of much of the microlevel research focused on electoral clientelism in political science. This existing work is compatible with my argument, in that many of these same actors are likely to have political interests at the supra-constituency level, and that in the pursuit of these ends, they coalesce and align with other actors at the regional scale of politics. As Mares writes of district-level and party-level explanations of legislators' behavior, "both can operate within the same case by capturing constraints on the activity of legislators that operate at different levels" (2015: 209).

Regional economic inequality itself is politically salient because it shapes not only interests but also *regional consciousness*. Positionality – that is, the relative political and economic clout of regions – informs ideologies of regional

---

[39] High regional specialization is expected to give rise to more homogeneous interests, while greater economic diversification should give rise to more heterogeneity in regional interests.

[40] As Rickard explains it, "Most voters work to earn a living and as a result, their personal economic prosperity is closely tied to the economic fortunes of their employer [or firm or sector ... People employed in a given industry share a common interest in the economic performance of the industry and government policies that promote its performance" (2018: 4). She takes it as axiomatic that, where sectors or industries are geographically concentrated and account for a significant share of local employment/livelihoods, we can expect voters and industries in that locality to have a political interest in the health and future of that sector. She argues that under territorial systems of political representation, politicians are likely to target generous subsidies at industrial sectors if and when "the potential beneficiaries are geographically concentrated" in the politician's district (14).

Conclusion: A New Model

entitlement or grievance.[41] Within a dynamic economy composed of regions that are differentially ranked vis-à-vis each other in terms of levels of economic development, and differentiated by sectoral specialization, the relative economic standing of regions and the expansion of gaps between them can become major *enjeux* in national political development. Relative standing influences a region's clout in present and future rounds of policy bargaining. The small gains of some may seem paltry in relation to the large gains of others. And as Frances Stewart (2000) pointed out, lagging groups tend to blame government for their relative disadvantage. She argued that "horizontal inequality" is almost always viewed in political terms.

CONCLUSION: A NEW MODEL

This work proposes a new model of structure and political cleavage at the national level in African countries. The focus is on political cleavages arising from regional economic differentiation and associated socioeconomic inequalities, as they are structured and channeled into the national political arena by strongly territorial institutions. My argument pertains to a level of politics – the regional level – that remains hidden in studies that rely solely on individual-level data, ethnic data that is stripped of geographic and economic content, and/or national-level aggregates. I aggregate up from the level of (voters in) constituencies to districts and provinces, revealing the geographic structure of political competition as it is visible at the national level. The relevant time period is decades, rather than the snapshot of a single election. This explanatory framework largely encompasses the observed phenomenon of ethnic clientelism at the individual and locality level, but it yields inferences about national politics that diverge from those rooted in micro studies. These inferences have to do with stability in national cleavage structures and cross-national variation therein, the conditions that give rise to and undergird political hierarchy and exclusion, and the salience of policy issues associated with divergent regional interests in national politics.

---

[41] Ideologies of regional entitlement include ideologies of "rightful" or natural leadership on the part of the most economically productive or advanced regions. Regional grievance is the focus of an outpouring of work in the late 2010s on "the politics of resentment" in left-behind regions. On political consciousness around regions' position in the national economy, see Alherup, Baskaran, and Bigsten (2016), Cramer (2016), Iammarino, Rodriguez-Pose, and Storper (2019), Burgoon et al. (2019).

3

Endowment, Institutions, and Spatial Inequality

Regions by Design

> Questions are geopolitical before they are political in the narrow sense.
>
> Le Roy 2011: 19

The term "regions by design" encapsulates the argument that economic development policy and institution-building under colonial and postcolonial rule promoted regionalization of national economies. Regionalization was an integral part – indeed a fundamental principle – of European efforts to restructure precolonial economies within the boundaries of the territorial units created by the Berlin Conference's partition of the continent into European colonies. Within each colony, administrative *découpage* – cut up, carve up, segmentation – created a template for territorially segmented strategies of imposition of colonial state authority, and for differential incorporation of regions into a colony-wide economy. Differentiated endowment (soil fertility, coastline) (Engerman & Sokoloff 2002) and preexisting variations in settlement patterns and political organization were thus overlaid by uneven patterns of colonial economic development, state-enforced impediments to population mobility, and territorially segmented forms of rule. This promoted stark patterns of economic differentiation across subregions of each colony.

In this chapter, I show that these same territorial political institutions – colonial Native Authorities (NAs) and cantons, districts (Admin2 units), and provinces (Admin1 units) – structured the integration of African populations into the colonial polity. Strong territorial administration served to structure the supply of the state (regulation, public policy, repression, local government), native populations' opportunities for legal recognition by the state (as collectivities, not individuals) and demand-making on the state (institutions for political collective action and representation). Colonial-era institutional channels for regionally differentiated economic development

48

Endowment, Institutions, and Spatial Inequality: Regions by Design 49

and political incorporation of the citizenry were largely *reproduced* in the postcolonial era.[1]

The chapter is divided into six sections. Together they argue that territorial strategies and territorial institutions forged in the colonial period have contributed strongly to regionalization of national economies, and to the territorially segmented and differentiated incorporation of populations into national political life. Section 3.1 places this analysis of territorial institutions in theoretical context and summarizes the chapter's main argument. Section 3.2, "regionalization of the economy," stresses the great extent to which colonial rulers employed territorial strategies of economic development, which were founded upon paradigmatic ideas of colonies as composed of different and unequal regional units. Boundary-drawing, regionally targeted administrative interventions to promote region-specific production profiles, and restrictions on inter-unit mobility were critical instruments. Colonial forms of spatial economic inequality were thus produced partly *by design*. Section 3.3, "regionalization of the citizenry," shows that delimiting "tribal units" within the same institutional grid created a political geography that corresponded to the economic one. Section 3.4 pulls together these two lines of argument to illustrate how the colonial states' institutional grids defined the building blocs of national political economies. Section 3.5 argues that these territorial institutions structured political mobilization in the nationalist era. While ethnic identities coalesced at the district level, regions served as templates for scaling up – that is, for building coalitions and political parties to compete in the national arena.

The last and longest section of this chapter, Section 3.6, extends these arguments to the postcolonial era. It begins by demonstrating the large extent to which postcolonial governments preserved the basic grid of territorial administration and political representation that they had inherited from the colonial era. I then show that national economic planning in the era of the postcolonial developmentalist state took this same territorial grid as the template for resource allocation, reinforcing the political salience of districts and regions as units of allocation and representation. The same state institutions and practices created political constraints and incentives that worked to channel territorial interests into national politics and to promote regional-level coalitions as main protagonists in national-level competition. The net effect is the "regionalization of politics" in postcolonial Africa which is the main subject of this book. Some important ways in which political bargaining, strategy, and identities contributed to regionalization of postcolonial politics are sketched out in the last segment of the chapter. These have to do with the politics of territorial unit persistence, incentives for regional coalition-building in electoral politics, and the rise of regional consciousness.

---

[1] It is true that there are strongly nationalizing institutions, too, and these have indeed received attention in the literature. They are strong national civil service, national education systems, national parties as in the era of one-party states, and presidentialism.

3.1 THEORIZING TERRITORIAL INSTITUTIONS

Territorial strategies of rule – the grounding of state authority in new divisions of space, and the establishment of new systems of rule within new local jurisdictions – were central to the making of modern African states. This is a classic strategy of empire.[2] Key technologies and practices were mapping, geographic classification of populations, segmentation of economic zones by functional activities, and constructing hierarchical authority by nesting subordinate areal units within larger territorial divisions (Sack 1986). It can be taken as an instance of a general phenomenon theorized by David Harvey as "the production of regionality" (2006: 102) by the state through territorial administration, workings of the regulatory apparatus, investment in built environment, and promotion of geographically differentiated modes of production and consumption. For Harvey, it is "a major determinant of uneven geographical development" (2006: 102).

This chapter argues that this is indeed what we see in the British and French colonies in Africa. Administrative boundaries and local units of political representation contribute to segregation of populations into subnational citizenship groups; impediments to the mobility of population, labor, and business activity; less-than-full integration of national markets; and sectoral differentiation of regional economies. This contributes to the regional economic heterogeneity and spatial inequalities that are at center stage in the present analysis.

The analysis of state institutions presented here focuses strongly on territorial administration (districts and provinces). There are large literatures on colonial officers themselves (district officers, *commandants*) and on the authoritarian legacies of this period of state formation. Yet the enduring institutional legacies of the colonial *découpage administratif* itself (carving up of national territory into administrative units), and indeed, the internal political structure and functions of these subnational units, have been largely invisible in the political science literature on Africa.[3]

Territorial administration, past and present, produces political effects by serving as an institutional template for structuring state action in the "regionalization" of economies, and as a planning framework and paradigm for state-led regional development. Administrative boundaries often serve as containers for policies, directives, and resource allocations that have shaped regions' and districts' distinctive producer profiles over time, often in line with regional economic "vocations" defined within colony-wide, spatial divisions of labor.

---

[2] See Barkey's (2008) study of the Ottoman Empire, Naseemullah's work on India and Pakistan (2022), and many works on nationalities policies in the former USSR (e.g., Martin 2001). Vandergeest and Peluso (1995) identify the "territorialization of rule" as a defining characteristic of British imperial rule in both Asia and Africa. They focus on Thailand, emphasizing territorialization as achieved by establishing control over natural resources – arable land, forest, grazing land – and, thus, power over the people who use them.

[3] Notable recent exceptions include Hassan 2020 and Wilfahrt 2021.

3.1 Theorizing Territorial Institutions

Boundaries and practices of territorial administration have also imposed impediments to market and other forces that might otherwise have done more to erode divisions among units over time, especially in the land tenure domain. Territorial administration also produces political effects as an "organizational actor" in national politics, conceptually akin to the military or the civil service (Branch & Cheeseman 2006; Hassan 2020).

At the same time, territorial administration shaped political communities themselves, and their strategies for pursuing representation and political power at the national level. Extensive historiographical literatures document the role of colonial Native Authorities (NA) and similar indirect rule jurisdictions in shaping political communities and identities in modern Africa. Here, I widen the analytic lens to bring into focus the institutional and economic–geography foundations of these NA jurisdictions and the political identities associated with them. Administrative institutions at the district and provincial (regional) level defined the geographic scale at which "politically relevant ethnic groups" coalesced in the national political arena.[4] Drawing a distinction also emphasized by Posner (2005), I argue that colonial states tailored ethnic identities to fit the administrative scale of *districts* (or subdistricts). In the anti-colonial (nationalist) period and postcolonial era, political entrepreneurs scaled up political mobilization and collective identities to the administrative scale of *regions* (provinces). Institutions of territorial administration and regional economic inequalities provided the political opportunity structure, the material bases of regional forms of political consciousness, and electoral incentives for the coalescing of regional interests and identities that aggregated or transcended the ethnic identities codified by colonial rulers. These form the principal building blocs of political coalitions, defining enduring lines of political cleavage at the national level.

My argument is that these institutional and historical processes work to bring territorial divisions to the fore. For analytical clarity, the institution-focused argument of this chapter is summarized in the three columns of Figure 3.1. Column I: Territorial institutions of the state are an instrument in bringing about the planned regionalization of the economy and segmentation of the population into discrete ethnicized units. Column II: These institutions structure the supply of government (repression, resource flows, local and regional authority), and shape the political organization of the citizenry. Column III: Institutions work to make territorial economic heterogeneity and spatial inequality politically salient, shaping the political expression of identities and interests.

Territorial institutions, defined in the early to mid-twentieth century, have remained largely intact over the last many decades. This goes far in reproducing the importance of regional inequality and regional economic heterogeneity in shaping patterns of coalition and cleavage in contemporary African

---

[4] On scale, I follow Agnew's (1997) work on Italy.

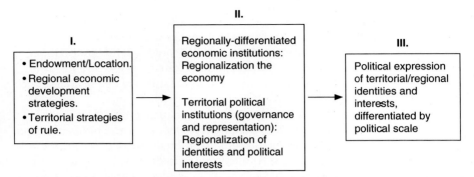

FIGURE 3.1 Uneven development and territorial institutions bring spatial inequalities to the fore in politics

countries. Institutional persistence itself is an outcome endogenous to politics (Knight 1992). Indeed, the enduring prominence on government agendas of initiatives to *redesign* territorial representation and administration is testimony to this (see Section 3.4 and Chapter 7).

3.2 COLONIAL PERIOD: REGIONALIZATION OF THE ECONOMY

> Rarely noticed by outside observers, the African countryside in the [first half of the] twentieth century became the scene of a long-term but radical change in spatial organization.
>
> Von Oppen 2006: 57

Colonial states in Africa were conquest states that employed geopolitical strategies to project and institutionalize their power. The model was fundamentally *spatial* in its logic of control, as emphasized in long-standing literatures on colonial rule and economic history, as well as in recent works by historians like Cherry Leonardi (2020) and Alden Young (2018). It consisted of dividing the governed territory into subzones or "sectors," and placing each under the concentrated authority of an appointed field agent of the center. The territorial grid imposed by the colonial state was its basic tool for segmenting space and conquered peoples into governable subterritories and subpopulations that could be dominated and exploited in differentiated ways in service to the colony and the metropole.

The basic architecture of the colonial state was built from the top down ("superimposed"). Regional and district officers commanded large territories delimited as the main territorial subdivisions of each colony (*cercles* and *cantons* in French West Africa, provinces and districts in most of British Africa). These provincial-level (Admin1) and district-level (Admin2) territories were basic units for maintaining territorial conquest; organizing resource extraction

3.2 Colonial Period: Regionalization of the Economy 53

and economic development; and grouping, classification, and control of populations (including disarmament, displacement and relocation, and mobility control). Subdivisions of the main provincial units generally served as arenas for constructing institutions of local administration, implementing economic policies, and building infrastructure. Regions and districts were the relevant units in which strategies of economic development, taxation, mobility control, and governability of local populations were formulated and implemented (Young 2018: 46–75).

Uneven economic development during the colonial period was therefore not a spontaneous result of uneven endowment and haphazard economic opportunity. Colonial regional economic planning and zoning aimed to develop strategies of exploitation and rule specific to each region. At the same time, policy and administrative practice intentionally enforced the separation and distinctiveness of regions through buffer zones, natural barriers, tribal boundaries, and restrictions on population movement (and trade) across internal borders within a given colony. Through these mechanisms, colonial economic planning and institution-building played a major role in producing the *particular forms of uneven economic development* that took shape in colonial Africa.

For the European colonial powers, claiming territory at the Berlin Conference in 1885 only set the stage for what was often a drawn-out process of actually taking control of territory and gaining acquiescence of populations through negotiation with existing political authorities (peace through protectorates, as in Northern Nigeria and Northern Ghana) or through sheer conquest. Military governors in the early decades of French and British rule delimited colonies into conquered and "unpacified" zones. In "unpacified" zones, populations were subjugated incrementally as colonial militaries moved inland, imposing overrule in what was often piecemeal or *tache d'huile* fashion, whereby establishment of a military command post created a hub for the gradual outward spread of domination through village-by-village threats and the violent crushing of resistance, as in central and western Côte d'Ivoire in the 1900s and 1910s.[5] Colonial regions or provinces were geopolitical territories under the control of military governors.[6]

By the 1910s and 1920s, colonial regimes were more secure in their control, and economic planning and governance became more earnest and systematic. Each colony developed as an economic entity in itself,[7] intended to

---

[5] See Kuba and Lentz (2003: 8) on Burkina Faso. On Malawi, from conquest to rule by District Commissioners, see Chipeta 1986.

[6] The basis of colonial state authority was conquest. This goes far in defining its essentially territorial character. Reliance on means of control and exploitation that are essentially territorial follows from this.

[7] Or, in the cases of Afrique Occidentale Française (AOF) and Afrique Equatoriale Française (AEF), each Federation.

54   *Endowment, Institutions, and Spatial Inequality: Regions by Design*

be both self-supporting (to "pay its own way") and to provide the benefits to the metropole – raw materials and markets – that colonialism's promoters and propagandists had promised. As Crowder wrote, "European governments [would play] a much more dominant role in the economies of their African colonies than they ever did at home" (1968: 275). Their ambitions increased over time.

Colonial territorial administrative grids of provinces and districts provided the spatial framework for the *mise en valeur* of the colonies. For agents of both the pre-WWII colonial extractive state and the post-WWII "colonial developmentalist state," the challenge was to expand the production of agricultural commodities of interest to the metropole where this was already well underway, and to bring forth such production – by direct coercion, if necessary – in zones seen as propitious for such development but that lay outside the reach of the colonial economy. This required, *inter alia*, the development of a grid of transport infrastructure of roads, railways, rail stations and trading centers, commercial depots, and ports. Commercial flows were shaped within provinces and districts through licensing, taxing, price setting and other forms of regulatory fiat.

Colonial state interventionism and activism was organized and executed by agents of the territorial administration – that is, regional governors and district officers who commanded, surveilled, oversaw the governing of, and taxed explicitly delimited geographic zones. They were stationed in administrative centers or posts that were networked vertically to colonial capitals and in downward fashion to lesser colonial agents and African agents of governance in district or subdistrict jurisdictions. This helps explain the strong tendency for crop development zones, sectoral projects, infrastructure development, marketing centers and catchment areas, and export-crop-marketing circuits to align with administrative regions. As the French Chef de Cercle de Louga in Senegal directed in 1927, "administrative division should correspond as exactly as possible to the economic regions created by colonial rule" (quoted by Wilfahrt 2021: 87).

As Ellen Basset wrote, "colonial planners' approach was top-down and almost exclusively spatial" (2015: 10). Regions and districts were delineated and ascribed an economic identity in a spatial division of labor, according to their location, endowment, population, and political makeup.[8] Deliberately nonuniform, location-specific economic development strategies were designed to draw separate regions into the emergent colonial economy and polity in

---

[8] Cresswall (2012: 65–70) associates this kind of regional development (or regional approach to development of the national economy) with the 1920s' concepts of planning, as epitomized by GOSPLAN in the Soviet Union. See also the contemporaneous case of the Tennessee Valley Authority (TVA) in the United States, originally conceived as a massive regional development agency that became a model for modernization of agrarian societies in the developing world after WWII.

3.2 Colonial Period: Regionalization of the Economy

differentiated, hierarchically ordered ways. Rambanapasi wrote that, in colonial Southern Rhodesia in the 1920s and 1930s, the regional development of the provinces "reflected a consistent attempt at differentiation of regions" (1989: 275) to draw out resources for transmission [to the center].

Region-making followed the contours of uneven natural endowment, locational constraints (distance from coast and ports), and the presence or absence of sociopolitical organizations that were (a) propitious for the expansion of smallholder export crop production and (b) could be incorporated into the colonial political economy at acceptable cost to the colonizers, calculated roughly in terms of capital, the need to balance the use of overt coercion against the cost of backlash, and planning capacity. Delimitation of borders and boundaries incorporated consideration of regional ecologies and natural limits, such as rivers, and what Dozon (2008) called "certain kinds of ethnographic and linguistic knowledge," prior contacts with African polities, and knowledge about their history. Administrative sectioning was refined and adjusted during the 1910s and 1920s "in the course of pacification, penetration, and administrative structuring of [each] colony."[9]

Planning took place almost everywhere via colonial forms of *regional development* by which regions "come to be defined in functional terms, in service of economic development. [The goal was] to make administrative and economic structure coincide."[10] *Regionalization* of the colonial economy was the explicit goal.

Highly interventionist forms of state activism were crafted to elicit particular forms of economic change. Rather than policy uniformity across each colony, the colonial authorities relied on policies and regulations that were regionally targeted. Taxation regimes were regionally differentiated, stipulating whether colonial taxes had to be paid in cash, kind, or labor, depending on whether districts were to supply cash crops, food crops, or labor to the colonial enterprise. Infrastructural development, compulsory export crop cultivation, export crop production induced by monetary incentives, movement and *"regroupment"* [regrouping] of populations, and forced labor regimes were constructed to bend existing economies and social systems to the "vocation" ascribed to each province or district. Regions that could not be profitably drawn into the

---

[9] From *Journal Officiel, Repertoire Administratif du 1925: Côte d'Ivoire, Circonscriptions Administratives*, p. 104. So it was that in Eastern Côte d'Ivoire, Cercle d'Indénié (one of the oldest in Côte d'Ivoire and comprising "all of the Comoé Basin") had in 1896 its chef-lieu at Zaranou and posts at Bettié, Zaranou, and Attakro. The northern part of the Cercle was attached to Bondoukou for five months in 1899, then became independent for a few years, but was then attached to the circumscription of Assikasso, Indénié Cercle, in 1910. The chef-lieu was transferred to Abengourou in 1915. The boundaries of the *cercles* of Bondoukou and Indénié were modified in 1919. *Journal Officiel, Repertoire Administratif du 1925: Côte d'Ivoire, Circonscriptions Administratives, Cercle d'Indénié*, p. 115.

[10] M. C. Maurel 1984 (cited by Médard 1999: 13–14), writing of planning philosophy in France and Eastern Europe after WWII.

56 Endowment, Institutions, and Spatial Inequality: Regions by Design

colonial economy were ignored, or governed with the goal of insulating them from the changes sweeping the more economically dynamic zones. This was regionalization by design.[11]

Within this spatial framework, colonial administrations targeted export-producing provinces or districts as the "core" or backbone of the colonial economy and prioritized these in the allocation of capital and infrastructural development. In much of colonial Africa, this meant zones producing agricultural commodities for export. The most widespread mode of export crop production was farming by smallholders or peasants – African farmers on their own land, working predominantly with family labor.

In some zones, smallholder **export crop production** was established in the mid- to late 1800s. Here, the colonial *mise en valeur* was largely a matter of expanding internal production and channeling it to the coast through state-regulated marketing circuits. This was the case in the cocoa- and palm-oil-producing regions of southern Ghana and southern Nigeria, for example. Elsewhere, it could be a process of introducing a crop the colonizers desired, such as cotton or tobacco, and coaxing, incentivizing, pressuring, or forcing people to produce it. In both situations, the task of the colonial administration was to organize the development of transport, marketing, and regulatory systems to structure the flow and resources in and out of the rural economy.[12] Policies to achieve this were designed and implemented at the district or multidistrict level.

Colonial planning paradigms defined particular provinces and districts as agricultural production units specialized in the production of a particular export crop. In Côte d'Ivoire in the 1920s, there were coffee *cercles*, cotton *cercles*, and *cercles* in which the production of cocoa was made compulsory (Crowder 1968: 283; Staniland 1970). In colonial Sudan, the Nuba Mountains Development Area was created in 1939 as an autonomous administrative region focused on the production of cotton (Young 2018: 60–66). The Provincial Administration itself undertook road building, the development and regulation of commercialization infrastructure and marketing circuits, and direct administration of the cotton scheme.[13] Large-scale foreign-owned **plantation, estate, and concessionary agriculture** developed in particular enclaves

---

[11] A familiar typology of colonial economies differentiates them into settler, peasant, and plantation types, depending on the Europeans' patterns of land use and how they structured colonial populations' incorporation as bearers of labor power into the colonial/cash economy (Amin 1974; Austin 2010). Iliffe and others employ this logic to analyze geographic differentiation that developed *within* each colony. The coastal colonies of West Africa were segmented into regions of "peasant export crop production" (coffee, cotton, palm oil), "labor-sending regions," food-crop-producing regions, and pastoral regions, each with its own "economic vocation."

[12] Organizing inflows of migrant labor to the more dynamic cash-crop-producing zones was part of this mandate.

[13] Officials decided which specific areas should be "reserved" for "the Nuba" for cotton cultivation, and set official production targets (Young 2018: 60–66).

3.2 Colonial Period: Regionalization of the Economy

in Central and Equatorial Africa and Liberia (for rubber), and East Africa (for tea and sisal). These were also circumscribed in administrative units for planning, labor regulation, marketing, and infrastructure provision. Zolberg wrote of the "regionalization of cash-crop development" (1966: 73).

Colonial planners intentionally designated some provinces and districts as "labor reserves" to play the peripheral role of providing a reliable flow of low-cost laborers to core smallholder export-producing zones, plantation agriculture, mines, or European settler agriculture. Often export crop production and interdistrict trade in food crops were banned or limited in "labor reserve" districts to close off alternatives to migrant labor. Regulations limited permanent migration of workers and families: Families were forced to remain in reserves in quasi-subsistence agriculture while the able-bodied traveled to zones of employment, returning home once a year for a few weeks.[14] In Uganda, "the imposition of a poll tax in West Nile in 1917 brought forth a stream of migrant labor into Bunyoro and Buganda [cash-crop producing zones] ... From here it was a short but highly significant step to the view that ... the less favored areas should remain underdeveloped in order to ensure the continued flow of [low-cost] labor to the cash-crop areas" (Jorgensen 1981: 110). Migrant labor flows were often organized, tracked, and regulated. In Senegal, migrant *navétanes* who labored in the groundnut fields of Sine-Saloum carried ID cards issued by the colonial administration that labeled, counted, and monitored them, and designated them as outsiders with only short-term permission to stay (David 1980). In Côte d'Ivoire, the colonial administration itself contracted with chiefs in *cercles* in the north to send an annual quota of laborers to the export-crop-producing *cercles* in the south.[15]

Mining enclaves developed in administrative regions such as the Copperbelt Province in Zambia and Katanga in the Congo. Development in zones peripheral to the mining enclaves was limited to promoting labor recruitment and commercial food crop production: Their economic vocation was to supply the mining enclaves with workers and cheap foodstuffs.

Colonies organized around European settlement, the settler colonies, were structured around racial divisions that were, first and foremost, spatial. Separation of space into white and African ("native") zones was paramount, with the white zones being those best endowed with land and minerals and the urban core of the colonial settler economies. The so-called White Highlands districts of Kenya, where land was expropriated from Africans and the indigenous owners were driven out, were separated from government-delineated "native reserves" by buffer zones of gazetted forest, and by provincial and district boundaries (Médard 1999). Labor and land use was structured along these lines. Taxation, forced labor policies, and land shortage drew men and women out of the reserves to work as laborers on settler farms and plantations,

---

[14] See, for example, Cordell, Gregory, and Piché (1996).
[15] On colonial southern Tanzania as a labor reserve for the north, see Becker 2019.

58 — Endowment, Institutions, and Spatial Inequality: Regions by Design

in mines, cities, and ports.[16] The circular migration model for ensuring a flow of cheap labor to the core settler economy reached its most elaborated form in South Africa's *apartheid* and pass-law system. A fundamental segmentation of territory along the lines of two different land tenure regimes – statutory for Whites versus "customary" for Africans – governed land access and use. This was the basic template for developing the agrarian economies of the settler colonies.[17] Even on land held under customary tenure in Kenya and Malawi, Africans were not permitted to cultivate the high-value cash crops that anchored the settler economies (coffee, tea, flue-cured tobacco) until the last decade and a half of colonial rule. It is clearly a mistake to see these colonial settler economies of East and southern Africa as market economies.

Pastoral zones were often rigidly delimited from agricultural zones and governed by distinctive spatial logics. The difficulties that pastoralism posed for colonial state-building are legion, precisely because colonial rulers found it difficult to extract value from this activity, and because production was nonsedentary. It defied the logic of spatial fixity that was the essence of colonial strategies of territorialization.[18]

The drive to spatial segregation found its highest expression in "**closed districts.**" These were created as "self-contained racial or tribal units," enclosed and separated from the rest of the territory. The classic example comprises the three southern provinces of Sudan. The "Southern Policy" articulated in 1930 "has been seen as a deliberate attempt to separate northern and southern Sudan" through the creation of "self-contained racial or tribal units" in the south (Leonardi 2013: 361). The entire province of Northern Kenya was also a closed district "which merchants and missionaries were forbidden from entering" (Young 2018: 60).

Mobility and trade controls helped to enforce and reinforce these segmentations. Movement between rural districts and regions was strictly regulated in many colonies. This was achieved through regulatory regimes not unlike China's hukou system or South Africa's pass system under apartheid. Mobility controls assigned individuals to particular local territories (native authority units) and imposed sanctions on those found to be present elsewhere without authorization, and reciprocally, tied access to land rights and to legal recognition under native authority systems to one's assigned home area. Colonial administrations feared "floating populations," "detribalized Africans," and "tribal interpenetrators," and were obsessed with fixing populations within

---

[16] In the farming areas of Kenya's White Highlands, until the late 1940s, workers were permitted to live as "squatters" on European farms, cultivating crops and raising cattle on their own account to subsidize what they earned in wages.

[17] In Malawi, by the 1910s, one-sixth of the total surface area of the country (3.75 million acres), concentrated in Southern Province, was held by settlers or companies under freehold or leasehold (Chipeta 1986: 32).

[18] See, for example, Ensminger (1992) on the pastoral Oromo in Kenya, Lane (1996) on Tanzania, and Hughes (2010) on the spatial dislocation and reordering of the Maasai.

3.2 Colonial Period: Regionalization of the Economy

prescribed administrative jurisdictions. This constrained movement from lagging to more prosperous regions (except in individuals' capacity as migrant laborers) and was essential both as cause and effect in upholding the neocustomary land tenure regimes that are discussed below.[19] Provincial boundaries between pastoral zones and agricultural zones, and district and intradistrict cordoning off of protected forests, parks, and reserves, further segmented space. Cross-district trade flows were also restricted. In Malawi, the colonial administration "prohibited cross-district trade in foodstuffs, unless licensed by the government for the purpose of feeding laborers employed on work of importance or work of public interest" (Chipeta 1986: 39). Access to the city was strictly controlled.

Differences in the timing, mode, and extent of incorporation of regions into the colonial economy produced strong patterns of economic differentiation. These were associated with predictable patterns of economic hierarchy between region types. Smallholder cash-crop-producing regions and zones of plantation export agriculture were the most favored. As Alden Young shows in his study of Sudan (2018, Chapter 2), there was a clear belief on the part of colonial officials that investment should be concentrated on the most developed and highest-potential regions. Regions that contributed heavily to the national (colonial) economy were favored with investment in transport infrastructure, marketing infrastructure, and post-WWII, agricultural extension services and credit for purchased inputs. In Sudan, this was the Gezira Plain, the stretch of land between the two Niles that was developed as colonial Africa's most extensive zone of irrigated export crop production (for cotton).

Commercially oriented food-producing regions, such as those that supplied food staples to mining enclaves in southern Africa (today's Zambia and Zimbabwe), were also subject to more favorable regulation and, in the Rhodesias and South Africa where white farmers were the dominant players in such markets, subsidized and protected.

By contrast, subsistence-oriented agricultural zones, where surpluses were mainly traded locally, were sometimes subject to predatory regulations that used sheer coercion to extract quotas of rice and other staples, or were treated as labor reserves. Pastoral regions were marginalized.

Highly uneven development of markets and sectoral differentiation across regions conspired to promote regionalization and drive spatial inequalities within colonies. Many colonies can be described as what Locke (1995: 28), writing of the "Third Italy," described as "composite economies," wherein regions were marked by very different patterns of economic development and regulation. In colonial Malawi, for example, modes of agricultural production and of incorporation into the colonial economy varied by province: The Shire Highlands districts were organized around plantation-scale export

---

[19] See Golaz and Médard (2016) on population density differentials along the district border between Kisii and Narok in Kenya.

60   *Endowment, Institutions, and Spatial Inequality: Regions by Design*

crop production (specializing in tea) controlled by settlers and international companies; the central districts developed largely around smallholder peasant production (cotton and air-dried tobacco); and the North was a labor reserve that was left economically undeveloped through the 1950s (Chipeta 1986: 30–42, 56).[20] As Chipeta explains, different modes of rural incorporation into the colonial economy gave rise to "distinct patterns of socio-economic differentiation and organization around socio-economic interests of the African population" (1986: 56–57): unionization in the case of workers in the southern plantation economy; cooperatives for smallholder farmers in central Malawi; and hometown associations for labor migrants from the North.

This left large zones that were not directly, or only marginally, incorporated into colonial economies. Writing of West Africa, Crowder emphasized that "[d]evelopment took place only in those areas that were of interest to the metropolitan economies, with the result that vast areas of West Africa remained untouched by the colonial régime [of economic planning]" (1968: 274) before the 1940s.

This is captured starkly in H. R. J. Davies' continent-wide *Tropical Africa: An Atlas for Rural Development*, which reported that, for Nigeria, in contrast to highly developed regions characterized by "favoured lands" with "accessibility to the coast or something special to commend their development," there are "problem areas that suffer from adverse physical conditions such as lack of rainfall or its unreliability," or areas "such as the Middle Belt in Nigeria, [where] no really suitable large-scale export crop has appeared. In general it will grow many crops, but it does not seem to grow cotton and groundnuts as well as the area to the north, and the conditions are not so favourable as further south for cacao, coffee, and palm oil" (1973: n.p.). The Middle Belt is thus a geographic zone that would be characterized by nonspecialization, the predominance of subsistence and locally traded agricultural production, and lesser and later levels of incorporation into the colonial economy.

3.3 COLONIAL POLITICAL INSTITUTIONS: REGIONALIZATION OF THE CITIZENRY

As military territories passed to civilian administration, *cercles* and districts were established and governing institutions and processes were imposed. *Cercles* and districts were subdivided into cantons or Native Authorities (NAs), which served as basic units of colonial governance and sociopolitical organization. Each defined a territorial homeland for a state-recognized tribe. Congeries of different collectivities were aggregated to the level of the new

---

[20] Chipeta explains that, by the 1930s, international and British companies had displaced settler capital as the dominant force in Malawi's economy. By then, over 90% of cotton and over 60% of tobacco were produced by peasants (1986: 56).

3.3 Colonial Political Institutions

colonial administrative unit (or larger polities were splintered into different units) and placed under the authority of a state-recognized chief. As in the USSR in the 1920s and 1930s, ethnicity was institutionalized and territorialized through the creation of administrative units that classified subject groups by ethnicity (or "autochthonous race" in the language of French administration). Native Authorities and cantons were coterminous with or nested within districts (or subdivisions), and ruled under the authority of one civilian colonial administrator. Regions brought districts (and NAs) and cantons together under a Provincial Commissioner or *Commandant de Cercle*. These pyramidal structures were anchored in administrative centers (often built out from original *postes militaires*) that served as nodes for resource flows between center and periphery.

Ethnic territories were tailored to align with the spatial organization of state administration. Small ethnic groups were amalgamated to create "tribes" that corresponded to the district level of colonial administration, and large states or ethnic groups were subdivided according to the same logic (Young 2012: 232–233). Amalgamations are extensively documented in the literature and well known to all students of colonial Africa. As Alden Young explained:

The British ethnographic literature acknowledged that the Nuba were not a single people, but the remnants of several distinct people eventually pushed into the hills and off the clay plain that dominated the landscape of Kordofan ... British officials [decided to] creat[e] policies to treat the Nuba as distinct from the Arabs [of Kordofan Province] ... [So it was that] administratively, the Nuba Mountains Development Area was created in 1939 as an autonomous region focused on the development of cotton. (2018: 60–61)

The Nuba community was thus coterminous with its designated area. Morris Nsamba (2013) writes that in northeastern Uganda, the "Karamojong" is an umbrella identity that refers to numerous indigenous or ethnic groups (Dodoth in the north, Jie in the center, Bokora, Metheniko, and Pian in the south), as well as five or more smaller ethnic groups who occupy the same colonial territorial space, Karamoja region. The people were named after the region, not vice versa. Writing of today's Burkina Faso, P. C. Hien (2003: 32) explains that, in an area of about sixty language groups, the French established seven *cercles* in 1919. Five were named after the preexisting capital cities of kingdoms (or subunits thereof), and two circumscriptions were given ethnonyms: "cercle de Lobi," "cercle de Gaoua." The Lobi *cercle* referred to the southwest and regrouped the Lobi proper as well as the Dagana, Birifor, Dyan, Gan, Teguessió, Padoro, and Phuo, among others. In 1918, one of the early *cercles* was suppressed and reattached to that of Ouagadougou, and renamed "Cercle de Mossi." In Côte d'Ivoire, small ethnic clans and collectivities were often grouped under overarching provincial- or district-level ethnic categories, giving rise to the Bété and Baoulé ethnonyms to match the administrative regions in which the constituent groups found themselves (Dozon 1985).

62 Endowment, Institutions, and Spatial Inequality: Regions by Design

Crawford Young describes how the "Bantu Kavirondo" group concept "applied to congeries of similar decentralized communities" (2012: 321) in Western Kenya that were later relabeled as Luhya, as well as "Meru" in Kenya, which is a blanket designation for eight different ethnic groups. Young identifies similar patterns of group amalgamation under "novel ethnic taxonomies" for the Kalenjin in Kenya, the Meru in Kenya,[21] the Mongo in DRC, and Bamilike in Cameroon ("a composite group in terms of modes of political organization and language ... with diverse origins") (Young 2012: 321). Similar of course is "Mijikenda" in Kenya (literally, "nine towns" or "nine tribes"). Posner (2005: 322 inter alia) describes the same process for the Bemba language identity group in Zambia, forged out of a myriad preexisting dispersion and fragmented identities and organizations. "In 1929, the Secretary of Native Affairs of Northern Rhodesia noted with satisfaction that '... a tribal organization had been created'" (Berry 1993: 28).

Sometimes territorialization strategies involved radical movement of populations and reordering of settlement patterns.[22] The Maasai were "removed" from their lush grazing lands in the central Rift Valley of Kenya and confined to much drier tribal reserves in the south. Creation of reserves for populations displaced by colonial land expropriation was standard practice in the colonies of white settlement in East and southern Africa, including Kenya, Zambia (Northern Rhodesia), Zimbabwe (Southern Rhodesia), and South Africa. Organized migrations from colonial Rwanda brought thousands of "settlers" to Kivu Province in eastern Belgian Congo. The *Terres Neuves* (New Lands) of *Sénégal Orientale* were cleared of pastoralists and opened to pioneer settlements devoted to the cultivation of groundnuts for export. In western Côte d'Ivoire and Gabon, defeated populations were regrouped along the main road axes after their villages were burned down by colonial troops. They were placed under the authority of cantonal chiefs appointed by the French. Forced displacements, directed migrations, and villagization policies were common.

Native Authority boundaries in British-ruled Africa were explicitly conceived as internal borders that would separate populations into government-certified ethnic groups, block "tribal interpenetration," and restrict mobility. In Kenya, an internal passport was required to travel across ethnic units. Native Authorities and district officers were empowered to evict "migrant foreigners" and interpenetrators who settled across internal borders (Parsons 2012; see also Médard 1999).

Differentiation of forms of rule across colonial subterritories compounded the processes of segregation, heterogeneity of units, and institutionalization of inequalities. Native Authorities and cantons were not uniform in their internal structure, or relations with the colonial state (Balans et al. 1975; Boone

[21] Meru is a blanket designation for eight ethnic groups.
[22] See Parsons (2012) on Kenya. See also Leonardi (2020: 224 inter alia).

3.3 Colonial Political Institutions

2003). Colonial rulers sought to preserve, accentuate, or create cross-unit difference, in accordance with their self-understanding as benevolent overlords who were preserving highly diverse precolonial political forms and cultures. Legal regimes of "customary law" were supposed to be unique to each "tribe" or ethnic group. Native Authorities varied in the extent of internal hierarchy and, as in the British Empire in India or the Ottoman Empire, enjoyed varying degrees of autonomy vis-à-vis the colonial state. Indirect rule took root to varying degrees even within a single colony: As Rotberg noted of today's Zambia, "indirect rule was never a reality in Northern Rhodesia except in Barotseland" (1965: 50). Closed Districts such as the three provinces of south Sudan and Kenya's Northern Frontier District were administered more as police zones than local government units.

Case histories of the creation of new state-recognized ethnic groups through top-down amalgamation strategies are well known to scholars.[23] My goal here is to highlight the role of state institutions, and specifically the geographic and scalar aspects of these, in defining structures of representation and the collective actors who emerged as contenders in nascent national political arenas. Colonial administrators often "employed kinship [or ethnic] terms to describe what was at bottom a *spatial reality*,"[24] which was defined with reference to a colonial administrative grid that was *prior* to it. The process also pushed a socioethnic "homogenization of space at the scale of the region" (Hien 2003: 32). Membership identities that were valorized as political identities under colonial rule (i.e., recognized by the state) were those defined at the district scale.

The extent to which colonial territorial jurisdictions overlapped with, or encompassed, precolonial African political entities or even collective identities is *variable*. Some Admin1 or Admin2 units did correspond roughly to the territory of a precolonial African entity, such as the Akan kingdom of Ashanti in Ghana (the core of which became the "Ashanti Region") or the Agni kingdoms of Abengourou, which became cantons in Indenié Cercle in Côte d'Ivoire), Barotseland in today's Zambia, or the Sokoto Caliphate in northern Nigeria. Yet the notion that, in general, colonial administrative grids merely sought to formalize preexisting or primordial ethnic divisions is not sustainable as an empirically based generalization. Establishment of the territorial grid of Admin1 regions often *predates* the political and social existence of the named ethnic collectivities that colonial authorities defined as indigenous to those units. Indeed, peoples assigned to a given territorial unit were often named after the unit, or took the name of the unit, rather than vice versa. Such was the case with Baouléland, which preceded the existence of "the Baoulé," and the Nuba Mountains, which preceded the existence of "the Nuba" as an ethnic group.

---

[23] On Tanzania, for example, see Iliffe 1989, Chapter 10, on the designation of tribes.

[24] Gray 2004: 239, writing of the French colonial state, citing Vansina 1990: 81.

3.4 INSTITUTIONAL BUILDING BLOCS OF THE COLONIAL ECONOMY

The work of building the colonial economy was executed within districts and the chiefly territories (NAs and cantons) that they contained. Boundaries and the hierarchical ordering of jurisdictions were tweaked and adjusted over time to bring units of economic planning and units of political control into alignment. Mobilization of land and labor for building the colonial economy happened through the authority and intergroup relations forged and institutionalized in the districts and NAs. District officers delegated to chiefs the onus of the jobs of extracting taxes, conscripts for forced labor, and colonial governments' production quotas for coffee, cotton, palm oil, wood, rubber, rice, other foodstuffs, etc. (Lawler 1990). Access to agricultural credit and farm inputs also passed though channels that were intermediated by chiefs, principally the agricultural producer cooperatives.[25] Districts and NAs thus functioned as conduits for the two-way flow of resources between the central state and the localities. The content, complexity, and volume of these flows – and their consequences for local political organization and prosperity – varied greatly across space within each colony.

Planning paradigms envisioned the creation of an "economic division of labor" among regions and districts. This led to zoning practices which promoted the specialized development of export-crop-producing *cercles* or districts (and other productive zones or enclaves, such as mining enclaves), labor-sending regions, and in some colonies, commercial food-crop-producing regions. The residual was comprised of zones of subsistence agriculture, agro-pastoralism, transhumant pastoralism, and "remote areas" on the far margins of the colonial economy. Economic development worked to forge a hierarchy of regions of greater and lesser significance in the functioning of the colonial economy.

Subnational administrative units distinguished by these differentiated "economic vocations" assumed a social identity as "local state" territories designated for state-recognized membership groups. Economic zoning was, in effect, a form of "livelihood zoning" along district lines (Nsamba 2013). Colonial authorities naturalized the political-cum-economic divisions by envisioning ethnic groups as inhabiting distinct "ecological niches" and pursuing differentiated but complementary livelihood strategies:[26] coffee growing in the eastern *cercles* of Côte d'Ivoire, cattle-raising in Maasai districts of Kenya, migrant labor to mines in southern Africa for "tribes" of northern Malawi. Mamdani cites Uganda's 1932 Acting Governor as looking across the fertile lands of the

---

[25] Chiefs' role in allocating land to "ethnic members" and conditional land-access permission to in-migrants was central in the expansion of commodity production. In labor-sending regions, the institution of chieftaincy was also pivotal: chiefs worked with colonial district officials to round up quotas of forced laborers or recruits, and worked to guarantee family and property rights for absent men.

[26] This is how Czuba (2019) put it, in a study of Northern Kenya.

3.4 Institutional Building Blocs of the Colonial Economy

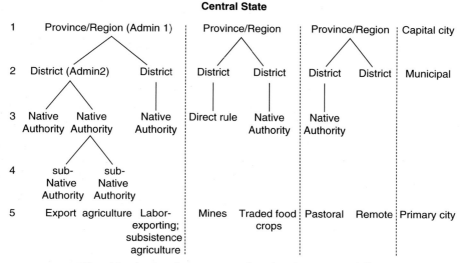

FIGURE 3.2 Tiered institutional structure and regional economic differentiation in an African colony
Notes: Schematic representation of nested institutional structure and its alignment with patterns of sectoral economic differentiation.

Protectorate and calling for "the development of tribes as agricultural communities producing raw materials for export."[27] District- and region-based colonial development projects, such as the Nuba Mountains Project, were seen as targeted at geographically delimited communities, usually referenced in terms of ethnicity (Tilly 2011: 115–169). Military recruits were provided by remote regions where men's labor was not channeled into colonial forms of commercial agriculture. In colonial Uganda, for example, "the Nilotic 'tribes' of the North were regarded as particularly suitable for recruitment into the King's African Rifles" (Mazrui 1988: 348–349). Ndlovu-Gatsheni (2009) describes the colonial ethnic hierarchy as an occupational caste system of agriculturalists, pastoralists, a military caste, and those recruited into the colonial civil service.

Figure 3.2 is a stylized depiction of regionally segmented economies that are subdivided into region (Admin1) and district (Admin2) units of territorial administration. It captures the overlapping and nested nature of political and economic institutions (and functions) that I aim to emphasize. Rows 1–4 represent layers of administrative hierarchy, in descending order from province or region (Admin1), to the district level (Admin2), to the Native Authority (NA, chieftaincy, or similar indirect rule unit), to the sub-NA level, representing

---
[27] Mamdani 1976: 254, fn.; see also 297, n. 62

66   *Endowment, Institutions, and Spatial Inequality: Regions by Design*

sub-chieftaincies. Row 3 draws attention to the fact that while most predominantly rural districts in most colonies were governed under some version of indirect rule, some were not. The so-called white settler districts of colonial Kenya were under direct rule, as were zones of plantation agriculture in Cameroon and the mining enclave in Zambia (and cities in all colonies).[28] Row 5 defines regions by their predominant "economic vocation."

The relative prosperity and economic dynamism engendered by colonial development were concentrated in particular geographic zones, just as especially destructive and disruptive effects (such as massive land expropriation and famine-inducing taxation) were regionally concentrated. Peasant producers of export crops and salaried workers were relatively prosperous vis-à-vis African populations in general from 1940 to 1970 (Jerven 2021: 132). Earnings were invested in better housing, schooling, business activities such as transport, and sometimes land acquisition and the in-hiring of agricultural labor. In the heartlands of cash crop production, on

> the cocoa farms of Ghana, and the cotton shambas and coffee smallholdings of Uganda, Kenya, and Ethiopia, [African] political power and agricultural productivity were greater. [T]he real wage in the heartlands of cash-crop production was, throughout the colonial period, approximately double that prevailing in the poor, labor-exporting regions such as the Upper Region of Ghana, West Nile in Uganda, and indeed in neighbouring Rwanda. (Bowden et al. 2008: 1067)

Impediments to permanent population mobility anchored inequality patterns in geography and administrative structure. Impediments included administrative restrictions on movement of persons, cattle, and crops; "members only" restrictions on rights of access to natural resources, especially land, in ethnic territories; and nonuniformity of the political character and regulatory systems across subnational government units.[29] Inequality across regions and districts reflected patterns of uneven development that arose within the gridwork of colonial territorial administration.

Socioeconomic organization and associational life developed around the producer profiles of regions and districts, and the flow of commodities, agricultural inputs, labor, and commercial circuits in and out of rural economies. In export-crop-producing regions, producer cooperatives and credit

---

[28] Pourtier (1989) argues that large parts of equatorial Africa, including most of Gabon and much of the Congo, were "direct rule" zones by default, since no structures of local authority offered footholds for colonial administration. On indigenous footholds for colonial administration, see Geschiere (1985). On bifurcated forms of rule, see Mamdani (1996).

[29] On nonuniformity of subnational units as a drag on the mobility of capital and labor, see Sack 1986: 165–166.

The effectiveness of land policy in restricting population mobility is evidenced in strong unevenness in population density on different sides of district boundaries. Rutten (1992) explains how the World Bank in the 1970s criticized Kenya's "tribal land policy" for impeding the rebalancing of population between areas of high density (Kisii district) and low density (Narok district). Golaz and Médard (2016) also documented this phenomenon.

3.5 *Political Mobilization in the Nationalist Era* 67

associations, local export-crop-processing centers, and local agencies of marketing boards took root within the territorial units and authority structures of Native Authorities and districts. "Hometown associations" brought migrants together around shared district- and subdistrict-level identities.

By contrast, colony-wide economic interests and identities developed at the nodes and nerve centers of the colonial economy, where unionized railway and dock workers, unionized miners, industrial workers, and African civil servants and professionals (lawyers) often parlayed their economic clout into organizations defined in proto-national (or even broader) terms, rather than with reference to a particular district or region.

3.5 POLITICAL MOBILIZATION IN THE NATIONALIST ERA

> Anti-colonial nationalisms were neither class nor ideological vanguards, but regional coalitions.
>
> Lonsdale 2015: 609

By the late colonial period, if not before, political mobilization began to coalesce within districts and regional units. Leonardi writes that, by the 1930s, "districts were becoming the primary territorial units not only of local government administration but also of emerging political organization and representation" (2020: 231). Early political mobilization often arose around issues related to government regulation of export crop production (pricing, market control, quality standards, enforced cultivation practices) and conflicts related to environmental and conservation matters (such as access to forests, destocking, terracing, forced crop destruction as a physiosanitary measure, and tsetse fly eradication), all imposed at the district or subdistrict level. This meant that patterns of agrarian activism and mobilization tended to track highly regionalized patterns of agrarian development. For example, in western Cameroon, where coffee had been grown since 1927, coffee producers "mobilized against the state in 1957" because of "mis-administration of the coffee sector" (Kuété 2008: 299). In an essay entitled "The commercialization of agriculture and the rise of rural political protest," Robert Bates (1983, 1989) showed how struggles over colonially imposed marketing monopolies and regulations, land-use regulations, taxation, and producer pricing schemes incentivized farmers and traders to combine in unions, producer cooperatives, trade associations, and other district-level, occupationally based interest groups to press their grievances and demands. They found common cause with emergent nationalist movements, linking rural organizations and rural activism to "the movements which made Africa ungovernable by foreign powers and thereby led to political independence" (Bates 1989: 92).

Collective action coalesced at the district and regional level – the state apparatus itself served as a framework for mobilizing collective action in ways that the European colonizers had not intended. As a national political arena emerged in the 1940s and 1950s, regional consciousness of uneven development and

68 *Endowment, Institutions, and Spatial Inequality: Regions by Design*

of positionality within national economies became a rallying point. Increasing regional disparities, combined with new colonial undertakings to open up previously "neglected" districts and regions, created focal points for political leaders and entrepreneurs to seek an expanded presence on the national stage by representing geographic units that transcended the district level. Regional identities like "the Coast," "the North," "the Muslim North," "backward regions," and corporate macro-identities (such as Hausa–Fulani) gained salience as idioms for demand-making and claiming a share of national power. Alden Young writes that, in Sudan, planning for the three southern provinces as a *region* around the development of the massive Jonglei Canal project in the 1950s "became a lightning rod around which southern politicians advocated for southern autonomy" (2017: 82). Questions of regional inequality, the distribution of state investment and state revenues across subnational units, and how the onward march of economic and political development would impact local autonomies and the regions' relative power on the national political stage were at the forefront of partisan mobilization (Young 2017: 145–146).

Mobilization built upon social solidarities and institutions imbricated in the local political economies and the networked administrative circuits of NAs, districts, and provinces. Districts and regions were increasingly conceptualized as subunits of the (emergent) nation-state. With the arrival of party politics in the late 1940s, there were heightened incentives for social and political identification with larger territorial circumscriptions. Political entrepreneurs encouraged populations to associate themselves with these regional entities. Maguire (1970) explains how in the Lake Region of Tanganika, leaders of cotton producer unions realized that the *Provincial Commissioner*, not the District Officer, was the linchpin of decision-making, and they targeted their demands accordingly. There was a scaling up of the politics of engagement with the colonial state.

Emergence of "Kalenjin" in Kenya as an umbrella ethnic identity was promoted by political entrepreneurs who wanted to unite the diverse groups indigenous to the farming districts on the western side of Rift Valley Province in the 1940s and 1950s, precisely to compete in the national political arena against regional rivals. Also in Kenya, the Luhya emerged as a "tribe" through local activists' efforts to forge a territorially based social collectivity that could claim the Nyanza North district as its homeland (Petersen 2012; MacArthur 2016).

Genesis of the Baoulé as a "politically relevant ethnic group" (PREG) in Côte d'Ivoire is another case in point. *Cercle-* and cantonal-level administrative divisions called "Baoulé" predate the existence of the colonial ethnic collectivity of this name (Box 3.1).[30] Colonial territorial institutions

---

[30] On PREGs, see Posner 2004a. Le Baoulé was one of the ten original *cercles* of Côte d'Ivoire (1896), comprising the posts at Ouossou, Kodiokoffi, and Toumodi (chef-lieu). These posts anchor circumscriptions. Bouaké circumscription was added in 1904. The *cercle* was divided into two in 1904. Baoulé Nord becomes Baoulé *cercle* in 1915.

3.5 Political Mobilization in the Nationalist Era

Box 3.1 Case study: emergence of Baoulé as a regional-level ethnic identity

The administrative military circumscriptions defined in the process of conquest, shifting from military to civilian command [*zones civils*] when pacification was considered complete, became containers that promoted the coalescing of state-recognized ethnic groups. In Côte d'Ivoire before 1910, "Baoulé" was one of ten administrative military *cercles* that enclosed approximately fourteen "tribes," or "Baoulé tribes" (1922) which, much to the chagrin of the administration, did not have real chiefs or even a hierarchical family structure that was deemed to be sufficiently robust to offer an adequate foothold for French authority. "We are standing in front of an amorphous population mass lacking all homogeneity" (1923). The administration struggled to regroup people into villages and to appoint local interlocutors. There was little commercial activity. Attacks on French posts continued into the early 1910s. There was a widespread insurrection in 1909–1910 and ongoing "*résistance violente*" in 1911 and 1912.

Baoulé *cercle*, like the other four original *cercles* of colonial Côte d'Ivoire, was divided into subdivisions, which were subdivided into cantons headed by cantonal chiefs – considered agents or "cadres" of the administration. They had very little authority up to the late 1940s and many of those appointed showed "complete lack of interest in the role." The administration recognized that these chiefs were exercising authority over people of "diverse tribes," some of whom argued that they "were not Baoulé" and were "implanted here before the in-migration of Reine Pokou" [the leader of the Akan migration from Ghana in the founding legend of the arrival of "the Baoulé" in Côte d'Ivoire].

With the arrival of party politics in 1949 and the territorially based political representation of indigenous population groups, there were heightened incentives for social and political identification with larger territorial circumscriptions – that is, for political entrepreneurs to encourage populations to associate themselves with these regional entities. Cantonal chief Kouakou Anoublé, using the title of "Traditional Chief of the Baoulé," carried the banner of the RDA which, he argued, "is supported by all the Baoulé." He asked to be recognized as "Chef Supérieur des Baoulés" because he and his supporters (fellow cantonal chiefs in Baoulé *cercle*) thought this would increase the stature and recognition of Baoulé *cercle* [one of 19 in 1960] throughout the colony.

Sources: Archives Nationales de la Côte d'Ivoire, Abidjan. *J.O. Repertoire du 1925*, Administratif: Côte d'Ivoire. Circonscriptions Administratives: Cercle du Baoulé, pp. 106–107, 122. Archives Nationales Côte d'Ivoire 1EE 29. Politique Général, Cercle de Baoulé, X-34-8, 2ème trimestre 1922, 5 juillet 1922, n. 664; EE 28 (4) X-47-16, Cercle de Baoulé Nord, Rapport sur la création d'un nouveau poste administratif, 1922, 1ère carte (X-47-16); Carton 14, dossier 568, "Notes sur les chefferies de Bouaké;" Carton 15, 568; Container 19, côte ref. 583, Affaires politiques, élection législative de 1956.

provided the political opportunity structure and incentives for the coalescing of what would become Côte d'Ivoire's most important PREG under the thirty-year rule of Félix Houphouët-Boigny, from 1960 to 1990. The logic of ethnic amalgamation was a strategy for increasing colony-wide political clout.

National political parties of the 1950s also coalesced within the territorial grid of districts and provinces. *Region* was the scale for claiming a seat at the national table and for collective action in the national arena. Parties built upon more local associations and networks anchored in the NAs or productive-sector associations (such as agricultural producer cooperatives), and scaled up to the provincial level of administration in response to electoral incentives for amassing clout at the national level. Hiribarren describes how "[i]t was behind the colonial limits [of regional boundaries] that political factions were entrenched in the 1950s [in Nigeria]" (2015: 170). In Northern Nigeria, after 1945, Amadou Bello, the Sardauna of Sokoto, pursued "the intense 'northernization' of the politics and administration of the Northern Region [aiming to achieve inter alia] the insertion of Borno into the wider Nigerian North" (Hiribarren 2015: 185–186). Crawford Young also believed that, in the crucible of nationalist-era and postcolonial party politics, colonialism's ethnicities were often absorbed in the larger identity groups that political and cultural entrepreneurs forged at the regional level around regional *lingua francas*. Four lingua francas served as reference points for regional political identities in Congo-Kinshasa. This also describes the Bemba lingua franca in northern Zambia, and "Kalenjin" in Kenya, mobilized more in the quest for a lingua franca than around an actual one, but definitely a regional group that found common cause in waging territorial politics on the borders of Rift Valley Province (Lynch 2011). When Britain's Kenya Boundaries Commission (1962) gathered local opinion on the setting of provincial-level boundaries in Kenya, on the eve of Independence, politically aligned groups, fearful of exploitation by larger, more educated, or wealthier groups, asked to be grouped together within the same province (Médard 1999: 63–65).

Administrative units served as electoral constituencies in the elections that brought African political parties and leaders to national power in the late 1940s and 1950s. In Côte d'Ivoire, Mali, Burkina, and rest of the AOF, *cercles* served as electoral circumscriptions. In Uganda, the district became the electoral constituency in the elections of 1958. In Ghana, Native Authorities became constituencies (or multiple constituencies) for the 1958 elections. Kenya's Northeastern Province, comprised of the Somali districts of Garissa, Wajir, and Mandera, formed a single electoral constituency in the pre-independence elections.

Regionally differentiated policies and practices structured the use of land, labor, and natural resources, and drove uneven processes of colonial market-building. Ethnic identities were constructed and reshaped through these same

3.6 Territorial Institutions and Regional Inequalities

processes of socioeconomic change. The net effect was regional economic differentiation, produced by variation in the timing, mode, and extent of incorporation of regions into the colonial economy. Patterns of uneven development were delineated largely within the grid of colonial territorial administration. Strong spatial inequalities associated with colonial economic development were thus aligned within the basic administrative and representative structures of the state. These defined the national space within which politics coalesced in the 1940s and 1950s. Section 3.6 of this chapter shows that after the end of colonial rule, many African governments retained the basic structures of territorial administration inherited from colonialism.[31] In most African countries today, these territorial grids constitute the basic institutional structure of governance, representation, land rights assignment, and state allocation of resources.

3.6 TERRITORIAL INSTITUTIONS AND REGIONAL INEQUALITIES IN POSTCOLONIAL POLITICS

> British spatial engineering left a deep mark in independent Nigeria. The territorial legitimacy sought after by the colonisers became part of the political game at a national level.
>
> Hiribarren 2017: 171

In most African countries today, territorial grids inherited from colonialism constitute the basic institutional frameworks of governance and economic development. Most also retained the territorial structures of political representation delimited in the 1940s and 1950s, as politics coalesced at the national level. What Esping-Anderson called "historical legacies of regime institutionalization" (1990: 20) have shaped the supply of government, conceptions of national space, construction of social subgroups and citizenship rights, and basic economic geography in postcolonial African countries. Expectations surrounding acceptable territorial bargains among subgroups of the national community were strongly shaped by the institutional framework within which parties formed and territorial bargains first emerged. Institutions and interests combine to bring regional politics to the fore.

Territorial Unit Persistence

Administrative units inherited from colonialism continue to serve as basic territorial units of provincial administration, policy-targeting, and policy

---

[31] Such a process of formation of national political and economic space is not unique to Africa: Indian nationalists also conserved the territorial map inherited from the British Raj (Breton 1991: 79–80; Naseemullah 2022).

Endowment, Institutions, and Spatial Inequality: Regions by Design

implementation. In predominantly rural regions and districts, they structure the "supply of government," allocation of central government resources, administrative allocation of access to natural resources including land, and the playing field on which interests are aggregated and advanced in the national political arena. Formal units of political representation are nested within the provincial and district grid.

Persistence of colonial-era internal subdivisions in postcolonial administrative grids is striking. This is dramatic at the provincial or Admin1 level. In Ghana, the Ashanti Protectorate became Ashanti Region in 1957. Gold Coast Colony was split into Eastern and Western Regions. The Northern Protectorate became the Northern Region (with the addition of a small slice of the former Trans-Volta region). Until the 2010s, Ghana retained this template of regions (and districts), modifying these units through subdivision. The six internal regions of colonial Côte d'Ivoire have been subdivided over time, but the colonial Admin1 boundaries have never been erased or overwritten. Malawi, Mali, Uganda, Zimbabwe, and Zambia retain their colonial provincial grid. Kenya retained the 1962 Boundary Commission Provinces until 2010, when a new constitution elevated the 1990 districts to first subnational-level divisions (as counties). Territorial divisions inherited from colonialism were decisive in the formation of national political space in the African post-colonies.

There is also strong persistence in internal ethnic boundaries and district (Admin2) units. In a study of ex-British colonies, we found that the vast majority of *internal ethnic boundaries* – that is, Native Authority unit boundaries – that existed in 1948 persist today as Admin2 administrative boundaries. Leigh Gardner and Jennifer Kohler found that, for Ghana, Malawi, Nigeria, and Kenya, about 70% of Native Authority boundaries persist as boundaries of contemporary district boundaries. In Ghana, the 1948 Native Authority boundary persistence rate (in current Admin2 boundaries, with a 0.5 km buffer) is 76%.[32] The corresponding figures are 77% for Malawi, 81% for Nigeria, and 68% for Kenya. In Sierra Leone, 99% of NA boundaries persist today as Admin-level 3 boundaries.

Figure 3.3 illustrates these overlaps. For Ghana, the top panel illustrates the extent to which contemporary (2000) district or Admin2 boundaries reproduce the old Native Authority lines. Seventy-six percent of Ghana's contemporary Admin2 boundaries correspond to 1948 Native Authority boundaries. For Nigeria, the lower panel illustrates the overlap of today's Admin1

---

[32] Kohler and Gardner, Preliminary boundary persistence results, LSE, August 23, 2018, presented as part of Boone, Gardner, Kohler, and Bolt, "Native Authorities and the Building Blocs of Territorial Representation," Workshop on Land Governance and Spatial Inequalities in Kenyan Politics, British Institute of Eastern Africa, Nairobi, June 7, 2019. See also Boone 2019.

3.6 Territorial Institutions and Regional Inequalities

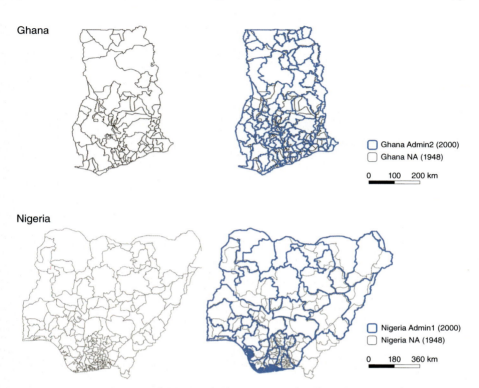

FIGURE 3.3 Persistence of Native Authority (NA) borders in 2012 Admin2 units: Ghana and Nigeria
Notes: In Ghana, 76% of current Admin2 boundaries correspond to Native Authority boundaries in 1948 (0.5 km buffer). In Nigeria, 57% of current Admin1 boundaries correspond to NA boundaries circa 1948.
Source: Shapefiles 1948, from Leigh Gardner; calculations from Jennifer Kohler and Leigh Gardner, August 23, 2018.

boundaries (states) and 1948 NA boundaries. The boundary persistence rate is 57%. Nigeria's structure of Native Authorities in 1948 remains almost perfectly intact, encased within today's Admin1 units of the thirty-six states of the Nigerian federal structure.

Today, electoral constituencies are very largely defined along these colonial-era administrative and ethnic boundary lines. Table 3.1 captures this. District (Admin2) units either serve as electoral constituencies or are subdivided into constituencies. In 1991–1992 for Zambia, Malawi, Kenya, Ghana, Tanzania, and Zimbabwe, as a cross-country average, 92% of all electoral constituencies were coterminous with or completely nested within one contemporary Admin2

74   *Endowment, Institutions, and Spatial Inequality: Regions by Design*

administrative unit (district).[33] Using the Ghana 2012 and Zambia 2016 electoral constituency units, the cross-national average for Table 3.1 is 70%.

Many electoral constituencies are descended directly from Native Authorities or subdivisions thereof, which are likely to have been sub-chieftaincies. In work with Gardner and Kohler, I calculated the percentage of electoral constituencies that are coterminous with or almost completely (i.e., > 85%) contained within, or "matched with," a single 1948 Native Authority unit. For Ghana's 2012 electoral constituencies, the figure is 58%. For Kenya's 1997–2007 constituencies, it is 69%. For Malawi's 1999–2004 electoral constituencies, it is 75%. For Nigeria's current senatorial constituencies, it is 60% – that is, 60% of the senatorial constituencies are coterminous with or contained within (>85% of constituency area) a 1948 Native Authority. For Tanzania's 2010 electoral constituencies, it is 80%. Of Uganda's 1994 constituencies, 67% are coterminous with or almost completely nested within the 1959 counties. Most electoral constituencies are strongly "matched" with colonial Native Authority units. They carry the DNA of the colonial ethnic homelands.

This type of boundary persistence and unit spatial overlap (i.e., nestedness) characterizes former French colonies as well. In a study similar to the one reported above, Joan Ricart-Huguet combined pre-WWII maps with 2016 GADM boundaries and calculated an Admin2 (*cercles*) boundary persistence rate for eight countries of the former AOF of 97% (compared to 77% for districts in eight ex-British colonies).[34] In Côte d'Ivoire, for example, the 1969 structure of Admin2s (*départements*) inherited from colonial rule has been preserved intact over time through multiple reorganizations of first- and second-level administrative divisions. New units have always been formed by splitting the original ones, preserving the boundaries between the original departments.[35] Colonial cantons became one or two *sous-préfecture(s)*, which served as electoral constituencies.

One implication is that ethnic voting observed today is highly likely to be at least partly epiphenomenal to these institutional effects – that is, to both the boundary effects and the ongoing effects of the authority and property institutions encased within those boundaries. Electoral constituencies also remain nested within territorial administrative units and subject to the top-down influence of agents of territorial administration, as was the case in the colonial period. In Kenya today, for example, divisional chiefs who are

---

[33] From Boone and Iddawala, "Note on Nestedness of African Constituencies within Admin 2 Regions," LSE, April 2019. This drops to 85% when we factor in Ghana's drop from 92% in 1992 to 63% in 2012. We used a 1 km buffer.

[34] Ricart-Huguet took each bilateral border as a unit of analysis, and if over 20% of it fell outside of the buffer, he coded it as changed (Joan Ricart-Huguet, personal communication, April 23, 2019, and November 20, 2021.)

[35] See Dozon 1985 (on cantonal units around Gagnoa), République de la Côte d'Ivoire 2011, Selanius 2017.

TABLE 3.1 *Constituencies (2000) nested within Admin2 units (2000)*

Country	Year	Total number of constituencies (n)	Coterminous or completely nested (n)	% coterminous or nested	Constit. includes area in two admin. districts (n)	Constit. includes area in three admin. districts (n)
Ghana	1992	179	164	92	13	2
Ghana	2012	270	169	63	88	8
Zimbabwe	2008	199	188	94	11	0
Zambia	1991	150	115	77	35	0
Zambia	2016	156	107	69	44	5
Tanzania	2015	228	220	96	8	0
Malawi	2004	192	190	99	2	0
Kenya	2013	285	262	92	19	1

Notes: Calculated by the author and Johan Iddawela, March 15, 2019, using GADM current series Admin2 shapefile and the reference constituency shapefiles listed in Appendix Section B.2. Constituency overlap calculated with 1 km buffer. We could not calculate an overlap rate for five Ghana constituencies and three Kenya constituencies. These are included in the total number of constituencies and percentage of nested constituencies reported in the table, however.

Endowment, Institutions, and Spatial Inequality: Regions by Design

responsible for local voting units report directly to district officers (Hassan 2020: 75–77).

Electoral systems established in the last decade of colonial rule further engrain the territoriality of representation into national politics. A total of twenty-two out of thirty-five sub-Saharan African countries that hold elections use SMD plurality (or mixed) systems for translating individual votes into legislative seats. Twelve use PR, and even in these, provinces often serve as multimember constituencies (as in Burkina Faso), or lower levels of political representation are defined on a territorial basis, as in Provincial Assemblies in South Africa and Mozambique (see Taggart 1995). Under the SMD systems, MPs represent constituencies that often contain both the skeleton (institutional structure) and the DNA (operating code) of colonial Native Authorities. As Rogers (2016: 71) summarizes it, voters in such electoral systems may evaluate their interests at the national level in territorial terms, and politicians have a clear mandate to bring resources back to their constituency. Politicians who appeal to ethnicity at the constituency level are engaging in what Rickard calls an "institutionally-generated electoral strategy" (2018: 3).

Regionalization of the "Supply" of Postcolonial Government: Territorial Administration, Planning, and Spending

Hierarchically structured territorial administrations comprised of provincial governors, district officers, *préfets*, and *sous-préfets* acted as agents of central Ministries of the Interior in many countries, reproducing colonial forms of government.[36] In strongly centralized unitary states, sectoral ministries (education, rural development, health) intervened along the lines of the territorial administrative boundaries, reinforcing this structure. Provincial administrations in Kenya and Côte d'Ivoire wield regionally specific powers of policing, regulation of access to resources, policy implementation, and election management.[37] Branch and Cheeseman wrote that Kenya's prefectoral provincial administration was bureaucratic-authoritarian in character, with "an extensive portfolio of responsibilities" (2006: 18) that included law and order functions, counterinsurgency, issuing of land titles and other aspects of land administration, allocation of trade licenses, and organization and supervision of elections. Hassan (2020: xvi, 18–19) described the districts as "units of government," each managed differently from the others (some much more repressive than others, for example). Tordoff (1968a, 1968b) made

---

[36] Most are unitary states. Nigeria, South Africa, and Ethiopia are the only explicitly federal states in sub-Saharan Africa.

[37] On Kenya, see Gertzel (1970: 26, 33), Bienen (1974: 87), Mueller (1984), Barkan and Chege (1989), Berman 1990, Berman (1992: 144, inter alia), Widner (1992), Bourmaud (2000), Branch and Cheeseman (2006), and Hassan (2020). On Côte d'Ivoire, see Boone (2003).

3.6 Territorial Institutions and Regional Inequalities

much the same argument for Zambia. Ladouceur wrote that in Ghana under Nkrumah, the agents of territorial administration, the Regional and District Commissioners, were essentially "political actors with considerable autonomy and independence of action" (1984: 152).

These structures and regional actors served as channels of resource distribution. As in the colonial era, postcolonial development policy itself has been predominantly territorial, rather than carried out within functional policy frameworks. Provincial and district units serve as units of economic planning and define frameworks within which policies and projects are implemented.[38]

Rural development policies in the 1950–1990 period were mostly project-based, and usually involved direct intervention in agricultural production, modification of farming techniques, application of government-supplied inputs or improved varieties, modification of settlement patterns, spatial demarcation of pastoral zones, etc. They were thus tailored for geographically specific areas according to their particular agrarian systems and economic specializations, often for export crops such as cocoa, cotton, or groundnuts.[39] "Sectoral governance" was the norm in the export agriculture sectors. "Integrated rural development policies" and Regional Development Agencies were explicit in defining administrative units such as districts (Admin2 units, overlapping as we have seen with electoral constituencies) as geographic zones of operation, concentrating rural development programs in specially targeted areas. As Bryceson wrote, donors such as the World Bank

had an exceptionally strong preference for development investment in rural rather than urban areas and ... [for] concentrating their aid efforts in specific parts of [each] country and building up ... that area to facilitate project operations. Donors became involved in a wide gamut of project activities in a specific region, which was intended to impart regional coherence to donor efforts but sometimes created national incoherence as each region evolved a different orientation and administrative organisation ... Aid-funded projects invariably involve spatial choices though prioritisation of a region or agro-ecological zone. (2006, para. 23–24)

---

[38] Regional Development Authorities have been a common mode of intervention. In Rhodesia (Zimbabwe), for example, regional and subregional parastatal development authorities, Sabi-Limpopo Authority and the South-Eastern Lowveld Authority, were created by the Ian Smith regime after 1965 to develop dams and irrigation schemes in these subdivisions of Masvingo Province. (Rambanapasi 1989: 278). Rambanapasi notes the influence of the US Tennessee Valley Authority on these ambitious, spatially targeted planning models. See Kanduza (1992) on "planning regions" in Zambia.

[39] An example from the traded food crop sector is Mali's Office du Riz Mopti, created in 1972. It is a state development agency, funded by the World Bank, charged with the mission of integrated rural development of the four *cercles* of Mopti, Djenné, Ténekou, and Youwarou, encompassing 190 villages. The objective is to boost rice-farming productivity and organize the rice value chain in the inland delta of the Niger River. Its operating mandate was renewed by state decree in 2008. It was originally called Opération Riz Mopti.

78 Endowment, Institutions, and Spatial Inequality: Regions by Design

In Kenya, the District Focus policy orientation in the 1970 and 1980s explicitly targeted the district as the unit of rural development (Barkan & Chege 1989). In the 1980s and 1990s, Development Authorities focused at the provincial level – Kerio Valley Development Authority, Coast Development Authority, Lake Basin Development Authority – were instituted under a Ministry of Regional Development Authorities. Writing of Kenya's rural development agencies of the 1970s through 1990s, Mwakubo et al. lament that "[A]ll too often, resource allocation is biased toward the most productive region" (1996: 49).

Resource-rich areas were in a privileged position in terms of investments, productive employment, services, and infrastructure. By the 1970s, regional redistribution policies designed to target lagging regions, and thus more balanced patterns of regional development, were considered best practice in national development planning. Ndulu et al. (2008) consider such policies so generic and widespread that they are identified as one of four anti-market syndromes of the developmentalist era (along with borrowing, corruption, and bad monetary policy). Structural Adjustment Programmes (SAPs) of the 1990s and 2000s took a principled stand against "regional balancing" as a policy objective, and emphasized spatially blind and market-based regulatory policies. Market-oriented policies aiming to "get the prices right" worked explicitly to bias growth toward tradable sectors, core regions, and large agglomerations (see World Bank 2009). Yet even of the post-SAP era, Philippe Lavigne Delville wrote that "'the project' or 'programme' remains one of the prime mechanisms by which 'development' is promoted in most African countries. [It is] delimited in space and time, regionally and sectorally targeted, externally-supported" (2011) and often focused on the *filière agricole* or particular agricultural commodity chain, rather than being sector-wide or national in scope.[40]

Various institutional mechanisms in export agriculture – cooperatives, cocoa-replanting schemes (in Western Nigeria, for example), agricultural development projects, marketing authorities, extension services – were and have remained channels for the dissemination of state resources (Bates 1981; Berry 1993; Rabinowitz 2018). After Independence, building economic institutions such as producer cooperatives and marketing boards in the countryside was standard development practice, promoted vigorously by the World Bank and the bilateral development agencies (as famously critiqued by Bates in *Markets and States in Tropical Africa* [1981]). In the most productive agricultural producer regions, cooperatives incorporated farmers and local communities into hierarchically networked commodity chains of national significance. In the new millennium, states remain key actors in structuring and regulating agricultural commodity chains in the export and commercial food crop sectors, even if most gave up direct control over marketing and processing in the 1990s and 2000s (Jayne et al. 2002).

---

[40] Cited by Sambou Ndiaye (2022).

3.6 Territorial Institutions and Regional Inequalities

At the molecular level of the administrative hierarchy, the ex-NAs and sub-cantons lived on as districts, subdistricts, and electoral constituencies. They remained economic institutions of high political salience, as well as political institutions of fundamental economic significance. Although chiefs' tax-collecting, labor mobilization, and judicial functions were generally suppressed after Independence, key aspects of NAs' internal institutional operating systems persisted, along with their territorial boundaries. Ethnic land units were preserved in most countries, with inherited boundaries continuing to demarcate divisions between different neocustomary land tenure units. (Notable exceptions are Tanzania, Mozambique, and Rwanda.[41]) Within units, rights to resource access that are contingent upon local (ethnic or sub-ethnic) citizenship status – that is, to land, pasture, fishing rights, forest products – often govern allocation between unit members and nonmembers. Locality-specific property rights thus tie individuals and families to particular territories, condition access to livelihoods and occupations, and constrain geographic mobility across rural regions.

State-led development in the 1960s to 1980s reaffirmed the centrality of government as allocator of capital across the national economy and as a driver of economic change in contexts of pervasive market imperfections and low degrees of market integration. This process tended to reinforce patterns of investment that were concentrated around agro-export sectors and mining enclaves, and thus, earlier patterns of regional advantage and disadvantage. This is true even though some compensatory development efforts were targeted at some lagging regions in the late 1960s and 1970s, often as deliberate efforts to promote national integration and the consolidation of ruling coalitions.[42]

Regionalization of National Politics in Postcolonial Africa

Territorial institutions shaped the construction of social groups within the polity, and how they were represented in politics. Government also continued to be "supplied" in spatially segmented fashion, compounding the salience of territorial political representation. These institutional factors contributed to the regionalization of politics in postcolonial African countries. Important

---

[41] Tanzania's partial divergence from this pattern of institutional persistence is registered in Figure 1.2. Tanzania is a counterfactual to the more general pattern in which neocustomary land tenure regimes contribute to the production of politically salient ethnic identities. Under the government of Julius Nyerere (1961–1985), the ruling party and central line ministries supplanted colonial-era provincial administration. On mainland Tanzania, it pushed a vision of uniformization of national policy and forms of rule. This entailed suppression of the NAs and their internal political structure, suppression of NA-level citizenship rights and promotion of individual rural-to-rural mobility, and suppression of producer cooperatives and other forms of civil society associationalism in the wealthier, export-crop-producing regions of the colonial-era Northern Region (Tordoff 1965; Boone & Nyeme 2015).

[42] An example is the investment by the Houphouët-Boigny regime in northern Côte d'Ivoire in the 1970s (Woods 1990, Boone 2007).

80 Endowment, Institutions, and Spatial Inequality: Regions by Design

mechanisms working to produce this effect include (1) the politics of subnational unit persistence, (2) institutionally induced strategies of political coalition-building within the national territorial grid, and (3) the synergistic relationship between regional consciousness and regional interests. Subsections below discuss each of these three mechanisms.

Politics of Territorial Unit Persistence

Defining the territorial structure of the state itself was a matter of high stakes, one of the major *enjeux* of national politics. Tracking the politics of internal unit boundary changes in postcolonial Africa countries yields up a rich record of political struggle over borders at all levels and over subnational unit creation, splits, and amalgamation. There have been some dramatic changes over time. Postcolonial incumbent rulers preserved, elevated, or destroyed NAs in competitive struggle with regional and other rivals. In Tanzania, NAs and territorial chieftaincies were abolished in the early 1960s by Nyerere's anti-chief modernizing government. Nyerere soon embarked on a reorganization of land tenure and settlement patterns, weaking the connection between ethnic identity and land rights and strengthening the prerogative of central state agents in land administration. In Ghana, Nkrumah endeavored to erode the correspondence between electoral constituencies and the chieftaincy domains (NAs) that served as the political fortresses of his main rivals. He was overthrown in 1966.[43] In Ghana and Kenya in the 1990s and 2000s, incumbents "promoted" old NA subunits containing loyal co-partisans to constituency status in order to win more seats in national legislatures (Hassan & Shelly 2016; Resnick 2017). A rich contemporary political science literature tracks "subnational unit proliferation," documenting, inter alia, recent chapters in the history of the persistence and fissioning of former NA units.[44]

Given this, the extent of subnational unit persistence at the Admin2 (or district) level that is demonstrated above, in the first part of Section 3.6, is striking. So is the persistence of the boundaries of colonial-era Admin1 units, even when these are subdivided. What Hiribarren referred to as the "spatial fossilization of the British administrative legacy" (2017: 170) in postcolonial Nigeria (with particular reference to Borno State) is an observation that applies to much of postcolonial Africa.

Strong patterns of boundary persistence that characterize the postcolonial state in most African countries must be understood as the outcome of competition and bargaining among collective actors constituted within these regional and district units, rather than as the product of inertia, inattention, or passive

---

[43] With Nkrumah's overthrow in 1966, his pro-chieftaincy successors appointed an electoral boundary commission that restored the old chieftaincy territories to their status as representative units in elections. This correspondence has persisted over time (Smith 2002).

[44] See Green (2008) and Grossman and Lewis (2014) on Uganda; Hassan (2016) on Kenya; and Smith (2002), Stacey (2016), and Resnick (2017) on Ghana. See also Chapter 7.

3.6 Territorial Institutions and Regional Inequalities

path dependency. Nationalist-era politicians and political parties "engineered their ascent into national political power" (Mavungu 2016: 189) in the colonial period on subnational playing fields defined with reference to colonial Admin2 and Admin1 units. Electoral constituencies were constituted along these lines and were thus rooted in local groups' defense of territory and property rights. Coalition-building proceeded within the same frameworks at the district level and the multidistrict level (often provincial or Admin1). Allies and contenders were anchored in organizations defined by the colonial administrative grid.

From a political perspective, the generally very high degree of postcolonial unit persistence can be regarded as the effect of a multi-scalar entente (or political equilibrium). National winners' incentives were structured around maximizing and locking-in their advantage. As Branch and Cheeseman put it, for Kenya, the inherited machinery of government was "too important for incumbent governments to dismantle" (2006: 28). In many or perhaps most countries, postcolonial ruling parties colonized the administrative apparatus of the state, including hierarchical structures of territorial administration, in ways that enhanced greatly their political–territorial reach and control. Many observers described this as the "rise of the postcolonial party state." One goal was to undercut rival parties. Undercutting was often most effective in parts of each country where rivals had few institutional footholds for political organization *other than* territorial administration itself, as would have been the case in many very poor and sparsely populated districts and regions.[45]

For ruling parties, maintaining the inherited template of territorial administration at the Admin1, Admin2, and even the former NA level (often with incremental subdivisions) was also critical to governing the economy. Rural development and export crop production were structured largely around institutions like producer cooperatives that were networked together and governed at the district level. They served as channels for two-way flows of inputs, credit, technical assistance, and cash crops between producers and the state. Marketing organizations such as the commodity marketing boards, which were literally the pumps by which the state drew revenue out of smallholder export agriculture, also operated at the district and provincial level. As Ludeki put it in a study of Kenya, "The supremacy of the bureaucracy [as an agent of rural development] lies in the fact that the private sector is not developed and spread out on such a scale as to be able to take an active role in the development of the

---

[45] The opposite case is also important for our analysis. As argued in Chapters 4 and 6, oppositional organizations and networks often *survived* in rich regions, where sectors vital to the national economy were embedded in producer organizations and marketing networks that could support political mobilization, and where sectors generated resources in the private sector that could be plowed into collective action and politics. This was sometimes the case in places where cash crop producers were organized into community-level organizations, cooperatives, and sector-wide marketing networks. This is consistent with Arriola's (2013) argument that economic liberalization in the 1990s gave private-sector actors resources that could be channeled into political action.

82   *Endowment, Institutions, and Spatial Inequality: Regions by Design*

rural areas" (1990: 17). Functional imperatives for maintaining inherited unit structures, in terms of both the unit boundaries and units' internal political structure, were compelling in land tenure administration as well (Boone 2014). Allocation and administration of land rights within and between territorially defined, rights-bearing groups happened within former native authority units (which were indeed sometimes riven by internal tensions that led to demands for subdivision). To sweep away these local jurisdictions would require complete overhaul of land tenure and local political structure. This was very rare indeed. It did happen in much of Tanzania under Ujamaa in the late 1960s and 1970s, but tellingly, the richest export-crop-producing zones in northern Tanzania were mostly not subject to this economically and politically disruptive reform (Cliffe 1973; Morse 2014).

Regional and constituency-level collectivities that found themselves on the losing side of politics in the decades after Independence, and thus at a political disadvantage vis-à-vis the winners of state power, also had stakes in territorial unit persistence. Institutions that segmented space and divided powers across different levels of the polity had value in defensive strategies. As Rodden suggests (2004), minority groups may prefer territorial to individual representation. A segmented and multitiered state structure in which the character of political authority varies across scales can serve as a device for accommodating imperfectly aligned interests, as in federal systems designed to reconcile nationalizing and regional interests (Bolton & Roland 1997), imperial state structures such as that created by the Ottomans (Barkey 2008), and China's "branch and bloc" system, which compartmentalizes local interests within strong top-down structures of control.[46] Such models of state structure can help buffer tensions arising in the relationship between "centralizing" and "peripheral" groups. Persistence of a multitiered structure with "heterogeneity of scale" can thus be understood as the outcome of a political standoff between central and various peripheral forces, constituted at multiple scales.

A theory of political equilibrium would suggest that *change* in territorial unit configuration would arise from shifts in the balance of forces as actors seek to gain advantage, or opportunistic exploitation of perceived moments of weakness. In the African context, this has usually occurred in piecemeal (localized) rather than systemic ways, often via the disaggregation of the largest administrative units along the lines of their own internal subdivisions to create smaller units, in ways that take advantage of the fractal structure of the inherited territorial matrix and exploit incumbents' prerogative to subdivide Admin1 units of territorial administration.[47] This way of viewing persistence

---

[46] See Mertha (2005) on the *tiao-kuai* system.

[47] Examples include the elevation of colonial Admin2 to Admin1 status, producing a "multiplication of regions" that could dilute very large units like "Northern Region" of Tanzania. Another example is local unit proliferation, one version of which was dilution of power of large NAs and "freeing" some subgroups from their subordinate status in relation to their former "overlords."

3.6 *Territorial Institutions and Regional Inequalities* 83

would account for the strong patterns of Admin1 and Admin2 (and electoral constituency) boundary persistence into the 2000s and 2010s.[48]

The Hierarchical Territorial Grid as a Template for Regional Coalition Building

The regional scale became a prime site for building national coalitions. A corollary of the persistence of inherited colonial territorial grids is that in many, perhaps most, African countries, administrative regions (or multidistrict clusters within them) often function as the constitutive units of the national polity. Admin1 structures serve as territorial frames for political coordination among politicians acting in the national political arena, both incumbents and main rivals, and as building blocs of the coalitions that underpin national regimes. The fractal structure of state – hierarchical administrative and representative institutions constituted within discrete state segments – creates an institutional frame for construction of political consciousness, interests, and strategy at *multiple scales* (see Czuba 2023). Aggregating at the supra-district level is an imperative for imposing territorial (or other) political interests at the national level.

Ethnic organizations or affinities can be a building bloc of regional coalitions, but ethnic and regional politics are constituted at different political scales, coalesce via different mechanisms, and are vehicles of different political logics and demands. Politicians and party builders can mobilize at both levels – at the level of the electoral constituency (generally corresponding to a former colonial NA) *and* the regional level. In a study of politics in Zambia, Posner (2005) made a similar case, drawing a distinction between politics at these two different scales. He conceptualized the political game in Zambia in terms of a politics within former NAs or districts based on "tribal" identity, and a politics at the provincial or regional level built upon linguistic identity. Posner argued that the same logic, the logic of ethnic politics, explains political mobilization and political coalitions at both levels. Here, I am arguing that ethnic and regional are *not* the same. The regional is not perfectly isomorphic

---

[48] More disruptive changes would scramble existing territorial configurations. There are some examples of this, including destruction of the NA as an ethnic landholding unit in much of mainland Tanzania under Nyerere (mentioned above), the territorial reorganization introduced after Nigeria's civil war, and new provincial structure introduced after the fall of the apartheid regime in South Africa (Mavungu 2016; see also Chapter 7). On Nigeria, Diamond (1988: 61–65) argued that, under the Second Republic, the creation of ethnic minority states added a swing factor in national politics that helped dilute regional polarization that had savaged the First Republic. Berry (1993: 58) notes the constant jurisdictional reordering in Nigeria in the 1960s, which she describes as driven by efforts to find a scale of incorporation/representation that would aggregate to some equilibrium power balance that the most powerful actors could subscribe to. Another type of change would involve moves toward *de*territorialization of representation or state function, as in Tanzania, or toward national economic *integration* in ways that promote commodification of factors or production and reduce market segmentation along regional lines, also seen in Tanzania.

to the ethnic, or simply ethnic politics played out on a larger scale. Differences of institutional scale, and their material and economic correlates, translate into differences in kind when it comes to mechanisms of coalition-building, animating interests, and the nature of political demands on the state.

Ethnicity that is politically salient in postcolonial politics is linked to neo-customary land rights and to membership in the former colonial NAs and cantons, most of which were defined in the 1920s and 1930s. Where ethnicity itself is rooted in claims to land and territory defined by state institutions, and where ethnicity is valorized through state practice, both state structure and state practice incentivize collective actors to organize themselves and press for demands as *territorially defined ethnic groups*. In many African countries, central governments provide ethnic services at the level of the "ethnic homeland" unit, including political recognition of groups, recognition of neocustomary land rights (i.e., an individual's birthright to claim land within a state-defined ethnic territory reserved for "members only"), and enforcement of these against rival group claims. Indeed, in many countries, defense of customary land rights within these units is a core expectation of government, constituting the base of the colonial and postcolonial "Magna Carta" or social contract at the molecular level (Boone 2014; MacArthur 2016: 74). Some political interests and expectations of the state are thus defined at the former NA or district level, and this contributes to political cohesion within these units (Boone 2014). Spatial economic inequalities also exist among ethnic homeland units, often aligning with and thus compounding regional inequalities.

Regional coalitions that define alliance and cleavage structures in the national political arena are analytically and empirically distinct from ethnic politics at the scale of the ex-NA or ethnic homeland. As Claire Médard (1999: 13) suggested, the classic form of ethnic politics is defensive – it *turns inward*. Within the fractal structure of the Native Authorities, subunits (sub-chieftaincies, lineages) seek the same club goods at lesser scales, along with recognition of some measure of functional and territorial autonomy. Regional administrative units, by contrast, offer wider territorial templates – both economic and political – for production of politics at a higher scale. This politics turns *outward*, to make claims and demands on the national state. Mega ethnicities – also referred to as conglomerate, confederal, or umbrella ethnicities, or "super tribes" – that coalesce at the regional level (e.g., Hausa–Fulani, Luhya, Bété, Bemba, and Kalenjin) may resemble more local, NA-level idioms of social collectivity, but they have different origins and political trajectories. Regional identities and coalitions date to the 1940s, 1950s, or thereafter, and are the construction of African political leaders and politicians jockeying for position on the national stage.[49] Regional identities and alliances form with explicit reference to territorial

---

[49] Regional identities thus defy the colonizers' attempts to confine political identities and participation to the level of the NAs. On the Bété, see Dozon (1985: 28, 312–320, 329, 337–338).

3.6 *Territorial Institutions and Regional Inequalities* 85

administrative units and natural regions that transcend the boundaries of ethnic homeland units. They refer to positionality and demand-making in the national arena. Posner made the same point when he observed that the groups in African countries that are actually doing the competing over national-level policy outcomes are not the local ethnic groups, but rather those that "fold themselves into broader political coalitions, often along regional lines" (2004a: 853).

Writing of Nigeria in the 1950s, Hiribarren (2015) describes the three-region structure of the 1951 constitution as more an *entente* around the goal of regional balancing – in this case, midwifed by the colonial administration – than the pursuit of "representation" or "ethnic representation" per se. Each of the three main regional blocs was highly ethnically diverse, with the East little more than a "territorial envelope" for myriad groups; the "Muslim North" not only ethnically heterogeneous but also divided by the rivalry between the Sokoto Caliphate and Borno State, and much of Nigeria not easily lumpable into meta-units by any ascriptive criteria. Similarly, the tripartite regional structure forged by Houphouët-Boigny in Côte d'Ivoire, 1960–1990, did not aim at ethnic representation. It grew out of geopolitics – the drive to secure hegemony through the alliance of two major regions against a third (Boone 2007). In Kenya, coalescing of the Kalenjin ethnic confederation in Rift Valley Province in the late 1940s and 1950s was driven by an effort to counterbalance the power of the political bloc rallying in the colony's Central Province. These regional coalitions are supra-ethnic, formed within colonial Admin1 units, and animated by the drive to compete for influence in the national arena. They do not arise from shared linguistic identities.[50]

Regional political coalitions are the work of nationalist-era and postcolonial African state-builders who operate within, and make use of, the territorial template of state institutions to construct political alliances of national standing and clout. They have strong roots in the spatial inequalities that arise from uneven development and the process of building national economies.

Regional Consciousness and Regional Interests
Keating wrote that in the "German Länder, mostly devised artificially after WWII, a sense of identity has been constructed by political institutions and by policy" (2003: 266). This is common in federal systems, as "even where subnational boundaries initially reflected purely geographical and not sociological features of the landscape, these political units tend to generate local identities and distinctive historical memories over time" (Whitehead & Behrend 2016: 296). It is true in African countries as well. Consciousness of "region" as a socio-spatial ensemble with distinctive interests and claims on the central state

---

[50] In the case of the Kalenjin, the attempt to forge a shared linguistic identity has been a key aspect of the political coalition-building strategy, but it has been only partially successful (Lynch 2011).

86 *Endowment, Institutions, and Spatial Inequality: Regions by Design*

has been constructed in large part by political institutions and policy. This is essential to the salience of region in defining national cleavage structure.

Regional identities anchored explicitly in Admin1 units include "Coastal" or Mijikenda in the Coast Province in Kenya; the identity of "northerner" in Ghana, Côte d'Ivoire, Nigeria, and Malawi; "Anglophone" identity in western Cameroon; Casamançais and *originaire* of the Région du Fleuve in Senegal; and Lozi in Zambia, which corresponds to the colonial Admin1 unit containing the Barotseland protectorate. As mentioned above, some wholly recent ethnic identities are regional identities crafted explicitly to rally collectivities to compete at the provincial level of national politics, as is the case for the Kalenjin and Mijikenda in Kenya, and Hausa–Fulani in Nigeria. National-level political actors themselves often treat regions as socio-spatial ensembles, and as constituent parts of the national territory and national community. This is true in political deal brokering as well as in discourse around national growth strategies. As Leonardi writes, "With regions and districts as the operational spatial unit of development planning and political action, planners and political leaders [themselves] often assumed a territorial definition of recipient communities or localities" (2020: 242). This contributes to making the region a framework for advancing claims on the center.

Regional consciousness can be defined as consciousness in relation to other subnational units constructed at the same territorial scale, within a single national framework. It is associated not only with generic demands for more schools, clinics, and roads (or for local club goods "here, rather than there"), as stressed in studies of electoral clientelism. It is also associated with particular, substantive regional interests, and ideologies of interregional advantage and disadvantage. These may coalesce around the terms of incorporation into the national economy, spatial–sectoral policies, regional autonomy versus centralization, and different visions of national growth strategy.[51] In Kenya, Sessional Paper #10 of 1969, which declared explicitly the government's intention to concentrate development efforts in "high growth potential regions" of the country, is an enduring source of bitterness among those in the "left behind places."[52] In Côte d'Ivoire, President Houphouet Boigny reminded his compatriots that his home region, the country's main coffee- and cocoa-producing region in the 1950s through 1970s, was "the udder of the national economy," thereby justifying its privileged economic and political status.

In a country's leading wealth-producing or growth regions, regional consciousness may find expression in a collective sense of entitlement to a disproportionate share of national wealth, and entitlement to national leadership.

---

[51] Spatial–sectoral policies often involve the delivery of "lumpy" public goods – investments, spatially targeted sectoral policy, or administrative practices (or dispensations) – that are supplied jointly at the regional level, or across multiple electoral constituencies within the same provincial-level or Admin1 unit (Saylor 2014).

[52] To use Rodriquez-Pose's (2018) phrase.

3.6 Territorial Institutions and Regional Inequalities 87

Where political and economic power align, regions may emerge as "drivers of national unity," as Bayart (2013) suggested. Regional ideologues may hold up the region and its inhabitants as the incarnation of "the nation" writ large.[53] Where wealth and national power do not align, there is likely to be resistance to taxation that siphons away wealth to fund development in poorer regions. Rich regions may press for autonomy and nonsharing of regional revenue, as in separatist regions like Katanga Province in Congo, and Nigeria's Biafra, in the 1960s. This same phenomenon is observed in wealthy regions that do not control national power in other parts of the world (Bolton & Roland 1997).[54]

Another form of regional consciousness may arise from defense of historically bargained arrangements with colonial state and rival domestic groups. One example is defense of gains in land tenure and territory vis-à-vis other regional contenders, such as those secured by the groups that rallied around Luhya identity in Western Kenya in the 1940s. In Zambia's agriculturally prosperous Southern Region in the 1960s, regional leaders and farmers feared land-grabbing by the UNIP government or by monied investors from other parts of Zambia. Another example is regional consciousness mobilized in defense of political autonomy won in the colonial period. This was the case in Zambia's Lozi region of Barotseland, where leaders sought for many decades to defend their measure of autonomy vis-à-vis the state and more politically powerful groups.

Consciousness of positionality in the national system may be acute in regions where populations perceive that they are exploited by the central state to enhance the wealth of other regions. This predicament may feel like "internal colonialism" (Hechter 2007). The term captures what has been felt by populations of Kenya's Rift Valley Province who, from the 1940s to the present, have resented the in-migration of Kenyan settlers from regions closer to the center of national power. As Rift Valley MP William Ntimama put it on the floor of Kenya's National Assembly in 2006, "we have finished with white colonialism and we are not going to have African colonialism in this country."[55] Where inhabitants feel peripheralized and marginalized, leaders may mobilize such sentiments to unify collectivities at the regional level around political grievances directed toward the center. This is what creates potential for the rise of regionalist ideologies in historically marginalized pastoral zones, where pastoralist and agro-pastoralist populations have been restricted to territories of inferior land quality and economic potential. Mavungu writes that

---

[53] This is consistent with Ahlerup, Baskaran, and Bigsten (2016), which finds that wealthier regions' populations (in level-1 GADM units, as gauged by advantage in nighttime luminosity) have stronger identification with the nation-state, based on Afrobarometer data. They interpret this as either consistent with modernization theory or possibly explained by the fact that wealthy regions are more likely to benefit from public services. See also Green 2020.

[54] An example is Spain's Catalonia. See Wallerstein (1967) on the "revolts of the privileged regions," and Ostby, Nordas, and Rod (2009).

[55] Kenya Hansard, June 20, 2006, p. 1448.

88 Endowment, Institutions, and Spatial Inequality: Regions by Design

in Congo, politicians' rhetoric justifying support for or opposition to the creation of new provinces is based on whether the new arrangements are likely to spark socioeconomic development "and spatial justice" (2016: 202).

CONCLUSION: WHEN POLITICAL INSTITUTIONS AND ECONOMIC GEOGRAPHY ALIGN

This chapter has argued that strong spatial inequalities associated with colonial economic development were aligned with the basic administrative and representative structures of the state. These defined the national space within which politics coalesced in the 1940s and 1950s. Most African governments retained the basic structures of territorial administration inherited from colonialism. These territorial grids thus constitute the basic institutional structure of governance and representation in most African countries today. *Alignment* of institutions of political representation with strongly regional patterns of economic heterogeneity and spatial inequality works to bring territorial interests to the fore in politics (Rogers 2016; Rickard 2018: 24). At the national level in many African countries, they bring regional interests to the fore.

These arguments resonate with works in economic history that underscore the importance of colonial institutions, including land tenure institutions, in shaping long-term patterns of economic growth, socioeconomic inequality, and political development.[56] In Africa, colonial patterns of regional advantage linked to export crop production and infrastructure provision have also proven to be enduring.[57] This chapter situates these empirical findings from economic history in an account of the formation of national economies and national political space in African countries, identifying forces that have worked over the course of the last century to promote the rise of the main regional contenders in national politics.

Provincial-level coalitions coalesced in the nationalist era of the 1940s and 1950s in the regions most deeply incorporated into national political economies. These were the political strongholds of the main regional contenders in the partisan contests of the early postindependence decades of the 1960s and early 1970s. After hiatuses in electoral competition in most African countries in the late 1970s and 1980s (when one-party regimes and military regimes held power in most of them), returns to multiparty competition in the 1990s made visible the *persistence* of these basic patterns of regional coalition and cleavage in national-level politics. The next chapters provide evidence of this in the regional voting blocs that structure national electoral competition in the

---

[56] See Engerman and Sokoloff (2002) and Banerjee and Iyer (2005). See also Müeller-Crepon et al. 2023.

[57] See Huillery (2009); Jedwab and Moradi (2016); Pengl, Roessler, and Rueda (2021); Roessler et al. (2022), and Ricart-Huguet (2022).

When Political Institutions and Economic Geography Align 89

1990s, 2000s, and 2010s (Chapter 4), the composition of national winning electoral coalitions (Chapter 5), the presence of stable axes of territorial opposition in the national politics of many countries (Chapter 6), and at the level of policy, in the enduring salience of demands for regionally tailored development policy, the politics of redistribution and national market-building (via land policy), and contestation around the territorial design of the state (Chapter 7). Negotiation around regional interests often emerges as a pivot of national politics.

4

Regional Blocs and Bloc Voting in National Elections

with Juliette Crespin-Boucaud, PhD

> In much of the developing world, regionalism prevails. It characterizes the political terrain.
>
> Bates 2017: 118

When geographic patterns of uneven development and territorial political institutions align, the *political salience* of spatial inequalities is enhanced. Interests and tensions arising from uneven geographic development can be channeled directly into national politics. In many African countries, inequalities and institutions coincide at the *regional scale* of politics, fueling regionalism in national electoral competition. This chapter shows that these patterns are visible in electoral cleavages in African countries post-1990, when most of them returned to multiparty competition after long interregnums of one-party rule in the 1970s and 1980s. Patterns of regional bloc voting that first appeared in national contests of the 1950s and 1960s have been perpetuated over time, often following lines of territorial division that were carved into national polities by the colonial state. This is in line with the observation made by Erdmann and Basedau (2008: 252) and others that the regional political cleavages observable in African countries today first emerged in the 1950s and 1960s.

Combining electoral and economic geography for twelve countries, this chapter identifies strong and persistent regional clustering in voting patterns that maps onto the uneven economic geography in each country. Most electoral clustering happens around historic, geographically concentrated zones of high-value crop production (or, less frequently, mining or labor-exporting zones), and maps roughly onto colonial-era units of provincial administration. In most cases, the sectoral economic specializations of the earlier era persist. Regional bloc voting is found in rural regions that are more deeply integrated in the national economy, wealthier, and more densely populated than other

Regional Blocs and Bloc Voting

rural regions. Uneven patterns in the presence and absence of regional bloc voting tend to follow lines of advantage and disadvantage rooted in long histories of uneven economic development. Chapter 5 shows that the most advantaged regional electoral blocs dominate politics at the national level in most (but not all) countries.

These arguments are developed through a series of comparisons and contrasts at different levels of analysis, working with a sample of twelve African countries that have all held multiple, multiparty presidential elections since the early 1990s. They are Côte d'Ivoire, Cameroon, Ghana, Kenya, Mali, Malawi, Nigeria, South Africa, Tanzania, Uganda, Zambia, and Zimbabwe. These countries are diverse in many ways, offering a wide range of values on attributes that are relevant to this analysis, including country size, national-level measures of both spatial and income inequality, colonial heritage, electoral system rules, the political salience of ethnicity, and profiles of main producer regions. Yet they are all marked by spatial inequalities that are high by global standards, and in all, a distinct regional cleavage structure is visible in electoral politics.[1] In all but one of the countries, the politicization of regional differentiation and inequality plays a strong role in structuring national politics. This exception is South Africa, where regionalism in electoral politics is overshadowed decisively by high levels of nationwide electoral support for the party that championed the anti-apartheid crusade, the ANC. It is the one country in the study in which the class-like cleavages arising from interpersonal income inequalities trump regional cleavages in national electoral politics (see Chapter 7).

Regionalism in electoral politics finds expression in regional voting blocs – what we call *persistent electoral blocs*[2] – that are defined here on the basis of electoral data from the mid-1990s to the mid-2010s. They are comprised of geographically contiguous electoral constituencies or districts that "stick together" as cohesive voting blocs in most presidential elections. They arise in predominantly rural regions. Distinct *oppositional zones*[3] *(opposition-leaning regions)* are visible in the electoral data in countries where hegemonic regimes have resisted electoral turnover in the multiparty era; we take this regionally distinct anti-incumbent voting as a type of bloc voting.[4] Regions *not* marked by such regional clustering are called the *non-bloc regions*[5] of each country.

---

[1] This invokes the logic of "maximum variation sampling" or a "method of agreement," whereby countries differ widely on many dimensions, but share a few key similarities that are correlated with similarity in the outcome of interest. For several reasons including sample size and measurement issues, this cannot offer a rigorous test of the theory, but it can support the plausibility of the argument.

[2] Defined below in operational terms.

[3] See below for operational definitions.

[4] It can be conceptualized as a diminished subtype of electoral bloc (Collier & Levitsky 1997: 437–438). We do not offer a separate theory of oppositional zones or opposition-leaning regions here.

[5] See below for operational definitions.

Non-bloc regions also provide leverage on the argument. They tend to be characterized by lower levels of economic development, lower population densities, and lack of sectoral economic specializations in agricultural production.

Our analysis offers a perspective on national-level voting patterns that is in tension with the most common lines of argument in the political science literature on electoral politics in African countries. The regional electoral blocs do not map onto what we would expect from mechanical ethnic voting, and they reveal spatial unevenness in electoral dynamics that cannot be explained by theories of retail-level electoral patronage. Shared ethnic identities surely contribute to the observed patterns of cross-constituency electoral cohesion documented here, but most of the regional electoral blocs are multiethnic – they coalesce at a political scale that transcends that of the "homeland" of a particular ethnic group. This is consistent with the argument made by Elischer (2013), Arriola (2013), Posner (2005), and others that winning electoral coalitions in presidential contests in African countries almost always need to be multiethnic, since it is rare for one ethnic group to include a majority of voters. Earlier arguments, however, do not tell us which ethnic groups vote together or why, or why stable patterns of alignment persist over multiple electoral cycles (or indeed, over many decades). Why do multiethnic electoral blocs emerge and persist over time in some parts of a country, but not in others? Why these particular lines of cleavage, but not others?

Identifying regional electoral blocs on the basis of geographically disaggregated electoral data provides a definition of their territorial extent that is independent of presuppositions about ethnic voting.[6] Focusing on these territorial units of analysis, we can identify their economic and institutional characteristics. We show that electoral blocs and oppositional zones are distinguished by economic characteristics that comparative political economy analysis has considered to be politically salient in other parts of the world: degrees of integration into the national economy, relative levels of wealth and prosperity, occupational profiles and policy interests related to these, and the presence of producer networks and organizations. The analysis thus supports a theory of bloc etiology that locates causes of regional bloc voting in uneven economic geography within countries – in particular, interest-based, institutional, organizational, and ideological correlates of sectoral differentiation and spatial (regional) inequality. This contrasts with voting theories that focus on ethnic affiliation alone, mechanical ethnic voting, or ethnicity-cued patronage-voting.

Section 4.1 introduces the cases and the data. There is very little subnational data for African countries, including constituency-level electoral data and subnational economic data, that is comparable cross-nationally and over time. This is surely one reason why few scholars have studied electoral geography in these

---

[6] As Andreas Wimmer (2009: 245, 262) argued, identifying territorial units of observation is a first step toward disentangling ethnic from nonethnic or more generic group processes, and thus avoiding "the ethnic lens" where this may be unwarranted.

Regional Blocs and Bloc Voting

contexts or matched electoral results to economic geography.[7] Section 4.2 lays out the analytic strategy by which regional electoral blocs were identified, and maps the blocs for each of twelve countries.[8] Section 4.3 describes socioeconomic attributes of electoral blocs and oppositional regions, focusing on spatial inequalities.[9] Section 4.4 traces the electoral blocs' histories as colonial-era producer regions and shows that most retain the same economic specializations today. Section 4.5 focuses on the geographic alignment of electoral blocs and the territorial gridwork of state administration. Most blocs have coalesced within the boundaries of Admin1 (provincial) units that were defined in the colonial period and that persist today, often with subdivisions. Section 4.6 takes up the related matter of the ethnic profiles of the regional electoral blocs, stressing their multi-ethnic character. Ethnic identity alone either over- or underpredicts the presence of regional electoral blocs and frequently fails as a predictor of constituency membership therein. Section 4.7 argues that *causes* of the observed patterns of regional-level electoral cohesion can be traced to multiple micro- and meso-level mechanisms that operate at the level of actors, collectivities, and organizations.

Drawing inferences from electoral bloc attributes, we theorize that blocs and oppositional zones arise as vehicles for the expression of sectoral and regional interests in national politics. The data suggest a strong relationship between historic export-producing zones, contemporary export-producing zones, and geographically cohesive political mobilization in the post-1990 years. Almost all of the electoral blocs and oppositional zones share a history of deep integration into the colonial economy and deep state penetration into the rural areas. They are historic targets of sustained government intervention in the rural sector to build export-crop-marketing organizations, input distribution channels, producer organizations, or systems for mobilization and channeling of migrant labor. Many are marked by histories of rural political mobilization and activism vis-à-vis the state that date to the 1940s and 1950s. They tend to be marked by several potential sources of persistent and cumulative advantage, both at the individual and household level in terms of education, and at the level of the locality in terms of local public goods, compared to predominantly rural non-bloc regions of each country.

The power of our argument is enhanced by the fact that we are using electoral data from the period spanning the early 1990s to the mid-2010s to identify persistent regional cleavages in electoral politics. A skeptical reader may

---

[7] As far as we know, this is the first over-time analysis of geographic voting patterns in multiple African countries. For earlier work, see Osei-Kwame and Taylor (1984) on Ghana, and Lawal (2019) on Nigeria.

[8] This section describes the electoral geography methods developed with coauthors Wahman, Kyburz, and Linke (2022) to identify persistent electoral blocs.

[9] In comparative politics literature, regions' *relative* positions in the national political economy are typically measured in terms of levels of development and prosperity or growth rates compared to a national average, or to national extremes (dynamic vs. stagnant regions, leading vs. lagging regions, rich vs. poor regions). See, for example, Massetti and Schakel (2015).

94 Regional Blocs and Bloc Voting

be willing to concede that regional cleavages were visible in national politics in many African countries in the early postcolonial years, but may doubt the claim that these same patterns are visible in electoral data four or five decades later. We show that these regional cleavages in national political competition do indeed persist, along with the underlying patterns of spatial inequality and sectoral economic differentiation that, according to our theory, give rise to them.

4.1 COUNTRY CASES AND DATA

The analysis here combines electoral geography, economic geography, and overtime analysis to propose a theory of geographic structuring in patterns of electoral competition in African countries. Tracking results in forty-four presidential elections at subnational levels of aggregation over time, we identify persistent regional clustering in all twelve countries.[10] We identify thirty-six persistent electoral blocs and persistent oppositional zones across the dozen countries and describe these in terms of relative economic advantage and disadvantage, historical sectoral profile, contemporary sectoral profile, congruence with territorial grid of state, and ethnic profile. Comparing these electoral blocs to non-bloc regions of each country offers clues to the causes of "bloc-ness."

The analysis is based on twelve countries that have gone through three or more presidential election cycles since the early 1990s: Cameroon, Côte d'Ivoire, Ghana, Kenya, Malawi, Mali, Nigeria, South Africa, Tanzania, Uganda, Zambia, and Zimbabwe. They were chosen to capture variation in inequality structure, as featured in Figure 1.1, which compares countries in terms of their Gini index scores (for interpersonal income inequality) and spatial inequality as measured across Admin1 regions. The twelve countries also represent a range of variation in the structure of national political economies, electoral system design, and variation in regime type along the spectrum from competitive electoral democracies to electoral authoritarian.[11] (See Tables B.1 and B.2 in Appendix B.) Half of the cases have experienced electoral turnover since 1990. Several have experienced coups either historically or since 2000, and six have experienced civil war in the form of insurgency or secessionism since the 1950s (Kenya, Cameroon, Nigeria, Zimbabwe, Uganda, Mali).

---

[10] For Malawi 1999 and 2004, Michael Wahman used legislative results to approximate presidential results. We used this work in Boone, Wahman, Kyburz, and Linke (2022) and do so here.

[11] Eleven of the twelve elect presidents directly. South Africa is the exception: The president is elected by parliament. Most of the countries hold plurality SMD elections for parliament. The exceptions are Côte d'Ivoire, Cameroon, Mali, and South Africa. The three former French colonies hold mixed elections that combine SMD or MMD elections with subsets of representatives selected by some other vote aggregation rule. In South Africa, the parliament is chosen through a list voting/PR system. See Table B.2 in Appendix B. Under South Africa's PR system, each party receives seats according to the number of votes it receives nationwide. Nine provincial-level governments with their own competencies are also elected via PR. These, in

4.1 Country Cases and Data

While varying widely on these dimensions, the countries share similarities that are important to this analysis. They are all relatively populous and subject to relatively deep patterns of colonial state penetration and economic development.[12] The combined population of the 12 countries in 2010 totaled 458 million, or about half of sub-Saharan Africa's total of 869 million at the time (WDI 2010). All had strong agro-export and/or mining sectors in the colonial era, with extensive labor mobilization within each colony to support the development of these productive zones. All except South Africa have electoral systems based strongly on territorial representation, wherein units of representation are nested within the grid of territorial administration. If we are to see the hypothesized effects of uneven development and strongly territorial institutions in the electoral arena, then these countries should offer fertile ground for doing so.

Data challenges are formidable when it comes to analysis of the countries studied here. The electoral data are heterogeneous in terms of coverage, quality, and level of spatial aggregation. In the best cases, we have constituency-level electoral data for four to six successive presidential elections, along with the constituency boundary maps (shapefiles) that allow us to map the electoral results and implement spatial clustering analysis. We have such data for the elections in Ghana, Kenya, Malawi, and Zambia. We will call these the A-list countries, based on the quality of the electoral data. There is also a B-list, which is made up of countries whose electoral data are less granular or less complete, or not available at the constituency level (or at the same level of aggregation) for all presidential elections, and available for fewer elections over time. Often electoral constituency maps and boundary shapefiles are missing. For these countries, we used the disaggregated electoral data that is available and administrative unit shapefiles to map electoral results[13] (see Table B.2 in Appendix B).

We describe blocs and oppositional zones in terms of relative economic advantage using geocoded nighttime luminosity data (NOAA), educational data (Demographic and Health Surveys, DHS), and population density data (AGILE), aggregated to the bloc level. The nighttime luminosity data make it possible to track constancy and change from 1992 to 2013. Sectoral profiles of the persistent electoral blocs and oppositional zones are developed from two sources of information. First, using 1960s-era atlases, we mapped colonial

---

turn, elect representatives to the lower house of the national parliament, the National Council of Provinces. At the municipal level of government, wards are SMDs (single-seat districts) elected by plurality vote. South Africa's electoral rules thus permit both territorial representation *and* representation of nongeographically concentrated minorities. See Chapter 7.

[12] This is compared to most of Afrique Equatoriale Française (the Congo River Basin states), the Mano River Basin states, most of the Sahelian states, or the countries of the Horn of Africa.

[13] We relied on constituency-level data that was spottier over fewer elections (Zimbabwe, Tanzania); electoral data aggregated to the Admin3, Admin2, or District Council level (Côte d'Ivoire, Uganda, South Africa); or Admin1-level results combined with district results where possible (Nigeria, Cameroon, Mali). See Appendix B.4.

96 Regional Blocs and Bloc Voting

"producer areas" (crop and mining areas) and then calculated the extent of areal overlap between the colonial producer areas and today's electoral blocs. Second, grid-cell-level data on harvested area by crop for Africa's twenty leading agricultural commodities (from IFPRI) were used to describe the agricultural production profiles of the electoral blocs in 2010. (See Appendix B, Section B.2.) Combined, the results strongly suggest that the economic advantages and contemporary sectoral profiles of the electoral blocs and oppositional zones are traceable to the colonial period. Using administrative maps, past and present, we also show that most of the blocs coalesce within the boundaries of colonial-era provincial units (Admin1 regions). Many Admin1 regions have been subdivided over time, but nearly all of today's Admin1 units fit wholly within colonial-era provincial boundaries. Finally, using individual-level DHS survey responses aggregated to the electoral-bloc-level data, we show that most of the electoral blocs and opposition zones are multiethnic.

4.2 IDENTIFYING ELECTORAL BLOCS: CONCEPTUALIZATION, ANALYTIC STRATEGY, AND MAPPING

Many scholars of politics in other parts of the world have used electoral returns to identify regional cleavages in national politics. This is the approach adopted here.[14] Yet we depart from the disciplinary tendency in political science to employ a party-centered approach to studying voting dynamics (a tendency followed by most earlier work on electoral politics in Africa). In many African countries, party labels change, and parties split, combine, and recombine. Personalistic political leaders defect from old formations to form their own parties. Fluidity in party labels can obscure overtime trends in the structure and organization of political competition in African countries. Since we are interested in the persistence over time of regional clusters of bloc voting, we depart from the default practice of defining bloc voting as "bloc voting for party A," and focus instead on bloc voting in the voter population (or voter base) over time, regardless of party. This gets us close to what Lipset and Rokkan (1967) theorized as "underlying social cleavages" in the electorate.[15]

To do so, we identify geographic clustering in constituencies that provide very high levels of support to a given party in election 1, and ask if that same geographic cluster of constituencies "sticks together" when voting in election 2, returning strong majorities – in most cases, around 70% or more of all votes – for a common presidential candidate in election 2, election 3, election 4, etc. (even if

---

[14] See Agnew (1996) on Italy, Flint (1998) and O'Loughlin (2002) on the Nazi vote, West (2005) on Turkey, and Harbers (2017) on Mexico. See also Osei-Kwame and Taylor (1984) on Ghana.

[15] West (2005:503) explains that Kitschelt (1992) criticized Lipset and Rokkan (1967) for not distinguishing between party and population. Kitschelt chose to focus his own research on the *party* rather than the "underlying social cleavage." While most literature on parties and elections in Africa has followed Kitschelt's lead, we take the other path, focusing on the "underlying social cleavage." See also Bornschier (2009).

4.2 *Identifying Electoral Blocs*

the electoral bloc is voting for a different party in each election). The minimum threshold for "sticking together over time" is set at two-thirds of observed post-1990 presidential elections.[16] Where these criteria are met, the cluster is designated as a *persistent electoral bloc*. Strong electoral majorities mean that most persistent electoral blocs are returning *landslide wins* for a shared candidate in most post-1990 elections.[17]

In countries with dominant, hegemonic, or electoral authoritarian party systems – Cameroon, Tanzania, Uganda, and Zimbabwe – incumbents win most constituencies in presidential elections and opposition candidates have limited chances for electoral breakthroughs. In these cases, we identify not only geographic clusters of constituencies that consistently return very strong support for a candidate at the 70% level, but also geographic clusters of persistently *opposition-leaning* or oppositional constituencies. Oppositional clusters are composed of constituencies that return a distinctively high vote share for opposition candidates (30% or more of all constituency votes). Where three or more such constituencies cluster together in two-thirds or more of the elections for which we have data, they are defined as a *persistent oppositional zone*. Oppositional zones are cohesive in that they persistently return distinctively high, anti-incumbent vote shares, even when constituencies within such zones opt for different candidates in a given election.

Persistent oppositional zones and persistent electoral blocs are considered to be variants of a single phenomenon – the electorally distinct and cohesive region. We refer to them generically as electoral blocs, mentioning both or drawing a distinction between the two where this necessary or adds useful information. The analysis shows that the electoral blocs tend to share similar, distinctive socioeconomic and sectoral attributes that distinguish them from the non-bloc regions of each country. Electoral blocs tend to be economically advantaged and sectorally distinctive, compared to the parts of each country not comprised within electoral blocs. Our theory is that regional bloc voting arises from these bloc attributes. The *non-bloc regions* of each country constitute a residual category that serves as a counterfactual in the analysis – these are the areas in which regional electoral blocs do *not* coalesce.

---

[16] That is, in 66% (2/3) or more of the elections we are able to observe for each country. Where we have four elections, the threshold is 3/4 (75%). See Boone, Wahman, Kyburz, and Linke (2022) for thresholds by country for Kenya, Zambia, and Malawi.

[17] Johnston et al. (2020: 189) define "winning by a landslide" as 20% or greater gap in the vote share of the two parties, in a two-party system. The term "landslide" is thus an apt description of winners' vote shares in the constituencies comprising the persistent electoral blocs that we identify here. Winners' vote shares generally range from 60 to 80%. For the elections included in the analysis, The average winner vote share in core constituencies in the electoral blocs in the A-list countries of Kenya, Zambia, and Malawi is 83, 68, and 70%, respectively. For the B-list countries, a margin of approximately 70% for a presidential candidate was the criterion we applied to identify constituencies "voting together" in a given election (except for constituencies comprising opposition zones, which returned anti-incumbent vote shares of 30% or more). There are some country-level exceptions. See Section B.4 of Appendix B.

Identifying Geographic Clustering in Electoral Results

To describe procedures for identifying geographic clustering in the electoral results, we divide the twelve countries into two groups, depending on the quality of the electoral data. The A-list countries are those with the best electoral data. They are Ghana, Kenya, Malawi, and Zambia. The other countries are on the B-list.

To detect *clustering* in the constituency-level electoral results for each of the elections for which we had data, we used basic measures in the electoral geography tool kit where the data permit: the Global and Local Moran's I measures of spatial autocorrelation.[18] The Global Moran's I shows high levels of spatial clustering in constituency-level electoral results for almost all the country elections for which we were able to calculate this statistic. (Results are in Table C.2 in Appendix C.) For the A-list countries of Kenya, Malawi, and Zambia, all Global Moran's I statistics indicate high levels of spatial clustering in constituency-level results for the top four parties across all elections in all three countries. In Ghana, also on the A-list, the Global Moran's I also indicates high clustering in vote shares for the two leading parties – it registers the "checkerboard pattern" of values where rival voting blocs are literally adjacent to each other in Southern Ghana (high and low vote shares for the same party in adjacent units).[19] For the B-list countries, the Global Moran's I could be calculated for Cameroon's 2011 election, Tanzania's 2010 election, and Zimbabwe's 2008 and 2013 elections. In Cameroon and Tanzania, levels of spatial clustering for both leading party vote shares are high and statistically significant.[20] Opposition party vote shares are also high and statistically significant.[21] In Zimbabwe, vote shares for the leading parties in 2008 and 2013 are also strongly and significantly spatially clustered.

A related statistic, the Local Moran's I, identifies subnational clustering in the electoral results.[22] For each election since 1990 for which we had adequate data, we calculated a Local Moran's I statistic for each party's vote share in

---

[18] We follow the analysis developed collaboratively in Boone, Wahman, Kyburz, and Linke (2022) for Kenya, Zambia, and Malawi. See Appendix B, Section B.3.

[19] Results for Kenya, Malawi, and Zambia are positive and statistically significant for all elections. For Ghana, the Global Moran's I is negative for both of the main parties in all elections (except 1996), reflecting the checkerboard pattern mentioned above. The results are statistically significant at the 0.05 level in 2012 (although in 2000, results for the NPP are close to this level). See Appendix B, Sections B.3 and B.4, and Appendix C, Table C.2.

[20] These parties are Cameroon's RDPC (led by Paul Biya) and Tanzania's CCM.

[21] The exception is Cameroon's SDF, whose voters are concentrated in the Western Region, but do not appear strongly clustered/concentrated due to competing votes for the other opposition party, the UDC.

[22] See Anselin (1995). The Local Moran's I detects specific geographic areas of spatial autocorrelation in constituency-level results for each election. Following standard practice, we include the constituencies on the outer edges of a cluster that return the same high vote shares for the cluster's candidate (i.e., the so-called neighbors of the cluster) as cluster members. See the Appendixes in Boone, Wahman, Kyburz, and Linke (2022).

4.2 *Identifying Electoral Blocs*

every constituency. For the A-list countries, we employed this method systematically to identify clusters of similar, high vote shares for the same winning party (i.e., positive and statistically significant spatial autocorrelation) in each election. In most constituencies, winners claimed the constituency with very high vote margins, usually over 70%. At least three contiguous constituencies with statistically significant spatial clustering in their vote shares constitute an "electoral cluster."

To detect *persistency* in the geographic clustering of constituencies over time, we compared the constituency makeup of each electoral cluster from one election to the next, counting the number of times a particular constituency is part of a given electoral cluster. This identifies constituencies that tend to stick together as a bloc over time – returning high vote shares for a candidate in a given election, even if the bloc as a whole votes for a different party in each election. A *persistent electoral bloc* is a statistically significant geographic cluster of three or more constituencies that vote together ("stick together") in at least two-thirds of the presidential elections since 1990.

For the B-list countries, due to the heterogeneity of electoral data availability and quality, it was not possible to use a single operational method to identify electoral clusters in all countries and elections. Where constituency-level electoral data was available for particular elections, we calculated the Global and Local Moran's I to detect statistically significant clusters (i.e., Cameroon 2011; Tanzania 2010; Zimbabwe 2008R1 and 2013R1) and combined this with simple serial mapping of available electoral results for the other presidential elections. Where such electoral data was not available, data at the most disaggregated level available (Admin3, Admin2, or Admin1) were used to identify geographic clusters of units returning high vote shares for a given candidate (higher than 70% in most blocs) and, in countries with hegemonic party systems, geographic clusters where opposition candidates' vote share (the anti-incumbent vote share) was persistently greater than 30%. Simple mapping of electoral results over time made it possible to identify persistent electoral blocs and oppositional zones in the electoral data. Additional sources of information aided in tracking geographic clustering in electoral returns over time (see Table B.2 in Appendix B). These methods are approximative in several respects.[23] Even so, when comparing the A-list countries to the B-list countries, we see no systematic variation in the average number of blocs, size of blocs, and fraction of the national territory comprised in blocs across the two categories of countries.

---

[23] For the B-list countries, although constituency-level data were available for some elections, results were often incomplete and impossible to map over time at this level. Results were aggregated to Admin2 or Admin1, but this washed out some variation in constituency-level vote shares. The types of errors that are most likely in B-list countries are thus erroneous inclusion or exclusion of constituencies/administrative units on the geographic edge of an electoral bloc (boundary error), or erroneous inclusion of a constituency/administrative unit in an electoral bloc (homogenization or leveling error). The margin of uncertainty is smaller for the A-list countries, given more granular and complete data.

Mapping Electoral Blocs and Oppositional Regions

The persistent electoral blocs, opposition-leaning zones, and the non-bloc regions that are defined by these methods are mapped in Figures 4.1–4.4.[24]

Figure 4.1 maps electoral blocs in Kenya, Malawi, Zambia, and Ghana. As explained above, the electoral blocs are composed of significant clusters of three or more constituencies with similar, high vote shares for the same party. The figure maps constituencies that vote consistently (more than 66% of all elections between 1990 and 2016) and strongly (a vote share of 70% or larger in most constituencies in most of the blocs) for the same presidential candidate in most or all elections. The constituencies rally together in each of a series of elections, even if the standard-bearer candidate, or party label, changes over time.

Readers will recognize Ghana's Central and Eastern electoral blocs. Four constituencies in Ghana's northwest corner also form a cohesive bloc. Kenya's Central, Western, Rift Valley, and Eastern electoral blocs will be familiar to those who know Kenyan politics. Malawi's four regional electoral blocs have been electorally distinctive for decades. For Zambia, the basic Copperbelt Northern and Southern bloc opposition is clear. These persistent electoral blocs hold up to alternative specifications of the criteria used for defining constituency clusters, with a couple of exceptions.[25] Case narratives of the development and persistence of "territorial oppositions" in electoral politics in Kenya, Malawi, and Zambia are featured in Chapter 6.

Figure 4.2 features Côte d'Ivoire, South Africa, Uganda, and Zimbabwe, four B-list countries that were mapped using administrative units (Admin1, Admin2, and/or Admin3 level) rather than electoral constituencies. In some cases, electoral results came from data reported at different geographic scales over time. The maps contain both persistent electoral blocs and oppositional zones in which the "anti-incumbent" (opposition candidates') vote share is persistently greater than 30%.

The Côte d'Ivoire map shows clearly three main persistent electoral blocs that have defined poles of regional competition in that country over time (Boone 2007). South Africa, which has been a hegemonic party system under much of ANC rule since 1994, has a strong, ANC-supporting persistent electoral bloc centered in the country's industrial and urban heartland. It extends across much of the national territory. There is also a persistent electoral bloc of opposition-voting constituencies in the Western Cape and an opposition-leaning

---

[24] Some gray-area cases are ambiguous due to weak electoral data or sensitivity to the cutoff years of our analysis.

[25] The most important exception is Zambia's Western bloc, for which the Local Moran's I does not generate stable results under alternative specifications. Even so, we see a distinct and cohesive voting pattern for ten Western constituencies for five of the six elections in our Zambia analysis. See also Boone, Wahman, Kyburz, and Linke (2022).

4.2 Identifying Electoral Blocs

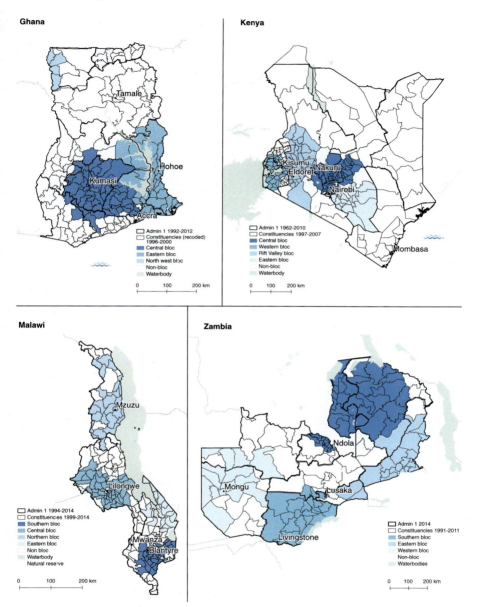

FIGURE 4.1 Ghana, Kenya, Malawi, and Zambia: Persistent electoral blocs
Notes: Electoral blocs defined on the basis of the Local Moran's I (constituency-level electoral data). Information on the constituency boundary shapefiles can be found in Appendix B.

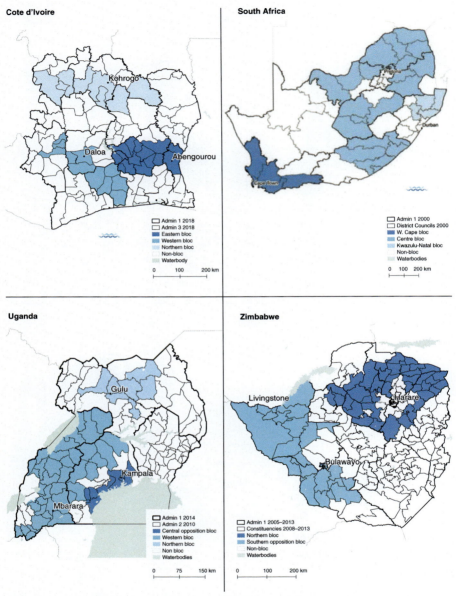

FIGURE 4.2 Côte d'Ivoire, South Africa, Uganda, and Zimbabwe: Persistent electoral blocs and oppositional zones

Notes: Côte d'Ivoire, electoral blocs drawn using Admin3 boundaries; South Africa electoral blocs drawn using District Council boundaries (and subdistrict council level for KwaZulu-Natal); Uganda, electoral blocs drawn using Admin2 boundaries; Zimbabwe, electoral blocs drawn using constituency boundaries. The oppositional zones are South Africa, part of KwaZulu-Natal; Uganda, Central oppositional zone; Zimbabwe, Southern oppositional zone.

4.2 *Identifying Electoral Blocs* 103

Nigeria

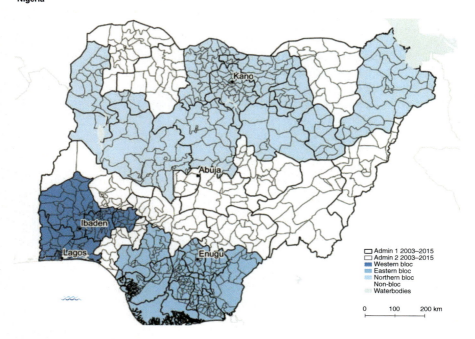

FIGURE 4.3 Nigeria: Persistent electoral blocs
Notes: Nigeria, persistent electoral blocs drawn using Admin1-level boundaries (i.e., states).

zone in part of KwaZulu-Natal.[26] The Uganda map shows the persistent electoral bloc composed of districts that have voted most cohesively for the country's long-time ruler, Yoweri Museveni, from 2001 to 2016, along with a Northern electoral bloc and an opposition bloc – that is, the Central oppositional bloc anchored in the region around the national capital of Kampala.[27] Zimbabwe's

---

[26] South Africa's electoral rules permit both territorial representation and representation of nongeographically concentrated minorities, via PR. As Ferree (2018) points out, this means that the electoral system would have permitted more strongly regional representation than we actually observe (i.e., more regional parties represented in the national parliament, more non-ANC controlled provincial legislatures) if underlying social interests were strongly organized on a regional basis. The ANC's national electoral dominance and its broad geographic base, depicted in Center electoral bloc in Figure 4.2, thus capture the dominant tendency for the contemporary political economy and electoral system to produce and give voice to divisions based on *nonterritorial* social cleavages in general, and to divisions based on interpersonal income inequality in particular (i.e., class and class-like divides). See Gethin 2020 and Chapter 7. Regional electoral blocs in Western Cape and in part of KwaZulu-Natal are exceptions to this dominant tendency.

[27] Uganda's Northern cluster returned anti-incumbent vote shares of over 50% in 3/4 elections between 2001 and 2016. (Gulu was the epicenter of conflict between the LRA insurgency and the government from 1986 to 2006.) Anti-incumbent voting was in the 60–70% range within

electoral geography shows two regions that have been consistently polarized since the country's struggle for national liberation from white minority rule in the 1970s. In elections from 2002 to 2013, under Mugabe's electoral authoritarian regime, Zimbabwe's Northern persistent electoral bloc was the most reliable base of the incumbent, while the Southern oppositional zone remained unsubdued. As the Zimbabwe map indicates, the region around the capital city of Harare remained a non-bloc region, where we do not see clustering in electoral returns because adjacent constituencies voted for either the opposition or the incumbent with highly varying margins.

Nigeria's persistent electoral blocs are featured in Figure 4.3. They are mapped at the state level (i.e., Admin1 level; B-list country). For Nigeria, we used state-level electoral results for all elections from 1999 to 2015 to identify geographically contiguous blocs of states that returned high vote shares for one of the three leading parties in three of the four elections for which we had reliable data.[28] Nigeria is often taken as a textbook case of regional bloc voting in the African studies literature, but such strong regionalism is often regarded as highly specific to Nigeria. The analysis here calls for a rethinking of that view: There appears to be as much or even more cohesion within persistent electoral blocs in most of the other eleven countries than there is in Nigeria. In Nigeria's Western and Northern blocs, vote shares for the winning candidate often hover around 60%,[29] whereas in many of the persistent electoral blocs featured in the twelve-country study, presidential candidates routinely win constituencies by vote shares that are considerably higher (often over 70%). This enhances our confidence in interpreting persistent electoral bloc voting across the other eleven countries as *at least as regionalized* as it is in Nigeria, if not more so.

Tanzania, Cameroon, and Mali appear in Figure 4.4. The first two are countries with dominant or hegemonic party systems. (They are all B-list countries.) In all three, levels of party competition are suppressed or subdued, electoral data are incomplete and difficult to map, and opposition presidential candidates win few constituencies. Here, we mapped persistent electoral clusters of high vote shares for the ruling party, as well as oppositional zones where opposition candidates appear to win at least 30% of the vote in at

---

this cluster of districts in 2001 and 2006, and fell to around 50% of the vote in several districts in this cluster in 2011 and 2016. By our criteria, it is in the gray zone between an "electoral bloc" and an "opposition zone." Because the obstacles to anti-incumbent mobilization under Uganda's dominant party regime are so high, we called it an *electoral bloc*. This does not affect the analysis: Electoral blocs and oppositional zones are considered to be two variants of the same phenomenon.

[28] Olanrewaju Lawal's (2019) spatial analysis of state-level clustering in the 2011 and 2015 presidential election results provided support for our description of electoral blocs in state-level voting results for 2011 and 2015.

[29] Electoral blocs were identified using a constituency margin of 60% as the threshold. For Western Nigeria, the criterion was a constituency margin of greater than 55%. Winners' vote shares in Nigeria's Eastern electoral bloc were often over 80%.

4.2 Identifying Electoral Blocs

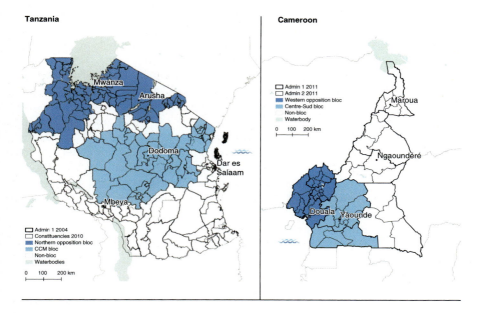

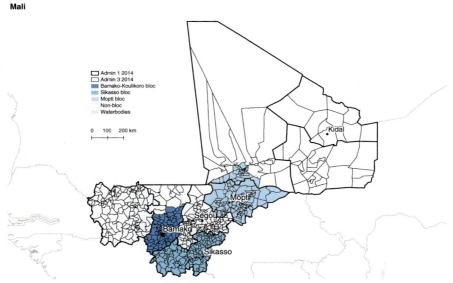

FIGURE 4.4 Tanzania, Cameroon, and Mali: Persistent electoral blocs and oppositional zones

Notes: Tanzania, electoral blocs drawn using constituency boundaries; Cameroon, electoral blocs drawn using Admin1 boundaries; Mali, electoral blocs drawn using Admin1 boundaries as well as Admin2 (for Bamako–Koulikoro bloc) and Admin3 (Mopti bloc) boundaries. Opposition zones include Cameroon Western oppositional zone and Tanzania Northern oppositional zone.

least two out of three of the elections for which we have data. For mainland Tanzania 2010, the electoral geography statistics show that spatial clustering for both CCM and opposition party vote shares was high and statistically significant.[30] This represents a geographic pattern that is discernible in elections since the mid-1990s, as the Tanzania map indicates. Mbeya may qualify as a persistent electoral bloc in the future – as of 2015, it did not fit the criterion of 30% level of anti-CCM voting in three or more contiguous constituencies. (However, this may be because of too much missing data for this region for earlier elections.) Zanzibar was not included in the analysis. Cameroon's map illustrates the stark cleavage between the regions that constitute a strong voting bloc for the incumbent in the Centre-Sud, and the highly and persistently oppositional zone of the West (based on a mix of electoral results at the province/region and constituency level over time).[31] Mali is where the over-time electoral data are the least complete and least precise. For Mali, electoral returns over time, patched together from different sources that reported results at different levels of granularity, indicate the presence of three electorally distinctive regions. Even though poor data make the depiction of Mali's electoral geography imprecise, it is clear that a large cluster of Mopti region constituencies – including constituencies in Gao and Tombouctou – has consistently diverged from most of the South, especially the Bamako–Koulikoro bloc. This appears to be the main line of electoral cleavage in Mali. The Sikasso region also exhibits a cohesive and distinctive pattern over time (not aligning with Mopti and the inland Niger Delta constituencies, or with the Bamako–Koulikoro bloc) and is thus designated on the map as a distinctive electoral region.

Non-bloc Constituencies and Capital Cities

Across the large and heterogeneous expanses comprised of rural non-bloc constituencies in each country, constituencies are more divided in their choices in presidential elections, either internally or vis-à-vis their neighbors, or both. They return lower vote shares for the presidential candidate who wins locally, and/or vote differently from neighboring constituencies some or most of the time. The non-blocs are significant in this analysis because they represent the counterfactual to bloc voting. One-half to two-thirds of the total area of each country (av. 57%), ranging from 83% (Mali) to 37% (Malawi), falls into the

---

[30] Zanzibar constituencies are not included in the spatial analysis.

[31] Cameroon's Western oppositional zone coincides with former British Cameroon (Southern Cameroon), which became the Western Cameroon federal state in 1961 (capital at Buéa), plus two regions in former French Cameroon – Western Region, capital at Bafoussam, and Littoral Region, capital at Douala. These were the locus of the Union des Populations du Cameroon (or Union of the Peoples of Cameroon, UPC) nationalist rebellion and insurgency and the French war against it. See Johnson (1970).

4.2 Identifying Electoral Blocs

rural "non-bloc" category in each country, wherein persistent regional clustering of electoral results in presidential elections is *absent*.[32]

In most cases, capital-city constituencies (and constituencies that make up two cities that perform capital-city functions, Abidjan and Dar es Salaam) are not part of the persistent electoral blocs (see Section B.5 in Appendix B on the capital cities). Most capital-city constituencies follow the widely documented tendency for African capital-city electoral constituencies to be electorally competitive.[33] Many capital-city constituencies vote against incumbent parties, and there is wide dispersion in voting results across and within capital-city voting districts. This is the case for eight of the twelve countries analyzed here. Capital cities in these countries are classified as "capital-city non-bloc" regions.

Exceptions exist, however. Capital-city constituencies vote cohesively with the larger Admin1 regions they are part of in Mali and Cameroon. For Cameroon, this may indeed be partly an effect of a high level of electoral authoritarianism – the ruling party has a tight grip on Yaoundé. In Uganda, the Central oppositional zone is anchored in Kampala. In Nigeria, the Western bloc includes Lagos, Africa's largest city (population estimated at 9 million) and Nigeria's capital until 1975. Even so, the persistent electoral blocs that include these primate cities remain predominantly rural in terms of their spatial extent and average population densities.

In a few countries, some constituencies on the peripheries of capital-city agglomerations are part of persistent electoral blocs. In Kenya, Nairobi's exurbs have encroached on Kiambu, which is part of the predominantly rural Central bloc of Kenya. In Malawi, a few Blantyre and Lilongwe constituencies vote with the Malawi Southern and Central blocs, respectively. In Ghana, three predominantly rural constituencies on the eastern side of Greater Accra are in the Eastern electoral bloc (anchored in Volta Region).

Most of the electoral blocs will seem familiar to long-time observers of these elections, even though earlier scholars have not used the electoral geography methods employed here, produced overtime mappings, or combined electoral and economic geography as this chapter will do. Our method avoids the common analytic shortcut of assuming that the ethnic map is what defines the electoral map. By working with spatial (territorial) units that are defined inductively from electoral data, we can underscore the extent to which aprioristic ethnic assumptions fall short, both as description and explanation of regional

---

[32] See Table C.3 in Appendix C. There is no systematic relationship between the method of bloc determination and size of the blocs as a percentage of the national territory. A-list countries cluster at the highest and lowest extremes of the range: 21, 22, 60, and 63% of national area for the persistent electoral blocs in Kenya, Ghana, Zambia, and Malawi, respectively. The countries in which "bloc area" includes opposition-leaning zones are Mali, Uganda, Cameroon, and Tanzania, and for these, "bloc areas" are 17, 39, 41, and 50% of the national territory, respectively.

[33] Constituency-level electoral returns confirm the competitiveness and cross-constituency fragmentation (dispersion) of voting in capital cities.

108   Regional Blocs and Bloc Voting

bloc voting. At the same time, this method opens the door to identifying bloc
attributes that may be prior, compounding, substitute, additional, or alternative sources of geographic clustering in electoral results.

4.3 ECONOMIC INEQUALITIES AND ELECTORAL BLOCS

Why do electoral blocs and oppositional zones arise in some parts of each
country but not in others? What differentiates blocs from one another? Why do
they emerge and persist? What is the relationship between economic inequality
and the patterns of political cohesion and cleavage that are revealed in persistent electoral bloc voting?

Sections 4.3 and 4.4 of this chapter begin to address these questions by considering how, and the extent to which, electoral blocs and oppositional zones
overlay the striking patterns of regional advantage and disadvantage that are
features of most national economies in Africa. While it is true that national capitals have strong advantages over the provinces in terms of levels of economic
development, the national capitals are not part of persistent electoral blocs in
most of the twelve countries in this study. Electoral blocs are predominantly
rural.[34] The analysis here shows that in terms of nature and levels of economic
development and advantage, they are different and unequal. Chapter 3 argued
that in African countries, cross-regional differences and inequalities are rooted
in economic and political geography – that is, in natural endowment, sectoral
specialization, employment and livelihoods, location with respect to each
country's main centers of urban agglomeration, and historical (1900–1990)
patterns of sectoral and spatial targeting in state allocation of public goods,
investment, and infrastructure.[35] Strong patterns of regional advantage and
disadvantage are traceable to the development of colonial economies and to
postcolonial development strategies that have tended to reinforce inherited
geographies of uneven development. These inequalities are strongly visible
today. They are picked up in variations across persistent electoral blocs and
the non-bloc regions in levels of wealth and economic development.

Most of the electoral blocs and oppositional zones (N=36) are economically
advantaged compared to national averages and compared to regions that are
not part of electoral blocs (i.e., the non-bloc regions).[36] These disparities are
captured in proxies for regional (bloc-level) GDP, indicators of educational
access and achievement, and population density.

Following the lead of economists and other political scientists, we use nighttime light emissions as a proxy measure for economic activity at subnational levels

---

[34] See below on the population density indicators.

[35] These findings are corroborated in Roessler et al., 2022.

[36] Capital cities are excluded from the computation of all indicators for the non-bloc regions in these
countries. However, including them would not bias our measures very much, given the small area
of the capital cities relative to very large areas of the non-bloc regions. The measure we are using
is *average pixel luminosity* in the areal unit of interest. See Section B.5 in Appendix B.

4.3 Economic Inequalities and Electoral Blocs

where systematic data from more accurate sources are missing (see, e.g., Chen & Nordhaus 2011; Henderson et al. 2012; Michalopoulos & Papaioannou 2013, 2014; Hodler & Raschky 2014; Pinovskiy & Sala-i-Martin 2016). These data provide a rough measure of gross product (level of economic development, or wealth) for each electoral bloc. We calculated average pixel luminosity at the bloc level for 1992, 2000, and 2013.[37] With the nightlight data, we can compare electoral blocs to one another, to non-bloc regions, and to national averages over time.

Educational achievement is another measure that captures the economic advantages of electoral blocs. It is a particularly sensitive gauge of socioeconomic advantage.[38] Pooled DHS survey data from the 2000s and the 2010s create a summary "snapshot" for each of two indicators for each electoral bloc: one for average numbers of years of education, and a second for the percentage of the local population that has completed secondary school.[39] Educational indicators tap into a confluence of national, regional, and community (and presumably household-level) advantages and disadvantages. They offer information on differences in the occupational profiles of regions, education provision across regions, and the socioeconomic status of individuals and families in given locales, regions, or electoral blocs. At the community level, education achievement can be considered a stock variable that gauges cumulative (dis)advantage over time in terms of social provision in localities, families' ability and willingness to keep their children in school, and the nature of local occupations (with more developed locales having higher proportions of occupations that require higher levels of literacy).

Most of the electoral blocs (including oppositional zones) contain significant secondary cities. For example, Ghana's Central bloc contains Kumasi, Kenya's Western bloc contains Kisumu, Zambia's Copperbelt Northern bloc contains Ndola, and Zimbabwe's Southern bloc contains Bulawayo. Presence of important "regional capitals" in electoral blocs is an indicator of their elevated levels of economic development. Even so, the bloc-level indicators overall are not driven by (strongly biased by) the presence/absence of a single large city.[40] Cities' weight in terms of nightlight and education levels is diluted by the geographic and demographic size of these large, predominantly rural units.

---

[37] A pixel is the smallest element in a digital image, corresponding to smallest observed areal unit in geographic raster data.

[38] Baleyte et al. (2020) treat educational disparity as a class-like cleavage in African countries.

[39] The data were pooled to achieve more even geographical coverage. See Table B.3 in Appendix B. The DHS data provide information on the location of surveyed villages and urban areas. Adult respondents are matched to a locale based on their place of residence, rather than on their place of birth (or schooling). Given that more educated persons are more likely to emigrate from their home region, the data may bias downward the measure of educational advantage in advantaged regions (blocs). (See Sahn & Stifel 2003: 589.) Emigrants often send remittances to families in their home region, which can further reinforce the advantage of these areas.

[40] The luminosity indicator is weighted by area. The education indicators are computed on a sample that is representative of the population. City values strongly influence the indicators only if the city makes up a large share of the area of the bloc (for luminosity), or a large share of the population within the bloc (for education).

Table 4.1 categorizes the electoral blocs in terms of these two indicators of economic advantage/disadvantage. By regional GDP in 1992 and/or secondary school completion, a large majority of the blocs (25/36) is more economically advantaged than the non-bloc area of the corresponding national unit. Sixteen electoral blocs are advantaged by both measures.[41] These results are robust to considering alterative time periods and years of education. The table uses the regional GDP measure for 1992, which was around the time of the return to multipartyism for most countries. It is safe to assume that the relative standing of blocs in 1992 was similar to what it was in the late 1970s, given the very low rates of economic growth in African countries from the late 1970s to the early 1990s (during the so-called lost decades). Fast-forwarding to 2013, the results hold. Twenty-five blocs are advantaged in either the GDP proxy or secondary education, and seventeen blocs are advantaged in both.[42]

Population density is another indicator of relative advantage and disadvantage across the electoral blocs and the rural non-bloc regions of each country (see Table C.4 in Appendix C). The population density advantage of the electoral blocs is remarkably consistent over time. Nearly all the electoral blocs (28/36) have higher population densities per square kilometer than the non-bloc areas in 1990, 2000, and 2015.[43] This contrast picks up the difference between more densely settled and commercially networked agricultural zones, on the one hand, and more sparsely populated zones of subsistence agriculture and pastoral areas, on the other. These numbers offer two additional pieces of information. First, they confirm the predominantly rural character of the electoral blocs. Cross-bloc population density averages for 1990 and 2013 are 50 and 95 persons per square kilometer, respectively. For 1990, the bloc range is from 3 to 263 persons per square kilometer: Côte d'Ivoire's Northern bloc is at the low extreme, and Kenya's Western bloc is at the high extreme (it is

---

[41] These results are robust to considering an alternative time period (2013) and/or our other education indicator. Notes to Table 4.1 indicate which blocs are classified differently when the indicators change.

[42] A few persistent electoral blocs are disadvantaged vis-à-vis the non-bloc regions. These tend to be colonial-era cotton-producing regions and labor-exporting regions. They were poor in the colonial era compared to richer producer zones, and fifty years later, they are poor in luminosity compared to the non-bloc regions. Northern Nigeria and Northern Côte d'Ivoire are cases in point. (On cotton in colonial Africa, see Issacman 2003; Bassett 2001; and Roessler et al. 2022: 12–13). The luminosity ranking of the Ghana East bloc vis-à-vis the non-bloc region may have been influenced by the decision to define the "capital city" as Metropolitan Accra. This pushed much of the larger Admin1 unit of Greater Accra into the non-bloc category.

[43] Twenty-four blocs had a higher population density than *the country average* without the capital city in 1990 and 2000. It was 25 in 2015. (See Section B.5 of Appendix B on coding capital cities and including or excluding them in calculating regional indicators.) The higher population density in the three blocs that do include capital cities is not coming solely from higher population density in the capital city itself. See Table C.4 in Appendix C. Because capital cities occupy a small share of an electoral bloc's total *area*, in almost all cases the main findings regarding economic (dis)advantage hold whether the capital is included or not.

TABLE 4.1 *Advantage of electoral blocs (including oppositional zones) over non-blocs in the same country*

Country	Electoral bloc		Nighttime luminosity		Education	
			1992	2013	Avg. no. of years completed	% completed secondary school
Blocs advantaged in light (1992) and education (secondary)						
Cameroon	Centre-Sud bloc		0.09	0.19	8.8	16.9
Cameroon	Western bloc		0.19	0.34	8.2	12.7
Côte d'Ivoire	Eastern bloc		0.21	1.06	3.6	6.2
Ghana	Central bloc		0.51	1.50	8.5	19.1
Kenya	Central bloc		0.51	2.01	9.3	36.4
Kenya	Rift Valley bloc		0.05	0.19	8.2	27.8
Malawi	Southern bloc	[3]	0.76	0.91	5.8	11.8
Mali	Bamako–Koulikoro bloc		0.15	0.57	4.1	9.1
Mali	Sikasso bloc		0.01	0.08	1.5	2.0
Nigeria	Eastern bloc		1.83	2.95	9.5	45.6
Nigeria	Western bloc		1.66	3.12	9.9	54.2
South Africa	West Cape bloc		1.59	2.21	10.9	47.7
Uganda	Central opposition bloc		0.72	2.44	8.8	22.1
Zambia	Copperbelt Northern bloc		0.17	0.29	7.8	20.4
Zambia	Southern bloc		0.10	0.24	7.4	13.5
Zimbabwe	Southern bloc	[1]	0.19	0.18	9.2	19.5
Blocs advantaged in light (1992), not in education (secondary)						
Côte d'Ivoire	Western bloc	[4]	0.10	1.42	3.5	4.9
Kenya	Western bloc	[4]	0.22	0.60	8.1	21.5
Mali	Mopti bloc		0.00	0.03	0.8	0.5
Nigeria	Northern bloc		0.24	0.40	4.1	18.5
South Africa	Center bloc		0.85	1.89	9.8	32.2
South Africa	KwaZulu bloc		0.76	1.80	9.5	36.9
Tanzania	N'rn opposition bloc		0.03	0.15	5.8	6.6

(continued)

TABLE 4.1 (*continued*)

Country	Electoral bloc		Nighttime luminosity		Education	
			1992	2013	Avg. no. of years completed	% completed secondary school
Blocs advantaged in education (secondary), not in light (1992)						
Malawi	Northern bloc		0.06	0.21	7.2	11.2
Uganda	Northern bloc		0.00	0.05	6.1	9.9
Blocs advantaged in neither						
Côte d'Ivoire	Northern bloc		0.03	0.32	2.0	4.0
Ghana	Eastern bloc		0.20	0.71	7.2	14.8
Ghana	NW bloc		0.07	0.35	4.9	15.2
Kenya	Eastern bloc	[2], [4]	0.03	0.26	8.2	23.1
Malawi	Central bloc		0.14	0.42	5.1	9.3
Malawi	Eastern bloc		0.06	0.14	4.2	4.7
Tanzania	CCM bloc		0.02	0.06	5.7	6.5
Uganda	Western bloc	[2]	0.00	0.07	5.5	5.9
Zambia	Eastern bloc		0.02	0.07	5.3	6.3
Zambia	Western bloc		0.01	0.03	5.8	9.4
Zimbabwe	Northern bloc		0.10	0.21	8.2	8.3
Sample average (all blocs)			0.32	0.76	6.6	17.2

Notes: Education measured by DHS merger of all geocoded rounds. For most countries, this is an average at electoral bloc level for the 2000s and 2010s. Luminosity is nighttime light data in 1992 and 2013, measured as average pixel luminosity within electoral blocs. The values for the non-bloc regions always exclude the capital city and can be found in Table C.5 in Appendix C. For data sources, see Appendix B.
[1] Bloc lost its advantage in luminosity in 2013; [2] bloc has an advantage in luminosity in 2013; [3] bloc is advantaged when we consider secondary school completion but not when we consider average years of education; [4] bloc is not advantaged when we consider secondary school completion but is advantaged when we consider average years of education.

4.3 Economic Inequalities and Electoral Blocs

one of the most densely populated rural areas in all of sub-Saharan Africa). Second, the figures register the high rates of population density *increase* that all the electoral blocs have experienced over the last quarter-century. On average, there is close to a doubling of population density.[44]

Figure 4.5 (a–c) captures these same values in the form of country-level scatterplots for Nigeria, Mali, and Tanzania. The scatterplots capture relations of advantage/disadvantage between the electoral blocs themselves and between these and the non-bloc regions of each country. Blocs' GDP proxy measures as of 1992 (i.e., levels of luminosity in 1992) are measured on the vertical axis, and levels of educational achievement on the horizontal axis. The regional GDP measure from 1992 provides a snapshot of spatial inequality in these three countries at the historical mid-point between the 1960s and the 2010s, and thus helps in capturing the continuities in relations of spatial inequality that are emphasized here.[45] The economically leading electoral blocs in each country are depicted in dark blue, and the next most advantaged electoral bloc is depicted in medium blue. The poorest blocs are in light blue. The size of the circles refers to bloc population size in 1990.[46]

Nigeria and Mali capture the dominant tendencies in the data that have been discussed so far. Most electoral blocs are advantaged vis-à-vis the non-bloc region of each country in terms of *both* luminosity and education. In Nigeria, both Eastern and Western electoral blocs have vast advantages relative to the non-bloc regions of the country. By these measures, the two leading blocs also appear nearly evenly matched in terms of luminosity (in 1992) and education.[47] Nigeria's Northern electoral bloc lags dramatically, even relative to the non-bloc regions.

Mali's leading electoral bloc includes the capital city of Bamako because Bamako votes consistently as part of the regional electoral bloc. It is hugely advantaged compared to the rest of the country. Yet even without the capital city, this bloc would have a large economic lead over the non-bloc region, as well as over the bloc ranked second in luminosity, the Sikasso bloc, which represents Mali's main cotton-producing region. (The values for Bamako city alone are depicted for reference in the scatterplot.)

---

[44] By contrast, the average population density per square kilometer across the 12 capital-city units was 1,579 persons/km^2 in 1990 and 4,095 in 2015.

[45] Corresponding values (as well as those for 2000 and 2013) are reported in Table 4.1 and Table C.5 in Appendix C.

[46] The GDP proxy (luminosity) and education scales are different for each of the graphs. In Nigeria, the country average (including the capital city) for percentage of adults having completed secondary education is 31.8%, whereas it is 3.5% in Mali and 8.4% in Tanzania. A logarithmic transformation of mean pixel luminosity is used to ensure a dispersion of values. The gap between the capital city and the first bloc is thus much greater, in absolute value, than most of the other gaps.

[47] Computations control for oil flares in the Niger Delta region.

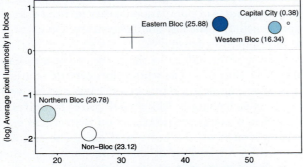

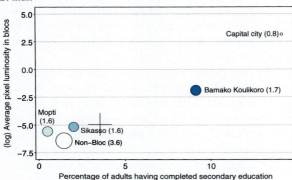

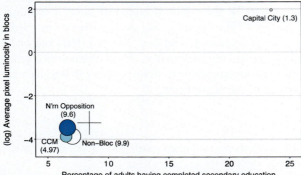

FIGURE 4.5 (a–c) Bloc advantage and disadvantage (composite 1990s through 2010s). Notes: Regional GDP proxy (log (average pixel luminosity)) for 1992 (x-axis) and % of adults having completed secondary education (pooled DHS, 2000s and 2010s) (y-axis). Scale varies by country (both axes). Circle size denotes relative bloc population in 1990 (total in millions, in parentheses). Corresponding values (luminosity and education) can be found in Table C.5 in Appendix C. Bamako city is part of the Bamako–Koulikoro bloc; values are reported for the capital city only (top corner) for reference. Crosses denote country averages.

4.3 Economic Inequalities and Electoral Blocs

Tanzania stands out because there is less socioeconomic disparity between its regional electoral blocs, and between these and the non-bloc region, than in Nigeria and Mali. Tanzania's most advantaged rural region is the Northern opposition zone, which includes the districts of Arusha, Kilimanjaro, Kagera, and most of Mwanza. It is depicted in dark blue. Its 1992 GDP proxy is 50% higher than that of Tanzania's other electoral bloc, the CCM bloc, in medium blue. The Northern bloc's advantage in education, compared to the CCM bloc, is slight. Fast-forwarding to 2000, we see evidence of a dramatic increase in the GDP gap between these two regional blocs. The Northern opposition bloc rebounds to its historically stronger position of regional advantage, registering a GPD proxy that is 2.5 times greater than that of the CCM bloc[48] (see Chapter 6, conclusion).

We can move from snapshots to something more like time-lapse photography by viewing the bloc-level descriptive statistics for different points in time. Table C.5 in Appendix C does this, showing that hierarchy among the blocs in terms of the GDP proxy is remarkably stable over the course of the 1992–2013 period. In most of the twelve countries (9/12), the electoral blocs that are ranked first in 1992 retained this lead in 2013.[49] Six of these blocs, including Tanzania's Northern opposition bloc, had an *even greater lead* by 2013.[50]

Although this cannot be demonstrated using this data, these rankings would hold constant in most countries for relative levels of economic prosperity and education going back to the 1950s and 1960s. Regions that were advantaged by the GDP proxy and education in the 2000s were among the economically leading regions in their respective countries in the 1950s, before the end of direct colonial rule. Agglomeration, path dependency, and lock-in effects have tended to reproduce the advantages of the leading regions, at one extreme, and "poverty traps" at the other. In the postcolonial era, the effects of these economic fundamentals have not been overpowered easily, even after state capture by incumbents whose main political stronghold lies in lagging regions. Opposition zones in Uganda, Tanzania, and Cameroon remain economically advantaged in 1990–2013, even though they have been out of power continuously since the mid-1960s.

---

[48] Proxies for spatial dispersion in regional wealth for 2000 resonate with the relatively high spatial inequality score for Tanzania in Figure 1.1, based on Lessmann and Seidel's (2017) adjusted nightlight data for 2012. The relatively small wealth gap observed in 1992 comes near the end of Tanzania's 25-year experiment with anti-agglomeration growth policies. One indicator of the Northern region's lead in the 1960s is the gap in infant mortality rates between Arusha (64 per thousand) and Dodoma (141 per thousand) reported in the Atlas of Tanzania, second edition, Republic of Tanzania, Dar es Salaam, 1976.

[49] In Côte d'Ivoire, Nigeria, and Zimbabwe, the second-ranked bloc in 1992 overtakes the first one by 2013. For Nigeria, correction for oil flares in the Eastern bloc may have affected the rankings.

[50] This refers to absolute luminosity values. When we consider *growth rates* of nighttime luminosity, most blocs grew faster than the bloc that was ranked first in luminosity in 1992, as luminosity levels were very low in these blocs in 1992 (for these blocs, more than doubling the 1992 levels is commonplace).

4.4 SECTORAL DIFFERENTIATION: ELECTORAL BLOCS' PRODUCER PROFILES, PAST AND PRESENT

> Once an area has gone ahead, it tends to preserve its advantage.
>
> (Bigsten 1977: 76)

The differentiated economic standing of the electoral blocs (and the fact that most are more economically advantaged than the non-bloc regions) is traceable to their varied sectoral profiles and degrees of incorporation into the national economy. Most of the electoral blocs map onto regions whose economic lead within the national economy is traceable to the 1930s and 1940s. The advantage of most of them is rooted in colonial-era export crop production, although a few have many decades of history as mining or labor-exporting regions. Most electoral blocs' colonial-era sectoral specialization has persisted over the course of the postcolonial period, along with the region's relative economic advantage vis-à-vis other rural regions. By contrast, most of the rural non-bloc regions are not specialized in the production of agricultural exports or nationally traded crops. Non-bloc regions tend to produce a range of food crops for local or household consumption and include the pastoral and subsistence zones of each country.

Congruence mapping makes it possible to describe the *economic* history of the *politically distinctive* regions that are the focus of this analysis. This involves overlaying maps of contemporary (1990s–2010s) electoral geography on maps of economic geography from the 1950s and 1960s. From this, we can assess the extent of territorial overlap between an electoral bloc and a colonial producer region. We then describe the contemporary economic profiles of the regional electoral blocs using 2010 data from IFPRI on the geographic distribution of agricultural production and cash crop specialization.[51] (Other sources provide information about whether colonial-era mining and labor-exporting regions retain this economic profile in the twenty-first century.) The results offer a strong sense of the extent of the *spatial overlap* between producer regions and electoral blocs, and *sectoral persistence* of blocs' producer profiles. Most of the regional electoral blocs are associated with colonial-era zones of high-value agricultural production (or mining), and most retained this sectoral specialization in the 2010s.

Atlases published from the late 1940s to the early 1970s outline colonial-era regions of export crop production (including coffee, tea, cocoa, cotton, palm oil), nationally traded food crops (maize, wheat, rice), and mining regions.[52]

---

[51] On IFPRI and other data sources, see Section B.2 in Appendix B.

[52] Nationally traded crops are those that are produced mostly for sale outside the district or province in which they are grown. Many are subject to national-level regulation, tax, and/or subsidies (including price controls, export restrictions, seed storage, input distribution). Commercial maize production in Zambia is an example. Anne Pitcher describes the ruling party's (MMD's)

4.4 *Electoral Blocs' Producer Profiles, Past and Present* 117

We used these to create GIS shapefiles defining the main colonial-era producer zones (agriculture and mining zones) across the twelve countries. This generated a dataset of forty-five colonial-era mining and agricultural zones.

Table 4.2 lists the colonial-era producer regions, classifies them by producer region type, and describes their *geographic overlap* with today's persistent electoral blocs or oppositional zones (i.e., percentage of the colonial-era producer region area located within an electoral bloc).[53] The table lists three mining regions, eight plantation agriculture zones, thirty zones of predominantly smallholder ("peasant") production of export crops or nationally traded food crops (maize or rice), and four zones of medium-scale commercial farming.[54] The latter were mostly zones of European settler agriculture in East and Southern Africa, including South Africa's grain- and fruit-producing regions, Zimbabwe's tobacco region, and Zambia's southern maize region. African smallholder production of these same high-value crops sometimes existed within the settler-dominated sectors; such zones are designated as "mixed" or combined in Table 4.2.[55] By the 1950s, for example, Central Kenya's coffee-, tea-, and pyrethrum-producing region included both colonial settler estates and plantations *and* African small- and medium-scale farms. Labor-exporting zones are not included in the dataset of forty-five colonial-era producer zones, but we bring them into the discussion below. In historical terms, we can say that most of these colonial-era producer regions "gave rise" to electoral blocs and opposition-leaning zones. Of the thirty-four colonial-era producer regions of smallholder or medium farms, twenty-six overlap geographically to a large extent (50% or more of the area of the colonial-era smallholder zone) with one or more of today's persistent electoral blocs or oppositional zones.

An example par excellence of a bloc arising within a colonial-era producer region is found in Ghana's Central electoral bloc. The colonial-era cocoa-producing region lies almost wholly within the electoral bloc, the core of Ghana's NPP party, which retains its historic specialization in cocoa production. Two mining regions overlap with – indeed, lie at the heart of – persistent

---

maize policies: "By 2006, the Food Reserve Agency [a marketing board resurrected in 1995 by President Chiluba] dominated the maize market as much as it had in the 1980s" (2016: 9). It acts as a major maize buyer, provides maize marketing and storage services, maintains a national strategic maize reserve, sets maize prices, distributes subsidized fertilizer, and regulates (limits) maize exports. This pattern of sectorally specific market governance for Zambia's commercial maize producers dates to the 1930s and 1940s.

[53] In Côte d'Ivoire, the colonial-era coffee and cocoa region as depicted in our source atlas overlaps with both the Eastern and the Western bloc.

[54] Peasant farming is household-based farming under customary or neocustomary land tenure, sometimes with some wage labor and/or tenancy arrangements. Commercial farming is based on freehold or leasehold land tenure with most labor provided by wage labor, often in the colonial era under labor-repressive regimes.

[55] See, for example, Doro and Swart (2022) who describe peasant production of tobacco in colonial Southern Rhodesia (today's Zimbabwe).

TABLE 4.2 *Colonial-era producer regions: Percentage of colonial producer region in a persistent electoral bloc or oppositional zone today, and continuing sectoral specializations*

Colonial-era producer region	% of colonial-era producer region in electoral bloc	Persistent specialization (2010) [1]	Type of production unit
Cameroon			
Cocoa	97.0	Yes	Smallholder
Cotton	0.0	Yes	Smallholder
Coffee	100.0	Yes	Smallholder
Palm oil	100.0	Yes	Smallholder
Côte d'Ivoire			
Cotton	52.6	No	Smallholder
Cocoa–coffee	53.5	Yes	Smallholder
Coffee	20.1	No	Smallholder
Ghana			
Palm oil	40.6	Yes	Smallholder
Rice	100.0	Yes	Smallholder
Cocoa	92.6	Yes	Smallholder
Kenya			
Coffee, tea, pyrethrum	94.2	Yes	Smallholder/mixed
Sisal	47.4	No	Plantation
Tea	55.2	Yes	Plantation
Sugar	93.2	Yes	Plantation
Malawi			
Coffee	49.1	Yes	Smallholder
Cotton	69.8	Yes	Smallholder
Tobacco	69.1	Yes	Smallholder
Tea	80.9	Yes	Plantation
Mali			
Groundnuts	33.6	Yes	Smallholder
Mopti rice	94.9	Yes	Smallholder
Cotton	85.7	Yes	Smallholder
Ségou rice	0.3	No	Smallholder
Nigeria			
Tobacco	48.5	Yes	Smallholder
Groundnuts	52.3	Yes	Smallholder
Cocoa	84.4	Yes	Smallholder
Cotton	85.9	Yes	Smallholder
Palm oil	99.8	Yes	Smallholder
Mining	4.5	n.d.	Mining
South Africa			
Grain	53.5	Yes	Med. farm
Sugar	56.2	Yes	Plantation

4.4 Electoral Blocs' Producer Profiles, Past and Present

Colonial-era producer region	% of colonial-era producer region in electoral bloc	Persistent specialization (2010) [1]	Type of production unit
Mining	74.0	n.d.	Mining
Fruit	78.0	Yes	Med. farm
Tanzania			
Cotton	78.5	Yes	Smallholder
Coffee	85.1	Yes	Smallholder
Sisal	82.4	Yes	Plantation
Cloves	0.1	n.d.	Plantation
Cashew	0.9	n.d.	Smallholder
Uganda			
Coffee	57.4	Yes	Smallholder
Tobacco	64.8	No	Smallholder
Cotton	12.6	Yes	Smallholder
Zambia			
Southern maize	81.9	Yes	Med. farm + smallholder
Mining	91.6	n.d.	Mining
Eastern maize	77.1	Yes	Smallholder + med. farm
Zimbabwe			
Tobacco	53.9	Yes	Med. farm + smallholder
Sugar	0.0	Yes	Plantation

Notes: Colonial-era producer regions from atlases (see References). Specialization from 2010 IFPRI data. N.d. = no data, that is, not included in the IFPRI data. Med. farm = medium-scale commercial farming.

[1] The colonial-era producer region is considered to be overlapping with one or several blocs if either the percentage of colonial-era producer region that is in electoral blocs is greater than 50 or there is at least a bloc whose overlap with the colonial-era producer region is greater than 50% of its area (results reported in Table 4.3).

[2] A colonial-era producer region is considered to be still specialized in the colonial-era crop if it produces more than 50% of the national output of the corresponding crop, or if its specialization ratio (share of national output it produces divided by its area, expressed as a percentage of the country area) is greater than 1.5.

Colonial-era producer regions associated with several crops (cocoa–coffee region in Côte d'Ivoire, coffee–tea–pyrethrum in Kenya) are still specialized in these crops.

electoral blocs today.[56] An example familiar to students of African politics is Zambia's Copperbelt Northern bloc. A history of sectoral specialization in mining and labor migration to the copper mines defines the bloc's economic and

---

[56] There are three mining regions in the dataset – South Africa's Rand, Zambia's Copperbelt, and Nigeria's Jos Plateau. The first two are associated with persistent electoral blocs in the 1990s–2010s.

120 Regional Blocs and Bloc Voting

organizational distinctiveness and cohesion.[57] Three additional colonial-era producer regions, not listed in Table 4.2, are colonial-era labor-exporting regions. They strongly overlap with Kenya's Western bloc, Ghana's Northwestern bloc, and Malawi's Northern bloc.[58] Some colonial-era producer regions did not "give rise" to blocs. We return to these cases at the end of this section.

In most of the colonial-era producer zones, *economic* legacies are strong: The original sectoral specialization persists today. Table 4.2 reports that of the forty colonial-era agricultural producer zones for which we have the data to make the calculation, thirty-five are still specialized in production of the same crop.[59]

Adding the *contemporary* production profiles of the electoral blocs to the analysis gives us a view of relationships between the economy and politics over time. Table 4.3 creates a typology of electoral blocs based on their profiles of producer regions, both past and present. Blocs are classified by two criteria – *spatial overlap* of bloc and colonial-era producer region, and *crop specialization* in 2010.[60] The spatial overlap is considered "high" if 50% or more of the bloc lies in the colonial-era producer region, or if 50% or more of the colonial-era producer region lies in the electoral bloc.[61] An electoral bloc is considered to have retained its colonial-era crop specialization if it produced 50% or more of national output of that crop in 2010, or if its share of national output is greater than 1.5 times its share of the national territory.

By these measures, more than two-thirds (27/36) of the blocs and oppositional zones "overlay" (are congruent with) colonial-era producer regions to a substantial extent. As of 2010, most also retain the economic specialization of the colonial producer zone with which they coincide (24/36).

---

[57] The northern part of Zambia's Copperbelt North bloc has a history as a labor-exporting region, sending labor to the Copperbelt.

[58] For Western Kenya, the connection between the region's history as a labor-exporting district in colonial and postcolonial Kenya, on the one hand, and the political, ethnic, and regional consciousness of its populations on the other, is richly documented by historians (Lonsdale 1969, 1971). Regional "nationalists" promoted the Luo ethnic identity as a way of bringing the region's populations together, politically.

[59] A colonial-era producer region is considered to be still specialized in the colonial-era crop if it produces more than 50% of the national output of the corresponding crop, or if its specialization ratio (share of national output it produces divided by its area, expressed as a percentage of the country area) is greater than 1.5, based on 2010 IFRPI data. If we raised the specialization ratio to 2.0, five colonial-era producer regions would no longer be considered "specialized" in 2010 (i.e., Côte d'Ivoire cocoa–coffee (for coffee); Ghana cocoa and palm oil; and Nigeria cotton and groundnuts.)

[60] That is, the bloc specialization (as of 2010) in the crop associated with the overlapping colonial-era producer region.

[61] Some overlap figures stand out. In Côte d'Ivoire, a large colonial-era coffee–cocoa producer region is associated with two different electoral blocs – that is, Côte d'Ivoire's Eastern and Western persistent electoral blocs. In this case, each bloc's overlap is a large percentage of the electoral bloc area, but a low percentage of the colonial-era producer region. In Western Kenya, the electoral bloc is much larger than the colonial-era sugar-producing region, but Western Kenya was also a strong labor exporter during the colonial period (see below). Sugar production expanded rapidly across Western Kenya in the 1960s.

4.4 Electoral Blocs' Producer Profiles, Past and Present

Table 4.3 is a typology of electoral blocs, based on these characteristics. The largest of five categories is made up of electoral blocs that have both strong spatial overlap with colonial-era producer regions *and* strong, ongoing specialization of the bloc in the colonial-era crop (Type 1, N = 24). This category includes twice as many blocs as the second-largest category. Type I blocs are persistent electoral blocs and oppositional zones that have arisen in colonial-era producer regions and that remain specialized in the same crop in 2010. Here we find many rural producer regions that feature in star roles in the making of states and national economies in modern Africa, including central Kenya's coffee–tea–pyrethrum-producing region; Southern Ghana's cocoa-producing region; Côte d'Ivoire's cocoa and coffee regions; southwestern Nigeria's cocoa bloc; the cotton-producing Sikasso region of Mali; central Uganda's coffee and cotton zone; Northern Tanzania's coffee and cotton blocs; and the tobacco producers of central Malawi and northern Zimbabwe. Three colonial-era regions centered on cultivation of nationally traded food crops – that is, on strongly commercialized production of food crops that are "exported" out of the local market area, via formal (state-regulated) marketing circuits – also overlap with the persistent electoral blocs, and retain the same specialization today. They are Zambia's Southern bloc (maize), Zambia's Eastern bloc (maize), and Mali's Mopti region (rice).[62]

Type II (N=3) includes persistent electoral blocs that have a high overlap with a colonial-era producer zone, but that have not retained this producer specialization in the 2000s. Northern Côte d'Ivoire is one. Cotton production zone in this region had extended beyond its colonial-era limits, and well beyond the bloc area, by 2010 (Bassett 2014: 413). Tanzania's CCM bloc is no longer specialized in sisal, and Ghana's Eastern bloc, although still a rice producer, does not register a 2010 specialization in this crop by our measure.

Type III (N=4) electoral blocs cover a smaller fraction (less than 50%) of a colonial-era producer region, which in turn constitutes less than 50% of the bloc's geographic area, but the electoral bloc is still strongly specialized in that colonial-era crop today. Emblematic of this category are South Africa's Central and KwaZulu-Natal blocs, which contain part of the country's mining and plantation sugar enclaves, respectively. Uganda's Western electoral bloc contains "islands" of coffee production that date back to the colonial period, but most of colonial-era production of coffee in Uganda was further east, in the regions bordering Lake Victoria.

Type IV (N=3) electoral blocs are those with limited geographic overlap with a colonial-era producer region, and in which colonial-era agricultural specialization, if it existed, has faded away. Some plantation crops which were highly circumscribed in geographic extent have declined over time in importance as

---

[62] On the distinction between commercially oriented food-crop-producing regions and subsistence-oriented food regions (i.e., those producing mostly local trading and household consumption), see Dercon and Gollin (2014) and Adam, Bevin, and Gollin (2018).

TABLE 4.3 *Producer profile of electoral blocs in 2010*

Country	Electoral bloc	Electoral bloc, % of national area	Colonial-era producer region	Crop	% of electoral bloc in colonial-era producer region	% of colonial-era producer region in electoral bloc	Electoral bloc, % of national output 2010	Specialization ratio
Type I. High overlap (>50%) and specialization (ratio >1.5)								
Cameroon	Centre-Sud bloc	24.8	Cocoa	Cocoa	95.6	82.1	61.1	2.46
Cameroon	Western bloc	16.3	Coffee	Coffee A	36.2	98.5	28.4	1.74
C. d'Ivoire	Eastern bloc	8.8	Cocoa-coffee	Cocoa	57.9	25.8	16.5	1.88
C. d'Ivoire	Western bloc	8.5	Cocoa-coffee	Cocoa	60.9	27	25.2	2.95
Ghana	Central bloc	18.1	Cocoa	Cocoa	61.5	85	33.7	1.86
Kenya	Central bloc	5.6	Coffee-tea-pyrethrum	Coffee A	28.4	94.2	74.1	13.24
Kenya	Rift Valley bloc	7.3	Tea	Tea	1.8	55.2	35.4	4.87
Kenya	Western bloc	2.1	Sugar	Sugar	3.9	86.5	74.1	35.36
Malawi	Central bloc	20.1	Tobacco	Tobacco	52.3	44.4	44.9	2.23
Malawi	Southern bloc	10	Tea	Tea	49.5	48.3	n.d	n.d
Mali	Bamako–Koulikoro bloc	3.6	Groundnuts	Groundnuts	69	33.4	15.8	4.45
Mali	Mopti bloc	7.9	Mopti rice	Rice	25.6	94.9	32.8	4.14
Mali	Sikasso bloc	5.6	Cotton	Cotton	78.8	76.3	62.9	11.14
Nigeria	Eastern bloc	12.2	Palm oil	Palm oil	25.7	99.8	66.9	5.48
Nigeria	Northern bloc	38.8	Cotton	Cotton	35.1	85.9	58.2	1.5
Nigeria	Northern bloc	38.8	Groundnuts	Groundnuts	27.1	52.3	62.8	1.62
Nigeria	Western bloc	6.8	Cocoa	Cocoa	54.9	78	51	7.47
S. Africa	West Cape bloc	7.4	Fruit	Fruit	53.7	77.9	74.4	10.08
Tanzania	N'rn opposition bloc	22.7	Cotton	Cotton	20.5	78.3	84	3.7
Uganda	Central opposition bloc	5.3	Coffee	Coffee R	53	36.8	10.2	1.92

Country	Bloc		Colonial-era producer region	Best match				
Zambia	Copperbelt Northern bloc	22.5	Mining		4.3	74.8	n.d	n.d
Zambia	Eastern bloc	12.1	Eastern maize	Maize	15.6	55.6	20.1	1.66
Zambia	Southern bloc	12.2	Southern maize	Maize	56.2	80.8	25.2	2.08
Zimbabwe	Northern bloc	19.4	Tobacco	Tobacco	50.2	53.2	51.6	2.66
Type II. High overlap but not specialized								
C. d'Ivoire	Northern bloc	14.3	Cotton	Cotton	58.5	52.6	3.8	0.27
Ghana	Eastern bloc	16.8	Rice	Rice	8	99.4	18.2	1.09
Tanzania	CCM bloc	28.6	Sisal	Sisal	5.4	83.6	1	0.03
Type III. Low overlap and specialized								
Malawi	Eastern bloc	10.0	Cotton	Cotton	11	11	22	2
S. Africa	Center bloc	42.0	Grain	Maize	24	47	63	1.5
S. Africa	Center bloc	42.0	Mining		3	38	n.d	n.d.
S. Africa	KwaZulu bloc	4	Sugar	Sugar	14	32	37	10.0
Uganda	Western bloc	28.0	Coffee	Coffee A	7	24	44	2
Type IV. Low overlap, not specialized								
Kenya	Eastern bloc	6.3	Sisal	Sisal	3.5	47	0	0
Malawi	Northern bloc	22.1	Tobacco	Tobacco	15.3	14.1	13.3	0.6
Uganda	Northern bloc	8.2	Cotton	Cotton	5.3	2.6	7.5	0.92
Type V: Does not correspond to a colonial-era producer region								
Ghana	NW bloc	2			0	0		
Zambia	Western bloc	15			0	0		
Zimbabwe	Southern bloc	23.9			0	0		

Notes: Table 4.3 reports the "best match" between the bloc and the colonial-era producer region (highest overlap as percentage of bloc area). For coffee, "A" and "R" refer to Arabica and Robusta. In specific cases, the table reports bloc overlap with producer regions of interest (rice in Ghana Eastern bloc, tobacco and groundnuts in Nigeria Northern bloc, mining in South Africa Center bloc, cotton in Uganda Northern bloc) rather than with the "best match." This does not change the results. The "specialization ratio," based on IFPRI 2010 data, is percentage of national output 2010 divided by percentage of national area. n.d. = no data. Tea in Southern Malawi and cashew were not included in the IFPRI 2010 data.

export commodities (e.g., sisal in Kenya's Eastern bloc). Uganda's Northern bloc overlaps with an area once associated with cotton and tobacco, but does not register an agricultural specialization in these crops today.

Type V (N=3) blocs are those for which there is no overlap with any colonial-era agricultural producer region. There is also no colonial-era history as a mining region. There are three electoral blocs in this category: Ghana Northwestern, Zambia Western, and Zimbabwe Southern. For these three, it will be impossible to claim that agricultural production profile per se, past or present, contributes to bloc-ness. Yet all three were distinct labor-exporting regions in the colonial period and continue in this today.

Country-level maps render these overlaps between colonial producer regions and today's electoral blocs in visual form and provide a reference point for discussing change over time in the agricultural specialization of particular regions. Figure 4.6 (a–b) presents these maps for Côte d'Ivoire and Uganda. (Similar maps for the other 10 countries appear in Appendix E.)

Côte d'Ivoire is a largely archetypical case that captures the tendencies in the data that we seek to emphasize, as well as some important nuances. Here, each of the country's three persistent electoral blocs overlap at the 50% level with colonial-era export-crop-producing zones. Most of Côte d'Ivoire's non-bloc region (the nonshaded region) does not share this history of colonial-era export crop production. Overall, this strongly conforms to our main expectation about the overlap between colonial-era producer regions and today's electoral blocs. There is something of a counterfactual here that actually helps to reinforce the argument. Forty-six percent of the colonial-era producer coffee–cocoa region lies in the non-bloc region (i.e., outside of Côte d'Ivoire's persistent electoral blocs), most of it in the extreme southeast.[63] This apparent anomaly can be accommodated easily within our explanatory framework: This region has not retained its former specialization in coffee and cocoa production. Since the 1970s, very high levels of economic diversification, including around other types of export-oriented industrial-scale plantation agriculture (bananas, palm oil, pineapples, hévéa), characterize this zone.

Uganda is featured in Figure 4.6 because the fit between producer regions and two of the three electoral blocs is low. (These discrepancies are leveraged in Chapters 5 and 6 to extend our theory.) Uganda has three electorally distinctive regions, one opposition-leaning zone and two electoral blocs.[64] Uganda's Central oppositional zone is almost completely within the colonial-era area of coffee and cotton production.[65] It overlaps at nearly the 100% level with the colonial-era export-producing region. Meanwhile, very little of the Western

---

[63] See Table D.1 in Appendix D for results and discussion of the non-bloc regions.

[64] Identification of the Uganda electoral blocs is based on aggregation of constituency-level results for 2001, 2006, 2011, and 2016 to the district level, and mapped manually onto the 2010 constituency map.

[65] Calculated on the basis of an anti-incumbent vote share of 30% or more of the vote in three of four elections since 2001.

4.4 Electoral Blocs' Producer Profiles, Past and Present   125

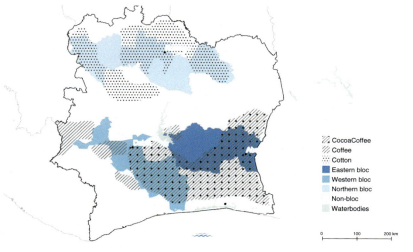

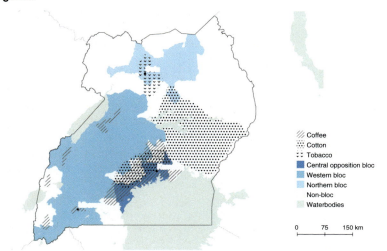

FIGURE 4.6 (a–b) Colonial producer regions and electoral bloc overlay (panels a and b).
Notes: See Appendix E for the full series of country-level maps.
Source: Authors' data.

bloc, which votes strongly for the presidential incumbent, Yoweri Museveni, is associated with colonial-era export crop production. (Colonial western Uganda contained only a few "islands" of coffee production.) The etiology of the Western electoral bloc clearly lies elsewhere (see Chapter 6). The overlap between the northern voting pattern and the colonial-era cotton and tobacco producer regions was considerable in the 1950s and 1960s, as expected, but it is reduced to about 20% for the Northern electoral bloc of the Museveni era. A plausible interpretation is that off-the-pathway changes (economic collapse, loss of the North's economic specialization in export crops, war, and postwar political reconstruction) disrupted the political and economic factors that produce stronger continuities in other regions.[66]

Labor-exporting regions and mining regions are not depicted in the twelve-country map series displayed in Figure 4.6 and Appendix E, but overlap with these, past and present, is a characteristic of several of the electoral blocs. A few electoral blocs are associated with production of export or nationally traded crops *and* labor export to other regions. Kenya's Western bloc is a sugar-producing region, but it was and is a strong labor exporter to the rest of Kenya.[67] In 2014, western Kenya had some of Kenya's highest rates of temporary out-migration of male workers and of female-headed households.[68] The Northern Malawi bloc is a labor-exporting region that also produces tobacco in its southern reaches. Most of this tobacco dates to the decades after 1970. The Northern part of Zambia's Copperbelt North bloc exports labor to the Copperbelt. A large share of the adult male population of Northern Côte d'Ivoire (also a colonial-era cotton producer) engaged in circular migration to work in other parts of the country in both the colonial period and recent decades. For mining, the most significant case here is the Zambian Copperbelt itself, which opened in the 1930s and still contributes 60% of total Zambian exports.

Considering the exceptions and counterfactuals that lie in the *absence of electoral blocs* also refines this analysis. Counterfactuals are found in colonial-era producer zones that retain their economic specialization, but do *not* overlap with (do not "give rise to") contemporary electoral blocs. Northern Cameroon is the most significant anomaly.[69] We might expect an electoral bloc here – either voting cohesively for the presidential incumbent or opposition-leaning – given the region's historical roots as a smallholder-based

---

[66] Electoral maps of Uganda in the early 1960s show a "northern voting bloc" with more extensive overlap with the 1962 cotton zone. This more extensive overlap is still perceptible in 2001 and 2006. Over time, the cotton zone and the Northern voting bloc contracted in opposite directions. As the limits of the cotton zone receded southward and Museveni made inroads in the Eastern Region, the northern voting bloc receded northward (see Chapter 6). Why the Northern electoral bloc persists is another question: This is an anomaly for the theory advanced here. Even so, historical legacies of state, regime, and political party formation, and persistent spatial inequalities, must be part of the answer.

[67] The geographic scope of sugar production in Kenya has spread dramatically since the 1960s.

[68] In Kenya in 2010, Siaya and Homa Bay had some of the highest rates in the country of female-headed households (43 and 44%, respectively). Kenya National Bureau of Statistics, 2014, Section 2:11. See Lonsdale 2012: 41–42.

[69] In northern Cameroon, cotton is produced by smallholders. The region accounts for 79% of national output. See Appendix D and Appendix E., Figure E.1.

4.4 *Electoral Blocs' Producer Profiles, Past and Present* 127

export-crop (cotton)-producing region, and its strong agricultural specialization in this same state-promoted and state-regulated export crop today, and strong continuities in the political history of the region. The repressiveness of the Biya regime, which is anchored in the South, combined with repressive social hierarchy in the North, may help explain both the limits of the ruling party's control over elections in the region and the extreme weakness of organized opposition.

Some colonial-era producer regions, or parts thereof, have lost their sectoral specialization over time, as noted in the discussions of southeastern Côte d'Ivoire and northern Uganda. These include the archipelago of palm-oil-producing enclaves across coastal Ghana, the sisal plantation zones of Tanzania, and the tobacco zone in northern Nigeria. Eastern Uganda also falls into this category: Along with much of Uganda's Northern Region, it was a major cotton exporter until production collapsed under the weight of economic and social strife in the 1970s and 1980s (although since about 1996, cotton production has been coming back in eastern Uganda).[70] These areas are non-bloc regions today. If there is a link between being a specialized producer region and electoral bloc-ness, then most of these cases are consistent with the theory.

Non-bloc regions in general are the most important counterfactual, in the sense that these are parts of each country in which electoral blocs are not present.[71] They strengthen our theory where there is no history of a colonial-era producer region (and thus, by definition, no continuing history as a colonial-era producer region), and no electoral bloc today. For the countries in our sample, this is as the theory predicts: There is limited overlap between a country's non-bloc area and a colonial-era producer region, and the non-bloc regions are much less likely than electoral blocs to have agricultural specializations in export crops or nationally traded food crops today (Appendix D). The most glaring exception, northern Cameroon, is noted above. In some countries, a colonial-era producer region expanded geographically in the postcolonial period, but the extension zones do not become part of the electoral bloc anchored in the older producer region (e.g., coffee in the Far West of Côte d'Ivoire; cocoa in much of western Ghana). These warrant more analysis. In the new zones of production in the Ivoirian and Ghanaian cases, land and labor issues cross-cut presumptively shared sectoral interests; they may constitute a

---

[70] Uganda cotton production peaked at 400,000 bales (of 480 lb. each) in 1969, fell to 14,000 in 1986, and recovered to 172,000 in 2017 (United States Department of Agriculture (USDA), Uganda cotton production by year).

[71] Table D.1 in Appendix D lists the twelve non-bloc regions (one per country, comprising, on average, 57% of the national territory). The table reports each non-bloc region's spatial overlap (the "best match") with a colonial-era producer region and its economic specialization in 2010. Despite the large size of most of the non-bloc regions, only three produce more than 50% of an export crop associated with a colonial-era producer region: cocoa in Tanzania's Mbeya region; cotton in northern Cameroon; and coffee in western Côte d'Ivoire.

special subset of cases.[72] In Tanzania's non-bloc region, the 2010 IFPRI data identify one new zone that has developed a strong export specialization in recent decades: the Mbeya cocoa-producing region.[73] Our theory predicts that it could emerge as an electoral bloc, and indeed, the electoral data put Mbeya (and the neighboring southeastern cashew-producing zone) near the threshold for inclusion as an opposition-leaning zone.

Eight non-bloc regions can be said to have an agricultural "specialization," based on our calculations using the 2010 data: The leading ones are Malawi (millet), Nigeria (bananas and teas), Tanzania (cocoa), and Zambia (barley).[74] The others specialize in millet, yams, and/or bananas. This supports our description of the non-bloc regions as comprised mostly of non-specialized food crop producer regions, pastoral zones, and other rural zones marked by lower levels of commercialization of farm output. Small farms in such regions would be expected to grow a diverse portfolio of food crops that are mostly consumed and traded locally, on markets in the same region (e.g., yams, bananas).[75]

In a study of regional economic disparities in Tanzania, Adam, Bevan, and Gollin (2018) contrasted the better-off, "well-connected, commercially oriented rural regions" to very poor "quasi-subsistence rural regions." We see this contrast in the rural regions studied here. Our analysis suggests that this *economic* distinction often correlates with a *political* distinction. Electoral blocs and opposition-leaning zones are likely to arise in well-connected, more specialized, more commercially oriented rural regions, especially those that are

---

[72] In such cases, producers in a new production zone may share commercial policy interests with farmers in the older production zone, but when it comes to land tenure relations and land policy, or labor relations, their interests may diverge. Another factor may be that the newer producer zones are not incorporated into the older marketing networks and organizations, or are incorporated into different (rival) ones.

[73] All of Tanzania's cocoa comes from the non-bloc region and is produced by small and medium growers around Mbeya. Although colonial-era atlases show an archipelago of cocoa-producing areas in Mbeya region, cocoa was not promoted as a major export crop then or after Independence. In 2020, Tanzania exported USD 18 million in cocoa beans (10,000 tons), much of it produced in the Kyela, Rungwe, and Busokelo districts of Mbeya region. IFPRI data do not include cashews, but if they did, this would appear as a significant specialization in southeastern Tanzania, which is also the colonial-era cashew zone. (See the Tanzania map in Figure E.2 in Appendix E.)

[74] That is, a specialization ratio above 1.5.

[75] The non-bloc regions contain predominantly rural economies at both extremes of the commercialization spectrum. At the low end are the weakly commercialized zones that are emphasized above. At the other extreme are hot spots within the predominantly rural areas that are highly commercialized, highly diversified, and highly networked into the national economy. Examples would be southeastern Côte d'Ivoire, mentioned above, and Ghana's coastal strip. These are zones of rapidly increasing population density and high employment shares in nonfarm sectors that lie within the gravitational pull of national capital cities. Because these highly commercialized rural zones occupy only a small proportion of total non-bloc area for each country, they do not affect non-bloc values on the statistical indicators very much.

4.5 *Territorial Institution and Electoral Blocs*

export-producing.[76] By contrast, regions not specialized in the production of high-value commercial crops tend to be found in non-bloc areas today – they are unlikely to be persistent electoral blocs or oppositional zones.

4.5 TERRITORIAL INSTITUTION AND ELECTORAL BLOCS: COLONIAL-ERA ADMINISTRATIVE REGIONS AS BLOC CONTAINERS

Chapter 3 argued that the territorial framework of the state has served as the template for "regionalization of the economy and of politics." State interventions aimed at promoting cash crop production were tailored for, and implemented within, particular subnational administrative territories (districts and provinces). Neocustomary rights to land were allocated primarily on the basis of state-recognized ethnic identity within territorial units (native authorities) that were nested within districts. Districts were nested in provinces.

Most of the persistent electoral blocs and oppositional zones are indeed largely congruent with (nested within) colonial-era Admin1 regions (see Table 4.4).[77] Over 80% of the blocs (29/36) are mostly contained within a single, colonial-era Admin1 region (i.e., 70% or more of the bloc is contained within a colonial-era Admin1 region).[78] Over half of the persistent electoral blocs and oppositional zones are wholly encompassed within a colonial-era Admin1 unit (at least 90% of bloc is contained within the colonial Admin1 unit). Strikingly, many of the boundaries of the colonial-era Admin1 units persist in exact form today. Others have been subdivided, but in almost all cases this has taken place *within* the inherited, colonial-era Admin1 borders.[79]

---

[76] The IFPRI data show that the electoral blocs clearly have strong profiles as agricultural producer regions today. Two-thirds (21/36) have a 2010 sectoral specialization in either an export crop or a nationally traded food crop (maize, wheat, or rice). All but two of the blocs (34/36) are *also* zones of high concentration of production of one or more of the "nontraded" food crops surveyed by IFPRI, including plantains, millet, beans, and yams. It is not surprising that ecological regions propitious for cash crop farming are also propitious for growing food crops. Self-provisioning and local trading of surpluses in basic food staples are characteristic of family farm ("peasant") production in Africa and elsewhere. This contributes to food security in cash-crop-producing zones.

[77] See Table C.1 in Appendix C for the correspondences between electoral blocs, colonial Admin1 units, and postcolonial Admin1 units.

[78] A focus on Admin2 or district units would make it possible to refine this argument about institutional effects, not only because there are cross-national (and overtime) variations in the distribution of powers and prerogatives across the Admin1 and Admin2 scales of territorial administration, but also because more disaggregated analyses would capture *within* Admin1 variation in how the political and policy pressures of territorial administration impact regional political economies. Such an analysis could help account for variation in the extent of bloc and Admin1 overlap.

[79] For Cameroon, the postcolonial Admin1 unit of Centre was the re-amalgamation of a German-era province anchored in Yaoundé (1912) that was divided in two in 1937 under the French mandate. For Kenya, colonial-era provincial boundaries were strategically modified in 1962, a year before Independence. For Zambia, the Copperbelt Northern bloc coincides with two colonial and postcolonial Admin1 units.

TABLE 4.4 *Electoral bloc overlap with colonial-era Admin1s*

Country	Electoral bloc	Admin1 name	% of electoral bloc in (colonial) Admin1	% of (colonial) Admin1 in electoral bloc
Cameroon	Centre-Sud bloc	Centre-Sud	100.0	100.0
	Western bloc	W, NW, and SW	73.7	100.0
Côte d'Ivoire	Eastern bloc	Eastern and Central	98.4	59.5
	Northern bloc	Savanes and Denguele	84.8	59.7
	Western bloc	Sassandra, Marahoue, Goh, Djiboua	85.6	61.6
Ghana	Central bloc	Ashanti and Eastern	79.9	79.9
	Eastern bloc	Volta	50.7	99.0
	NW bloc	Northern	100.0	~ 20.0
Kenya	Central bloc	Central Province	69.7	87.0
	Eastern bloc	Eastern	99.7	23.8
	Rift Valley bloc	Rift Valley	99.9	23.3
	Western bloc	Nyanza, Western	99.9	49.1
Malawi	Central bloc	Central	99.9	46.6
	Eastern bloc	Southern	99.8	25.7
	Northern bloc	Northern	99.5	67.0
	Southern bloc	Southern	100.0	25.1
Mali	Bamako–Koulikoro bloc	Koulikoro	99.5	49.2
	Mopti bloc	Mopti	81.8	100.0
	Sikasso bloc	Sikasso	100.0	100.0
Nigeria	Eastern bloc	East	25.7	100.0
	Northern bloc	NW and NE	79.9	57.8
	Western bloc	West	100.0	81.0

South Africa	Center bloc	NW and Gauteng	77.8	88.2
	KwaZulu bloc	KwaZulu-Natal	100.0	47.3
	West Cape bloc	Western Cape	100.0	70.1
Tanzania	CCM bloc	Central	58.1	74.3
	N'rn opposition bloc	Lake and Nrn Provinces, 1948	65.8	71.5
Uganda	Central opposition bloc	Central	100.0	20.6
	Northern bloc	Northern	99.8	23.2
	Western bloc	Western	70.6	85.8
Zambia	Copperbelt Northern bloc	North Copperbelt	99.8	73.3
	Eastern bloc	Eastern	65.3	84.3
	Southern bloc	Southern	92.3	98.7
	Western bloc	Western	66.5	59.1
Zimbabwe	Northern bloc	Mashonaland	92.4	59.5
	Southern bloc	Matabeleland	99.2	70.7

Notes: This table reports territorial overlaps between electoral blocs and colonial-era Admin1 units. The bloc–Admin1 pairs are determined by selecting the Admin1 for which the overlap (as a part of the bloc area) is the greatest. See Appendix C, Table C.1 for Admin1 unit notes.
Note 1: For Ghana: The exact boundaries of the Northern Admin1 were not determined.
Note 2: For Kenya, we report the overlap with the 1962 provincial boundaries except for the case of Central Province, where we use the 1960 boundary.
Note 3: For Zambia: The Admin1 "Copperbelt" was a district within what was the colonial-era Western Province, the capital of which was Ndola. (Barotse was a separate colonial-era Admin1.) This table reports the overlap with the 1964 Western Admin1 (renamed Copperbelt in 1969) and colonial Admin1 of Northern.

Regional Blocs and Bloc Voting

This evidence supports the claim that most blocs' origins are traceable to regionally specialized patterns of economic development that were established during the colonial period, within the territorial administrative grids created by colonial states.[80] Blocs' spatial–sectoral profiles developed over time *within* the territorial administrative grid of provinces, districts, and subdistricts (Native Authorities, in the colonial period) that structured both colonial economic development and the categorizing and governing of native populations. Provinces and districts (or more generically, Admin1 and Admin2 units) function as containers for the "supply of government" and frameworks for political representation, and these functions have persisted over time.[81] Administrative units supply government via policy implementation, spending to promote government objectives, and political control. They also structure political representation – the "demand for government"– by serving as administrative containers for the electoral constituencies nested within them.

Four persistent electoral blocs correspond to colonial-era producer zones that developed in regions of historical statehood *that were encapsulated within* colonial Admin1 regions. These are Nigeria's Northern bloc, centered on Islamic emirates; Uganda's Central oppositional zone, which is Buganda; Ghana's Central bloc, arising from the core of Ashanti; and the more marginal case of Zambia's Western bloc, comprising Barotseland. This fact points to some of the endogenous links between colonial-era sectoral specializations, natural endowment, and centralized indigenous (precolonial) institutions. Centralized precolonial institutions arose in well-endowed regions that could support higher population densities and wealth accumulation, and/or in regions that attracted gains from trade.[82] Some of these offered political conditions conducive to cooperation with colonial regimes to promote the rapid expansion of smallholder commodity production in the twentieth century (Nigeria's northern emirates, Buganda, and Ashanti). Barotseland sent skilled workers to the Zambian Copperbelt (Ranger 1968). Other blocs that might be considered to fit into the category of zones of "historic statehood" encapsulated within Admin1 regions are Nigeria's Western bloc (Yoruba states), Côte d'Ivoire's Eastern bloc (Agni kingdoms), and Mali's Ségou/Mopti region. Yet looking at the entire list of persistent electoral blocs and opposition zones, it is clear that historic statehood is not a necessary condition of bloc-ness. The analysis here stresses an attribute that most of the blocs and

---

[80] Some colonial-era Admin1s were actually separate colonies. Northwest and Southwest Cameroon and the Volta Region of Ghana comprised, respectively, the British Cameroons and British Togoland. Both were former German territories which became League of Nations mandates in 1914. They were eventually absorbed into postcolonial Cameroon and Ghana. This is a potentially compounding source of regional political distinctiveness and cohesion. Many studies of the political distinctiveness and secessionist inclinations of state-segment territories have made this point.

[81] On Kenya, see Lonsdale (1969, 1971), Branch and Cheeseman (2006), MacArthur (2016), and Hassan (2020). On colonial Tanzania (Tanganika), see Maguire (1970).

[82] See Bandyopadhyay and Green (2016). On legacies of precolonial statehood, see also Wilfahrt (2021).

4.6 ETHNICITY AND ELECTORAL BLOCS

oppositional zones have in common, which is a history of deeper incorporation into the twentieth-century colonial economy, especially through engagement in the agricultural export economy (and mining economies).

4.6 ETHNICITY AND ELECTORAL BLOCS

The finding regarding the institutional correlates of the electoral blocs and oppositional zones bears directly on the question of the ethnic profile of the blocs. Provinces and districts served as the template for the colonial project of attempting to assign particular regions a functional economic role within the national economy. These same administrative units also served as the template for delimiting ethnic territories and applying policies of ethnic recognition to collectivities contained therein (King & Samii 2020). Combined, the net effect was to assign many ethnic groups "a vocation" in the colonial economy. Colonial NAs and districts often became electoral constituencies after Independence. This means that we should expect considerable endogeneity (or reciprocal causation) in the relationship between higher levels of export crop production, the geographic boundaries of export-crop-producing administrative units, and particular, politically salient ethnic identities, as indeed has been found to be the case (Pengl, Roessler, & Rueda, 2021). Lonsdale argued that "[p]olitical ethnicity ... is formed relationally in the national economy as much as in the national electoral arena" (2012: 22, 47), and this is our argument here.

Self-reported ethnicity data from DHS surveys from the 2000s can be used to describe the ethnic makeup of the persistent electoral blocs and oppositional zones, as well as the ethnic makeup of the constituencies or districts that comprise them.[83] This makes it possible to ask whether the persistent electoral blocs are monoethnic and whether they correspond to the "ethnic homelands" of particular ethnic groups.

Across the twelve-country study, we find great heterogeneity in the population share of the largest ethnic group in each electoral bloc and oppositional zone. Figure 4.7 reports results for the twenty-nine electoral blocs for which we have data. (Tanzania, South Africa, and Zimbabwe DHS surveys do not report ethnicity data.[84]) The share of the largest ethnic group ranges from 15% (for Cameroon's Centre-Sud bloc) to 94% (for Ghana's Northwestern bloc). Many blocs appear not to have a majority ethnic group (no group's population share

---

[83] This builds upon the analysis proposed by Boone, Wahman, Kyburz, and Linke (2022) for Kenya, Malawi, and Zambia and extends it to the other countries for which ethnicity data is available. See Table B.3 in Appendix B on the DHS data. For earlier work using DHS surveys to code the ethnic composition of constituencies or more disaggregated subnational units, see Jablonski (2014), Wilfahrt (2018), and Beiser-McGraph et al. (2021).

[84] Absence of DHS ethnicity data for Tanzania, South Africa, and Zimbabwe does not bias our estimates strongly in one direction or the other. Tanzania's two blocs and two of South Africa's are strongly multiethnic, while Zimbabwe's two blocs and South Africa's KwaZulu-Natal bloc are strongly associated with an ethnic identity (Shona and Ndebele, and Zulu, respectively).

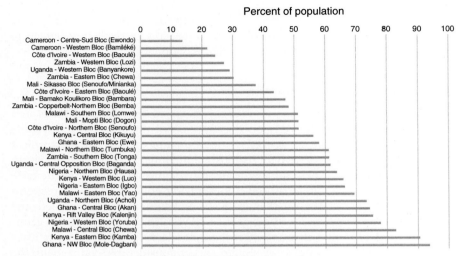

FIGURE 4.7 Ethnic profile of the electoral blocs (2010s)
Notes: Blocs are ranked in increasing order of the largest group population share. Name of the largest group is indicated in parenthesis. Results are based on the most recent DHS survey round for each country (see Appendix Table B.3: DHS surveys for details). The ethnic categories are those reported in the DHS.

exceeds 50%).[85] Note that these percentages are based on DHS reporting categories that may *combine* ethnic groups, as is the case for not only the Mole-Dagbani in Ghana's Northwestern bloc, but also for Zambia's Bemba group, Malawi's Lomwe, Kenya's Kalenjin, and Ghana's Akan. Reporting categories are shaped by country-level reporting conventions and government choices. (For example, "Akan" first appeared as a DHS reporting category for ethnicity in Ghana in the 2000s; it replaced Ashanti, Akwapin, Fante, and "other Akan" that had featured in DHS surveys in 1993 and 1998.) Several ethnic groups featured as DHS ethnic categories do not share a common mother language. These include Mole-Dagbani, Bamiléké, Kalenjin, and Lomwe. Ethnic categories used in DHS surveys, and also often used in scholarly analysis of ethnic voting in African countries, are not exogenous to country-level administrative decision-making and politics.

Table 4.5 describes the ethnic makeup of the constituencies and administrative units that *compose* the persistent electoral blocs and oppositional zones.[86]

---

[85] The average ethnic group share is 55.1%, and the median ethnic group share (within blocs) is 56.1%.
[86] Countries for which electoral results are reported at Admin1 level may be seen as biasing the results in favor of the multiethnicity argument, since the large size of the unit of observation and the nesting of Admin2s (which often defined the homelands of state-recognized ethnic groups in the colonial period) within Admin1s makes it less likely that units outside the electoral bloc will have the same ethnic plurality.

TABLE 4.5 *Ethnic profile of units comprising the persistent electoral blocs (2010s)*

1	2	3	4	5	6	7
				No. of units that have same plurality as bloc		
Country and unit level	Electoral bloc (number of units)	Largest ethnic group in bloc	Ethnic group size (% bloc pop.)	In bloc	In non-bloc	Bloc is multiethnic
Cameroon	Centre-Sud bloc (2)	Ewondo	13.6	1	0	Yes
Admin1	Western opposition bloc (4)	Bamiléké	21.7	2	0	Yes
Côte d'Ivoire	Eastern bloc (14)	Baoulé	43.3	9	16	Yes
Admin3	Northern bloc (8)	Senoufo	51.4	4	5	Yes
	Western bloc (11)	Baoulé	24.2	4	16	Yes
Ghana	Central bloc (48)	Akan	74.3	43	54	Yes
Constituencies	Eastern bloc (27)	Ewe	58.0	17	3	Yes
	NW bloc (4)	Mole-Dagbani	93.8	4	26	No
Kenya	Central bloc (45)	Kikuyu	56.1	33	9	Yes
Constituencies	Eastern bloc (14)	Kamba	90.5	14	5	No
	Rift Valley bloc (27)	Kalenjin	75.4	26	5	No
	Western bloc (30)	Luo	65.8	21	0	Yes
Malawi	Central bloc (36)	Chewa	82.8	35	25	No
Constituencies	Eastern bloc (15)	Yao	69.2	11	5	Yes
	Northern bloc (22)	Tumbuka	61.1	16	6	Yes
	Southern bloc (27)	Lomwe	51.2	19	13	Yes
Mali	Bamako–Koulikoro bloc (21)	Bambara	47.1	17	28	Yes
Admin3	Mopti bloc (36)	Dogon	51.3	14	0	Yes
	Sikasso bloc (35)	Senoufo/Minianka	37.4	14	4	Yes

(*continued*)

TABLE 4.5 *(continued)*

1	2	3	4	5	6	7
				No. of units that have same plurality as bloc		
Country and unit level	Electoral bloc (number of units)	Largest ethnic group in bloc	Ethnic group size (% bloc pop.)	In bloc	In non-bloc	Bloc is multiethnic
Nigeria	Eastern bloc (11)	Igbo	55.3	5	0	Yes
Admin1	Northern bloc (9)	Hausa	63.7	6	2	Yes
	Western bloc (5)	Yoruba	77.9	5	2	No
Uganda	Central opposition bloc (5)	Baganda	61.9	5	7	Yes
Admin2	Northern bloc (4)	Acholi	73.3	3	2	Yes
	Western bloc (22)	Banyankore	29.5	9	1	Yes
Zambia	Copperbelt Northern bloc (44)	Bemba	48.1	31	12	Yes
Constituencies	Eastern bloc (19)	Chewa	30.3	6	0	Yes
	Southern bloc (19)	Tonga	61.1	16	3	Yes
	Western bloc (13)	Lozi	27.2	3	6	Yes

Notes: This table reports the results for the ethnic makeup of the units used to draw the blocs (i.e., relating to the shapefile used to define the blocs which, for most countries, corresponds to the level at which the electoral data were reported for most countries). The relevant units are reported in column 1. The number of units for which there is at least one DHS cluster in the pooled data (see Table B.3 in Appendix B) included in each bloc is reported in column 2. Discrepancies between the number of units reported here and those visible in the maps are trivial except for the case of Mali, where DHS survey clusters were located in only 20% of the Admin3 units. Blocs are considered to be multiethnic either if there is no majority ethnic group in the bloc or if at least 10% *of the units that make up the bloc* have a different ethnic plurality than the bloc. The information reported in column 4 is the most important for our argument.

4.6 Ethnicity and Electoral Blocs

Overall, for most blocs, the largest ethnic group in the bloc *does* represent a plurality of the population in most of the units that comprise the bloc. But the ethnic head count leaves a lot of variance to be explained. The electoral bloc's largest ethnic group comprises a plurality in 70% or more of the bloc's constituencies (or alternative administrative units used to draw the blocs) in only about half of the blocs for which we have data (16/29).[87] At the same time, there are constituencies (or administrative units) that might be expected to be bloc members, based on the ethnic identity of a majority of residents and adjacency to a bloc, but are not. (Column 5 reports the number of non-bloc units that have the same ethnic plurality as an electoral bloc; most are adjacent to the bloc.[88])

Another counterfactual is the clusters of three or more constituencies with the same ethnic majority that do *not* form blocs. If dominating a large contiguous cluster of electoral constituencies or districts was the "cause" of persistent electoral blocs, then all such clusters would be persistent electoral blocs or opposition zones. Yet this is not the case. For example, the Fulbe (Peuhl) comprise the largest group in the three Admin1 units of Northern Cameroon, but these do not correspond to a bloc. Several such examples in Kenya, Malawi, and Zambia are noted below.

For three county cases that are considered by many political scientists to be countries in which ethnicity is highly politicized, even by African standards – Kenya, Malawi, and Zambia – the findings reported above hold true (see Boone, Wahman, Kyburz, & Linke 2022). They are also the countries (along with Ghana) for which our electoral bloc definition is based on the most complete and granular electoral data for the longest series of elections, and where we detect electoral clusters for all elections using classic electoral geography methods of spatial autocorrelation. The risk of inclusion or exclusion errors when identifying bloc boundaries is lower in these cases, and corresponding results can be interpreted with more confidence. The analysis shows that, although many of the electoral blocs in these three countries *do* have clear ethnic attributes, the persistent electoral blocs cannot be explained as the mechanical effect of ethnic voting.

Across the twelve persistent electoral blocs in Kenya, Zambia, and Malawi, all but three are *multiethnic*, as recorded in the DHS ethnic categories.[89] Blocs

---

[87] Ichino and Nathan (2013) find that in multiethnic localities in central Ghana, non-coethnics may vote with the ethnic plurality (or majority) out of a rational calculation about which candidate will best serve the locality. The authors use this finding to critique ethnic determinism in explanations of voting in African countries. Their findings and the inferences drawn from it dovetail with the argument here.

[88] These constituencies (or administrative units) must be adjacent to the electoral bloc or opposition zone in order to be "picked up" either by the Local Moran's I or by serial mapping analysis.

[89] Earlier work that suggests that *group size* determines the political significance of particular ethnic groups (Posner 2004a) has prima facie plausibility. Yet where the acquisition of political power is associated with ethnic group size, endogeneity concerns are strong: Politics may drive group amalgamation and the formation of (umbrella) ethnic identities, rather than the reverse.

are considered to be multiethnic either if there is no majority ethnic group in the bloc, or if at least 10% of the constituencies that make up the bloc have a different ethnic plurality than most of the other units in the bloc. The three "monoethnic" blocs are Kenya's Eastern bloc in which 91% of the population identifies as Kamba and whose constituencies all have a Kamba majority; Kenya's Rift Valley in which 75% of the population is Kalenjin and all constituencies but one have a Kalenjin plurality, and Malawi Central, in which 82% of the population identifies as Chewa.

One example of the multiethnicity of blocs is the Kenya's Western bloc. Luo make up about 65% of the bloc's total population and constitute a plurality in 70% of the bloc's constituencies (21/30). In Malawi's Southern bloc, the Lomwe are about 51% of total bloc population, and make up the plurality in about 70% of the bloc's constituencies. In Zambia's Eastern bloc, the Chewa are 30% of the bloc's population and the plurality in about 30% of the constituencies. Multiethnicity is strongest in Zambia's electoral blocs. In three of the four persistent blocs we identify in Zambia, three have no majority group. Moreover, not all constituencies that are composed mostly of members of one of the large ethnic groups vote persistently with the electoral bloc that most of their coethnics choose (Table 4.5 and Boone, Wahman, Kyburz, & Linke, 2022). In Kenya, for example, not all Kikuyu-dominant constituencies are part of the Central persistent electoral bloc.

Clusters of coethnic constituencies that do *not* form persistent electoral blocs are also present. In Kenya, at least three groups that comprise more than 60% of the population in geographically contiguous blocs of nine or more constituencies but do not form electoral blocs: the Kisii, Somali, and Mijikenda/Swahili. In Malawi, the Ngoni and the Sena are such counterfactuals. In Malawi, the Ngoni and Sena comprise more than 60% of the population in geographic clusters of eight constituencies each, but neither engages in persistent bloc voting. In Zambia, there are no such counterfactuals, but Zambia's persistent electoral blocs themselves do not pass this 60% threshold that would define these as "ethnic blocs."[90]

Ethnicity is not a mechanical predictor or mechanical cause of bloc-ness: It is either underdetermining, in that it does not predict the presence of the large, multiethnic coalitions that we actually see, or it is overdetermining, in that it predicts

---

See Ericka Albaugh (2011: 392) on how membership in the Beti ethnic group in Cameroon expanded after Paul Biya, who identified as Beti, came to power. See also discussion of the Baoulé in Chapter 3 (Box 3.1).

[90] Boone, Wahman, Kyburz, and Linke (2022) offers an analysis of the extent of territorial overlap between electoral blocs and putative ethnic homelands in Kenya, Malawi, and Zambia. We found that most of the electoral blocs are not coterminous with ethnic homeland territories. The average overlap between the "ethnic blocs" and the electoral blocs for these three countries is 62% by number of constituencies, 64% by population, and 67% by territory. This may be enough to support a layman's intuition about the ethnic character of blocs, but it leaves a very wide margin unaccounted for, and a great deal of cross-bloc variation to be explained.

4.7 Explaining Bloc-ness: Theorizing Bloc Cohesion

many more electoral blocs than we actually observe. It does not distinguish between blocs and non-blocs, or offer a theory of multiethnic alliances across the constituencies (or administrative units) that make up blocs, or explain persistent alliances between blocs with different (or non) ethnic profiles. As Kanyinga wrote, patterns observable at the national level "call for categories of explanation independent of theories of electoral patronage and ethnicity" (2000: 85).

The large historiographical literature on Africa shows that many of today's "politically relevant ethnic groups" emerged as such in the twentieth century in response to the economic and institutional drivers of bloc-ness. Even in Kenya, Zambia, and Malawi, three countries often considered to be among those with the strongest patterns of ethnic voting in sub-Saharan Africa, at least several of the politically salient ethnic identities that are prominent in the national arena – including Kalenjin, Luyha, Luo, Bemba, and Chewa – are identities that have coalesced around regional cleavages and regional interests, rather than the reverse. They are "composite," umbrella, or super-ethnic identities that have coalesced in the course of competition against other regional groups in the national political arena. This logic would lead us to expect that the ethnic identities claimed by the most important "politically relevant ethnic groups" are often associated with the distinctive political projects of regionally defined groups that are able to incorporate neighbors into effective political coalitions, and are thus on a par with political identities that are expressly regional: "Northern" in Ghana, Nigeria, Côte d'Ivoire, and Malawi; "Le Grand Ouest" in Côte d'Ivoire; Eastern Province in Zambia (as argued by Posner); "Anglophone" in Cameroon, etc.

Constituency or district membership in an electoral bloc appears to be an effect of political and economic organization, shared regional interests, *and* some ethnic identities and affiliations. The findings from the DHS analysis suggest that politically salient ethnic identities may interact synergistically with political drivers to contribute to bloc voting, but in most cases, bloc voting transcends ethnic lines. In some cases, such identities are clearly *produced by* the larger institutional and economic forces that contribute to regional cohesion and cleavages in politics.

4.7 EXPLAINING BLOC-NESS: THEORIZING BLOC COHESION

Today's persistent electoral blocs and opposition-leaning zones are electorally distinctive. They are also *economically* distinctive. They are economically advantaged vis-à-vis other rural regions, and in most cases, this is traceable to economic specializations that date to the colonial period. These findings point to mechanisms of electoral bloc formation and persistence. Our theory is that, in most cases, the *sectoral profile* of the electoral blocs and oppositional zones is key to explaining *why* they are electoral blocs (i.e., their bloc-ness). Sectoral profile is associated with relative economic and collective action advantages, including institutional and organizational correlates of sectoral economic specialization in export crops and nationally traded food crops like commercial maize, wheat, and rice. Sectoral profiles capture features of local economies that give rise to joint economic interests, membership in producer associations, jointness of supply of public goods related to the sector, and shared exposure to the regulatory structures and processes of government (supplied via Admin2 and Admin1 institutions). *Relative* position in the national political economy is a politically salient dimension of regional economic heterogeneity that contributes to the formation of regional consciousness and regional ideologies (Ahlerup, Baskaran, & Bigsten 2016). Interests may coalesce around positional advantage or "positional deprivation" relative to other groups.[91] Nesting of electoral constituencies within district and provincial units (Admin2 and Admin1 institutions), and the presence of national legislatures based on territorial representation (except in South Africa), also provide resources and incentives for regional political coordination. Institutional factors shape political entrepreneurialism, electoral brokerage, and strategies of political control at all levels.

A range of meso- and microlevel mechanisms is compatible with this general theorization of the sources of bloc cohesion. As Isabela Mares has insisted, those operating at different levels of the political system may be different: Political action across levels of a political system – micro, meso, macro – "may not be regulated by a singular logic that applies across all territorial units" (2015: 213–215, 233). Shin and Agnew made the same point, saying that studying electoral politics geographically makes it possible to see multiple mechanisms at work at different scales of analysis (2007: 291).[92] Mechanisms may be described in generic terms of interests, organizations, strategy (brokerage, coordination, scaling up), and ideology. They work through individual, collective, and elite agency. All are conditioned by the institutional structure of the state. Where state institutions structure interests, organization, and strategy along territorial lines, and regions are economically differentiated and unequal, regional interests are likely to be salient in politics.

Although our arguments are cast at the level of social aggregates, the agency-based, interest-based, and micro- and meso-level foundations of this theory are not far from the surface. Constituency- and district-level electoral data, combined with data on the sectoral profile of blocs, brings us close to voters, households, and communities.

Interests

Most of the sectoral data refer to specialization in household-based ("peasant" or smallholder) cash crop production. Where family farming prevails, a significant share of the electoral bloc population is likely to be engaged in occupations that are linked to this sectoral specialization. In predominantly rural electoral

---

[91] As documented in the EU context in the work of Iammarino, Rodriguez-Pose, and Storper 2018.
[92] Indeed, McDoom (2020) explains that sensitivity to scale can help to arbitrate between different causal theories of what we take to be the same phenomenon. The different explanations may apply at different scales of analysis.

4.7 Explaining Bloc-ness: Theorizing Bloc Cohesion

districts, we can infer that many voters are members of farming families whose livelihoods are, directly or indirectly, at least partially dependent upon the production, processing, and commercialization of these crops.[93] Much comparative political economy work uses occupational and sectoral attributes of individuals and groups to draw inferences about political behavior and vote choice (Rogowski 1987; Rickard 2018). Scholars often associate the interests of voters with those of the firm or sector in which they are employed, and argue that, in localities in which most livelihoods depend on a given industry or sector, voters' fortunes and interests are tied to those of that sector. We also know that individuals' fortunes can be tied to sectors prominent in their communities and localities, even when they themselves do not work in that sector (Scheve & Slaughter 2001; Broz, Frieden, & Weymouth 2021).

For productive sectors of national significance, policy itself links producers to government and works to "produce politics."[94] In the agricultural sector, export crops and nationally traded grains (commercial maize, wheat, and rice) are subject to state-regulated pricing, storage, conditions of sale, and quality controls, as well as trade and exchange rate policies. In mining and labor-sending regions, government policies around wages, working conditions, labor mobility, taxation, rules and land tenure rights in migrants' home regions all bring producers and households into direct engagement with the state. Following Rogowski (1989) and Rickard (2020), we should expect high *specialization* in the regional economy to be associated with more homogeneity in public policy preferences than would be expected in economically diverse regions.

At the level of localities, sectoral specializations can generate both shared interests and capacity for collective action. Within the villages and districts that make up electoral constituencies, communities and producer groups are likely to be interlinked by multistranded interdependencies in the control and use of productive resources. Producers of export crops or other nationally traded crops are linked by jointness of supply in inputs, infrastructure, and policy. This may include group-level interests in political conditions that affect land rights security (Boone 2014). For miners, relations of codependency and co-positionality in the regional and national economy are built into the job. For households and communities in some labor-exporting regions, there are bridging ties to producer regions and social networks around long-distance logistics and reciprocities. These economic interests and relationships can produce the potential for collective demands on the state, as well as capacity for engagement in partisan mobilization and electoral politics.

Individual and group-level political preferences and grievances may also take shape around more general, contextual conditions that characterize regional

---

[93] Boone, Crespin-Boucaud, and Kim (2021) find that 35% of DHS respondents in the electoral blocs in Ghana, Kenya, Malawi, and Zambia work in the agricultural sector.

[94] That is, interest groups may coalesce and mobilize in response to public policy (Skocpol 1992; Pierson 1993: 599).

economies. European Social Survey data reveal the impact of contextual economic conditions (such as unemployment rate within localities and regions, exposure to trade shocks) on social attitudes measured in individual-level opinion data, as well as in voting.[95] It is likely that these effects also operate in African countries.

Organizations and Associational Ties

Organizations and institutions at multiple political scales persist over time, embedding individuals in communities that are centered around particular types of livelihoods, producer organizations, marketing networks, and formal and informal associations based on religious, ethnic, or familial group membership. These, in turn, are often embedded in sociopolitical hierarchies rooted in specific productive sector relations (such as relations of access to land, markets, credit, and labor). These organizations and associations can contribute to bloc-ness: They shape individuals' voting preferences, incentives to vote, vote choice, and capacity for collective action.[96] Organizations often aggregate across political scales – from the local, to the district, to the multidistrict scale – following the lines of administrative structures that nest the former colonial chieftaincies (often contained in today's electoral constituencies) into district and provincial units.

Producer cooperatives and farmers' associations are canonical examples of hierarchically organized producer organizations. They often provided the building blocs of political parties in the nationalist era. Bates (1983) explained that farmers' associations in export crop sectors provided urban politicians with the organizational structures and issues they used to build political parties of regional and national scope, and eventually "to sweep the colonizers from power." In the nationalist era and after independence, these were absorbed into political parties, just as labor unions were in Tanzania, Zambia, Zimbabwe, and many other countries. Neoliberalizing reforms of the 1980s and early 1990s scaled back the state's role in creating and maintaining such organizations, as well as state monopolies in input distribution and marketing. Even so, cooperatives, producer organizations, and agricultural commodity chain sectoral institutions remain present as economic and political actors in many important sectors and in the post-1995 period, especially in key export crop commodity chains and in sectors organized around food crops of national importance.[97] Kenya's National Bureau of Statistics reported that there were 20,000 registered agricultural cooperatives and societies in Kenya in 2019.[98] Nine major export or

---

[95] See Burgoon et al. (2019: 52).

[96] On organizations (associationalism) as building blocs of collective group identities vis-à-vis other societal groups and the state, see Putnam (1993), Eaton (2016: 388–389); Levitsky et al. (2016), and Poertner (2021).

[97] Poulton 2014. On producer cooperatives in agriculture in the post-2000 era, see also Wayama, Develterre, and Pollet (2009), Poulton and Kanyinga (2013), Treakle (2016), Bolton (2019), and Wedig and Wiegratz (2018).

[98] KNBS Economic Survey (2019: 117).

4.7 Explaining Bloc-ness: Theorizing Bloc Cohesion 143

commercial food crops were sold through marketing boards: maize, wheat, rice, tea, coffee, cotton, sugar cane, pyrethrum, and sisal. Many such producer organizations in Kenya and elsewhere are descendants of organizations that date back several decades, with long histories of political action aimed at influencing policy actions of the central state (Schulz 2020).

Labor unions in mining districts are analogs. Mining unions have been visible in their high activism around sectoral policy, regulatory issues, and indeed, electoral politics since the 1940s. Families and communities located in distant labor-sending regions can be linked into the same social and political networks, as is documented in a large literature on the political ties between Zambia's Copperbelt and the labor-sending region of Zambia's Northern Province.

Political parties as organizations play a key role in cross-constituency coordination and in scaling-up interest representation to the regional level. Indeed, party organization, action, and strategies, and the sedimenting of these over time since the 1940s, contribute directly to defining territorial extent and political character of the electoral blocs and oppositional zones. Economic geography, sectoral profiles of producer regions, and spatial inequalities help explain where parties build political machines and gather support, and how they do so. Presidential candidates themselves, past and present, often appeal to regional interests. In Ghana's 2008 the presidential elections, the NPP's Akufo-Addo appealed to his core supporters in the country's main export-producing region (the Central electoral bloc) with a rallying cry against the rival party: "We are not going to put our nation in the hands of these inefficient, unproductive persons!"[99]

In rural non-bloc regions, by contrast, absence of a sectoral specialization in export crops or nationally traded food crops implies absence of the types of rural organizations that contribute to bloc-ness. Social groups are less likely to be organized into producer organizations that aim to represent sectoral interests in interaction with the state. Other factors associated with the non-bloc areas – remoteness, low population density, high levels of poverty, low levels of connectivity – may also impede the formation of organizations and associations that transcend the local level to express wider shared interests, consciousness of shared positionality in the national political economy, and collective claims on the state.[100] High levels of ethno-linguistic fractionalization (ELF) can be a historical outcome of such conditions, including of low growth itself.[101]

---

[99] Jarreth Merz, *An African Election*, 2011, min. 51.

[100] Urban non-bloc regions also do not exhibit the patterns of cross-constituency cohesion that characterizes the rural electoral blocs. This can be understood as an effect of economic heterogeneity, defined in terms of sectoral and occupational profiles, and of income and class differences. This results in heterogeneity of interests and in networks of associational life. In urban areas, these differences can be reinforced by residential segregation and sorting by socioeconomic status (Resnick 2014; Nathan 2019; Paller 2019).

[101] Historians have made this argument for much of the African continent for many centuries prior to the twentieth.

Other analysts have drawn a causal connection between the economic advantages of the most productive agricultural regions of Africa, on the one hand, and the density of associational life, political capacity, and collective action on the other. Binswanger and Deininger (1997: 1981–1985) suggested that rural areas of higher population density are associated with more trading organizations, more independent local associations and institutions, and information-sharing advantages, all of which translate into bargaining advantages for local groups in relation to the state. Poulton (2012:12) also observed a positive relationship between higher levels of education and higher population density and rural political capacity and collective action. Population density creates the conditions for cooperation around public goods and collective action, and education produces what Poulton called "awareness of political processes." These advantages tend to result in greater "policy supply" and, as Poulton put it, greater accountability of leaders to their supporters in advantaged regions.

The historical record is also compelling in this regard. Many of the electoral blocs and oppositional zones are marked by long histories of political organization, mobilization, and activism in pushing demands on the state. Zones of peasant commercial hold-ups, boycotts, tax strikes, rebellion, or insurgency in the late colonial period include what is now the Cameroon Western bloc, Ghana Central bloc, Kenya Central bloc, Nigeria Western bloc, and Zimbabwe's Northern and Southern blocs. The mining regions corresponding to Zambia's Copperbelt Northern and South Africa's Central bloc were hotbeds of political mobilization in times of nationalist struggle. Nationalist and postcolonial political parties were often erected on these foundations.

Strategy, Politicians, and Political Parties

Strategizing, coordination, and constituency-building by local elites and elected political representatives play a role in shaping and aggregating voter preferences and behavior. Political entrepreneurship and elite coordination happen at the constituency, district, and regional levels, playing a role in the supply side of ethnic and regional identities, in shaping group preferences, and in political organization and mobilization. As Shin and Agnew (2007) argue, politicians and political parties may *propose* territorial framings of the political questions and dilemmas that animate national life.

The segmented and multitiered structure of national political systems plays a role in shaping coalitional structure, political party organization, and politicians' strategies. Distinct mechanisms of voter aggregation and distinct appeals to interests may predominate at different political scales, working separately or in tandem to produce bloc voting at the regional level. A political party trying to compete nationally may offer a bland appeal at the national level, where it may indeed follow a party platform that is "everything to everyone" (Resnick 2014: 48). Within *subnational* electoral areas, however, the party's appeal may

4.7 Explaining Bloc-ness: Theorizing Bloc Cohesion

be strongly regionalist. There may even be strong tensions between the two (see Fabre & Swenden 2013).[102]

Regionally based parties (such as the UPND based in the Southern Province of Zambia, Chadema in Tanzania, or the FPI in Côte d'Ivoire) are evidence of collective action on the part of regionally based leaders and political entrepreneurs to both mobilize and represent regional constituencies. Many ostensibly or aspirationally national parties, including incumbent parties, have strong regional bases (strongholds) that serve as the hub of coalition-building strategies (Arriola 2013; Elischer 2013). Political networks formed within Admin1 structures can mobilize regional interests: Hiribarren (2017) writes of the "Northernization" effort that drew together the rival emirates of Sokoto and Borno in Nigeria's colonial Northern Region in the 1950s, as the Sarduna of Sokoto sought to consolidate and enhance the bargaining power of the North vis-à-vis southern interests in the 1950s.[103] Since the returns to multipartyism in the 1990s, there are many instances in which regional caucuses of MPs coalesce around regional policy interests. Examples include Northern Kenya's pastoralists' caucus, district caucuses of MPs in Uganda (Green 2008: 11–12), and the regional caucuses that mobilized in the making of Côte d'Ivoire's 1998 land law (Boone 2018). That MPs seek reelection by appealing to particular constituency or sub-constituency interests (those of coethnics, or voters in more populated locales) does not preclude the possibility that they also appeal to regional interests, and do so by working within regional networks. Their own career ambitions to ascend within party hierarchies may incentivize them to do so.[104]

Territorial features of electoral systems shape politician and partisan strategies, voter mobilization, campaign dynamics, and the internal organization of political parties themselves. Where MPs are elected under SMD electoral rules (or modified PR rules that provide for territorial representation), as is the case for eleven of the twelve countries featured here, political parties will almost inevitably organize their own organizational structures around territorial constituencies, and mobilize voters at the constituency level.[105] Electoral apportionment of seats in national legislatures favors rural districts, in some countries very

---

[102] An example of such contradiction was visible in Kenya in 2017, when the ruling party, Jubilee, campaigned on a platform of respect for private property rights in land, while the Jubilee-aligned MP in Laikipia North constituency campaigned on a platform promising to expel white landowners and return the land to indigenous communities.

[103] See Maguire (1970) on Lake Province in Tanzania. Leaders of the influential cotton cooperative unions in the early 1950s realized that their grievances had been targeted at the *Provincial* Commissioner, not his subordinates. A similar dynamic united various proto-nationalist and nationalist groups on the Kenya Coast, who joined forces at the provincial level of politics (Mambo 1987: 107–108).

[104] On the distinction between politicians' constituency-level work and their national-level career goals, see also Fiorina and Rohde 1989.

[105] South Africa is the outlier: Here, a strongly national (territoriality-mitigating) proportional representation voting system predominates, but this coexists with features of the state design and the electoral system that provide for territorial representation at the subnational levels.

146 Regional Blocs and Bloc Voting

strongly so (Boone & Wahman 2015). These features of electoral system design create opportunity structures for the expression of territorial interests. Yet where presidents are elected de facto from a single national constituency, SMD rules *in themselves* do not induce politicians and parties to organize regional bloc voting in presidential elections. This outcome must be explained with reference to additional institutional and organizational features of national and subnational contexts, and/or underlying commonalities in social or socioeconomic context, that produce persistent clustering of constituency vote shares in some regions but not others. By the same token, PR rules will not produce "nationalized" political strategies or electoral results when the underlying social context is characterized by strongly spatially concentrated interests (Ferree 2018; Rickard 2018; Selway 2015: 14) (see discussion of South Africa in Chapter 7). This means that, in presidential elections, electoral system design per se does not explain regional clustering (or the absence thereof) in presidential results.[106]

Regional Ideology and Regional Interests

Ideology is critical in the transformation of socioeconomic inequalities into *political cleavages*, as Lipset and Rokkan (1967) and other political economy scholars have emphasized. Regional and ethnic identities, as ideologies of belonging and shared fate, can be such a force in politics. The analysis here emphasizes the large extent to which the identities that become salient in national-level politics are endogenous to political economy and institutional variables, and to the competitive interaction of groups within the national political arena.

National identities are defined partly in terms of long-standing *regional* identities and ideologies of belonging. These are shaped by shared experiences in relation to the state, relative position in the national political economy, and distinctive sector-based identities. These may indeed be associated with, or partially rooted in, territorially defined ethnic identities, which are themselves animated in part by relative advantage/disadvantage vis-à-vis others. John Lonsdale (2015: 623) has written that "inequality" is a dominant theme in African political thought, and that regional inequality heightens and politicizes ethnicity.[107]

Shared political and policy interests arising from the sectoral profiles of regional political economies, and the positionality of regions in the national political economy, also provide the basis for multiethnic regional alliances and

---

[106] The number of candidates on a presidential ballot, rules that require a presidential winner to show significant support across most national regions (as in Kenya and Nigeria), and concurrency of presidential and parliamentary elections are electoral system features that can shape electoral dynamics and affect winners' margins at the constituency level. Côte d'Ivoire, Mali, and Zimbabwe hold runoff elections in presidential contests when no candidate commands a national majority in the first round. Kenya adopted such a rule in 2010. Where there were two rounds of voting, we used R2 results in identifying electoral blocs, but we used R1 results for rougher calculations when only these were available. (See Table B.2 in Appendix B.)

[107] For Lonsdale, responsibility/accountability and "difference" are also dominant themes.

Conclusion

the coalescing of regional identities and ideologies that express these. Related arguments were made by an earlier generation of Africa scholars. In a study of Zambia, Robert Moteno (1974: 87–93) argued that nested supra- and subgroup ethnic identities may be activated strategically, in response to electoral and policy incentives. In the national political arena, these may find expression as mega- or supra-ethnic identities that are *an effect* of electoral incentives and shared policy interests, rather than the effect of preexisting or free-floating ethnic identities. Posner (2005) provided evidence of just such activation of supra- and subgroup identities in Zambia, showing inter alia that shared membership in the same province (Admin1) could provide the basis for electoral alignment.[108] In accounting for such alignments, this book emphasizes drivers of regional alignments and regional ideologies that arise from economic geography, uneven development, and regional inequalities (rather than ethnic identity per se). The territorial extent and demographic weight – and the political salience – of ethnic and language groups are often endogenous to these underlying political economy aspects of national life.

In studying European electorates, Burgoon et al. find that there are "positional or relational group-level political preferences" that develop around "positional deprivation (or advantage)" relative to other groups (2019: 52). This chimes with some literature on the politics of ethnic inequality in African countries. What the European comparison suggests is that "ethnicity" is not a necessary ingredient (a sine qua non) in these processes.

CONCLUSION

This chapter identifies regional bloc voting in twelve countries and shows that its incidence varies across space within countries. Persistent electoral blocs and persistently opposition-leaning regions tend to be more economically developed and to have better-educated populations, higher population densities, and long histories of deep incorporation into national economies dating to the 1930s and 1940s if not before. In most cases, bloc-ness is related to long-established sectoral specialization in the production of high-value crops. These variables all capture accrued and cumulative advantages over time. Among blocs, economic hierarchies (inequalities in bloc rankings) also tend to be stable over time.[109]

---

[108] Posner (2005) focused his analysis of the formation of winning electoral coalitions on the role of social identity in promoting cohesion. He attributed regional-level alliances to shared language, which he defined as a type of coethnicity. "Tribal affiliation and language group" were defined as "two bases of social identity that constitute the complete menu of social identity available to Zambian political actors when they try to build and secure membership in winning political coalitions" (Posner 2005: 88).

[109] From a regional economics perspective, this is not surprising. In OECD countries and within the European Union, policy alone does not reverse entrenched patterns of spatial inequality, even if income transfers, etc., can mitigate income inequality across regions. See McCann (2020) on Britain, and on cohesion policy within the OECD, Iammarino et al. (2019).

These data show that persistent electoral blocs map onto persistent patterns of regional advantage and disadvantage in national political economies.

Significance of the blocs is cast into stark relief by the existence of large expanses of each country in which cohesive, geographically defined voting clusters *do not emerge*. These comprise the residual category that we have called the "non-bloc" parts of each country, which are generally poorer, less specialized in high-value crops, and lower in population density than the persistent electoral blocs and oppositional zones.

Earlier scholars have picked up on the geographic dimensions of inequality in African countries in "ethnic inequality" arguments cast at both the individual level (Houle et al. 2019) and across geographic units (Alesina et al. 2016). Yet in emphasizing the ethnic correlates of inequality, its sectoral, institutional, and electoral correlates remained invisible, as did the multiethnic character of both richer and poorer regions. By placing this information in a larger context – temporal, geographic, institutional, and electoral – this analysis can identify enduring *regional interests and political cleavages* that are immanent in the findings of earlier work.

There is a good rationale for including all twelve countries in the electoral bloc study, in spite of unevenness in the data and thus in the precision of the analysis. With all twelve countries in the mix, it is possible to expand analysis beyond the countries that offer the most complete and transparent sets of electoral results, and thus to have a larger, more diverse, and arguably more representative sample of countries. The validity of the arguments here does not rest on the precise boundaries of the blocs. Indeed, given our criteria for bloc inclusion, incorporating more or future elections into the analysis could modify the shape of some of the blocs.[110] Our substantive claims about bloc attributes are expected to be robust to some changes in the parameters of particular blocs. One prediction derived from our main argument is that bloc modifications will arise from changes in regional economic geography and inequality structures, and that these may produce, or contribute to, impactful changes in national political alignments. By this reasoning, such changes may affect observed political cleavages, but regionalism will remain a strong feature of national politics as long as economies remain strongly regionally differentiated, institutions remain strongly territorial, and spatial inequalities persist.

---

[110] For example, in Malawi, the Southern and Eastern blocs would appear to be a single electoral bloc in an analysis that included the 2019 (annulled) and 2020 elections.

5

Regional Hierarchies and Winning Coalitions

> Regional inequality became the basis for dividing power from opposition.
>
> Lonsdale 2015: 620

Chapter 4 showed that regional electoral blocs and opposition-leaning zones map onto the uneven economic geography of countries, largely following the delineation of colonial-era units of territorial administration. Blocs and oppositional zones tend to be economically advantaged over non-bloc regions in terms of general levels of economic development, wealth indicators, and the sectoral division of labor within national economies. Economic advantage in most of these regions is correlated with, and indeed traceable to, spatial–sectoral advantages that date to the colonial period. Most are leading export-producing regions that have benefited from the forces of economic agglomeration over time: They are sites of the greatest concentrations of economic growth in the rural regions of each country. This finding departs from much political science work on Africa that attributes regional economic advantage to capture of government itself – that is, to the pattern of central government allocation of development spending (Franck & Rainer 2012; Archibong 2018). Our data suggest that the causal arrow runs in the reverse direction: Economic dominance facilitates state capture.

This chapter shows that the economically leading electoral blocs[1] are indeed the dominant *political* players in most of the countries considered in this study. They have been incumbent strongholds (regional bases of incumbents) in most of the 12 countries considered here for much of the postcolonial period.[2] Tanzania and Uganda, where "poor regions" have provided the regional bases

---

[1] As measured by nighttime luminosity, compared to the non-bloc regions.

[2] This generalization holds for 8 or 10 of the 12 countries, depending on whether we consider the entire postcolonial period or post-1990 only, and how we regard the case of Zimbabwe. In Zimbabwe, the Northern electoral bloc, which does not include constituencies in the capital

149

for incumbent regimes since the 1960s and 1980s, respectively, are the clearest exceptions.

Relationships between economic advantage and political advantage are explored in this chapter. There are two main arguments. The first, laid out in Section 5.1, is that political hierarchy among regional electoral blocs, defined in terms of *relative political advantage*,[3] tends to map onto the *economic* hierarchy of regions. This conforms to a default theoretical expectation, derived from comparative studies of regionalism in the European context (Gourevitch 1979), that the politically dominant blocs tend to be economic leaders as well. A corollary to this is that when relatively advantaged regions are out of power, they are likely to rival or push back against the incumbent regime: Such regions are likely to constitute a rival electoral bloc or an opposition-leaning zone. We use the data from Chapter 4 to propose a typology of four bloc types that are distinguished by where they stand in the national distribution of political and economic advantage.

The second argument, developed in Part 5.2, analyzes the formation of national winning electoral coalitions. Evidence from the 12-country study suggests that national electoral coalitions are built mainly via the ability of *incumbent blocs*[4] to mobilize electoral support among the weakly organized non-blocs. The most common alliance structure in the African countries examined here is alliances of the extremes (richest and poorest regions) against the middle. Similar patterns of alliance between rich and poor regions have been noted for countries cleaved by high spatial inequalities in other parts of the world. For Latin America, for example, Gibson (1997) and Gibson and Calvo (2000) argued that regionally segmented coalitional structures – one coalition based in a country's most prosperous region and the other based in its peripheral provinces – underpinned winning national electoral coalitions forged by long-lived ruling parties in Mexico and Argentina (by the PRI and the Peronist Party, respectively).

The chapter's conclusion argues that in African countries, this winning coalition structure reinforces regionalism by lowering coalitional pressures on government in policymaking. Rival blocs tend to be left out of the winning electoral coalition, and they rarely successfully ally with each other to challenge leading regions.

5.1 HIERARCHY AMONG THE BLOCS: BLOC DOMINANCE

Regional economic differences and economic inequalities are politically salient in African countries partially because they are so entrenched. Figure C.5 in

city of Harare, has not held an economic advantage (as measured by our GDP proxy, which is nighttime luminosity) over the non-bloc region since 1994.

[3] "Political advantage" is registered in percentage of time (% of elections) that the bloc is aligned with the winner in the 1990 to 2016 presidential elections. Politically dominant electoral blocs are defined as those that are aligned with the winner in at least half of the presidential elections between 1990 and 2016.

[4] Defined in operational terms below.

5.1 Hierarchy among the Blocs: Bloc Dominance

Appendix C captures the fact that, for most countries, they have remained very stable over time.[5] Across the 12 countries in this study, there is extraordinarily little movement in the relative ranking of blocs in terms of economic hierarchy (proxied by mean luminosity) and education scores over the course of the 1992–2013 period. In many or most cases, the same rankings have existed since the 1940s and 1950s. In Kenya, for example, the wealth disparity between colonial-era Central Province and all other Kenyan Admin1 regions may be as great now as it was in 1964, when the country became independent. At the same time, in Kenya and in the other countries studied here, there are significant populations living in regions that have been persistently marginal or lagging – economically, demographically, and in terms of natural endowment – over the course of many decades. In Cameroon, school enrollments in the North were one-quarter of those in the West, the former Anglophone region, in 1970. For the Far North of Cameroon today, there is a gap of almost exactly the same magnitude.[6] This phenomenon is also observed in other parts of the world. Regional economic disparities tend to persist even in spite of governments' attempts to support lagging regions through infusions of state-directed investment and regulatory supports.[7]

Persistence in the economic ranking of electoral blocs and oppositional zones is due largely to limited structural transformation of national economies since the 1950s, and to agglomeration factors that tend to reinforce the advantage of already-leading regions. Export agriculture and extractive sectors continue to predominate in most national economies. In most countries, the leading rural producer zones are sectorally differentiated (in terms of crop specializations, agrarian production systems, and marketing networks), geographically concentrated, and distributed unevenly in space. Over time, growth and forces of agglomeration have tended to favor already-leading predominantly rural regions vis-à-vis the lagging ones, as well as to favor primate cities and other urban agglomerations.

Gourevitch (1979: 306) sets the baseline expectation that economically leading blocs are also politically dominant ones, based on his study of the modal cases of regional alignment in European political development in the late nineteenth and early twentieth centuries. He defined the modal cases as countries in which the "political core" and the "economic core" coincide, such that the

---

[5] There is a stable economic hierarchy among the blocs (1992–2013), measured in terms of mean bloc luminosity and educational advantage. In Côte d'Ivoire, Eastern and Western switch places. In Tanzania, the CCM bloc rises above the non-blocs, and in Kenya, Eastern and the Rift Valley bloc switch places. In Zimbabwe, the non-blocs overtake both of the electoral blocs.

[6] Ndiva Kofele-Kale (1986: 59) and author's data.

[7] This conforms to what has been observed in US and EU settings since the 1970s, where investment and employment tend to be concentrated in the more advantaged regions. See McCann (2020) on the United Kingdom and Rodriguez-Pose (2018) on EU countries.

152   *Regional Hierarchies and Winning Coalitions*

country is "dominated politically and economically by the same region."[8] Do the African cases examined here evince the same generic pattern?

The electoral data suggest that this intuition does hold up for many of our 12-country cases. To test for the type of congruence that Gourevitch identifies in the African cases analyzed here, an inverted tree chart is presented in Figure 5.1. The first branching of the tree describes each electoral bloc and opposition-leaning region as either economically advantaged or disadvantaged vis-à-vis the non-bloc region of its country, proxied by each electoral bloc's luminosity measure in 1992.[9] Economically advantaged blocs are on the left branch, and those that are disadvantaged compared to the non-bloc region are on the right. Next, each branch subdivides to distinguish between blocs that are "in power" for half or more of the post-1990 period (i.e., incumbent or incumbent-aligned blocs) and those that are not. Operationally, "in power" is defined as aligned with the election winner in half or more of the national elections since 1990 (see Table F.1 in Appendix F). Calculations are made using the electoral data employed in Chapter 4.[10] This generates four bloc types:

I. Economically strong blocs that are also politically dominant blocs (stronghold of the winner or aligned with the winner in 50% or more of presidential elections since 1990).
II. Economically strong blocs that are almost never or never aligned with the national election winner (i.e., rival contender or opposition blocs).
III. Economically weak blocs that are sometimes aligned with the national winner (swing blocs) or always aligned with the winner.
IV. Economically weak blocs that are never in power (i.e., never aligned with the presidential election winner) from 1990 to 2016.

Figure 5.1 categorizes each of the blocs in terms of this conceptualization.[11] On the left half of the figure are the 22/37 blocs that are more economically developed than the non-bloc area of each country, measured by mean pixel luminosity in 1992. All of these have been economic leaders over the course of the period covered by the luminosity data, and indeed since the 1950s, if not before.

---

[8] Gourevitch (1979: 315). Gourevitch defines the political core as the region corresponding to the regional identity or regional base of the rulers, controlling common national institutions, and predominating in setting policy in key areas of state competence (defense, army, trade, taxation, police, bureaucracy). The economic core is the economically leading region, defined by Gourevitch (1979: 312) as the "industrial core." He seeks a model that will explain cross-national variation in the strength of peripheral nationalism.

[9] The luminosity measure is used as a rough proxy for regional GDP; the measure is average pixel luminosity.

[10] See Table B.2 in Appendix B on electoral data. There are 14 elections for which we can link electoral data to the blocs in a statistical analysis. The others are figured manually.

[11] This includes oppositional zones, which are considered to be a bloc subtype.

5.1 Hierarchy among the Blocs: Bloc Dominance

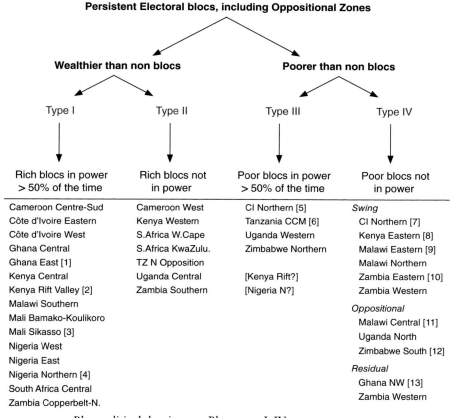

FIGURE 5.1 Bloc political dominance: Bloc types I–IV

NOTES: Wealth comparisons based upon average pixel luminosity (as of 1992) within blocs. "Rich blocs" are those with mean pixel luminosity that exceeds that of the non-blocs. "In power" means incumbent or incumbent-aligned in more than 50% of post-1990 elections for which we have data. "Political dominance" is based upon results summarized in Table F.1 in Appendix F. Notes provide additional information on the classification decisions.

[1] Ghana E bloc includes three constituencies within the Greater Accra region, but they are predominantly rural. The bloc as a whole is actually slightly below (but almost indistinguishable from) the non-bloc region in average pixel luminosity, but this may be affected by including the rest of Greater Accra (Accra Admin1) in the non-bloc area.

[2] Kenya's Rift bloc is barely in this "advantaged" category by mean pixel luminosity. In 1992, it is almost indistinguishable from the non-blocs. Average pixel luminosity tripled by 2013, but it is still only 10% of that of the Central bloc. It could also be considered a type III bloc as denoted by the bloc name in brackets in type III. Its average pixel luminosity was 1.25 of that of the non-blocs in 1992 and 1.9 of that of the non-blocs in 2013.

[3] Mali Sikasso is very marginally above the non-blocs in terms of mean pixel luminosity.

FIGURE 5.1 (Continued)

[4] Nigeria Northern bloc is barely advantaged compared to the non-blocs. Its mean pixel luminosity was 14% of that of Western bloc in 1992 and less than 10% of that of Western in 2013. However, its mean pixel luminosity was 1.6 and 1.2 of that of the non-blocs in 1992 and 2013, respectively. It could also be considered a marginal type III bloc.

[5] Côte d'Ivoire Northern incumbent after 2010.

[6] Tanzania CCM is borderline by luminosity.

[7] Côte d'Ivoire Northern is swing before 2010.

[8] Kenya Eastern: mean pixel luminosity surpasses that of non-blocs in 2010.

[9] Malawi Eastern: poor bloc aligns with winner 50% of the time.

[10] Zambia E: aligned with winner in 50% of elections.

[11] Malawi Central was poorer in mean pixel luminosity than the non-blocs in 1992. However, the disparities in Malawi are less extreme than in most of the 12 countries.

[12] Zimbabwe Southern: the southern Admins of Matabeleland N, Matabeleland S, Masvingo, and Manicaland voted en bloc for the opposition MDC in the first round of the 2008 elections. This is the poorest part of the country, a fact not captured well in bloc luminosity score because the bloc includes Bulawayo. I classified this bloc as type IV to reflect the non-Bulawayo part of the bloc.

[13] Ghana NW bloc always votes with Ghana Eastern bloc. However, with only 4 constituencies and a population of only 300,000 (2000), it cannot be considered a leading bloc. It is an anomaly. One would expect an electorally cohesive small bloc to swing.

Type I, the largest category, is comprised of 15 blocs that are *economically leading* and also *politically leading.*[12] The blocs are advantaged over the rural non-bloc regions in luminosity, population density, as producers of relatively high-value crops, and by having the largest absolute increases in luminosity since 1992.[13] Their relative economic advantage is traceable to the colonial period. They are also politically leading blocs, in the sense of having been aligned with the presidential winner in half or more of the presidential elections since 1992. Economic and political advantage thus align. Kenya's Central bloc is the archetype. It is an example of what Jean-François Bayart meant by regions as "drivers of national unity" (2013: 21).

---

[12] This is also the largest category when we use the luminosity measures for 2013. The overall findings hold for 2013 as well. For 2013, taking average luminosity rank as the proxy for relative level of economic development in that year for the 9 of the 12 countries (i.e., excluding Côte d'Ivoire, Mali, and South Africa; see below), blocs that won at the national level in more than half of the elections (N=14), had an average luminosity rank (2013) of 1.5. For blocs that won (at national level) in fewer than half of the elections (N=6), the average luminosity rank (2013) was 3. (See Table C.5 in Appendix C.) In Côte d'Ivoire, Mali, and South Africa, blocs in power for more than half of the time since 1995, 2002, or 1994, respectively, have also ranked first or second in terms of luminosity.

[13] All these blocs (except South Africa Center bloc) spatially overlap with a colonial-era producer region to a large extent (> 50%) and are still specialized in the corresponding crop ("type 1" producer profile). South Africa Central retains its historic producer profile ("type 3" producer profile).

5.1 Hierarchy among the Blocs: Bloc Dominance

Our cases thus generally conform to Gourevitch's default expectation at the bloc level and the country level. Congruence between the political and economic core is strong. This is a strong suggestion that, in the main, the patterns of national political consolidation are not so different from what historical evidence from other world regions would lead us to expect. Yet although spatial inequality is a strong predictor of patterns of political dominance in these African countries, the relationship is not deterministic. The presence of type II blocs attests to this.

Type II includes seven electoral blocs (including opposition-leaning zones).[14] These are economically advantaged blocs and regions that have almost never or never been aligned with the national winner in elections from 1990 to 2016. Here, there is weak or noncongruence between political core and economic core: An economically dynamic region is "left out" of national power. Gourevitch (1979: 306) argues explicitly that this may produce regional nationalism with or without ethnically distinct regional identities. Several of the type II blocs were out of power not only from the 1990s to 2016, but also from the 1960s. They are Kenya's Western bloc, South Africa's Western Cape, Zambia's Southern bloc, Cameroon's Western opposition region, Tanzania's Northern opposition region, and Uganda's Central opposition region. It is clear that zones of persistent oppositional politics have formed in rural regions of *relative economic advantage* compared to the non-bloc average, and even compared to some of the other electoral blocs. Uganda's Central bloc is a case in point: It is Uganda's wealthiest region by far, even when the city of Kampala is excluded from the calculations,[15] but it failed to capture national power in the 1960s and has been held at arm's length under the Museveni regime which came to power in 1986. This region cannot be said to have ever controlled the national government in postcolonial Uganda (see Chapter 6). In an analysis of Bolivia in the early 2000s, Eaton (2016: 387) suggests that the underrepresentation of a country's leading export-producing regions in national politics is a recipe for unstable politics, and this observation rings true here.

On the right half of Figure 5.1's inverted tree, there are 13 blocs that were ranked lower than the non-blocs in terms of luminosity in 1992.[16] Almost all were still disadvantaged by this measure in 2013 (see Table C.5 in Appendix C).

Type III blocs are the most anomalous from the perspective of Gourevitch's baseline hypothesis. These are the relatively disadvantaged blocs that have

---

[14] The oppositional zones are pure type II cases. They are defined by their anti-incumbent leanings (i.e., either voting against the incumbent, or returning weak majorities or mere pluralities for the incumbent in hegemonic party regimes).

[15] The total luminosity of the Central opposition-leaning region (minus Kampala) was 4 times that of the Western bloc in 2013 (24,000 vs. 5,600). Kampala itself accounts for about 30% of the luminosity of the Central opposition-leaning bloc.

[16] This includes the oppositional regions, which are considered to be a bloc subtype.

been the political base of the incumbent for all (or most) of the time period under review. As Gourevitch put it, "The nation builder and economic leader differ" (1979: 316). In these cases, there is a strong polarization between the holders of economic power and the holders of political power. Uganda under Museveni is a good example. It is a civilianized military regime that came to power through guerrilla war. Another clear case is Tanzania under the CCM. Gourevitch uses the term "revisionist coalition" (1979: 314–315) for political blocs that seek to undo or overturn a prevailing distribution of political and economic power. This term seems to apply in these cases. These are regimes that are "ruling from the periphery."

Type IV is the category that contains most of the economically disadvantaged blocs (with average 1992 pixel luminosity below that of the non-blocs). They have been nonincumbent for most of the period under review (i.e., aligned with the national winner in fewer than half of all the 1990–2016 elections for which we have data). They are economically weak and politically weak. Of these, four can be considered "swing regions." They are junior partners that have aligned with rival incumbents in the period under review: Northern bloc in Malawi, Eastern bloc in Kenya, Eastern bloc in Zambia, Northern Côte d'Ivoire. (Eastern bloc in Malawi either aligned with Southern or fronted its own candidate.) The remaining blocs are definitely marginalized: Western in Zambia, Southern in Zimbabwe, Northern in Uganda.

Some electoral blocs are indeed hard to subsume into this schema.[17] Northern Côte d'Ivoire is a type IV persistent electoral bloc that moves into the type III category in 2011, when Alassane Ouattara came to power.[18] This happens thanks (in part) to military action. But it also reflects the fact that Ouattara's base of support was widely diffused countrywide, in the form of a multiethnic internal diaspora of *originaires* from the North who became an economically leading stratum of landholders and business owners in Western Côte d'Ivoire. Côte d'Ivoire may thus hold clues to how internal migration can shift regional interests and balances of power, or even dilute regionalism.[19] Nigeria's Northern electoral bloc is also not easy to fit into these categories. It is very slightly advantaged in luminosity, our regional GDP proxy, relative to the non-blocs, but it falls far below Nigeria's other two persistent electoral blocs by this measure of economic strength.[20] Yet it has been "in power" (aligned with the winner) in 50% of the national elections considered here.

---

[17] In Mali, the Mopti bloc also has a higher mean bloc luminosity than that of the non-bloc area. From the electoral data, I could not determine whether it could be considered as "incumbent-aligned" for the three elections for which we had results. Eastern in Kenya is a "swing" bloc.

[18] See Banégas and Popineau 2021.

[19] Indeed, violent attempts to expel Northerners from Western Côte d'Ivoire (and annul their claims to be holders of property rights) in the electoral cycles of the 1990s were an explicit attempt to prevent this from happening.

[20] The nighttime luminosity measure controls for flaring of oil fields in Eastern Nigeria.

5.2 A Theory of National Electoral Coalitions

From this perspective, Nigeria's Northern bloc could be considered a type IV "revisionist" bloc, rather than a relatively advantaged incumbent: It has used the power of numbers (in population) to offset the power of the economically predominant South. This is indeed a classic interpretation of Nigeria's independence bargain, which ensured the populous North an electoral advantage over the far wealthier South.

Difficulty in fitting Malawi's Central bloc into the schema raises a related issue. Elections in our dataset go back only to the early 1990s. This lops off the preceding period, generating anomalies like depicting Central Malawi as a disadvantaged bloc never in power, when in fact it was the ruling bloc for 1964–1994.[21] For the 1964–1994 period, it could be described as a type III revisionist bloc. During this period, Hastings Kamuzu Banda was in power and sought to elevate the Central bloc to a position of national economic as well as political preeminence (see Chapter 6). Yet in 1994, Banda and the Central electoral bloc that was aligned most closely with his regime lost power in Malawi's first election of the multiparty era. For 1994–2016, Malawi's Central bloc is an electoral bloc that is both out of power and less wealthy (as registered in nighttime luminosity) than the non-bloc regions of Malawi (see Chapter 6).

5.2 A THEORY OF NATIONAL ELECTORAL COALITIONS IN AFRICAN COUNTRIES

Taking the persistent electoral blocs as the starting point for analysis, we can combine the disaggregated electoral data with data on regional economic heterogeneity to test theories of national coalition structure.

Melissa Rogers' (2016: 172) analysis of coalition-building in "regionally unequal countries" shows that winning parties build national coalitions by taking advantage of interest heterogeneity across regions, regional disparities, and the overrepresentation in national legislatures of the least populous provinces. Politically leading regions often align with hinterland regions to build national electoral majorities. Work on agrarian and semi-agrarian developing countries in different world regions provides concrete instantiation of this. Gibson and Calvo (2000) argue that in countries with competitive electoral systems and strong regional inequalities, *economically dominant* regions often align with the *poorest regions* against the middle-income regions.[22] They offer Argentina and Mexico as cases in point. Brazil was characterized by Guillermo O'Donnell in the same terms. Writing about Sri Lanka, Mick Moore (1997) observed the same alliance structure in the 1980s and 1990s: The wealthier, core constituencies of the incumbent provide the party's organizational and

---

[21] Even so, after 30 years in power, the mean pixel luminosity of Central bloc in Malawi did not exceed that of the non-blocs. Many of the Lilongwe constituencies are not members of the persistent electoral bloc.

[22] See also Gibson (2004), Chhibber and Kollman (2004), and Diaz-Cayeros (2006).

158 *Regional Hierarchies and Winning Coalitions*

ideological base and are beneficiaries of regime policy, while the much poorer, "peripheral component" of the ruling coalition provides a vote reservoir in exchange for patronage.[23]

For the 12 African countries studied here, a breakdown of the distribution of the winning party's national vote across the electoral blocs and the non-bloc regions reveals a strong pattern. Politically leading regions tend to align with non-blocs to win national elections, rather than to combine with other blocs (Table 5.1).[24] This is consistent with what scholars have found in regionally unequal developing countries in other parts of the world.

A politically dominant bloc in combination with the non-bloc part of the country emerges as the dominant type of winning coalition in most presidential elections in most countries in our sample. In 28 of the 40 elections for which we have enough data to make the call (i.e., the elections listed in Table 5.1), the winning party gains 70% or more of its total votes from the electoral bloc most closely associated with the presidential candidate (the president's "home region") plus the non-blocs (Table 5.1).[25] That is about 72% of the elections for which we can make a call. Raising the threshold to 80% of all votes coming from the winner's regional stronghold plus the non-bloc constituencies, the pattern remains strong. At this high cutoff point, at least 16 of 40 elections, over 40% of those for which we can make the call, fit the pattern.[26]

This pattern is clear in Kenya.[27] In four of five fiercely contested elections held between 1992 and 2013, the winning party has gathered over 70% of its total votes from the (multiethnic) "home bloc" of the presidential candidate and

---

[23] Munro (2001) makes a similar argument for South Africa in the late 1990s, arguing that the pattern was like the one observed by Moore (1997) for Sri Lanka. See Boone and Wahman 2015.

[24] This pattern holds for 11 of the 15 elections we consider for Kenya, Malawi, and Zambia.

[25] The analysis considers election results for 48 elections across the 12 countries (Table B.2 in Appendix B). Six of those do not appear in Table 5.1 because we could not confidently report enough of the necessary information (i.e., Mali 2007R1, Nigeria 1999, Tanzania 1995 and 2005, Uganda 2006, and Zimbabwe 2002R1). Côte d'Ivoire 2010 appears twice; both parties claimed to have won this election. For the five South Africa elections, estimates were made as follows: Over the last five elections, the ANC has gathered 62–72% of all its votes from the Center bloc (which excludes the metropolitan core). About 10–12% of the ANC's national vote appears to come from the non-bloc district councils of KZN – that is, Ugu, Harry Gwala, uMgungundlovu, iLembe, and eThekwini (metro Durban), all returning high vote shares for the ANC. (eThekwini is the most competitive of these. Here, ANC shares are 62%, 64%, and 60% of all votes over the last three elections.) By this calculation, all five South Africa elections cross the 70% threshold used in the test above, by a wide margin, with at least two approaching 80%.

[26] Malawi is an important exception. In three of the four elections considered here, the incumbent depended on a swing region to build a national coalition. Also noteworthy is that in Tanzania in 2010, Malawi 2014, and Côte d'Ivoire's flawed 2010 election, most of the winner's votes came from non-bloc constituencies, not what we would consider as the winner's party's "home region" or electoral stronghold.

[27] See Boone and Wahman (2015) and Wahman and Boone (2018).

TABLE 5.1 *National winning coalitions: Winner bloc plus non-blocs*

Country	Election year	Winning party/ candidate/ bloc	Share of winner's votes from the following:			Vote share >70%	Remaining votes from bloc (%):	Notes
			Electoral stronghold (home) bloc	Non-bloc	Stronghold (home) bloc + non-bloc			
Cameroon	1992	Biya/RDPC	49	46	85.6	Yes	W (14)	
	2004	Biya/RDPC	27	49	76.5	Yes	W (23)	
	2011	Biya/RDPC	24	48	73.75	Yes	W (26)	
Côte d'Ivoire	2010	Gbagbo/FPI	~20%	74	94	Yes		1
	2010	Ouattara votes	~25%	~65	~80	Yes		2
Ghana	1996	NDC	21	45	66	No	Central (20), Accra (~10)	
	2000	NPP	43	40	83	Yes	Accra (~10)	
	2004	NPP	44	39	83	Yes	Accra (~10)	
	2008	NDC	20	47	67	No	Central (~19), Accra (~10)	
	2012	NDC	18	50	68	No	Central (~21), Accra (~10)	
	2016	NPP	42	43	85	Yes	Accra (~10)	
Kenya	1992	Moi/Kanu	30.4	50.8	81.2	Yes	E (8.2)	
	1997	Moi/Kanu	31.3	45.4	76.7	Yes	Central (8.8)	
	2002	Kibaki	28	30.9	58.9	No	W (18.6)	
	2007	Kibaki	56.8	31	87.8	Yes	Rift (5.2)	
	2013	Central	42.2	33.8	76	Yes	Rift (19.2)	
Malawi	1999	S'rn bloc	26.2	39	65.2	No	E (17.1)	
	2004	S'rn bloc	24.6	41.4	66	No	E (13.2)	
	2009	S'rn bloc	23.2	38.7	61.9	No	N (16.6)	
	2014	S'rn bloc	34.1	46.2	80.3	Yes		
Mali	2002	ATT	25.9	27.7	53.6	No	Bamako-K. (23.7)	
	2013 R1	IBK/RPM	52.8	26	78.8	Yes	Sikasso (12%)	3
Nigeria	2003	PDP	18.4 (N)	37.3	55.7	No	E (34)	
	2007	PDP	29.5 (N)	26.9	[61.6]	No	E (34)	4
	2011	PDP	49.3 (E)	27.1	76.4	Yes	N (17.4)	
	2015	APC	53.8 (N)	33.5	87.3	Yes	W (8)	

(continued)

TABLE 5.1 *(continued)*

Country	Election year	Winning party/ candidate/ bloc	Share of winner's votes from the following:			Vote share >70%	Remaining votes from bloc (%):	Notes
			Electoral stronghold (home) bloc	Non-bloc	Stronghold (home) bloc + non-bloc			
South Africa	1994	ANC	71.9	[10]	>80	Yes		5
	1999	ANC	70.5	[11]	>80	Yes		5
	2004	ANC	69.1	[12]	>75	Yes		5
	2009	ANC	65.6	[19.3]	>75	Yes		5
	2014	ANC	62.4	[22]	>75	Yes		5
Tanzania	2010	CCM	20.1	38.7	59.68	No	N'rn opposition (32.8)	
Uganda	2001	NRM	29.7	44	73.7	Yes	Central opposit. (22)	6
	2011	NRM	27.9	58.8	86.7	Yes		
	2016	NRM	26.3	60.7	87	Yes		
Zambia	1991	MMD, Chiluba	55	28.7	83.7	Yes		
	1996	MMD, Chiluba	43.7	29.5	73.2	Yes		
	2001	MMD,	47.9	29.1	77	Yes		
	2006	PF Sata	24.6	41.4	66	No	E (13.7), W (12.8)	
	2011	PF Sata	58.1	31	89.1	Yes	E (17.4)	
	2016	PF Sata	42.8	34.4	77.2	Yes	E (17.9)	
Zimbabwe	2008 R1	MCD	11.5	58.9	70.4	Yes		7
	2013	ZANU PF	32.7	55.7	88.4	Yes		

[1] Provisional results, reported at Admin2 level. Gbagbo/FPI did not win this election. Ouattara's votes were disqualified for Gbagbo to be declared the winner. These results did not stand.

[2] Provisional results, reported at Admin2. Disputed election.

[3] For 2002, the Mopti bloc is considered to be ATT's stronghold region. Bamako-K = Bamako–Koulikoro bloc. The regional base of IBK, the RPM candidate in 2013, is considered to be Bamako–Koulikoro. We do not have absolute vote counts for 2007 to test H12.

[4] Flawed election.

[5] Vote share in brackets in Col. 5 refers to votes from the non-bloc districts in KZN.

[6] Based on 2001 district results, with districts categorized as bloc or non-bloc units based on a 2010 district map (UGA_admin2.shp). Support for NRM for 2001 by former Admin region (not electoral blocs) is W, 26.5%; E. 16.79%; Central, 29.03%; N., 17.5%.

[7] ZANU PF's votes were 32% from the N bloc, 5% from the S bloc, and 57.2% from the non-bloc.

5.2 A Theory of National Electoral Coalitions

the non-bloc constituencies. In 1992, 81% of Moi's votes came from the Rift Valley electoral bloc plus the non-bloc parts of the country. In 2007, 88% of Uhuru Kenyatta's vote came from the Central electoral bloc plus the non-blocs. The exception was the turnover election of 2002, where the "winner's electoral bloc plus non-bloc" combination generated only 59% of winner Mwai Kibaki's total votes. In that election, 40% of the votes in the national winning coalition that ousted Daniel arap Moi came from Kenya's other persistent electoral blocs.

Strong economic inequality characterizes the modal alliance structure. Abdul-Garfaru Abdulai (2017) wrote that winning majorities in Ghana are coalitions of areas with "a strong bimodal distribution of GNP per capita," and this appears to be typical of the elections studied here. Most persistent electoral blocs that capture the presidency repeatedly (i.e., most of the time since 1990) are economically leading regions.[28] Of the politically and economically leading blocs for which we have the data to estimate a result, 8 of the 12 blocs win national elections by gathering votes from the non-bloc areas of the country, rather than by aligning with other blocs.[29] At the national level, this describes the national-level pattern in Cameroon, Côte d'Ivoire (2010, R1), Ghana, Kenya, Zambia, and South Africa.

Such strongly asymmetric alliance structures between richer, politically leading blocs and non-bloc constituencies can be called "coalitions by cooptation" (Wahman & Boone 2018) that create national majorities in presidential elections. Coalitions by cooptation *with non-bloc constituencies* appear to be the dominant pattern – that is, the dominant type of national winning electoral coalition – in the cases surveyed here. There are indeed a few cases of durable coalitions by cooptation *between persistent electoral blocs*. These are coalitions between a leading and a less wealthy electoral bloc. One example is Côte d'Ivoire under Félix Houphouët-Boigny. A strong and stable coalition between Côte d'Ivoire's wealthy Eastern bloc (the incumbent bloc) and the lagging Northern bloc underpinned regime hegemony for three decades, from the 1960s to the 1980s.[30] Western Côte d'Ivoire – the middle region in terms of economic ranking – was frozen out of power. Collapse of this alliance in 1992 turned the Northern bloc into a true swing bloc for a few brief years in the first

---

[28] In the sense that they are advantaged compared to the non-bloc part of the country.

[29] These eight are Côte d'Ivoire Western bloc (2010 only), Cameroon Centre-Sud, Ghana Central, Ghana Eastern, Kenya Central, Kenya Rift Valley, Zambia Copperbelt Northern, South Africa Central. See Table 5.1. The exceptions are Southern bloc in Malawi, which has allied with other blocs to win in three of the four elections for which we have data. For the Nigeria blocs, see below.

[30] Mali may also be a version of such a model. The Bamako–Koulikoro and Sikasso blocs appear to usually pull in the same direction, electorally. This could be seen as a durable alliance between a dominant bloc (which contains the capital city, in this case) and a producer region. By contrast, there appears to be a distinctive pull in opposite directions between most of the South and the northern regions of Mopti–Tombouktou–Gao (and Kidal), depicted as the Mopti bloc in Figure 4.4. (On Mali electoral data, see Appendix B, Table B.2 and Section B.4.)

162   *Regional Hierarchies and Winning Coalitions*

half of the decade, when each of the two leading blocs vied for alliances and voters (Boone 2007).

Explaining "Coalitions by Cooptation"

Three convergent and complementary lines of theorizing in political science offer possible explanations for the "coalitions by cooptation" alliance structure. First are minimum-winning coalition theories that highlight the strategic logic of forging (minimum) winning coalitions with "cheap" coalition partners who are in a weak position to demand programmatic concessions, or costly policy or economic payoffs. Incentives for this kind of coalition-building are amplified by malapportionment, which raises the electoral value of poor, sparsely populated regions.[31] In our cases, these poor and sparsely populated territories tend to be concentrated in the non-bloc category. They are favored by malapportionment (Boone & Wahman 2018). This is what Rogers' (2016) general theory would lead us to expect.

Second is a line of coalition theory that focuses on policy coalitions, and policy competition among sectorally based interest groups. Applied to the African context, Eun Kyung Kim (2017, 2018, 2020) shows that in Kenya, Zambia, and Ghana, electoral/party coalitions (1) respond to strong, regionally specific sectoral interests, and that (2) to build national coalitions, they mobilize the electoral support of "unattached voters" – that is, voters who are not aligned with the sectoral or ethnic affiliations of the party's core supporters, or with those of its main partisan rival (Kim 2020: 368). Kim argues that incumbents elicit the support of such voters, who would be concentrated in what I call non-bloc constituencies, through strategic targeting of clientelistic individual or club goods (see also Hern 2020). The findings here suggest that this logic can be transposed from the individual level, where Kim's analysis operates, to the constituency level, and to national-level coalition-building. Such an argument was advanced by Edward Gibson, who argued that in Argentina and Mexico in the 1990s and 2000s, "policy blocs" were composed of the economically leading interests and social groups that were the major beneficiaries of the government's economic policy orientation aligned with poorer, peripheral regions that benefited from government patronage, rather than policy. The poorer, marginal regions provided the electoral weight necessary for victory in national elections (see also Mick Moore on Sri Lanka).

Third is Guillermo O'Donnell's theory of the structural role that "brown areas" (i.e., regions where the level of quality of democracy is low, compared to "blue areas" marked by strong civil society and civic associations) can play

---

[31] See Eaton (2001), Boone and Wahman (2015), and Rogers (2016: 53). Regional representation rules can also play a role. Examples are Kenya's pre-2010 rule, whereby the winner must gain at least 25% of the vote in five of the seven provinces (or post-2010, at least 25% in at least 24 of the 47 counties), and Nigeria's rule by which the winner must gain at least 25% of the votes in two-thirds of Nigeria's 36 states.

5.2 A Theory of National Electoral Coalitions

in democracies in which the quality of citizenship varies across space. The poorest and least politically organized rural areas can provide easily controllable vote reservoirs for electoral authoritarian regimes. Mai Hassan provided an example of this in a study of the 2007 Kenya election. She argued that the incumbent PNU regime used the Provincial Administration in the 2007 election to bully and intimidate voters, and to facilitate "vote rigging" in "nonaligned constituencies" that were neither PNU nor opposition party (ODM) strongholds (Hassan 2015: 596; 2020: 217–220).

Alternative Patterns: Unstable Alliances *between* Electoral Blocs

An alternative pattern is the alliance between nonincumbent blocs, or *contender blocs* (Wahman & Boone 2018). These consist of two persistent electoral blocs that ally with *each other* to challenge an incumbent bloc. These are not very common and are typically one-off alliances, as the comparative politics literature on "opposition party fragmentation" in African countries suggests.[32] In our dataset, there are some spectacular one-off instances of electoral alliances among contender blocs. These are the grand opposition alliances that overturned one-party states in the multiparty elections of the 1990s in Malawi and Zambia, and in Kenya in 2002. Another successful case of "coalition by alliance of contender blocs" is Malawi 2020, where the Northern bloc voted with Central to overturn the long-time Southern-based incumbent. Eastern Ghana and Northwestern Ghana offer another possible example of a long-standing "coalition by alliance" – the alliance endures over time as the Eastern bloc has cycled in and out of incumbency.

There are some one-off cross-bloc coalitions involving an incumbent-aligned bloc and a *swing bloc*. Some politically dominant blocs (i.e., aligned with the presidential winner in at least half the elections since 1990) align with other blocs to win, but not always with the same one. Malawi is an example of an incumbent bloc involving the swing blocs. Malawi's two secondary blocs are Northern and Eastern. In all elections over the last three decades, they have "swung" their support between one of the two main contenders.

Nigeria is often taken in the African politics literature as the archetypical case of regionalism in national electoral competition, but its alliance structure does not fit the modal pattern that emerges in the other country cases examined here. Many have described Nigeria's North and West as persistently aligned against the oil-rich East, whose wealth sustains the national federation as a whole. The wealthy Western bloc has been aligned with the national winner in 100% of the elections for which we have data, and by this measure, it would be considered politically dominant. The economically lagging Northern bloc, rich in population and social cohesion if not in luminosity or education, has traditionally allied with the West to win. Since the 1990s, it has been with the

---

[32] On the syndrome of opposition fragmentation, Wahman 2017.

national winner in 60% of the elections in our dataset. By this reading, the 2010–2015 presidency of Goodluck Jonathan (preceded by his vice presidency from 2007 to 2010), an Easterner, was an anomaly. In Nigeria's 2015 election, Nigeria's Northern and much of the Western bloc (plus Lagos State) coalesced against the Eastern bloc to oust Goodluck Jonathan and elect Muhammadu Buhari, and the dominant pattern reasserted itself. The equilibrium pattern may well be one in which a wealthy core (the West) aligns with the poor periphery (the North) as electoral ballast, in this case in exchange for concessions, such as the North's regional "special status" under Sharia law. Eastern Nigeria put up a strong showing in the 2023 elections. Perhaps a longer time horizon will reveal an unstable pattern arising from a situation in which the regional locus of "political and economic dominance" cannot be unambiguously defined. In Nigeria, the North has wealth in population, the East is wealthy in natural resources, and the West is wealthy in private capital – each possesses a *richesse* by which it outshines the others.

5.3 CONSIDERING GAP MAGNITUDE

Table F.2 in Appendix F considers variation in the *degree of economic dominance* of the leading region in each country. Sticking with nighttime luminosity as the GDP proxy, we can look at the size of the economic gap between the two most important electoral blocs in 2013. This invites further speculation and hypothesis-generating about how asymmetries in economic clout can shape the political balance of power. One prediction is that where there is greater balance in the distribution of economic clout between the top two blocs, the more likely it is that there will be *political alternance* (trading places, or electoral turnover) between the two. This seems to be true for Côte d'Ivoire's Eastern and Western blocs, where there is indeed *alternance*, and for Ghana's Central bloc and Eastern bloc. Côte d'Ivoire and Ghana figure as two of the four "most symmetric" countries – that is, with the smallest gap between leading blocs as measured in terms of nighttime luminosity.[33] South Africa and Zambia are also in this group: They are among four countries in which the distribution of economic development across the two leading blocs, proxied by the nighttime luminosity measure, is *least* asymmetric in 2013. In Malawi, Central and Southern could be considered rather closely matched (when both are compared to the non-blocs, and given that Malawi's overall measure of cross-regional inequality is one of the lowest in the 12-country sample).[34] There was no

---

[33] Western and Centre-Sud in Cameroon can also be considered to be somewhat matched, in the sense that both are strongly advantaged in terms of luminosity compared to the non-blocs, although in Cameroon there has obviously been no *alternance*. The intuition captured in the hypothesis does resonate in the Cameroon case, however: The economic weight of the western Anglophone region is invoked consistently in support of regional claims for more political power. The West has capacity to advance claims against the Centre-Sud, if not to prevail.

[34] See Figure 1.1.

Conclusion: The Modal Coalitional Structure

electoral *alternance* in Malawi and Zambia during the time period covered by the electoral data used here (which ended in 2016), but there was indeed turnover in both countries in 2020 and 2021, respectively.

As a thought experiment, consider an economically determinist, *real politic* or "balance of power" notion of regional politics. This might suggest that in the long run (over decades), where there is more economic *in*equality between blocs, *alternance* is less likely. We would predict that the Central bloc of Kenya would dominate Kenyan politics. And indeed it has for most of the postcolonial period. Viewed in this way, Daniel arap Moi's presidency in Kenya from 1979 to 2002 would be an "unlikely" (not predicted) outcome, given that Moi represented the Rift Valley bloc, a stronghold that is far less advantaged by all measures of economic development (as well as total population) than the Central bloc stronghold of both his predecessor and his successor.[35] Other mismatches between what an economically determinist theory would predict and actual outcomes are visible in the type III cases: Uganda West, Côte d'Ivoire North, Zimbabwe North, CCM in Tanzania. Côte d'Ivoire North and the Tanzania CCM bloc have neither population advantage nor economic advantage over the rival bloc(s). Centre-Sud bloc in Cameroon, although itself advantaged over the non-bloc part of the country, is another case of the domestic use of force to dominate or overpower an economically advantaged region (the Cameroonian West). Nigeria's civil war, which crushed the secessionist Eastern region (Biafra), is another case of the use of military force to offset the power of an economically strong region.

CONCLUSION: THE MODAL COALITIONAL STRUCTURE CONTRIBUTES TO REGIONALISM

The structure of the modal winning coalitions may work to reinforce the political–economic asymmetries that fuel regionalism by lowering coalitional pressures on government in policymaking. In the dominant mode, coalitions by cooptation, coalition pressures on government are low. The "electoral ballast" provided by very poor and, in most cases, politically unorganized, non-bloc regions can be bought fairly cheaply through top-down patronage transfers and cooptation of regional elites. Political scientists' characterizations of elections as low in issue salience and high in one-off clientelistic electioneering may best apply in these places – that is, in parts of each country that are made up of non-bloc constituencies. Within persistent electoral blocs, by contrast, electorates are more organized, demanding, and anchored in policy interests, including interests in sectoral policies that promote the specialized needs of regional economies.

---

[35] Total population of the Rift Valley bloc in 2000 was 3.68 million, just over half of Central bloc's 7.3 million. Western bloc's population in 2000 was 4.3 million.

When national winning coalitions *are* built by long-term alliance between persistent electoral blocs (e.g., Eastern and Northern Côte d'Ivoire under Houphouët-Boigny, 1960–1990), concessions that work to reduce the asymmetry of policymaking may prevail. Persistent alliances may lead to more concessions, or more institutionalized concessions, such as Houphouët-Boigny's agreement to respect prevailing forms of neocustomary land tenure in the North, and to target the North for large-scale development projects in agriculture and agro-processing.[36] Yet insofar as regional political leaders are incentivized to maintain electoral bloc coherence, the underlying regional template of policy bargaining may be maintained. This may also play into regionalism, as bloc leaders and voters may be better off if the bargaining power of the bloc as a political collectivity is maintained.

Cheeseman and Ford (2007: 2) speculated that an emergent pattern in national-level voting in African countries was the coalescing of large, dominant multiethnic winning coalitions at the expense of excluded ethno-regional groups. This squares with the argument advanced here. By mapping the coalition structure that Cheeseman and Ford describe, the analysis here takes us several steps forward. Mapping reveals the spatial structure of the vote, showing how it aligns with socioeconomic inequality and sectoral differentiation. We see persistent territorial oppositions among electoral blocs, as well as coalitions between leading and lagging groups that produce electoral victories at the national level. The politically dominant electoral blocs and persistently opposition-leaning regions are distinctive – they tend to be more economically developed, better educated, to have higher population densities, and have long histories of deep incorporation into national economies, dating to the 1930s and 1940s, if not before. There are a few notable exceptions in which a poor region dominates national political life for decades, as in the case of Tanzania's CCM bloc, but such exceptions defy a pattern that is considerably more prevalent (see Chapter 6). Politically dominant blocs tend to stay in power by winning votes in non-bloc constituencies, rather than by entering into long-term alliances with other electoral blocs.

As shown in Chapter 4, the non-bloc constituencies lie in the large swaths of each country in which cohesive voting clusters *do not emerge*. Non-bloc regions are the predominantly rural regions of each country in which constituencies do *not* cluster in predictable, cohesive electoral blocs. Most non-bloc regions are poorer, less educated, and less specialized in the production of high-value crops than the predominantly rural constituencies that coalesce into persistent electoral blocs and oppositional zones. Non-bloc constituencies are highly likely to provide the vote reservoirs that incumbents need to win national elections.

Many of the persistent electoral blocs are based on stable multiethnic coalitions. This suggests that the common assumption in the literature on African

---

[36] See Woods (1990) and Boone (2007).

Conclusion: The Modal Coalitional Structure

politics that multiethnic alliances are unstable does not apply as a blanket rule. Rather, the observation about instability appears to describe most alliances *among* persistent multiethnic blocs. In most countries, these are rare or one-off. The argument about unstable alliances also applies to the one-off electoral alliances between dominant blocs and constituencies in non-bloc regions. These are common and are indeed shifting in nature. It may well be that these forms of instability are fostered by nationally dominant political actors. Incumbents clearly do work to disrupt coordination among contender blocs (regions), as well as the crystallization of rival blocs. They employ divide-and-rule tactics, successfully coopting one bloc or another, and use carrot-and-stick tactics to disorganize non-bloc and opposition-leaning regions. Many observers of African politics have emphasized such divide-and-rule tactics, usually applying the argument generically to describe competition among ethnic groups. The analysis here suggests that such tactics operate unevenly across space, playing upon regional economic inequalities and disparities in national economic standing.[37]

---

[37] Kent Eaton (2016) made a similar argument for Bolivia, where Evo Morales in the 2000s successfully used a combination of economic concessions and political sanctions to disrupt the formation of an eastern regionalist party that could rival the dominance of the ruling Movimiento al Socialismo (MAS).

6

Territorial Oppositions in African Politics

> The early growth of national states and bureaucracies produced mainly territorial oppositions.
>
> Caramani 2004: 29

Chapters 4 and 5 focused on persistent electoral blocs and the regional bloc hierarchies that underpin national winning electoral coalitions. This chapter considers the structure of territorial cleavage from the national perspective. It examines how a country's leading blocs may align vis-à-vis each other to produce strong axes of territorial cleavage that persist over the course of many decades.

Persistent polarities between two leading blocs are visible in many of the countries in the 12-country study. I argue here that such patterns of regional competition and polarization are isomorphic to those described by Lipset and Rokkan (1967) and others as characteristic of countries in the early stages of national state-building and national market integration.[1] A broader implication is that territorial oppositions that arise in African countries are often understandable in terms of theories that have been invoked to explain sectionalism in other parts of the world. These generic patterns have common roots: uneven regional development, including strong agglomeration forces that tend to favor already advantaged regions; power struggles over political consolidation and the growth of national bureaucracy; and the institutional design of power relations between the national and local state (the distribution of powers). Ethnic identities that have featured prominently in much political science writing on African politics are forged in these contexts; their political meaning

---

[1] Like other critics of 1960s' modernization theories, I do not embrace the teleologies that motivated and informed these theories.

Territorial Oppositions in African Politics

is defined in relation to interregional inequalities and uneven development. They do not, in themselves, constitute an explanatory force that can trump or operate independently of these deeper, more structural drivers of national-level political competition, especially in an analysis that spans decades and is pitched at the national level.

Territorial cleavage structures in African countries take forms that are structurally analogous to those observed in many non-African developing countries. In their classic work on territorial oppositions in national politics, Lipset and Rokkan (1967: 41) identified three types of core–periphery cleavage: the dominant (or core) region versus the periphery, the leading region versus a "growth region" in the provinces, and competition between "rival cores."[2] These differ according to the nature and degree of dominance of the economically leading region vis-à-vis regional contenders. This chapter proposes Kenya, Zambia, and Malawi as archetypes of each of these three forms. Gourevitch (1979) suggested a fourth type, in which the regional base of the incumbent regime is a *lagging* region. The lagging region provides the regional base for a "revisionist regime" that is able to exclude a wealthy region from political power.[3] Here I take Uganda under Museveni as an example of a revisionist regime that defines just such an axis of territorial opposition.

Visual depictions of electoral blocs' relative position within the national economy help tell the story of regional inequalities and territorial oppositions. The chapter includes country-level scatterplots that plot each bloc's GDP proxy (average pixel nighttime luminosity) on the vertical axis, and average levels of educational achievement on the horizontal axis (Figures 6.1 through 6.4). Color-coding distinguishes the economically leading bloc from the second most-advantaged electoral bloc in each country. The axis dividing the two is the line of "territorial opposition" that I emphasize in the case studies in this chapter. The scatterplots also enable rough, cross-country comparison of the magnitude of the economic inequalities among blocs.

Following Bensel (1984: 4–6), I take *consistency of the shape* of sectional cleavage across diverse policy issues and over time as evidence of sectionalism that is rooted in functional differences and economic inequalities across regions. In the case studies examined here, the cleavage between two opposed regional blocs defines competition around issues spanning multiple policy areas over many decades.

Parts 6.1–6.4 of this chapter consider each of the four country cases as archetypes. The conclusion extends the argument to the other countries in the 12-country study.

---

[2] A similar conceptualization is Locke's (1995) tripartite distinction between national coalitional structures that are unipolar, or marked by a single, clearly dominant party or region; polarized between two contender blocs; or multipolar in structure, with no clearly dominant party or region.
[3] Gourevitch (1979) distinguishes between politically leading and economically leading regions.

6.1 "OPPOSITION BETWEEN THE LEADING REGION AND POORER PERIPHERY": KENYA

Kenya fits the classic pattern of territorial opposition in which a country's economically advanced areas are pitted against politically mobilized parts of the poorer periphery.[4] Political and economic dominance coincide in a strong core region that exercises hegemony as a self-designated "nation building region" (Gourevitch 1979: 313). National politics revolves around a very strong juxtaposition between this dynamic center and "regions that remain inferior in income and growth" (ibid).

Spatial inequalities in Kenya are among the highest of the countries featured in this study. There is a steep concentration of national wealth and economic production in the Central region, and roughly coterminous with the Central persistent electoral bloc. It is adjacent to Nairobi and, together with the capital city, it forms a powerhouse which contributed an estimated 60% of Kenya's GNP in 2018 (Kerosi 2018; Wankuru 2019). The economic lead of Kenya's Central region is reflected at the micro level in its lead over the other blocs, and over the national average, in education, health indicators, and DHS asset and consumption scores, and at the aggregate level in regional GDP (as proxied by nighttime luminosity).

Export crop production (coffee, tea, pyrethrum), first by colonial settlers and then by African smallholders from the late 1940s, food production for Nairobi markets, and wage employment in agriculture, government service, and the service sector have generated the wealth of households in this region. Its rural populations hold a lead over those in other parts of Kenya that dates to the 1920s. Commercial agriculture in Kenya's colonial-era Central Province created dense networks of associational life rooted inter alia in producer associations and schools, and a broad base of prosperity that boosted living standards and education levels relative to the rest of Kenya.

Historically, the Central region has been at the leading edge of economic development, education, proto-nationalism in Kenya, the internal diaspora, and both the radical and moderate wings of the nationalist struggle. It was the electoral stronghold of the country's founding president, Jomo Kenyatta, who ruled from 1963 to his death in 1979. Kenyatta commanded a political party, the Kenya African National Union (KANU), that traced its lineage as the vehicle of the interests of Central Province's cash crop peasantry and petty bourgeoisie to precursor organizations in the 1920s and 1930s. A successor party to KANU reclaimed power in 2002, passing the presidency to Jomo Kenyatta's son, Uhuru, in 2013, who retained this position until 2022. The

---

[4] For Gourevitch (1979: 311) and Lipset and Rokkan (1967: 41, 43), France was the paradigm. Paris was the archetypal case of a region "without serious competitor for economic, political, and cultural power ... There was no basis for durable alliances against the center" (Lipset & Rokkan 1967: 43).

6.1 Leading Region and Poorer Periphery: Kenya

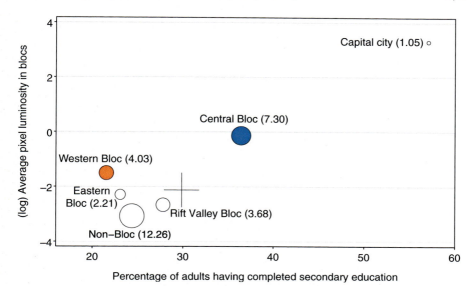

FIGURE 6.1 Kenya electoral blocs, disparities in regional GDP proxy and education
Notes: X-axis is average pixel luminosity in 2000, a rough proxy for regional GDP. Y-axis is percentage of adults having completed secondary school, from the pooled DHS data. Country averages, denoted by the cross, include the capital city. Circle size denotes population size (numbers reported in millions of persons).

Central region, corresponding with the colonial-era Admin1 that included the flanking districts of Embu and Meru, has been the electoral base of the country's ruling clique for 40 of the 60 years of Kenya's independence.

The huge advantage of the persistent Central bloc in Kenya relative to the other predominant rural electoral blocs in the 2000s is captured in Figure 6.1.[5] The economically leading Central electoral bloc (depicted in dark blue) is considerably advantaged over the next most-advantaged electoral bloc, Western (depicted in red), and also strongly advantaged over the non-blocs region. The bloc depicted in dark blue is also the politically leading region of Kenya. Kenya's capital city of Nairobi is far and away the richest part of the country. It displays constituency-level voting patterns that are typical of the capital-city non-bloc regions in this study – electoral results are highly heterogeneous across the Nairobi constituencies.

Since the 1960s, there has been a strong and persistent axis of territorial opposition between Central region and Western region. This appears in the post-1990 electoral data as the juxtapositioning of the Central and Western electoral blocs. Rift Valley leaders and constituencies have also been locked in a bitter standoff over land and territory with leaders of central Kenya since

---

[5] Earlier versions of Figures 6.1–6.3 appeared in Boone, Wahman, Kyburz, and Linke, 2022.

the decolonization era. This cleavage was sublimated and defused within the Kenyatta regime's one-party state in the early postcolonial decades, and later, for a second time, in a tense electoral alliance with the Central bloc in 2013–2017 (the Jubilee Alliance).[6]

The Western electoral bloc spans much of the colonial-era Western Province, which was divided in 1962 into Nyanza and Western Provinces. Of the 20 poorest electoral constituencies in Kenya in 2008, 14 are located in these two provinces.[7] Measured by individual- and household-level indicators, including secondary school completion rates, its lagging status vis-à-vis the Central electoral bloc is stark (Figure 6.1).[8] The regional GPD proxy measure is little more than half of Central's. This position of structural disadvantage relative to the Central region has been pronounced since the 1920s and 1930s. Under colonialism and until the 2000s, household economies of western Kenya have relied heavily on subsistence agriculture and remittances earned through labor out-migration for wage employment in other parts of Kenya: on the plantations of eastern Kenya, in industry in Nairobi, and on the railway as workers and clerks. There is a distinctive (but spatially concentrated) regional agricultural specialization in sugar, produced on plantations and, since the 1960s, on outgrower schemes, but otherwise commercial agriculture is weak.

Modern ethnic identities coalesced in the 1930s and 1940s around material interests arising from incorporation into the colonial economy. Proto-nationalist and nationalist-era political leaders in western Kenya mobilized new ethnic identities at the district level around economic organizations that leveraged wealth from wages (savings and lending associations for Luo) and around land issues (in the case of the Luhya) as bases for collective action and, eventually, partisan mobilization and opposition to colonial rule.[9]

---

[6] Other writers have stressed what is fluid, rather than what is persistent, in this coalitional structure. Elischer (2019: 125) described Kenyan politics as revolving around "unstable and fluid multiethnic alliances" based on short-term deals brokered by ethnic strongmen. Tice (2020) described Kenyan politics as "a game of musical chairs with extreme dispersion of power amongst competing factors of the elite." These statements do capture the sense of within-election and election-to-election maneuvering, and the swing role played by the Eastern bloc and, in some elections, the Rift Valley (and the shifting or fractured politics among the non-bloc constituencies, as argued in Chapter 5). When Kenya's political alignments are viewed in a longer historical perspective, the enduring oppositions and substantive stakes become clearer.

[7] That is, 10 in then Nyanza Province and 4 in Western Province (Elischer 2013: 231).

[8] The Western bloc's disadvantage is also reflected in DHS asset scores (averaged across pooled rounds), which are 25% lower for the entire bloc than they are for rural Central bloc. Rates of access to electricity are much lower in the Western bloc than in the Central bloc (9.4% vs. 32.2% based on DHS data [averaged over georeferenced DHS rounds covering the years 2003–2016]) (Boone, Wahman, Kyburz, & Linke, 2022).

[9] See Lonsdale (2012) on the connection between Western/Nyanza's history as a labor-exporting region and the political, ethnic, and regional consciousness of its population. Luo leaders emerged at the helm of Kenya's Nairobi-based trade union movement, Tom Mboya first among them. Class-based identities competed with ethnic identities. On Luhya nationalism, see MacArthur (2016).

6.1 *Leading Region and Poorer Periphery: Kenya*

In an alliance that helped to bring independence from Britain in 1963, Western Kenyan electoral constituencies were brought into the dominant KANU party by the already-iconic regional leader, Oginga Odinga. This partnership was shattered in 1966 when Kenya became a one-party state and Odinga was expelled from government. Resurrected in the multiparty era of the 1990s under the banner of the Orange Democratic Movement (ODM), the Western electoral bloc remained in a standoff against the Central electoral bloc until 2022.[10] It has been frozen out of power since 1966.

Like the Western bloc, the Rift bloc squares off against the Central bloc as an enduring rival. In the 1963 independence bargain, constituencies in this region lost their bid to reclaim land lost to white settlers under colonial rule, and their bid for a measure of territorial power through a federal constitution. A Rift bloc leader, Daniel arap Moi, served as vice president under Kenyatta. He inherited power upon Kenyatta's death in office in 1979, and he held onto it as head of the one-party state until 2002. Castigated by a punishing electoral defeat in that year, the Rift electoral bloc constituencies were mobilized anew around historic grievances. After the violent presidential elections of 2007, Rift Valley electoral bloc leader William Ruto entered into a brittle alliance with President Uhuru Kenyatta, at the head of the Central electoral bloc, as a *frère ennemi* from 2013 to 2018.

The enduring rivalry between the Central bloc and Rift Valley bloc is also marked by great economic asymmetry. Rift electoral bloc populations remain far poorer than those of the Central bloc by all economic indicators.[11] In the political arena, this line of regional cleavage has been structured around land competition since the 1950s.[12] Rift constituencies resent the central-government-sponsored in-migrations of land-seeking settlers (mostly Kikuyu) from Central Province. Collective consciousness of regional disadvantage on the part of the poorer, less educated, politically fragmented, mostly agro-pastoral groups of the Rift crystallized in the 1950s around "Kalenjin" as a confederal ethno-political identity pushing for a decentralized, devolved political system that would guarantee their claims to land.

Cleavage structure within the electorate follows the lines of these regional oppositions. Rural non-bloc constituencies – poorer than all the blocs by most measures – are key in producing the winning national vote at the national level.[13]

---

[10] The 2022 Azimio coalition between Raila Odinga and Martha Karua attempted to bridge this line of opposition for the first time since the early 1960s. See Mueller (2022).

[11] The Rift electoral bloc populations are poorer (as measured by DHS asset scores, nightlight per capital, poverty index, and educational levels) than the Central bloc. The DHS asset score is almost 30% lower in the Rift Valley bloc, and nighttime luminosity per capita is 1.1 in Rift Valley versus 4.5 in the Central bloc. Only 14.7% of people have access to electricity, against 32.2% in the Central bloc (see Boone, Wahman, Kyburz, & Linke 2022).

[12] See Boone, Lukalo, and Joireman (2021).

[13] The disparities would be clearer if we excluded the Orange Democratic Movement (ODM) Coast Province constituencies and/or Mombasa from the non-bloc category. See Boone, Wahman, Kyburz, and Linke, 2022, Appendix A17.

Rural non-bloc constituencies in Kenya are, taken together, poorer than all the blocs (in 2008 and 2014). Put in electoral terms, we could say that the politically dominant and wealthy Central bloc rules by aligning with poor non-bloc constituencies.

The Eastern persistent electoral bloc is a swing bloc (Poulton 2012; Kim 2017a; Nzau 2020).

If territorial politics is typified by conflict around the structuring of authority in the state, then it is clearly manifest in bloc oppositions in Kenya. Kenya has been racked for 60 years by the centralization–devolution struggle that has pitted the Central bloc against the Rift Valley bloc and entered national politics in late 1950s around demands for "majimboism" or regional devolution. In the national referendum on a new, devolved constitutional structure in 2010, the Central electoral bloc was the only regional bloc to vote no.

The growth–redistribution opposition also follows a core–periphery line of cleavage. Political representatives of the Central persistent bloc, the economically leading region adjacent to the massive Nairobi growth pole, have been steadfast champions of pro-growth policy.[14] The poorest electoral bloc, the Western (comprised of constituencies in the former Nyanza and Western Provinces), has been led by politicians who have consistently demanded redistribution. In the 1960s, this opposition found expression in "capitalism versus socialism" idioms. The leaders of the Western persistent electoral bloc and the political parties drawing most of their support from its constituencies, CORD and ODM,[15] have advanced calls for redistribution (including universal social protection) in both regional and populist terms. Western leaders have also championed a national minimum wage. The stance of leaders of the rival Central bloc has generally been that these demands are parasitic.

Sectoral interests give rise to different and competing regional policy preferences. These are a constant in Kenyan history. Kanyinga and Poulton (2014) and Eun Kyung Kim (2019) show that the constituencies of Central, Western, and Rift Provinces are represented by different parties that lobby for different sectoral interests. Sectoral policies around maize, cotton, meat, sugar, and dairy have highly uneven regional effects, and affect regional constituencies in highly uneven ways (Kanyinga & Poulton 2014). Kim tracks what she calls partisan "policy favoritism." Governments anchored in the Central electoral bloc have consistently advanced policies promoting leading-growth industries around Nairobi and Central Province's agricultural sectors (dairy, pyrethrum, nuts, tea, coffee). For Kim (2019), these are policy issues that are "owned" by the governments and parties representing the Central electoral bloc. Kim also

---

[14] Sessional Paper N. 10 of 1965 has long been viewed as the "turning point" at which the Kenyatta government committed itself to directing resources to Kenya's "high potential regions," reinforcing inherited spatial inequalities.

[15] That is, the Coalition for Reform and Democracy (CORD) and the Orange Democratic Movement (ODM).

6.2 *"Center versus Growth Area in the Provinces"*

tracks Central bloc incumbents' systematic embrace of trade and investment policies that *disfavor* Kenya's sugar industry, which is concentrated in the Western Province, the heartland of the Western electoral bloc. Political leaders representing the West fight for protection of the sugar industry against import competition, and the jobs it creates in the region.[16] She suggests that having a common interest in *economic policy* may intensify the political salience of ethnic difference (Kim 2019: 963).

Land policy preferences of constituencies in the Central electoral bloc and the Rift bloc have been directly contradictory since the 1950s. Rift bloc voters were dispossessed by colonial land alienation policies – they claim much of the former "White Highlands" as their ancestral land. They have been demanding restitution since the 1960s. Central bloc leaders, who captured control of the postcolonial state, have resisted these calls, biasing postcolonial land allocation policy in favor of their own constituents. Favoritism in central state distribution of land has indeed resulted in what appears to many as "colonization the Rift" by Black settlers originating from Kenya's Central Province.[17] Resulting antagonisms and zero-sum policy conflicts have fueled bloody confrontations since the return to multiparty competition in 1991.

Regional ideologies relating to positionality within the postcolonial state are embedded in the modern ethnic identities that have coalesced at the regional level in Kenya. In Kenya, core electorates in the dominant Central bloc have long been associated with an ideology of leadership entitlement and a vision of themselves as rightful heirs to the colonial state. Regional leaders have rallied under the trans-ethnic identities of GEMA (the Gikuyu, Embu, Meru Association) and the "Mt. Kenya group." Rival regional ideologies center on resistance to subordination, exploitation, and "internal colonialism."

6.2 "CENTER VERSUS GROWTH AREA IN THE PROVINCES": ZAMBIA

In Zambia, a persistent territorial opposition has structured national politics since the 1960s. It juxtaposes the core of the national economy – the Copperbelt North region centered on mining and the adjacent mining-labor-exporting regions, plus the urban population of Lusaka, the capital – to the main region of commercial agricultural production, the Southern region. This juxtaposition

---

[16] In National Assembly debate in 2006, Moses Masika Wetangula, MP from Sirisia (Bungoma), advocated for the sugar-growing areas: "It is totally unacceptable to those of us who come from the sugar-growing areas to remove the [import tax] on the importers of sugar. [S]ugar-cane is the most taxed crop in this country. Why are we not taxing other crops like tea, coffee or pyrethrum? Why are we targeting the sugar industry; an industry that people of Western and Nyanza provinces live upon? This is something that is totally unacceptable to us and we shall resist it by all means." Kenya Hansard, Debate on Ministry of Finance Budget Proposals, June 20, 2020: 1447–1448.

[17] See the mapping and analysis in Boone, Lukalo, and Joireman (2021).

176　　Territorial Oppositions in African Politics

is grounded in two dominant electoral blocs that have defined electoral cleavages at the national level since the 1960s. Given the overwhelming predominance of the Copperbelt in Zambia's national economy and its upper hand in electoral politics since the 1960s, and the lesser but still strategic role of the South as a food producer and homebase of Zambia's strongest opposition party over the same period, the national alignment arguably qualifies as an instance of what Lipset and Rokkan called an axis of cleavage between "the center and a growth region in the provinces" (1967: 41). A large political science literature supports this characterization.[18] Cheeseman and Hinfelaar, for example, write that "Zambian politics has long been divided between the interests of the Copperbelt and its 'labor reserves' in Northern Province and the Southern Province, where commercial agriculture dominates the local economy" (2009: 69). Bates (1976, 2019) described this as an agriculture–industry or rural–urban cleavage, a classic axis of core–periphery opposition. Ethnic politics interpretations are often considered not to apply very well in the Zambian context, notwithstanding the association of some prominent contributions to the country literature (Posner 2005) with ethnic politics theory.[19]

The powerhouse of the Zambian economy since the 1930s has been the mining industry concentrated in the Copperbelt, which generated 64% of all exports in 2015. From the 1950s to the 2010s, the labor-sending electoral districts of the colonial-era Northern Province voted consistently with the Copperbelt.[20] This political connection has a material base: The two are joined in a single, sectorally based economic system. Households in the overwhelmingly rural electoral constituencies of the northern region have depended heavily on mining and other Copperbelt wages for their livelihoods: By a 1980s' measure, 60% of all adult males worked in the Copperbelt. What became the Copperbelt North electoral bloc led the nationalist struggle for independence in the late 1950s and early 1960s. It fell out of the ruling coalition in the 1970s as the United National Independence Party (UNIP), the ruling party, embraced growth strategies that were designed to milk the Copperbelt to fund state-building and development in other parts of the country. Copperbelt labor unions provided the organizational base for the pro-democracy movement

---

[18] See Molteno (1974), Bates (1976, 2017), Cheeseman and Hinfelaar (2009), and Macola (2010).

[19] Posner (2005) advanced a linguistic-regional cleavage theory, which attributed political/electoral cohesion to shared ethno-linguistic identity among demographically large groups. He explained that colonial rulers in Zambia promoted vernacular lingua francas within colonial Admin1 units (provinces). His work aligned with theories that consider language groups to be one type of ethnic group (see, for e.g., Chandra 2012).

[20] This follows much precedent in the Zambia politics literature in depicting the Copperbelt and Northern Region as one ensemble, based on the empirical observation of political cohesiveness in partisan alignment (Posner 2004a; Elischer 2013: 211; Bates 2019: 104); theories of cohesion pointing to a unifying Bemba language or ethnicity (Posner 2005; Lindemann 2011); *or* theories of regional unity arising from shared socioeconomic interests (Bratton 1980; Macola 2010: 96 inter alia; Gould 2010: 46; Bates 2019). These are not necessarily rival theories of regional coherence.

6.2 "Center versus Growth Area in the Provinces"

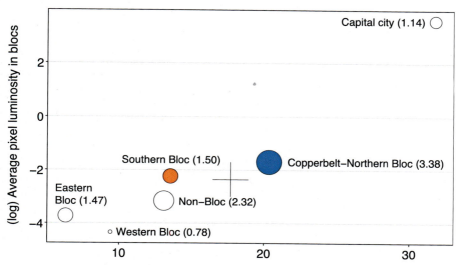

FIGURE 6.2 Zambia electoral blocs, disparities in regional GDP proxy and education
Notes: X-axis is average pixel luminosity in 2000, a rough proxy for regional GDP. Y-axis is percentage of adults having completed secondary school, from the pooled DHS data. Country averages, denoted by the cross, include the capital city. Circle size denotes population size (numbers reported in millions of persons).

that forced a return to multipartyism in 1990 (Ihonvbere 1996; Larmer 2006). From the return to multipartyism in 1991 to 2015, national power resided in the coalition that commanded the Copperbelt North plus Lusaka, which together comprise about 40% of the national vote. Five out of six elections between 1992 and 2015 featured this urban-mining alliance.[21]

Figure 6.2 offers a view of spatial inequalities in Zambia, highlighting the Copperbelt North's very strong advantages. The Southern bloc, ranking second by the regional GDP proxy and educational achievement, also enjoys a strong lead over the other electoral blocs.

Southern Province, coinciding closely with the Southern electoral bloc, is Zambia's leading agricultural region. It has long been the main locus of large- and medium-scale commercial agriculture in Zambia and is the richest predominantly rural province of Zambia.[22] Large- and medium-scale commercial

---

[21] The copper industry declined sharply in the 1990s, but recovered (under a neoliberal labor regime) in the 2000s.

[22] Boone, Wahman, Kyburz, and Linke (2022), Table 11, shows that the Lusaka constituencies and the Copperbelt sub-bloc constituencies are, on average, twice as urbanized as the constituencies of the Southern bloc. Comparing the Southern bloc to the northern part of the Copperbelt Northern bloc, and to the Eastern bloc, underscores the strong economic advantages

178   *Territorial Oppositions in African Politics*

maize production developed along the line-of-rail in the 1930s, supplying food staples to the cities and Zambia's mines. A relatively prosperous and politically engaged peasantry emerged under colonial rule. In the 1950s, it provided the political base for regional political parties that vied with Copperbelt-based parties, especially UNIP, for national preeminence. Its political expression in 1991–2015 is the Southern persistent electoral bloc (10% of the national vote). Loss of national leadership to UNIP in 1964 marked the beginning of what would be over a half-century of opposition politics for Southern. Davies observed that "a striking spatial arrangement of partisan alignments is the manner in which they divide the country into two single-party areas" (1971: 55).

Both of Zambia's two main producer regions were alienated by the statist and centralizing regime of UNIP in the 1970s and 1980s. Wealth produced by the Copperbelt and its miners funded the quest for state-led economic development, and this sector bore the brunt of volatile swings in world-market prices for copper, which trended sharply downward from 1975 to the early 2000s. UNIP's highly interventionist maize-sector policies aimed to keep maize prices low, and to block Zambian farmers' ability to sell maize exports to neighboring countries. This penalized maize producers.

The Eastern electoral bloc, largely coterminous with the Eastern Admin1 region, has been consistently present in national politics as a distinctive region. In the 1970s, as UNIP lost support in the Copperbelt North, Eastern served as UNIP's regional stronghold.[23] In terms of economic structure, Eastern is a poor region that combines characteristics of Zambia's two main economic poles. It has resembled the labor-sending Northern Province, with a partially proletarianized rural population, weak peasant economy, and dependence on out-migration to the Copperbelt and Lusaka. Eastern also has zones of large-scale maize (and tobacco) production, similar to Southern Province. As in Southern, the roots of large-scale commercial agriculture lay in European settler agriculture, but Eastern region is strongly disfavored economically by its off-the-line-of-rail location. Large-scale commercial agriculture declined dramatically in most of the province after the 1950s, but regained some momentum in the 2000s.

Eastern's populations were politicized in the colonial era by the experiences of land alienation and European settler agriculture, and labor out-migration to the Copperbelt. Rural activism powered Eastern region's incorporation into the nationalist coalition that brought UNIP to power in 1964 (Bratton

of Southern: Southern is more urbanized and has a higher population density, higher rates of household access to electricity and DHS asset ownership scores, and higher levels of adult education achievement. Luminosity per capital is the quadruple in Southern of what it is in Eastern and in the northern part of the Copperbelt Northern bloc.

[23] The Eastern bloc was part of the UNIP-led nationalist front in the 1960s and was the rump (i.e., what remained) of the regional political base of the UNIP regime in the 1970s and 1980s. In terms of socioeconomic indicators, the Eastern bloc looks similar to the Northern part of the Copperbelt Northern bloc, except that the Eastern bloc is even less urbanized.

6.2 "Center versus Growth Area in the Provinces" 179

1980). Decline of large-scale agriculture in this part of Zambia in the 1960s created opportunities for UNIP to reallocate state land to peasants and subsistence farmers. Lacking a strong producer profile, Eastern was perhaps the region most apt to support the statist, redistributive politics that UNIP came to represent.

Zambia's two main producer regions, Copperbelt North and Southern, aligned in 1991 to overthrow UNIP, but the alliance dissolved after 1996 and the cleavage line between the Copperbelt North and Southern was visible in electoral politics for the next 20 years. After 1996, the incumbent Movement for Multiparty Democracy (MMD) party attempted to rule against the Copperbelt North, as UNIP had. It mobilized support in the Eastern persistent electoral bloc and attempted to rally a broader rural electorate around family-scale agriculture, focusing on maize subsidies (Kim 2017: 30; Jepson 2020: 177). A Copperbelt North-plus-Lusaka coalition pushed back in 2011, propelling the Patriotic Front (PF) to power and ushering in policies "prioritizing mining and the urban areas" (Cheeseman & Hinfelaar 2009: 65).

Ideologies of regional consciousness animate Zambia's politics. They run along a strong axis of regional cleavage that juxtaposes the Copperbelt North and the Southern electoral blocs. Classic lines of sectional tension are visible around growth strategy, with UNIP and its populist successors strongly associated with statism, and the UPND, the party of Southern Province and the Southern electoral bloc, consistently advocating "liberalism" in opposition to the statism of Zambia's ruling parties.[24] The Southern bloc is typically characterized as the locus of national "business interests" and large- and medium-scale agriculture (Macola 2010), pushing back against Zambia's populist leaders. Hallink and Siachiwena (2023) describe this ideological opposition as a constant in Zambia's political history and root the divergence in the different sectional imperatives and interests of the dominant electoral blocs.[25]

Sectoral policy conflicts run along the lines of these territorial oppositions. They revolve around redistributive taxation; formal-sector wages and labor regulation, especially in mining; regulation of the maize sector; policies targeting the urban poor; and land policy. Macola identified regional tensions around land policy in the 1970s, when Kaunda allowed his voters in Eastern Province to colonize abandoned white-owned lands in this region. Southern

---

[24] Macola 2010: 90. The UPND is the United Party for National Development.

[25] The PF promoted a pro-poor agenda rooted in normative ideas of statism and "Zambianization" similar to the political ideology promoted by President Kenneth Kaunda and the United National Independence Party (UNIP) during Zambia's immediate postindependence era. The PF's ideological positions are popular among poor urbanites in the two economically strategic provinces, Lusaka and Copperbelt, and in the northern region, where support for the party is strongest. The UPND, on the other hand, articulates a "ruralist liberalism" that prioritizes individual economic achievement and self-reliance, which draws support from the rural areas in Zambia, especially in Southern and Central Province. It is a direct continuation of Zambia's African National Congress (ANC) led by Harry Nkumbula.

180   *Territorial Oppositions in African Politics*

and Western politicians pushed back, fearing that squatters and wage-rich buyers from other regions would attempt to buy or otherwise occupy land in Southern Region. Macola reports that smallholders in Southern Province were "united in fighting off perceived land encroachment from other parts of Zambia" and "feared and opposed central state control over land occupation" (2010: 90).

Territorial politics around questions of state design have played a permanent but subdued role in Zambia. Demands for special semi-autonomous status for Western region and the Western electoral bloc, the most political and economically peripheral of Zambia's electoral blocs, have been constant since the mid-1960s. These demands have been invoked by successive challengers in presidential elections since the 1990s in bids to win Western support (Englebert 2005).[26]

The breakthrough victory of the UPND's Hakainde Hichilema in the 2021 presidential elections, in his sixth bid for president, was achieved with the strong support of Western region and the Copperbelt. This is the third time in Zambia's electoral history that such a coalition has emerged to overturn an entrenched and highly unpopular regime (1964, 1991, and 2021). Time will tell whether the long-standing territorial opposition will reemerge, as it has in the past. Notable in 2021 is that while the Copperbelt voted for the opposition, the Northern region leaned marginally toward the incumbent. The Copperbelt and Northern constituencies did not vote as a bloc. Perhaps urban Copperbelt populations have gradually become more like Lusaka populations and less like the "circular migration" workforce of the twentieth century, eroding the coherence of a long-standing regional voting bloc.

6.3 COMPETITION BETWEEN RIVAL CORES: MALAWI

Malawi's persistent electoral blocs map onto an economic landscape polarized around two competing provinces, both centered on urban agglomerations that are roughly equal in terms of population.[27] However, the regions are very

[26] The Western persistent electoral bloc is the smallest and poorest of the four that appear in the 1991–2015 electoral data. The political cohesiveness of the core of the bloc is attributable in part to its former status as the semi-autonomous Barotseland Protectorate under indirect rule, when its Lozi leadership promoted education and a eventually a territory-wide (pan-Zambian) political outlook. Under colonialism this region was an exporter of skilled labor to the Copperbelt mines ("clerical class"), but regional advancement postindependence did not happen. Frustrations were heightened by UNIP's refusal to accord the region status as a semi-autonomous province (Ranger 1968). Since the mid-1960s Zambia's Western bloc has maintained an autonomy-seeking stance vis-à-vis national rulers. See Englebert (2005). In the elections considered here, it aligned mostly with the UPND, but was part of the winning coalition in three of the six elections between 1991 and 2015.

[27] In 2013, Southern bloc's luminosity score was still two times greater than Central's. By other measures, the gap is not so large. Access to electricity is slightly higher in the Southern bloc (8.8%) compared to the Central bloc (5.3%) across the pooled DHS rounds reported in Boone,

6.3 Competition between Rival Cores: Malawi

different in terms of agricultural sector composition, agrarian social structure and demands for state support arising from the agrarian interests, levels of urbanization and proletarianization, political organization, and state-society linkages. Differences fuel rivalry over the uses of state power that is reflected in what is basically a bipolar structure of competition (plus two swing blocs) that maps onto two persistent electoral blocs that are rooted in colonial-era Admin1 regions. Other scholars have noted the very high levels of regionalism in Malawian party politics, and several write that ethnicity either serves as a proxy for regional identities or that regional identities simply predominate.[28] Malawi evokes what Lipset and Rokkan called "competition between potential centers of political control" (1967: 41).

Regional GDP as proxied by nighttime luminosity shows the developmental lead of Central and Southern electoral blocs over the other two blocs (Figure 6.3). That Southern holds the upper hand is, however, unmistakable.

The Southern electoral bloc is grounded in the formerly white-settler-dominated Shire Highlands districts that contain Malawi's colonial-era commercial and administrative capitals, Blantyre and Zomba.[29] These remain the locus of private business, and the expatriate and corporate tea plantation sector that dates to the colonial era. The rural population is largely made up of smallholder and peasant worker classes on extremely small plots of customary land (median size =.06 ha) and/or engaging in wage and tenant labor on tea plantations owned by expatriates and international corporations (such as Lonrho). To a large extent, this is the economic model laid down under colonial rule.[30] In the rural sector, land and labor issues in the Southern persistent electoral bloc remain strongly politicized around land and labor grievances, including demands for land redistribution. These forms of politics are part of a lineage traceable to the well-organized Southern-based rural political mobilizations and rural militancy that helped propel Malawi to independence (Palmer 1973).

Malawi's Central bloc, by contrast, is anchored in a political economy built after Independence as the power base of Hastings Banda and his MCP ruling

---

Wahman, Kyburz, and Linke, 2022. Yet compared to other African countries, spatial inequality as measured by asset inequality is low (ibid.). The urban primacy ratio (between Blantyre and Lilongwe) is much lower here than in most other countries. (See the last column in Appendix B, Table B.1.)

[28] See, for example, Kaspin (1995), Kalipini (1997), Ferree and Horowitz (2010: 537–539), and Posner (2004b: 542, n. 32). Amundsen (2015) writes that "each party has a strong regional home turf ... Party leadership is also, generally, from the same region, making the party easily identifiable with the region. What matters most [for the voter] is ... that you are from here, that you are one of us, that you are not one of the others. It is for instance necessary to be a Northerner who knows the hardships and the marginalization of the North, or a Muslim who knows the Muslims of the East."

[29] The Shire Highlands is the region east of the Shire River, including the Southern Region districts of Blantyre and Zomba, the tea districts of Thyolo and Mulanje, and Phalombe and Chiradzulu.

[30] Agriculture provided over 80% of Malawi's exports through the 1980s.

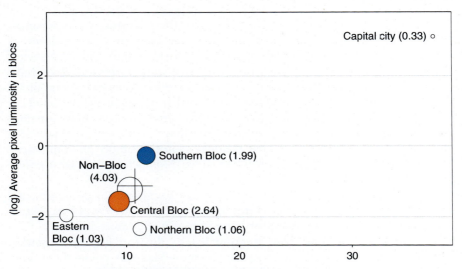

FIGURE 6.3 Malawi electoral blocs, disparities in regional GDP proxy and education
Notes: X-axis is average pixel luminosity in 2000, a rough proxy for regional GDP. Y-axis is percentage of adults having completed secondary school, from the pooled DHS data. Country averages, denoted by the cross, include the capital city. Circle size denotes population size (numbers reported in millions of persons).

party.[31] This province remained a hinterland of Southern Region throughout the colonial era and remained very much on the sidelines of the anti-colonial nationalist movement. Once in power, Banda acted on this regional split.[32] He moved Malawi's capital 300 miles to the north, to Lilongwe in the Central Region, and developed it as a new growth pole that competed with Blantyre and Zomba in the South. His postcolonial economic development policy concentrated on developing a tobacco estate sector in Central Region, with several hundred large estates (hundreds of hectares each) owned by MCP elites who benefited from government patronage, protection, and financing. In the 1980s,

---

[31] MCP is the Malawi Congress Party.
[32] Of "the 1964 constitutional crisis, as McCracken has written that, 'the division reflected interregional divisions.' The north, though agriculturally poor, was educationally rich and provided a high proportion of the middle level administrators; many in the south, profiting from the cash crop revolution and the existing system of communications, were also expanding into bureaucratic positions. The central region, on the other hand, had not only been less involved in the nationalist movement, it had also missed out on the educational and economic ladders to power ... The forces which swung behind [Banda] were the less educated, the less economically successful, those older politicians ... and the chiefs and headmen whose authority the nationalist politicians had done much to weaken. Such individuals were to be found especially in the central region" (Hodder-Williams 1974: 92, citing McCracken 1968: 207).

6.3 Competition between Rival Cores: Malawi

the Central Region tobacco economy expanded to include about 30,000 small- and medium-scale estates (10–20 ha) through the conversion of customary land to leasehold. Central Region's population, largely dependent on labor migration in the colonial era, became a population of tenants and sharecroppers producing tobacco for estate owners.[33] Vertical ties bound tenants and peasants in Central Region to the MCP political machine. Banda promoted the "Chewa" ethnic identity as a regional unifier and as the core Malawian identity. Under Banda, the tobacco sector became the source of Malawi's wealth, producing 60% of Malawi's exports and 70% of all foreign exchange in 1990. As Chinigò put it, Banda's strategy of agricultural modernization "had very different impacts in different parts of the country" (2016: 289).

Malawi's 1994 election ended the 30-year rule of Hastings Banda and the MCP. A coalition of the South, East, and North, anchored in the Southern Region, defeated the Center.[34] Governments based in the Southern persistent electoral bloc, centered in Blantyre, ruled Malawi from 1994 to 2020 (first as the UDF, then after 2005, as the DPP).[35] They systematically dismantled the tobacco-estate-based political and economic hegemony of Central Region. Tobacco production and marketing liberalization started in 1994. By 2000, most of the old tobacco estates in Central Region had collapsed or been abandoned and 70% of Malawi's tobacco was produced by 350,000 smallholders. State-backed smallholder production targeted Southern Region in the first five years of reform – 75% of state investment to support new tobacco farms went to this region.[36] Land tenure reform has also been a signature issue of governments of the Southern electoral blocs – this aims most urgently at taking the edge off long-simmering grievances of Southern smallholders and tenants in the tea-producing "land pressure districts" of the Shire Highlands (Thyolo, Mulanje, and Chiradzulu).[37]

Malawi's Northern persistent electoral bloc reflects constituency-level voting patterns in an economically marginal, labor-exporting, low-population-density

---

[33] Peasant producers on customary land were banned from tobacco cultivation.

[34] Led by Muluzi, a leader and candidate of the UDF. Muluzi passed power to Bingu wa Mutharika, his chosen successor, in 2004. President Mutharika split from the UDF and founded the DPP in 2005. The DPP won the 2009 and 2014 elections.

[35] UDF is the United Democratic Front. DPP is the Democratic Progressive Party.

[36] Tobacco is "the country's primary source of wealth" (Jaffee 2003: 1) and for Jaffee, the structure of access to land, capital, and markets is a main mechanism in determining the distribution thereof. Malawi's post-1994 governments, representing southern business and southern rural populations, undertook sweeping reforms to open tobacco farming to smallholders (favoring those in the southern region with new quotas in 1994–1996), and to reform the marketing system. Jaffee writes of "on-going state policy paralysis characterized by on-going struggle to maintain, undermine, or otherwise redirect earlier policy reforms in the tobacco industry" (2003: 3). This intensified in 2004 under Mutharika, who targeted the tobacco auction house system. It was dismantled in 2012 and replaced by contract-buying.

[37] The government undertook to address land tenure issues (most acute in the South) with a Land Commission in 1996 which gave credence to southern concerns around land held by tea estates.

(2.4 persons per sq. km) region, where the typical household depends on subsistence agriculture and wage remittances.[38] A distinctive export of the North has long been semi-skilled and skilled workers, many as teachers and civil servants to other parts of Malawi. In the nationalist era and the Banda years, they were stereotyped as Northern intellectuals.[39] Banda branded the North as untrustworthy and oppositional and targeted Northerners for political repression. Northern (and Southern) teachers were expelled from Central Region in the 1980s, as Banda promoted Chewa-ization of the populace. Writing in the early 1990s, Kaspin identified the source of the region's political unity as "30 years of marginalization under Banda's rule" (1995: 618). The Northern electoral bloc has been represented by a regional party, the People's Party (PP), since 1994. It joined the anti-Central coalition as a junior partner in 1994, 2009, and 2014.[40]

The Eastern persistent electoral bloc emerged as a distinctive cluster of constituencies in our 1994–2015 electoral data because of the 2005 splintering of the Southern bloc.[41] It retained the UDF party label. The distinctiveness of this zone has roots in political history and economic geography. Machinga and Mangochi districts lie outside the Shire Highlands' commercial urban areas and away from the tea plantation economy and the struggles of its semi-proletarianized and land-hungry rural population. They are the two Southern region districts that are most suitable for smallholder tobacco production, and that benefited from the pro-smallholder politics of Southern incumbents in the 1990s.[42] Mangochi's history of anti-regime politics and repression in the Banda era, along with its Yao Muslim identity, is a source of sociopolitical identity and cohesion. After the split with the rest of Southern, the Eastern persistent bloc swung to align to the Central electoral bloc in the 2009 and 2014 elections and then realigned with Southern Region in the 2020 elections.

---

[38] On the North as a labor reserve, Green 2011: 147. In the 1990s and 2000s, unavailability of land for smallholders in Southern Region led to in-migration of land-seekers. Potts (2006) explains that this reversed the North's historic status as a labor-sending region. As the region's southernmost districts were drawn into the tobacco economy, land competition intensified.

[39] In the 1960s, Northerners were indeed overrepresented in the national civil service. High levels of education in the North are traceable to long-term effects of missionary activity, sustained by reinvestment by families in education (Posner 2004b: 536, citing Vail 1981: 144).

[40] The PP has never won an election, although the People's Party's (PP's) Joyce Banda assumed power when Bingu wa Mutharika died in office. Although the PP fielded its own presidential candidate in 2014, the DPP won in the North in that election. North and East did not align together in post-1994 elections. Both fielded regional parties in 2014. In 2020 (not in our electoral dataset), the North voted with Central. See Wahman (2023).

[41] The split was initiated by the sitting president, Bingu wa Mutharika, who was elected as the UDF candidate as the chosen successor of Muluzi. Mutharika created the Blantyre-based DPP.

[42] In contrast to the Shire Highlands, a more historically legitimate form of customary land tenure under Yao chiefs prevails in Manchinga and Manchogi, where lower population densities and lower land pressure presumably contribute to land (tenure) priorities that differ from those driving land-related rural political mobilization in the Shire Highlands districts.

6.3 Competition between Rival Cores: Malawi

The MCP, anchored in Central Region, won back power in July 2020 in an electoral alliance with Northerners, reproducing the stark polarity between Central and Southern Regions that had structured Malawi politics since the time of Independence.

A stable axis of territorial opposition divides the Southern electoral bloc and the Central bloc. These electoral blocs represent the two growth poles of the postcolonial economy. This territorial opposition that was stark in Malawian politics from the 1960s to the 2000s was, to a significant extent, an expression of competing interests over not only who controls the state and competition for position in the business sector, but also how to use state power to structure and regulate different sectors of the agricultural export economy.[43] Here, different histories of agrarian mobilization in both Southern and Central around issues of tea and tobacco production, respectively, and different land policy concerns, are rooted in very different grassroots organizational structures (cooperatives, unions, and land militancy) that can socially embed political party networks (Chipeta 1986: 56–70; Kishindo & Mvula 2017). After 2000, long-standing rural issues have perhaps been compounded by issues about regional trade-offs in the promotion of maize production (Malawi's staple food crop) as this has become more of a national priority (Poulton 2012: 15–16). Land demands have flared up as well.

The case of Malawi points to ways in which economic geography itself has been shaped by the use of state power. From the starting point of the inherited colonial economy, segmented by region as described by Chipeta (cited in Chapter 3), postcolonial rulers undertook to build up Central Region as the new national capital and the core of the tobacco-producing economy. This was territorial politics writ large by the Banda regime: The incumbent promoted the rise of a region to rival the colonial-era political and economic core in the South.

In the national political area, the politically salient ethnic identities are those that have coalesced at the regional level.[44] Northern identity spans ethnic distinctions, and Kalipeni writes that even Tumbuka is a "super-ethnic identity" (1997: 154). "Chewa-ness" was promoted by Banda as an Admini-level ethnic ideology of the Chewa farmer as the ideal Malawi citizen. Southern Region is strongly multiethnic. The UDF and DPP do not claim a particular ethnic profile (Elischer 2013: 203–204). Lomwe is a modern identity held by migrants from diverse ethnic backgrounds who in-migrated from Mozambique to work on southern tea plantations during the colonial era (Chinigò 2016).

---

[43] Writing in the early 1990s, Kaspin (1995: 614) suggested that regional identities and voting blocs in the multiethnic Southern and Northern Regions solidified *in opposition to* the MCP.

[44] See Kaspin (1995), Erdmann (2004: 71, 80), Posner (2005), and Ferree and Horowitz (2010: 537–539). See also Kalipeni (1997: 154), who says that Chewa and Tumbuka are "super-ethnic" identities.

6.4 REVISIONIST REGIME: UGANDA UNDER THE NRM

Uganda under the National Resistance Movement (NRM) is a country ruled by a regime with a political base in a lagging, peripheral region, in opposition to the indisputable "core of the country," the Buganda region, long institutionalized in the colonial-era province of Central Region (Low 1988: 52). The country exhibits the classic core–periphery structure, with the asymmetry between the core and the rest of the country the most extreme in our 12-country study. The political history of Uganda is structured around this territorial opposition. All of Uganda's leaders have ruled from the periphery, relied on the military to centralize power, and built up independent bases of political power in the state to check the prerogatives and influence of Buganda. Of these, Yoweri Museveni has been the most ambitious and successful. Southall writes that "[a]fter the failure of two disastrous northern-dominated regimes of Amin and Obote to unite Uganda," the West represented a "reservoir of possible alternative power" (1988: 61). It provided a regional base for the rise of Museveni.

Museveni's NRM is more than "a low-income coalition against a wealthy region" in the general sense.[45] It is a revisionist regime, in Gourevitch's sense: It challenges and dilutes the power of the economically leading region. It undertook, through mobilization of the NRM and the 1980–1985 bush war, to "create a new society" in Uganda (Southall 1988: 61, 65) by reconfiguring grassroots political structures and local territorial institutions. The NRM built alternative participatory structures in the West and the Luwero Triangle reaches of Buganda to undercut local elites linked to Museveni's predecessor regimes, and to neutralize the representative political structures of the earlier era. New district creation and population resettlement have segmented local authority, land rights, and territorial claims in new ways.

Anthony O'Connor writes that "Uganda gained independence in 1962 with a space-economy that offered a classic example of a core and periphery structure" (1988: 85; s.a. Bakwesegha 1974). Ugandan politics since the 1950s have been constituted along this regional axis. Spatial inequalities were and are extreme.[46]

The Central Region has towered over the rest of the country by all economic measures since the 1920s. In 1904, the British selected the Buganda aristocracy as its privileged intermediary to conquer and rule the rest of the protectorate, making Buganda a sub-imperialist power that was widely "feared and resented" (Low 1988: 40) in the rest of the colony. In the 1960s, the Buganda region, institutionalized as one of four colonial Admin1 regions, contained 75% of the colonial coffee-producing area and 50% of the cotton-producing

---

[45] "A successful low-income coalition against a wealthy region" is, for Kyraicou and Roca-Sogales (2014: 186) a "low-income coalition that has been able to lock in a system of redistributive transfers, as in Canada and Spain as well as many centralized states."

[46] See also Wang, Rafa, et al. (2019).

6.4 Revisionist Regime: Uganda under the NRM

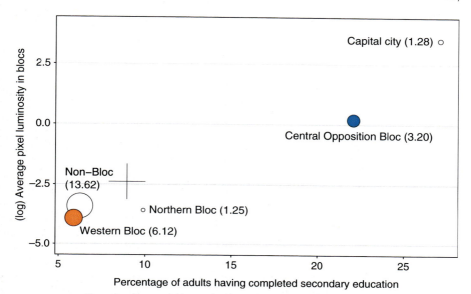

FIGURE 6.4 Uganda electoral blocs, disparities in regional GDP proxy and education
Notes: X-axis is average pixel luminosity in 2000, a rough proxy for regional GDP. Y-axis is percentage of adults having completed secondary school, from the pooled DHS data. Country averages, denoted by the cross, include the capital city. Circle size denotes population size (numbers reported in millions of persons).

zone. The other half of the cotton zone was in the Eastern Region, starting near the Nile's headwaters and heading along the White Nile to Lango.

Most of the Northern and Western regions constituted underdeveloped periphery, serving as labor reserves in the colonial economy. These were the poorest parts of colonial Uganda. Southernmost reaches of Northern Region – the southern part of Acholi district – were pulled into the colonial economy as cotton (and tobacco) producer zones in the 1930s. With the exception of some compact coffee-producing enclaves in Bunyoro and Toro (which produced 25% of Uganda's coffee in 1960), much of the Western Region was a noncommodity-producing backwater.[47]

The core–periphery structure that was striking circa 1960s is evident in data that describes spatial inequalities in Uganda 50 years later. Figure 6.4 plots socioeconomic indicators for the persistent electoral blocs that we identified in the 1996–2015 electoral data for Uganda. The Central oppositional bloc, comprising Kampala and the most developed parts of Central region, is light-years ahead of the rest of Uganda.

---

[47] Toro and Ankole in the southwest were mostly noncommodity-producing districts and were incorporated into the colonial economy as labor reserves (Jorgensen 1981).

188   *Territorial Oppositions in African Politics*

Uganda since Independence has been ruled by four regimes – under Obote I, Amin, Obote II, and Museveni – that have all arisen from regional bases "in the periphery" to rule the country. They have all relied on the military and strongly statist, centralizing policies to sideline Buganda with the aim of redistributing wealth, investment, and political clout to other regional constituencies.

Milton Obote, who led Uganda to independence in 1961, rose to power at the head of a coffee–cotton producer coalition anchored in Central Region, Eastern Region, and parts of Acholi district (in the Northern Region). His party, the Uganda People's Congress (UPC), was strong in the cash crop areas, the cooperatives, labor and producer unions, and among the nonhereditary Buganda elite ("opponents of the Mengo hierarchy").[48] A rival party, the DP, formed around the pro-monarchy faction of the Buganda elite, drawing support from the mostly noncash crop, more peripheral, areas of Uganda, including Ankole and Toro in the West and part of Acholi in Northern region.[49]

The UPC allied with a faction of the Buganda elite (the Kabaka Yekka, or KY party) to defeat the DP in the election that gave it control of the postcolonial state in 1962. The split within Buganda would be decisive for Uganda, for it ensured that this region, so advanced both politically and economically over the others, would fail to establish control over the postcolonial state.[50]

The split between Obote and factions of Buganda tied to his government came in the constitutional crises of 1964–1966. Obote turned against the Buganda establishment, centralized power in the presidency, severed off three western counties from Buganda control, and abolished all Uganda's kingdoms in 1966. He expanded the state apparatus and the parastatal sector, and asserted state control over marketing circuits for cash crops. He deepened the ruling party's alliance with Asian capital, sapping the economic base of the Bugandan economic elite. Obote tried to build a broad populist alliance bridging the North and South. Meanwhile, the regime became more repressive, coming to rely more and more on the machinery of state to gather power, and on the military, 70% of whom were northerners, most from Lango and Acholi (Mamdani 1975).

---

[48] See Jorgensen (1981: 194), Southall (1988), and Mutibwa (1992: 13). The UPC's predecessor party, the Uganda National Congress (UNC), was anchored in the agricultural cooperatives – led by heads of prominent families and locally influential leaders – and the ginneries. The cooperatives and ginneries in this region, and in Teso in particular, flourished (but became more corrupt) in the late 1960s (Mamdani 1976; Jorgensen 1981: 241–244).

[49] These were areas in which the Catholic Church was indeed the strongest local organization and Catholic teachers formed the node of organizing. The only commodity-producing peasant zone in which the DP had a hardcore base was Acholi (Mamdani 1976: 219).

[50] There were deep divides between aristocracy–monarchy vs. the Buganda bourgeoisie vs. tenants, and a religious split between Catholics and Protestants. Buganda and Central Region also had ethnically heterogeneous populations, 45% of which was non-Bugandan in 1960 (Jorgensen 1981: 191–193). A quarter of the Central Region population was made up of people from Rwanda and Burundi.

6.4 Revisionist Regime: Uganda under the NRM

Obote was overthrown by Idi Amin in 1971. Amin established a bloody dictatorship, expelled the Asians, massively expanded the regime's reliance on the army from the North, split Buganda into separate administrative districts, and destroyed the cotton export sector which was heavily reliant on state-coordinated finance and marketing. Coffee was driven into the informal, underground economy.[51] Large parts of the economy were near collapse by 1980.

Obote came back in 1979 in a military invasion from Tanzania that was coauthored by Museveni. Museveni lead his FRONASA army up through Western Region, recruiting fighters along the way, up to West Nile, for the multipronged attack on the Amin government.[52] Upon the ousting of Amin, Museveni contested the ensuing 1980 elections at the head of his newly formed party, the Uganda Patriotic Movement, with a regional base in the Southwest (in Toro and Ankole), noncommodity-producing, labor-exporting areas historically aligned against the Obote I regime (Jorgensen 1981: 339–340). Yet Obote won the flawed elections of 1980.

Museveni spent the next five years under the Obote II regime forging a regional base in the Southwest and raising a fighting force, the NRM – composed especially of Toro, Ankole, and refugees (in-migrants) from Rwanda – to take power by force. He forged an alliance between these bush fighters, partisans in core "liberated areas" of the Luwero Triangle of Buganda, and "a significant part of the Ganda and other southern intelligentsia and propertied classes [who] came to look upon Museveni as their saviour from what they privately regarded as barbarian northern domination" (Southhall 1988: 62).

In 1985 all major towns of the West fell to the NRM. Museveni then took Kampala and drove Obote's successor, Okello, and the rest of the Ugandan army into retreat to Teso and Acholi (Gulu).

With NRM victory, the power balance in Uganda shifted for the first time to the South. Southall (1988: 61) wrote that, although Museveni is "not a westerner by principle or intention," he did raise his army in the West and *began to create his new society* in the West during five years of war (1980–1985). The West provided "a supportive context" (ibid., p. 64) where Museveni built new political structures at the grassroots, starting in the Lowero Triangle and then more broadly throughout the West, incorporating lower-level chiefs and wealthier peasants into elective decision-making bodies and new administrative structures, sidelining higher-ranking chiefs and the existing local

---

[51] See Low (1988: 46) and Kasfir (1988: 164–165).

[52] The Front for National Salvation (FRONASA) invaded Uganda with Obote loyalists organized as the Uganda National Liberation Army (UNLA) and Tanzanian government forces in 1979. FRONASA was responsible for the western axis of the attack on Amin's government – Mbarara, Fort Portal, Masindi, and West Nile – and recruited fighters as it moved through the country (Brittain 1986). In the subsequent 1980 elections, Museveni ran at the head of the newly formed Uganda Patriotic Movement, which had its regional base in Toro and Ankole, and thus cut into a region that had historically been aligned with the DP as a Catholic, noncommodity-producing, labor-exporting region (Jorgensen 1981: 339–340).

190   *Territorial Oppositions in African Politics*

administration. The NRA built up the National Resistance Council at the supra-local level as a political structure to form the core of a new government (Weinstein 2007: 175–180).

Once in power, Museveni rebuilt state structures from the bottom-up. The NRM rebuilt the central state and built up the Western Region as a political base, building on the resistance councils created during the war and strategically deploying state resources, indigeneity issues, state investment, and new subnational unit creation. Playing to land issues, the government attempted to orchestrate land allocations and resettlement politics to build support and weaken opposition, often siding with indigenous demands for land rights over immigrants and landlords (as in Ankole, Kigezi, Kibaale),[53] often through new district creation which divided land and territory among communities.

The war in the North (in Acholi, and Teso in the Eastern Region) against the rump of the Obote–Okello government and security forces routed by NRA continued from 1986 to 1990. This was followed by another decade of counterinsurgency to defeat the LRA, allowing Museveni and the NRM to extend military hegemony over this vast territory.

Ruling from a regional stronghold in Uganda's periphery, as Obote and Amin had, the NRM pursued the same centralizing, statist drive as its predecessors. Museveni embraced anti-federal policies, new administrative unit creation, and reliance on the military to rebuild the state and economy and check Buganda. NRM growth strategies are reminiscent of those of Obote: build up the parastatal sector, and forge alliances between the state, foreign capital, donor capital, and state-linked Asian capital to fund state investment and expenditure, and to check domestic private capital.[54] The regime did not focus on building up smallholder production (in coffee, for example), small landlords, and private business in parts of the country where these had been historically strong, but that it did not control (Kjaer 2015).[55] Development policy funds were channeled to the West. The end of the war in the North was followed by infrastructure investment in that region and the promotion of large-scale agricultural investments linked to the state.

---

[53] In Ankole (Mbarara and Bushenyi districts), places with some of the highest population densities in the West, there was intense land pressure and a history of bitter land enclosures of public land by Obote I and Amin, and displacement of smallholders. Museveni aligned with the immigrant populations in Mbarara district who had suffered land seizures under Obote II (Lemarchand 2000: 11–12). Mamdani (2001) describes the first crisis of the NRM regime as culminating in the expulsion of the Banyarwanda from the SW districts of Kigezi and Mbarara and denial of their land ownership rights (see Mamdani 2001: 289). Kjaer (2015) describes the subsequent buildup of dairy ranching in Museveni's home region. In 1993, Museveni resettled Kigezi populations in Banyoro. Cattle-keepers were settled in Kasese.
[54] See Mamdani (1976: 246, 259).
[55] The coffee sector came back under Obote II, with devaluation, etc., and climbed back up to earlier levels in the 1990s. See Wedig and Wiegrast (2018) and on cooperatives, Ayeko-Kümmeth and Schlichte (2021).

Conclusion

In Central Region, the NRM's connections with Buganda frayed in the 1990s and thereafter. Museveni provoked a major show-down with Buganda landlords by backing user rights against their ownership claims, refusing the political decentralization they demanded, and delaying the opening up of the political arena to party politics until 2006.[56] Buganda interests in Central Region have been denied both leadership and autonomy.

The persistent electoral blocs identified in Chapter 4 are based on Uganda election results since 2001, mapped at the district or Admin2 level on the basis of vote share for Museveni. This allows us to gauge the strength of the vote for and against Museveni in 2001, when independent candidates (not parties) stood against Museveni in no-party elections, as well as pro-NRM voting in 2006, 2011, and 2016. This method identifies persistently high levels of electoral support for Museveni throughout most of the Western Region, as well as strong oppositional voting (persistently more than 30% of the vote for candidates other than Museveni) in the core of the Central Region, corresponding to Buganda and including the capital city of Kampala. It also identifies a persistent Northern voting bloc, centered on Gulu, in Acholi, representing the remnants of the old Obote coalition, now embittered by war.[57] If only the 2001 and 2006 electoral results had been considered, Teso would have appeared as a much more important part of this anti-NRM geographic cluster.[58] It is striking that these polarities and territorial oppositions are clearly visible more than half a century after Uganda's Independence.

CONCLUSION

Persistent electoral blocs are evidence of *regional* cleavage patterns in national electoral politics, as argued in Chapter 4. They map onto the uneven geography of regions, and onto the differential positioning of these regions in terms of wealth, distribution of productive assets, productive capacity, and sectoral division of labor within national economies. In most countries, the distribution of wealth and the distribution of political power overlap, and leading regions

---

[56] See Green 2006, 2008.

[57] The Lord's Resistance Army (LRA) in Acholi declared a cease-fire in the 2006 elections to allow people to vote for the DP (*Africa Confidential*, February 3, 2006, "Uganda: Making the President Nervous," pp. 1–2).

[58] Sjogren (2015) considered Acholi and Teso to be opposition strongholds. Perrot (2014: 375–376, inter alia) describes how Teso voted heavily for the opposition in 2006, and then swung back to the NRM by a narrow margin in 2011. As elections became more competitive in the 2000s, Museveni relied more on the non-bloc constituencies in the former Eastern Region to solidify his majority (see Table 5.1). New district creation, cattle stocking, development initiatives, party infrastructure development, and peace itself (defeat of Karamojong insurgency) helped pull support to Museveni. Nevertheless, there were still "wide local disparities" in pro-NRM voting in Teso in 2011 (Perrot, 385). This shift over time is visible in the electoral data: The "Northern bloc" that is visible in 2006 shrinks in 2011.

often dominate politically without building coalitions with other persistent regional blocs (Chapter 5). In such situations, instability in coalition-building is not *tous azimuts*, but rather structured in a particular way: Incumbents' winning coalition-building strategies tend to fragment the least politically organized regions of the national polity (probably through elite deals and one-off patronage), while reinforcing regionalism by holding the best-organized regional blocs at arm's length (Chapter 5).

Regional polarization along a single national axis of cleavage is visible in many countries. This chapter illustrates this point using four country case studies, arguing that variations in core–periphery dynamics observed at the national level are isomorphic to those identified in generic terms by Lipset and Rokkan (1967) and Gourevitch (1979). Territorial oppositions between and among economically leading regions in Kenya, Zambia, Malawi, and Uganda illustrate these canonical variations. Tracking these cases over time, we see the remarkable extent to which the basic structures of political regionalism in each country persist over the course of many decades. Uganda is a country case that defies the theoretical expectation that economic and political power will tend to coincide. Here, the region that is the clear economic leader does not rule – representatives of Central Region have failed to capture state power. Revisionist regimes, including the one headed by Museveni since 1985, have tried to harness the state and its resources to build alternative bases of political and economic power (with only partial success).

Similar patterns of territorial opposition are observable in other countries in the 12-country study. Ghana is similar to Kenya in the political and economic preeminence of a distinctive regional core. In Ghana, however, the rest of the country is less strongly segmented into potentially contending blocs. Ghana's Eastern persistent electoral bloc, anchored in a colonial-era Admin1 region, can pull much of the non-bloc region into electoral coalitions that act as a counterweight to Central bloc. Cameroon's structure of territorial opposition is similar to Malawi's "rival cores." In Cameroon, there is a persistent polarization between the Yaoundé-centered Centre-Sud bloc, which is the ruling electoral bloc, and the Douala-centered Western electoral bloc, a rich and sectorally diverse region that has been excluded from leadership, to put it mildly, since the 1960s. In Nigeria's territorial opposition between West and North, we see the juxtaposition of two very different sources not only of economic power but also of political legitimacy and social power. Their rivalry is tempered by their shared interest in checking the East, a potentially powerful region in its own right, as demonstrated by the secession of Biafra in Nigeria's 1966–1969 civil war, and by the Eastern electoral bloc's electoral weight.

The "growth center in the provinces" that has been a persistent pole in Zambian politics finds an analog in Western Côte d'Ivoire, a strong growth center "in the provinces" that was repressed politically for three decades under the rule of Houphouët-Boigny, even as the economic lead of the politically

Conclusion

193

dominant producer regions narrowed. Western Côte d'Ivoire was able to assert itself on the national stage in the 1990s and 2000s.

Tanzania, like Uganda, diverges from the general tendency in the 12-country study in that its ruling party has long been anchored in an economically disadvantaged, lagging region, rather than in an economically leading region. And similar to the Ugandan case, its ruling party, the Chama Cha Mapinduzi (CCM), has been "revisionist." With a political base in the central region of the country, the CCM successfully imposed its political hegemony over the wealthier, cash-cropping Northern region which, inter alia, had been the cradle of the independence movement (Maguire 1970). The Northern oppositional bloc that is visible in Tanzania's post-1990 electoral data – including the Arusha, Kilimanjaro, and (most of) Mwanza districts – is the most developed rural region in the country, measured in terms of nightlight and education.[59] It is an export-crop-producing region specialized in coffee and cotton that corresponds to the colonial-era Northern Province.[60] Tanzania's politically dominant electoral bloc, the CCM bloc, is disadvantaged in both luminosity and education compared to the North. Over the course of the late 1960s and 1970s, the CCM built its territorial political base around the subsistence-farming peasantry in the geographic center of the country, which was drawn into the party state's embrace through the policies and institutional structures of Ujamaa. Under Nyerere, spatial and political reorganization of rural populations (through resettlement and replacement of colonial indirect rule structures with the ruling party apparatus) created a new mesh of rural political and economic institutions that anchored the party in the central region of Tanzania.[61] This territorial base shows up in the electoral data as the CCM bloc.

In Tanzania, regional disparities have not been as great as in Uganda or Kenya, and the Northern opposition-leaning electoral bloc is widely dispersed across space and segmented into different cash crop zones, rather than united around a singular specialization. By the theory advanced here, these factors would have been a drag on attempts to mobilize this region as a counterweight to the ruling CCM. The ruling party, for its part, has used strongly centralizing administrative, economic, and property rights (land tenure) institutions to impose its national predominance.

---

[59] In 1990, our GDP proxy put the Northern oppositional bloc ahead of the CCM bloc by about 50%, but by 2000, this advantage had more than doubled. See Figure 4.5(c) and Table C.5 in Appendix C. On *Chama cha demokrasia na maendeleo* (CHADEMA) and its rise, see Paget (2019, 2022).

[60] Divided into the Northern and Lake Regions in 1948.

[61] On institutional reordering in Tanzania, see details in earlier chapters (Sections 1.2 and 3.6). See also Boone and Nyeme (2015); Collord (2024). The analysis here focuses on mainland Tanzania. When Zanzibar is factored in, we have a case of high spatial inequality and economic differentiation, combined with strongly territorial political institutions, that is highly conducive to political regionalism. See Myers (2000), Fouéré (2011), and Moss and Tronvoll (2015: 94 *inter alia*) on Zanzibar politics and the Civic United Front (CUF).

194   *Territorial Oppositions in African Politics*

The territorial distribution of political power in Kenya under the presidency of Daniel arap Moi (1979–2002) was also structurally similar to that in Uganda under Museveni. Low (1988: 52) drew this analogy, writing that under Moi, a "lagging region" in Kenya (the Rift electoral bloc) found itself as the regional base of the incumbent party and ruler, pushing against a historically economically and politically dominant region. An indignant letter-to-the-editor in Kenya's *Daily Nation* in 1997 likened this political status quo to one in which "the wealth-creating area of the British heartland is in perpetual slavery to political bosses from the remote Welsh valleys."[62] This arrangement did not last in Kenya. The historic pattern was reasserted in 2002 when Moi was ousted by a political coalition rooted in the wealthy Central bloc, which retained power for the next two decades.[63]

This chapter identifies regional oppositions and core–periphery dynamics in national-level politics in four African countries, leveraging the analysis of electoral blocs and electoral coalitions presented in Chapters 4 and 5. Case studies underscore the extent to which observed lines of political cleavage map onto underlying patterns of regional economic inequality and sectoral differentiation. Viewed over time, rulers' economic growth strategies and the guiding logics in state-building exhibit strong regional biases that are molded by spatial inequalities, and by territorial oppositions that arise more or less directly from underlying patterns of uneven development. National trajectories cannot be understood merely in terms of inertia (passive path dependency), elite deal-making, patronage politics, or electoralism.

This combination of political and economic geography opens the door to bringing economic policy and issue salience back into the study of African politics. Such an approach unlocks the potential of Posner's insight, mentioned above, that the politically relevant ethnic groups in African countries are those that "fold themselves into broader political coalitions, often along regional lines, when it comes to competing over resources and national-level policy outcomes ... [These are] groups *that are actually doing the competing over policy*" (2004a: 853, emphasis in the original). Territorial oppositions that structure electoral competition reflect in part sector-specific policy preferences, regional interests, and even distinctive national projects. This is the focus of Chapter 7.

---

[62] Cited in Kenya Institute for Education in Democracy (1998: 5).

[63] In Mali and Zimbabwe, deep and persistent North–South lines of territorial opposition are clear. Mali's North does indeed have a long history of autonomy-seeking vis-à-vis Southern-based governments. A Mopti "persistent electoral bloc" that reaches up to Timbuctou is discernible in electoral returns, but it is not very clear (Figure 4.4). Zimbabwe is clearly polarized between a Northern and Southern electoral bloc; the south was the victim of violent repression by the ruling party in the 1980s. In South Africa, regional electoral dynamics are subordinated to stronger nationalizing forces. Even so, we do see voting patterns at the provincial level that are distinctive, with persistent electoral blocs that fit the definition of blocs advanced in Chapter 4 (see Figure 4.2). On South Africa, see Section 7.1.

7

Regionalism and the National Agenda

> The land question ... formed the central axis of the 2007 campaign [in Kenya].
>
> Kagwanja and Southall 2010: 10

> [In 2013 in Kenya] the main parties differed widely over land ownership and control, and over the new devolution of powers to the 47 counties.
>
> Africa Confidential, March 15, 2013

> They also differed over minimum wage.
>
> Githuku 2013: 1

In African countries, regional economic inequality and economic differentiation give rise to cross-regional interest heterogeneity and power differentials. This chapter shows that regional competition and tensions shape policy and policymaking, much as they do in other parts of the world, and are manifest in analogous policy domains.

Rogers (2016) focuses on how territorial institutions shape politics and policy in "territorially divided states." In her analysis, strongly territorial institutions in interaction with underlying spatial inequalities work to channel regional interests into the national system, magnify territorial heterogeneity of interests, and narrow the space for (or displace) truly national policy coalitions. Territorial segmentation tends to produce a heterogeneous or fragmented policy space in which interregional distribution is a pivot of national politics, and regional policies and pork-barrelism feature strongly. When the president is elected from a single national constituency and levels of party and levels of party nationalization are low, countries experience more extreme deviations in policy when there is electoral turnover.[1] The analysis here shows that these

---

[1] On the effect of how the president is elected (and presidentialism) on targeted regional spending, see Rogers (2016: 158–159).

effects are clearly visible in the politics of many African countries, as theories of politics in territorially divided countries would predict.

Territorial and indeed regional cleavages around policy manifest much as they do in countries in other parts of the world with salient regional tensions: that is, in policy domains in which the distribution of costs and benefits of national-level policy choices – such as trade, sectoral, regulatory, labor, fiscal policies – are distributed unevenly across regions, or across regionally concentrated sectors of the economy. Regional actors also bargain over the rules of the game when the outcome of *future* bargaining rounds is at stake. Regional economic heterogeneity and inequality are likely to give rise to regionally specific and sometimes divergent preferences over (a) questions of redistributive policy, (b) productive-sector policies, (c) matters that have to do with national market integration (in African cases, this is visible in land policy issues), and (d) questions of state structure and national design (i.e., the territorial form of the state) (Beramendi 2012: 40; Rogers 2016). This chapter deals with each of these in turn, underscoring the extent to which regional inequalities and uneven development heighten the salience of these types of policy issues, largely because of their territorially uneven distributive implications. The net effect is regionalism in the national policy arena.

In cross-national comparisons, the intensity of regionalism in shaping the national policy agenda should vary as a function of the weight of spatial inequality (compared to interpersonal inequality), and the salience of territorial institutions, including institutions of political representation (compared to nationalizing and centralizing institutions). Across African countries, we do see the expected cross-national variation in the domain of redistributive social policy, where outcomes can be compared cross-nationally in terms of simple metrics, and a key cross-country difference in institutional design is visible in the classic contrast between SMD and PR electoral systems. By these measures, South Africa offers support for the theory advanced here by way of counterfactual (see below). Yet in general, for the other three policy areas, the fairest tests of the theory's capacity to predict outcomes (i.e., to predict cross-national variation) may lie in wide-angle comparisons of sub-Saharan African countries to those in other parts of the world, rather than in explaining variations among African countries. Most African countries stand out in global comparisons for their high levels of spatial inequality and strongly territorial institutions. This chapter examines debates over redistributive policy, sectoral policy, land policy, and constitutional design, and shows that, in many African countries, regional tensions produce strong and politically salient regional divisions in all these domains. The many similarities across countries and across these policy domains support the expectations of the theory.

Scholars have often explained clientelism in African politics as the consequence of the overwhelming weight of ethnicity in national political life. Ethnic clientelism, it is argued, relegates redistributive policy and other substantive policy issues to the sidelines of national and electoral politics. This chapter

Regionalism and the National Agenda

offers an alternative analysis. I aim "to put ethnicity in its place" by showing that it is not a sufficient explanation or perhaps even necessary to an explanation of electoral clientelism in settings with strongly territorial institutions (including SMD electoral systems) and high spatial inequalities.[2] At the same time, the discussion shows that substantive policy issues *are* prominent on national policy agendas in many African countries, including in national electoral contests. Policy issues that are salient on the national agenda are often those arising from the interaction of territorial politics and uneven development, as is the case in other regionally divided countries around the world.

One reason for the systematic sidelining of these nationally salient policy issues in research on African countries lies in conceptual framings that downplay policy. Stark juxtaposition of *programmatic* and *clientelistic* attributes of parties, policies, and/or practices is a common move in a large body of survey, electoral, and experimental research on African electoral politics. "Programmatic" refers to parties, policy, and politics that are nationwide (universal, or state-wide), and that do not entail or allow for electorally advantageous political bias or discretion in implementation. Programmatic or nationwide means *not* regionally, geographically, village-, or individually targeted or biased.[3] "Clientelistic" functions as the conceptual opposite of programmatic: It can refer to any distributive practice that is individually, locally, or geographically targeted in a discretionary way. This categorical distinction between "programmatic policy of national scope," on the one hand, and clientelistic policy and practice, on the other, leaves a vast gray area of regionally targeted policy in between. Everywhere in the world, productive-sector policies, including land use policies, are geographically targeted, due to the spatially uneven distribution of economic activity. This is especially true for natural-resource-based sectors, including mining, agriculture, and pastoralism. Regional policy may thus be targeted for functional reasons, rather than, or in addition to, clientelistic or pork-barrel reasons (e.g., opening a new port, hospital, or road).[4] Policies that revise the territorial division of powers also have geographically targeted and uneven effects, by definition. Leaving this vast gray area unexamined has caused many scholars to miss much of the actual policy content of political competition (including competition via elections) in African countries, and thus to miss important drivers of national politics.

---

[2] See Rogers (2016: 10–11 inter alia).

[3] Garay, Palmer-Rubin, and Poertner (2020, n. 136) define discretion as existing where rules of allocation are opaque or do not follow known formal rules. Selway (2015: 52) defines programmatic policy as "geographically dispersed" and affecting the whole country. Programmatic *parties* are "mass-based." By this reasoning, those that have "a narrow geography" are, by definition, not mass-based.

[4] Stokes et al. (2013: 7–8) address this ambiguity by stressing that classification of a particular regionally targeted policy as "programmatic" depends on whether the policy is subject, in practice, to discretionary individual or geographic targeting for electoral ends. See also Kitschelt and Wilkinson (2007:1–49).

198   *Regionalism and the National Agenda*

Analysis in this chapter is structured around four substantive policy domains. Section 7.1 focuses on the question of redistributive social policy. This policy domain gives rise to the puzzle that has motivated decades of the work on democracy in Africa: Why is there so little programmatic social policy aimed at redistribution, especially after the return to mass electoral politics in the 1990s? I argue that redistributive issues *are* highly salient on national agendas, but in most countries, demands for *regional* redistribution trump demands for class- or income-based redistribution. Where both regional inequalities and territorial institutions are strong, the politics of territorial redistribution comes to the fore. Part 7.2 takes up the politics of productive-sector policy, the salience of which defies the oft-repeated argument that, in African countries, competition in elections is rarely policy-based. Part 7.3 examines the politics of national market integration. Land policy serves as the case in point. The stakes here lie not only in the uneven distribution of gains and losses in particular acts of government land allocation, but also in questions having to do with the role of the state in promoting land markets, and the rise of *national* land markets. Regionally uneven risks and gains of such proposals have stoked regional cleavages in many African countries over the last three decades. Part 7.4 concerns debates over national state design and constitutional structure. Charged issues around the territorial division of resources, powers, and prerogatives emerge and reemerge in different forms and at different administrative scales, from federalism to subnational administrative unit creation. The Conclusion stresses that policy competition often cleaves along regional lines. Uneven development itself gives rise to distinctive regional dynamics that mark national political systems as a whole.

7.1 REDISTRIBUTION: UNIVERSAL SOCIAL POLICY VERSUS REGIONAL REDISTRIBUTION REGIMES

For countries with high inequality, a technocratic remedy is income distribution on the basis of universalistic, need-based criteria. In the real world, however, the relationship between inequality and the rough-and-tumble of redistributive politics is highly conditional on the nature of inequality and its distribution across territory. This is especially true in political systems with elections based on territorial representation, where the combination of high levels of spatial (interregional) inequality and strongly territorial institutions predicts low levels of interpersonal redistribution (Beramendi 2012). This goes hand-in-hand with high salience on the national agenda of demands of interregional redistribution (Rogers 2016).[5] We see both effects in redistribution politics in African countries.

---

[5] In an empirical study of 22 OECD countries (1996–2005), Kyriacou and Roca-Sagales (2004) argue that in countries marked by high disparities in the regional distribution of wealth (and where the public sector accounts for a large share of employment), voters and regional politicians in poor regions (i.e., regions wherein average per capita income is below the national mean) are incentivized to focus their political efforts on demands for *interregional* redistribution.

7.1 Redistribution: Universal Social Policy

The emblematic case of programmatic policy deficit in African countries is found in anemic demand for policies that redistribute wealth from rich to poor. This is a puzzling outcome when we consider that these are some of the world's most unequal countries. Nita Rudra (2015: 465) pointed to the same paradox for the developing world as a whole. In democracies with mass franchise, demands for programmatic social policy should surely be high. In African countries, the paradox of lower-than-expected demand for redistributive social policy is often explained as a product of ethnic politics, which saps the drive for all forms of programmatic policy. There is, however, little in the comparative political economy literature or in worldwide data on social spending that would lead one to expect most African countries to invest strongly in programmatic redistributive social policy.

Worldwide, low levels of GDP per capita and high levels of regional inequality are strongly correlated with lower levels of redistributive spending. Both levels and types of social safety-net spending in African countries conform to this worldwide pattern.[6] The World Bank's *Atlas of Social Protection Indicators of Resilience and Equity* (ASPIRE 2015) compares African countries to other low and middle-income countries in terms of social-spending effort. ASPRIE data show that in African countries, social policy's contribution to Gini index inequality reduction is indeed very low: It averages only about 0.07% for sub-Saharan Africa (minus South Africa), compared to about 1.9% for Latin America.[7] The worldwide average is about 1.8%. The negative correlation of *spatial inequality* with redistributive social spending worldwide also holds in African countries, on average. Sub-Saharan Africa's high levels of spatial inequality (Figure 1.1) predict relatively low levels of Gini index reduction through social-policy-spending, low universalism in social policy, and pork-barrel-type targeting, and this is indeed what we see.[8] Even within the OECD, high spatial inequality predicts lower levels of redistributive spending aimed at mitigating interpersonal inequality.[9]

World Bank ASPIRE data also allow for country-level comparisons. For GNP per capita, the countries at the very high end of the distribution – South Africa, Swaziland, Botswana – score high on social policy effort and outcomes,

---

[6] ILO data from 2011 show that 5–10% of national populations in East and West Africa are covered by social policy in the form of pensions or insurance. Coverage has long been higher in southern Africa (Hujo 2013).

[7] World Bank, ASPIRE, 2015. South Africa and Botswana are strong outliers in the sub-Saharan Africa sample, with comparable scores of 8.7 and 3.9%, respectively.

[8] For the theoretical argument, see Rogers (2016). For African countries, analysis of the composition of social transfers is also suggestive of low programmatic redistributive commitment. Unconditional cash transfers, the gold standard for tax-and-transfer policy in countries of the Global South since the mid-2000s, make up a low share of all social safety-net spending (World Bank 2015). Targeted and conditional social safety-net spending accounts for the lion's share, as has long been the case for social-policy-spending in African countries.

[9] See Beramendi (2012) and Rogers (2016).

as predicted. But for the rest of Africa, variation GDP per capita does not offer much leverage on predicting cross-country variation in "redistribution effort."[10] The same is true for spatial inequality: countries with lower spatial inequality score just about the same on the Gini index reduction measure as those with higher spatial inequality. Yet when sub-Saharan Africa (SSA) is placed in worldwide context, the expected relationship holds.

South Africa as a Counterfactual: Strong Programmatic Redistributive Policy

In the sub-Saharan African context, South Africa is the counterfactual case that helps to prove the rule.[11] Its inequality structure distinguishes it from most African countries: South Africa is marked by lower-than-average spatial inequality across Admin1 units, compared to other African countries, but it has a devilishly high national Gini. Measured by interpersonal income inequality, South Africa is one of the most unequal countries in the world. This inequality structure placed South Africa in the upper left quadrant of Figure 1.1.[12] Meanwhile, South Africa's political institutions, including its electoral institutions, are also anomalous in the context of the rest of sub-Saharan Africa: They are strongly nationalizing, rather than territorializing, as captured in Figure 1.2. As CPE theory predicts, programmatic redistributive social policy in South Africa, in terms of coverage and share of GDP, is the most highly developed on the continent.

South Africa's basic inequality structure is endogenous to the country's high levels of urbanization (68%, compared to an all-SSA average of 46% in 2020), industrialization, proletarianization, service-sector development, and internal population mobility. Peasant agriculture accounts for a small share of livelihoods, compared to other African countries. Only about 25% of the population lives in the rural areas in zones where neocustomary-type land tenure prevails, and many rural households depend mostly on remittances and

---

[10] Countries like Kenya and Nigeria with higher GDP per capita do not appear to invest proportionally more in Gini index reduction than much poorer countries. Yet the role of external financing of these programs is a confounder. Donor funding accounted for over 50% of all social safety-net spending in African countries in the ASPIRE dataset in 2010, and this was targeted disproportionately at very poor countries of the Sahel G-5 (Burkina Faso, Chad, Mali, Mauritania, and Niger) and war-affected Liberia and DRC.

[11] Namibia also has very high GDP per capita, a very high Gini, a highly urbanized population, and relatively high levels of social spending. It has a political system with nonethnic parties. See Elischer (2013: 227 inter alia).

[12] See Ahlerup et al. (2016: 8), who also measure spatial inequality across provinces using nighttime luminosity. Measuring spatial inequality across South Africa's 354 magisterial districts, Naudé and Krugell (2006) find highly divergent subnational growth patterns over the 1998–2002 period. More than 70% of GDP is produced in 19 urban areas. Meanwhile, there are entrenched enclaves of wealth and poverty within each South African city and province (Moyo 2014: 11), and territorial "ethnic enclaves" as defined by the ex-Bantustans.

7.1 Redistribution: Universal Social Policy

transfers.[13] The legacy of *apartheid* – institutionalized denial of political and economic rights to Black South Africans from 1948 to 1994 – is surely what accounts for South Africa's *extreme* level of interpersonal income inequality. Its Gini index score is the world's highest.

Socioeconomic structure and institutions prevailing in South Africa today are the outcome of the rise of a national economy and society over the course of the twentieth century, fueled by the forceful integration of four distinct political entities into the Union of South Africa in 1910.[14] Forging of national *racial* identities (black/white) was part and parcel of this process – it contributed to nationalization of the political economy and worked to dilute the political salience of ethnicity, region, and language, albeit unevenly so. By the 1930s, industrialization, urbanization, and white solidarity had produced a strong, national social welfare system for whites, who made up about 26% of the national population when the system of apartheid ended in 1991.[15] The postapartheid regime inherited a strong national economy, a strong central state and progressive national tax system (Lieberman 2003), a relatively balanced urban system compared to other countries of sub-Saharan Africa (Behrens & Bala 2011: 166), and a programmatic national social policy regime.

As South Africa's economy is strongly nationalized, so too are its politics. While the South African population is racially and indeed ethnically heterogeneous, many political scientists have questioned or rejected the argument that "racial (or ethnic) census politics" defines the political system in general or the electoral system in particular.[16] At the same time, at the national level, the South African political system offers few institutional opportunities for the expression of regional interests.[17] The federal structure that was instituted at the end of apartheid to *protect* regional interests has been a weak federalism, but has served its purpose insofar as each provincial unit "contain[ed] no majority ethno-racial community" (Berman 2014: 190).[18] An electoral system

---

[13] Jacobs (2018: 885) reports that the general scholarly consensus is that the South African peasantry was almost completely proletarianized as of the 1970s. Approximately one-quarter to one-third of the Black population is still in the ex-homelands. These are zones of out-migration.

[14] By the 1850s, there were two British colonies (Cape Colony, Natal) and two sovereign Afrikaner states (Transvaal Republic, and Orange Free State).

[15] Only 10% of the white population was rural in 1980 (Cell 1982: 9).

[16] Nyenhuis and Kronke 2021; Ferree 2006, 2010; Piombo 2005.

[17] Lieberman 2003: 83, sa. 4. Lieberman draws the contrast with Brazil, where regions and regionalism are highly politically salient (2003: 4).

[18] Redrawing provincial units for the post-1994 era broke up the former Transvaal Province (the bulk of the pre-1910 South African Republic), which contained five of the Bantustans. The new boundaries placed former Bantustans in four (of nine) post-1994 provinces such that these high-poverty enclaves were not concentrated within a single jurisdiction. Although poverty is entrenched in the former Bantustans, representative institutions and territorial administration (party system, district and provincial units, powers of chiefs in the ex-Bantustans as endorsed by the ANC) do not concentrate these political units in a single territorial "container," and do not create a political opportunity structure that incentivizes the pooling of grievances across

based on list proportional representation was adopted at the same time to ensure the representation of minorities, both scattered (such as Afrikaners) and geographically concentrated (such as Zulu in KwaZulu-Natal). Even so, the ANC has been hegemonic virtually nationwide, and electorally dominant at all levels of government.[19] The ANC and the main opposition party, the Democratic Alliance (DA), are both structured as national organizations (Holmes 2020).[20] The ANC has a strong presence throughout South Africa and has driven the strong centralization of national politics.[21] Two arguably regional parties are present: the DA, which controls the Western Cape provincial legislature, and the Inkatha Freedom Party (IFP), which is anchored in its KwaZulu-Natal enclave. These are visible in the map of persistent electoral blocs in South Africa (Figure 4.2). Only the IFP has a truly regionalist agenda (it has supported devolution since the 1990s, inter alia).[22]

Since 1994, the ANC has placed addressing economic inequality within South African society at the center of its agenda. It is perhaps the clearest example among the Third Wave of Democratization countries of a mass-based, poor-people's party coming to power with a strong redistributive agenda. Known as the "party of the welfare state," the ANC ushered in a massive expansion of the tax-and-transfer system of social spending (Paret 2018; Schneider 2018). There has been a sharp increase in the social wage since the mid-1990s. In 2015, 3.3% of GDP was devoted to social spending, most of this in the form of unconditional cash transfers (World Bank 2015; Schneider 2018), which reached about 45% of households nationwide in 2015. Generous social policy coexists with urban housing grants for the urban poor. In South Africa, class and income inequality trumps spatial inequality in defining the character and extent of redistributive politics. It is the clearest example in our 12-country study of class politics, as opposed to regional politics, played out at the national level.

(or within) former Bantustans *as* territorial grievances. (The KwaZulu-Natal districts that are IFP territory are an exception.)

[19] The party system is nationalized to a much greater extent than the designers of the PR electoral system had anticipated it would be (Ferree 2018: 946). Ferree explains that the system would, in theory, produce an effective number of seat-winning parties of about 6.4, but "has hovered at 2.3 or lower" (2018: 946). She attributes this discrepancy to the fact that electoral rules interact with social structure to produce outcomes.

[20] In 2014, 20% of DA votes came from Black voters. Regional clustering is visible in the DA's high vote shares in the Western Cape and its control of the Western Cape provincial legislature. Yet this party has not advanced a territorial agenda.

[21] Bruce Berman writes (2014: 190) that in South Africa's devolved union, domination of the central state by one party has actually increased centralized state control over the federal units. And federalism "can do little to deal with the internal movement of peoples and loss of territorial focus of increasingly hybrid and intermarried populations, especially in the urban areas."

[22] As of the mid-2010s, IFP was the only regional group (2020) to have invested in regional/territorial claims for autonomy or regional carve-outs. See Munro (2001). The newer, Afrikaner-based Freedom Front (FF) also supports devolution. The EFF has challenged the ANC from the Left. It is a Black, ethno-populist party that supports land redistribution, inter alia.

7.1 *Redistribution: Universal Social Policy* 203

Most African Countries: Regional Redistribution Regimes and "Social Policy by Other Means"

In most African countries, by contrast, levels of redistributive effort are extremely low, compared to both South Africa and other low- and lower-middle-income countries (Haggard & Kaufman 2009). Seekings (2017) and Hickey et al. (2019) argued that actual levels of redistributive spending in Africa are even lower than what structural economic indicators (i.e., GNP per capita) would predict. To explain this, Hickey et al. point to social-structural features of African economies, elite attitudes, and the existence of other forms of social support. Low levels of redistributive effort are also predicted by most African countries' high levels of spatial inequality, and strongly territorial systems of political representation. These features of African countries' policymaking contexts – high regional inequalities in the context of strongly territorial political institutions – are similar to those that produce lower-than-expected levels of redistributive social spending in other parts of the world (e.g., United States, Spain). Regional inequality dampens the appetite for redistribution between rich and poor when this is expected to come at the expense of economically leading regions (through taxation, mostly).

Since the end of the colonial period in Africa, high spatial inequality has found expression in national debates and conflicts around *regional* distribution, as well as in distributive politics at the constituency level (as emphasized in many political science studies of local electoral clientelism). At the national level, the pervasiveness of the politics of *regional* distribution and redistribution in growth and spending policy in African countries was captured by Ndulu and O'Connell (2008: 61–63) in a cross-national study of 35 countries from 1960 to 2000. They find "Regional Redistribution Regimes" – in which the "basic units of redistribution" are regional – to typify national spending investment patterns in Africa in the 1970s and 1980s (but to have been curtailed under structural adjustment in the 1990s). Allocation is distributive or redistributive across regions, either in that central state resources are allocated by region, or in the zero-sum sense of redistributing wealth from the richest regions to poorer ones. Ndulu et al. (2008) stress that regional redistribution is most obvious and extensive in oil- and mineral-exporting countries such as Cameroon, Nigeria, Zambia, and the DRC. Such spending also figured into national development planning in agricultural commodity exporters such as Côte d'Ivoire and Ghana. Elsewhere, development spending targeted at lagging regions was financed largely by external borrowing (Senegal, Tanzania). Some scholars suggested that the rollback of regional redistribution policies from the late 1980s onward contributed to the state fracturing and civil wars of the 1990s and 2000s (Azam 2001, 2008; Reno 2008).

Regional redistribution from richer to poorer regions could aim to draw less productive regions into the national economy (as in the case of 1970s' investments in developing the cotton sector in Northern Côte d'Ivoire) and/or to shore up national cohesion ("to buy peace").[23] In this double sense, regionally targeted investment and subsidies often served the same function as "territorial cohesion" policies in the European Union.[24] Such distributive spending has often entailed patronage-based distribution (e.g., in allocation of government jobs), but the patronage aspect of regionally targeted investment and subsidies can coexist with the policy, functional, and territorial aspects that are the focus here. Regional redistribution regimes are a territorial strategy of economy- and state-building. They respond to regional tensions and demands, and also help to consolidate regions as distinct actors in national politics (Keating 2009) and *regional identity* as a citizenship category (Cammett & McLean 2011).

The visibility and salience of regional revenue-sharing institutions and formulae are markers of the prominence of regional distribution issues on national political agendas. In Kenya, Nigeria, Ethiopia, Sudan, and DRC, transfers from central to regional governments are a centerpiece of national fiscal contracts. In Nigeria, this consists of sharing-out oil rents extracted from the Southeast. Kenya's 2010 Constitution created a regional redistribution regime based on transfers from the national budget to 47 new counties, following a revenue-sharing formula that takes Kenya's stark regional inequalities into account explicitly.[25] Regional disadvantage is measured in terms of variation across counties in economic context, captured in population density and a county-level poverty index.

Recent studies of social policy in African countries emphasize the significance of "social policy by other means."[26] This consists largely of measures associated with what Seekings and Natrass (2005) and Hickey et al. (2019) call "agrarian welfare regimes" (or agrarian distribution regimes) because they are centered on the rural smallholder or peasant household, rather than on the urban worker, or the urban poor.[27] Agrarian welfare regimes seek to provide a subsistence floor for most of the poor by upholding the rural household as a functioning unit of consumption, production, and social reproduction. Prime instruments for doing so are land policy, regionally and locally targeted "rural development" schemes (including farm input subsidies), locally targeted social-service delivery (especially schools and health facilities) and, in some circumstances and places, food transfers and food subsidies. Land access via

---

[23] Woods 1990, Boone 2007.

[24] Crezensi et al. (2015) report that "An equitable territorial distribution of the benefits of the integration process is a founding principle of all EU policies" (Art. 75 of the EU Treaty). See Iammarino, Rodriguez-Pose, and Storper 2019: 287–288 on spatial-redistribution-cum-equity policies in Europe (a.k.a. equity through territorial redistribution).

[25] The new counties were defined along the lines of old districts, following the lines of the old native reserves. On devolution in Kenya, see Kanyinga (2016) and Ngigi and Busolo (2019). Laji (2019) situates the 2010 devolution in the context of a long history of regional planning strategies in Kenya.

[26] Mkandawire 2016: 11; Seekings 2017; Ayeko-Kümmeth and Schlichte 2021.

[27] Seekings and Nattrass 2005; Seekings 2008; Lavers 2019: 66, 67; Lavers 2023.

7.2 Sectoral Policy and Regionally Specific Policy

neocustomary land tenure regimes has long been the anchor of such a social model. A family landholding under a neocustomary land tenure regime is a kind of asset-based entitlement that is immobile, formally nonalienable, and allocated through membership in a state-recognized social collectivity tied to an ethnic homeland. Since the 1990s, many African governments have responded to electoral incentives to invest in agrarian welfare regimes, including in farm subsidies (Seekings 2019: 67) and in measures that defend neocustomary land tenure.

These policy instruments – land tenure policies, rural development programs, agricultural subsidies, state investment in rural health and rural education – have strong distributive and redistributive content.[28] All are spatially targeted, both regionally and locally. They are not necessarily clientelistic in the narrow sense of electoral clientelism (i.e., individual or brokered exchange, conditional on individual or polling-station-level voting behavior). Indeed, over the course of the postcolonial period, *most* land allocation in policy and practice has not conformed to the classic logic of electoral clientelism: State-backed neocustomary land tenure regimes are supposed to underwrite entitlements, rather than contingent, revocable transfers. (Where neocustomary land tenure prevails, it is the *exceptions* to this rule or norm, which may come in the form of land takeaways or new allocations, that may entail high-stakes political clientelism.[29]) Even where "agrarian model social assistance" serves as a vehicle for clientelism at the point of delivery to an individual, household, or locality, it is embedded in larger choices over policy and geographic targeting that are made by government at the regional and national scales of politics, where wider considerations of regional distribution are at play.

7.2 SECTORAL POLICY AND REGIONALLY SPECIFIC POLICY INTERESTS

> Allocation on a functional basis is not territorially neutral.
>
> (Keating 2003)

Because most productive-sector or sectoral policy in African countries is not nationwide in scope (because economic activity is distributed unevenly across space), it is excluded from the "programmatic policy" category in many political science analyses and often treated, ipso facto, as clientelistic policy. Political science studies often assert that electoral politics in African countries revolves

---

[28] Social-service spending on health and primary education, and electrification and roads, are types of territorially targeted pork-barrel spending that have strongly redistributive effects. However, these vary greatly in their progressivity. See Rogers (2016: 70).

[29] Land is most likely become an instrument of political clientelism where it is controlled directly by the state (i.e., where the state recognizes neither neocustomary tenure nor private property). See Boone (2014).

mostly around valence issues (i.e., issues everyone agrees upon, like being pro-development or anti-corruption), rather than substantive policy issues. This section advances a different view, highlighting the salience of sectoral policy in the supply and demand for government, and on national policy agendas.

Sectoral policy issues are critical in coalition-building in electoral politics, and in tying voters to persistent electoral blocs and to political parties. The electorally salient issues often pertain to agricultural-sector regulation – producer prices, marketing and market regulation, subsidies and inputs, and protectionism. This should not be surprising. In many African countries, agriculture weighs heavy in overall GDP and employment profiles and provides a large share of exports. This is the case in most of the countries featured in the 12-country study presented in Chapters 4–6.

Although modalities of state intervention in agricultural markets and productive sectors changed in the structural adjustment era of the 1990s, the general importance of such policy to national and regional economies remains high. Fox and Jayne reported in 2020 that "Africa's agricultural exports have increased substantially in the last two decades … The region's lower-middle income countries, led by Côte d'Ivoire, Ghana, and Kenya, have become export powerhouses, with net agricultural trade surpluses of more than $5 billion/year. SSA's top [agricultural] exports are mainly tropical commodities such as cocoa, coffee, tea, and cotton" (p. 1).[30] Regionally focused agricultural commodity policies remain essential to quality standardization and control, input distribution, and crop-processing and commercialization in sectors that involve tens of thousands of household producers. Traders, transporters, processors, and input suppliers are also highly sensitive to price, tax, tariff, regulatory, and crop-processing policies. While the political marginality (and poverty) of the most remote rural areas of many countries appears to have worsened since 2000, policy competition among the better-resourced and mobilized producer regions appears to have increased.[31]

Colin Poulton (2012: 9, 10, 14) stresses the politically strategic nature and stark *regional* targeting of agricultural policy, as well as the critical role of political "championing" by senior politicians in bringing such policy to the cabinet table, and then taking it through the legislative process, and to actual implementation. As Poulton argues, such policies are highly salient in mobilizing electoral support at the regional level and in building national coalitions, including by "forming alliances of regional voting blocs, in which case different

---

[30] In Mali, cotton seed production tripled between 1995 and 2005, "providing the main source of livelihood for one-quarter of the Malian population" (Behrendt 2006: 1).

[31] Potts 2019. On the renewed salience of agricultural policies since the 1990s, both in terms of proactive producer policies and for mobilizing political support, see also Bates and Block (2013), Poulton (2012, 2014), Whitfield et al. (2015), and Schulz (2020). On cotton and cotton producers in Mali, see Behrendt (2006), Roy (2010), and Serra (2014). On Zambia maize, see Sitko and Jayne (2014).

7.2 *Sectoral Policy and Regionally Specific Policy*

[sectorally targeted policy] 'offers' can be made to each bloc."[32] Poulton writes that regional constituencies can be "brought into" an electoral coalition either through credible policy offers *or* through payoffs to individual, high-status regional leaders. This distinction would seem to apply to the different types of constituencies identified in the 12-country study presented here. The *absence* of electorally salient sectoral policy is more likely in *non-bloc areas*, which are not specialized producer regions and do not display a pattern of regionally cohesive voting. Electoral mobilization is likely to happen around ad hoc political organizing efforts and electoral appeals that are specific to particular localities and/or aimed at local political elites, rather than designed to appeal to the occupational interests of significant regional populations. From this perspective, in regions with strong producer profiles, shared ethnicity is a resource in electoral mobilization, but not a necessary ingredient.

Much evidence from Kenya, Ghana, and other African countries connects the *timing* of critical policy announcements or legislative votes on policy to the electoral cycle. This is further evidence in support of the argument that career politicians engaged in successive (repeated) cycles of electoral competition believe that delivering policy helps to build coalitions and win votes.

Potential agents of such regional coordination are identifiable at multiple levels of government. Regional caucuses of MPs are common.[33] Regional political parties can serve as vehicles for the coordination of regional interests. In Kenya, following the constitutional replacement of the former 7 regions with 47 new counties, there has been an informal reconsolidation of provincial-level regional delegations of elected politicians (see Hassan 2015: 601). At the cabinet level, ministries connected to agriculture, mining, livestock/pastoralism, and industry are often highly regionally focused and often champion regional sectoral interests.[34] Studies of the politics of sectoral policy in Africa offer support for these claims. Clearest evidence of a link between policy interests of voters and electoral mobilization/politics is found in work that shows that parties in power do indeed deliver targeted sectoral policies to their main blocs of supporters.[35] In a tough test of the hypothesis, change of the incumbent party in the presidency leads to shifts in policy. This would confirm the salience of

---

[32] These are communicated through credible local (regional and local) intermediaries or "regional leaders" and "district-level elites." See Poulton (2012: 11, 12, 15, 19), citing Keefer and Vlaicu (2008) on credibility.

[33] See Green (2008: 11) for Uganda, Kerosi (2018) for Central Kenya, and di Matteo (2022) for Northern Kenya's Pastoralist Coalition.

[34] For Kenya, Kanyinga, and Poulton (2014: S167).

[35] Low levels of constituency competitiveness mean that voters in a given constituency may not be invited to choose between two alternative sets of policies. All politicians campaigning in a constituency may promote the same broad policy agenda, just as they are likely to be members of the same ethnic group, as Ferree (2012, 2022) has pointed out. This means that it is often not possible to compare the vote shares of two candidates who offer rival policy packages, just as in most or many constituencies it is not possible to compare the vote shares of candidates of different ethnic groups.

both policy and of elections. Actors interested in policy would have reason to believe that the party in power can deliver policies that affect their interests.[36]

A series of articles analyzing the politics of sectoral policy in Ghana, Kenya, Malawi, and Zambia by Eun Kyung Kim (2017, 2018, 2019, 2020) shows that incumbent parties do provide agricultural policies that cater to the interests of producers of crops concentrated in their geographic strongholds. Policies that favor producers in a particular sector may come at the expense of opposition parties' backers. Opposition parties, for their part, often promise policy that will favor distinctive producer interests in their own stronghold regions.[37] For the case of Ghana, Kim shows that upon coming to power in 2001, Ghana's NPP, strongly aligned with cocoa-sector interests, raised cocoa farmers' share of export prices from 65% in 2001 to 80%, and created a cocoa export revenue set aside as development funds for infrastructure, input subsidies, and technical assistance for the cocoa sector. These policies "significantly improved productivity and farmers' well-being in the cocoa sector" (2019: 967). At the same time, NPP oversaw a surge in rice imports, which increased more than ten-fold from 2000 to 2005. In 2008 it removed the import duty on rice. This militated against the interests of domestic rice producers, concentrated regionally in Eastern Ghana, aligned with the rival party, the NDC. Rice-sector fortunes declined under NPP tenure, but recovered under NDC presidents (2009–2016), who emphasized the need to increase local rice production under several rice-related projects, imposed a substantial duty of 20% on imported rice, and provided support in the form of extension services and inputs to smallholder rice farmers. These policies restrained rice imports and "allowed well-protected domestic rice producers to increase output in 2009–2011" (Kim 2019: 969). Kim uses the concept of "issue ownership" to describe parties' sector-based policy platforms, insisting that the sector orientation of leading parties' policy platforms is stable over time, and that this contributes to building multiethnic electoral coalitions.

These findings add to those of Kanyinga and Poulton (2014) and others on Kenya, Zambia, and Malawi, inter alia. Studies of Malawi show tight connections between sectorally and regionally targeted productive-sector policy on the one hand, and party-building and partisan mobilization, on the other, especially for the Central Region where tobacco reigned supreme from the 1960s to the early 1990s, and around highly charged tea sector issues in the 2000s. Studies of the politics of key sectoral policies in other countries in the 12-country study featured in earlier chapters include coffee policy in Cameroon, cocoa policy in Côte d'Ivoire, sugar and coffee in Kenya, cotton in Mali, and coffee, cotton, and cashews in Tanzania. In Malawi, Kenya, and Zambia, maize policy is often a high-profile issue, although the territorial reach of maize

---

[36] Deviations in sectoral policy brought on by electoral turnover were also observed in country case studies presented in Chapter 6.

[37] Kim 2018, 2019.

7.3 *Land Tenure Policy*

policy is generally more diffuse than that of export crops (given that maize is widely grown in these countries as a subsistence crop as well as a nationally traded commercial crop).

Employing individual-level survey data to get a closer look at the behavior of Ghanaian voters living in areas specialized in either cocoa or rice production, Eun Kyung Kim (2018) matches Afrobarometer survey data on respondents' voting intentions in the 2004–2012 elections to districts' industrial and agricultural profiles, and their ethnic makeup.[38] She shows that living in a district that is specialized in cocoa or rice production is a significant predictor of consistent support for the political party associated with one or the other sector-based policy platforms. Being in a cocoa-producing district in Ghana predicts support for the NPP, while being in a rice district predicts support for the NDC (Kim, 2018: 40), even among individuals who are not members of the ethnic groups that predominate in those regions. She concludes that parties provide both ethno-clientelistic *and* policy-based appeals, and that in specialized agricultural regions, the latter are effective in bringing non-coethnics into the party coalition. This is consistent with Poulton's (2014) arguments about the political salience of sectorally targeted producer policies.

7.3 LAND TENURE POLICY

Land policy plays out as distributive politics in African countries because of its strongly allocative character. This makes land activism by national government a political lightning rod, often defining highly salient issues that can mobilize or even polarize parts of the electorate in national elections. Land issues were highly salient in national elections in Kenya in 1992, 1997, 2008, and 2013; in Zimbabwe in 2000 and 2008; in Uganda in 2010; and in Côte d'Ivoire throughout the 1990s and 2000s. In Kenya, for example, "[t]he land question … formed the central axis of the 2007 campaign."[39] In 2013, the main parties again "differed widely over land ownership and control, and over the new devolution of power to the 47 counties."[40] Nationwide land law reform via legislative or constitutional change has burst onto the national stage as a contested issue in almost every one of the twelve countries featured in Chapters 4–6 at one or several moments in the postcolonial era.

In most African countries, law and administrative action segment national space into distinct territories or land units that fall into one of three land tenure

---

[38] Kim 2018: 40. (See also Ichino & Nathan 2013, who draw analogous inferences from electoral data at the polling station level.) Individual-level data on agricultural policy preferences is very hard to come by. Most Afrobarometer survey results pertain to the national level, although some are valid at Admin1. Poulton (2014: s110) notes that "Unfortunately, Afrobarometer surveys do not contain questions specifically about agricultural policies."

[39] Kagwanja and Southall (2009).

[40] Kenya, "The closest of shaves," *Africa Confidential*, 56/6, March 5, 2013, p. 1

types: neocustomary land tenure, state land, and statutory private property (freehold or leasehold).[41] These categorical distinctions often fall along the lines of administrative divisions. Neocustomary tenure accounts for approximately 80–85 percent of all farmland in African countries (as a rough, cross-country average) (Boone 2014: 22–23). Under this form of tenure, governments have allocated (conceded) the right to access land to collectivities recognized by the state as holding "customary" or ancestral rights to the land. Where this is the case, land administration is segmented into locally specific jurisdictions that usually correspond to units of territorial administration that are traceable to colonial Native Authorities and sub-units thereof (chieftaincies), or to ethnic reserves in former settler colonies such as Kenya. The *raison d'être* of forms of neocustomary tenure that are descended from colonial indirect rule is to protect group land access, entitlements, and territory; and to impede permanent transfers of land (i.e., land alienation) to nonmembers of the entitled community. Land rights are often rented out or leased (or sold informally), but the scope of market forces is constrained by the neocustomary nature of tenure. Today, the majority of all adults in most African countries depend upon a neocustomary landholding for their livelihood, a subsistence floor or livelihood supplement for themselves or for family members, or de facto social insurance.[42] On state land – such as in national forest reserves, national parks, or on state-owned land – neocustomary rights are not recognized. Governments can elect to transfer portions of the state's domain to individual users or groups, or to grant or revoke the legal forbearance that allows residents to use state land provisionally (as "squatters"). In most countries, private property in land has long been concentrated in municipal jurisdictions; districts where colonial regimes had created private freehold tenure (for European settlers only, at the time); highly commercialized periurban areas or transport corridors; and enclaves zoned to attack outside investment (in tourism, agro-industry, or industry, for example).

Postcolonial governments have been remarkably activist in the land politics and policy domain. Land activism revolves largely around the allocation and reallocation of land across and within land tenure categories, and sometimes across user groups. Central state powers to allocate and reallocate reside mostly in executive branch agencies (the president's office, Ministries of Land or the Interior), making the president's office and agencies of territorial administration the focal point of land allocation politics. Between the state and entitled collectivities, what is at stake is demands for new land allocations or the defense of past allocations. Allocation from the state's reserve of land is common. This includes degazetting state forests to give forest land to villages or displaced communities; allocation of plots on settlement schemes that have

---

[41] See Boone 2014.
[42] De facto social insurance includes a place to live and subsistence in retirement for themselves or their dependents. See above, on social policy by other means.

7.3 Land Tenure Policy

been carved out of the state land domain to individual claimants, or to add to the territory of ethnic homelands; and the "return" of state-owned land to collectivities.[43] State activism also includes redividing land among communities, such as the recognition of carve-outs for subgroups along the lines of subdivisions within the ex-Native Authorities. In the former settler colonies of Kenya, Zimbabwe, and South Africa, the national agenda is profoundly shaped by ongoing contestation over lands expropriated by white settlers from the 1880s to the 1950s. In Kenya and Zimbabwe, land struggles have formed the main axes of national politics, including electoral politics, since national Independence.

Economic inequalities and grievances serve as the justificatory basis of particular group claims, and these often follow the fault lines of territorial administrative divisions of provinces, districts, former native reserves, and electoral constituencies. The state's territorial grid often defines the ethnic and supra-ethnic identities that are mobilized in demands for land (such as Kalenjin, Northerners in Ghana, and Mijikenda at Kenya Coast), as well as the boundaries of the territories and land domains that are objects of contention.

The kind of land tenure reform that has been on the agenda of many African governments since the late 1990s aims at tenure uniformization and the development of nationally-integrated land markets through the registration and titling of neocustomary land. Conversion of neocustomary tenure to private land tenure erases the customary claims and entitlements of collectivities, families, and households. This raises the spectre of new winners and losers that are likely to emerge along existing lines of economic inequality within communities, as well as along the lines of inequalities between regions. While tensions within communities are most likely to turn inward, tensions between regions can find expression at the national level in classic forms of conflict over national market integration.

Regional Claims and Regional Cleavages in Land Policy

In the national arena, land politics often finds expression in *regional* claims. This is because of the overlapping of territorial institutions of land governance, regional inequalities which provide ideological and material justification for claims, and structures of political representation that bring regional interests to the fore.

Examples of *regional* land interests that are advanced in the national political arena are visible in almost every country examined in the 12-country study. In Malawi, land reform was a high-salience political issue in the election of Southern politicians in the late 1990s and 2000s. In Côte d'Ivoire, land issues

---

[43] See Boone 2014. In addition, forbearance shown to politically protected groups around local invasions of, or encroachments on, state land and idle private land has long been very common. See Holland 2017.

mobilized regional constituencies in the West long before they exploded onto the national stage in the 1990s. Northern Uganda's oppositional stance vis-à-vis the Museveni regime in the 1990s crystallized around land issues in the North. In 1979, to get Northern support, the Ghanaian government made a constitutional change to concede to Northern demands "to return land to its owners" (Lund 2008). At the Kenya Coast, by the 1980s, reform of land tenure to deal with landlessness and squatting "had become the single most important issue around which support was mobilized by Coast politicians" (Kanyinga 2000: 118). In Tanzania in the 1970s, the CCM built its regional base in the central part of the country through Ujamaa policies of rural resettlement, leaving land tenure in the country's most prosperous agricultural regions in the North largely undisturbed. In Zimbabwe, Mugabe consolidated support in the north of the country in the 2000s under his Fast Track land allocation program. *Regional* land interests are advanced/articulated at the national level by *regional actors*, including MP caucuses in Kenya, Uganda, and Côte d'Ivoire, emirates' networks in Northern Nigeria, and regional alliances of hierarchical chieftaincies in Ghana.

In many African countries since the 1990s, the specter of programmatic policy change in the land tenure sector has ignited regional cleavages that are clearly visible in the national arena. Proposals for the creation of nationwide land markets have acute distributive implications because the risks and benefits of land commodification are spread unevenly across regions. Homogenization of the land tenure regime via the creation of national land markets would, by definition, do away with the locally protectionist land tenure regimes that mediate the access of most of the population to land in most countries. Such debate came to a head in many countries in the 1990s and 2000s, when donors threw their weight behind large-scale tenure reforms aimed at universal land registration and titling.[44]

Land tenure reforms of the 1990s and 2000s aimed explicitly at eroding neocustomary land tenure regimes and moving toward national uniformity in land administration, with the goal of expanding and stimulating national land markets. Land parcel demarcation and registration in Kenya, Côte d'Ivoire, Zambia, Malawi, and many other countries aimed to replace family entitlements with private land titles.[45] This change would shift the locus of authority around land from extended family (or chief) to the state. It also redefines who holds land rights within families and communities. Viewed more broadly, commodification also alters the balance of power in competition for land

---

[44] See Wily 2001, Manji 2006, Chauveau 2000, Boone 2019, and Lavigne Delville and Moalic 2019.

[45] In Ethiopia, where registration aimed at individualization of ownership (at the family level) and expansion of the state's land administration powers at the expense of local authorities, the drive to full land commodification was strongly attenuated. See Lavers 2013, 2023. In Ghana, land tenure reform aimed at bureaucratizing the powers and prerogatives of neocustomary authorities.

7.3 Land Tenure Policy

access within countries. It empowers holders of capital who have state connections to buy land, and who can master the bureaucratic machinery of titling, at the expense of holders of historical and neocustomary entitlements who may lack both. Land markets raise the specter of dispossession through land tenure conversions in which the decks are systematically stacked in favor of wealthier, better-connected individuals and groups.[46]

Because rural regions of African countries are marked by unevenness in the extent of rural class differentiation, market integration of rural economies, and land market development, there is a lack of territorial uniformity in the potential impact of proposals to pursue state-wide policies that aim at land commodification. Interests diverge across regions, and in some cases, within them.

Resistance to programmatic registration and titling has found expression at the regional level in *lagging* regions. These are the most at risk of loss of asset entitlement, erosion of local protection in land allocation, erosion of local protectionism in land transactions, and erosion of downwardly accountable local authority over land. In such regions, neocustomary land tenure and some modicum of subnational political autonomy are interlocking, with local land authorities and local landholders jointly exposed to the risk that land commodification represents. In national political arenas, regional-level actors and organizations responded defensively to the specter of programmatic land tenure reform in lagging regions in several of the country cases considered here, including in northern Kenya, northern Uganda, and northern and western Côte d'Ivoire. Regional leaders are incentivized to retain local support and capacity to mobilize constituencies by protecting existing land entitlements, via mobilization of credible political threats if need be (Azam 2001).

By contrast, leaders and wealthy citizens in regions with high market integration (and with better connectivity, higher incomes, more education) have been national drivers of a push to market expansion in Kenya and Côte d'Ivoire. In Kenya in 2013, for example, the dominant players within Kenya's Jubilee Alliance, anchored in central Kenya, campaigned on "unlocking the economic potential of land" through nationwide titling. By contrast, the rival coalition, CORD, pushed for the opposite – land grants to land-hungry Rift Valley Province communities.[47]

Within advantaged or advanced regions, tensions around land commodification are more likely to take class-like form. Local authorities with land powers may transfer land to wealthier members of their own communities and share in the "bonanza" of primitive accumulation generated in this process. In such regions, individualization and demarcation of holdings are likely to already be more advanced. Full land commodification, registration, and titling require little or no administrative pressure. This is the case in the Agboville

---

[46] For regional dynamics in Côte d'Ivoire, see Boone (2018) and Boone, Bado, Dion, and Irigo (2021). On Uganda, Green (2006) and Gay (2016).

[47] CORD is Coalition for Reforms and Democracy.

region of Côte d'Ivoire. It is less than 50 miles from the capital city of Abidjan and the target of a land rush of salaried sons-of-the-soil who are eager to acquire land.[48]

Divergence of regional preferences around nationwide land commodification helps to explain the rocky course of titling initiatives in African countries since the late 1990s, and the eventual backing-off of programmatic land registration and titling drives by international donors. In Kenya and Côte d'Ivoire, extreme deviations in policy were driven by electoral turnover, as control of the presidency alternated between regional electoral blocs with rivalrous land policy preferences. In Zambia, less extreme deviations in land policy, but highly significant shifts nonetheless, coincided with the coming to power of the MMD in the early 1990s and its subsequent disintegration (Englebert 2005; Boone 2007).

South Africa again provides a counterfactual. Land politics as played out in the national political arena expresses tensions by race and class, rather than region. The ANC government has adopted a "willing buyer, willing seller" approach to land (re)distribution. Redistribution is understood to mean "from white to Black owner." Any Black person can acquire land anywhere in the country. The DP has resisted any land allocation that impinges on property rights. To the political left of the ANC, since 2010 the Economic Freedom Fighters (EFF) party has made the slow pace of land transfer an electorally salient issue at the national level, but neither the EFF nor its land demands have a particular territorial base or target. It calls for accelerated land redistribution nationwide. On the far right, Afrikaner landowners, who are regionally dispersed, have gravitated to the Freedom Front, which categorically opposes the ANC's land reform agenda.[49]

7.4 STATE STRUCTURE/NATIONAL DESIGN

> Federalism politicizes inequality "in a uniquely geographic manner."
>
> (Bakke & Wibbles 2006: 14)

The final instantiation of our argument lies in struggles over state structure itself. For many African countries, competition and conflict around constitutional and administrative design have been a persistent feature of national politics over the last half-century. As in other parts of the world, conflict over state design is often driven by distributive concerns. As Markus Kurtz writes,

the institutions themselves become part of the redistributive struggle among contending political parties and social actors, rather than channels that shape the form that redistributive conflict takes ... [A]dministrative development itself thus becomes the terrain on which political conflict is fought, with [elites] seeking to retrench or transform

---

[48] Boone, Bado Dion, and Irigo (2021).
[49] On South African land reform politics, see Dyzenhaus 2022.

7.4 State Structure/National Design

important institutions and [their rivals] seeking to use and expand them to enforce redistribution or development goals. (Kurtz 2013: 178)

In African countries, where spatial inequality is high and institutions are strongly territorial, state design and redesign are often driven by competition and conflict over distribution *across territorial units*. This is visible in conflicts around unitary versus segmented state structure, centralization and devolution, subnational unit breakup and creation, market segmentation (local protectionism) or market development (unification). These may be fought over as matters of constitutional choice or policy choice, or play out in executive strategy.[50] Contending players are territorial groups, often defined in terms of the national administrative grid, rather than income groups, or rival political parties of national scope. Outcomes affect not only the distribution of resources across regional units, but also the distribution of power across tiers of government.

Nationalist struggles that emerged in the 1950s and 1960s over unitary versus regionalist state structure (Kpressa et al. 2011) would define cleavage lines in national politics for many decades. As argued in Chapter 3, protagonists in the decolonization-era politics of national design were leaders of, or were bidding to represent, regional units that had been administered as distinctive entities (districts or Native Authorities) under colonial rule. These territorial units were economically heterogeneous in terms of the nature and extent of their contribution to, and integration into, the national economy.

Many regional actors fiercely defended powers, prerogatives, and forms of local government that were institutionalized in colonial indirect rule. This was true for Ashanti, Buganda, Lozi (Barotseland), and the Northern Nigerian emirates. Northern Nigeria under the British was governed as a separate colony, "indirectly" through the hierarchically ordered Sokoto Caliphate and the cooperating Borno emirate. For leaders of provinces of the Northern region, the stakes of independence within a united Nigeria were two-fold. First was preserving their political power vis-à-vis both their own populations and the wealthier but less populous South. Second was preserving the inflow of southern resources that subsidized the North as a region, and the favorable policy regime that protected northern domestic-market-oriented manufacturing and agricultural interests.[51] In some countries, wealthy regions wanted either regional autonomy or to go it alone. They wagered that a smaller, independent, wealthy polity was better off than a rich region serving as a "milch cow region" in a large poor country governed by their political rivals. Katanga in Congo in the early 1960s is an example.[52]

---

[50] There may be constitutional or legal concessions to actors advancing explicitly regional interests, as in Ghana 1979 over land policy in the North, as described by Lund (2008). Kanyinga (2016) discusses "patronage politics" in geostrategic, regional terms, rather than as relations among individuals (or relations between MPs and voters at the polling station level).

[51] Harnishfeger 2018: 177, 185 inter alia.

[52] On Katanga, Lemarchand 1962.

For the most part, postcolonial governments have upheld the neocustomary land entitlements created under colonial rule. In doing so, they confirmed the subnational territorial jurisdictions that defined these, in their territorial extent, local specificities, and land governance structure. Government recognition of ethnic groups and ethnic homelands has thus constituted a kind of constitutional settlement (representing what has served as a credible commitment) between state-recognized ethnic collectivities and the postcolonial state. The central state became the (provisional) guarantor of boundaries and allocations inherited from colonial rule. This kind of "social contract" not only divided the land itself and land governance authority between the state and subnational collectivities (by ethnic homeland boundaries, often coinciding with districts and subdistricts), but also divided land and territory between different subnational collectivities. Tanzania was an exception. Nyerere expressly rejected the colonial-era ethnic division of the land and made the state itself the direct administrator of a de-ethnicized form of customary land tenure (Boone & Nyeme 2015).

Wibbles (2005), Rodden (2009), and others have argued that high regional disparities shape the "original federal contract" in political unions. "Holding together" unions may be based on cooptation of subnational units on terms that preserve the political cohesion of distinct regions, rather than (or as much as) on regional wealth-sharing agreements.[53] This choice is itself shaped by regional inequalities (as was the case with the United States, India, Spain, and Canada). These rules then shape patterns of coalitional politics that emerge in regionally unequal polities.

These generalizations hold for many African countries. Independence bargains were struck among contending social and regional interests, and indeed between new national leaders and various regionally and ethnically identified populations. In effect, the de facto equilibrium outcome for nongoverning regions was acquiescence with central government (over)rule in exchange for government recognition of distinctive communities, a measure of local self-rule (via central recognition of local neocustomary authority), and reaffirmation of the central state's commitment to neocustomary land tenure regimes within colonial land units. In many countries, however, where regions were too weak vis-à-vis the center (northern Tanzania, especially Bukoba) or too strong (Western Cameroon, Central Uganda anchored in Buganda, Ashanti in Ghana), no such equilibrium emerged, and either political undermining of the weaker unit or conflict among regions ensued.

---

[53] See Diaz-Cayeros (2006: 12 inter alia) on cooptation and enforcement mechanisms in federal contracts. Cooptation by the center may mean that the center guarantees the political power of regional leaders and allocates resources to them. Contract enforcement may require that regional actors retain the power to politically mobilize their territorial constituency. As Amuitz Garmendia Madariaga (2014) suggested for Europe, in postcolonial Africa an important part of the constitutional pact may be not interregional redistribution, but rather guaranteeing regional autonomy arrangements among the units.

7.4 State Structure/National Design

In many countries, nationalist-era struggles over state structure proved to be only the first round. Politics around defining constitutional order, including the rise and repression of secessionist bids, was a focal point of 1960s–1980s' national consolidation. In the post-1990 period, Kenya held constitutional referenda over devolution in 2005 and 2010. Côte d'Ivoire's national territory split in two along the North–South divide from 2000 to 2010. Mali undertook territorial repartition of powers in 1991 and 1992, offering a regional autonomy to the North and then extending a measure of this nationwide through devolution over the course of the 1990s. Mali then faced secessionist conflict in the 2000s (Seely 2001; Hesseling & van Dijk 2005: 180). Nigeria's 1993 constitution has been sorely tested by the rise of a separate legal order in the Northern region (Sharia law), insurgency in Borno in the Northeast, and in ex-Biafra in the Southeast. Cameroon has faced renewed mobilization by regional groups advancing demands for federation or secession.[54]

Agents advancing regional demands for (re)design of national institutions are often *political parties*. Many enduring partisan formations in the countries featured in Chapters 4–6 built their identities as political organizations around demands for constitutional configurations that would protect or advance regional interests. Programmatic, territorial demands often figure in parties' electoral appeals to regionally concentrated voters. This can happen alongside the clientelist promises of boreholes and electrification that are featured in studies of electoral behavior. In Kenya, the political party representing the Central bloc was the only one to campaign against the 2010 Constitution, which devolved power to 47 new counties. In Ghana, the party representing the Ashanti region, the core of today's NPP, emerged in the 1950s to demand federalism and devolution to preserve its wealth and autonomy. In Cameroon, the UDF is the party of the anglophone provinces which have demanded federalism and regional recognition since the Independence era. In Côte d'Ivoire, the FPI has consistently, since the 1990s, pushed for devolution that would push power and resources away from the long-dominant Abidjan–Yamoussoukro axis and toward the politically marginalized West (and southeast). In Nigeria, the nationalist-era NPN and its post-1993 incarnation, the NPC, both built regional cohesion around explicit calls for constitutional engineering to advance Northern interests. The IFP in South Africa has called for devolution since the 1990s.

Predicting Divergent Preferences over State Design

CPE literature conceptualizes the territorial dimension of politics as the allocation of power between center and regions, or periphery[ies]. The default move

---

[54] Civil wars along territorial lines scarred Nigeria, Congo, and several others. The Kenyan and Zimbabwean national armies fought regional wars of mass repression, the so-called Shifta War in the 1960s and the Gukurahundi in Zimbabwe from 1983 to 1987.

		Economically	
		leading	lagging
Politically	leading	**1.** centralization anti-redistribution	**2.** centralization/ pro-redistribution
	lagging	**3.** decentralization/ anti-redistribution	**4.** decentralization/ pro-redistribution

FIGURE 7.1 Regional preferences over state design
Notes: Expectations based upon a region's position as economically leading or lagging, and politically leading (dominant) or lagging (not dominant), in the national setting.

is to frame this territorial dimension of politics as orthogonal to the redistributive dimension, which is defined along a right–left dimension. Yet in some countries, the two dimensions align (Rovny 2015). When they do, the politics of distribution and redistribution of both wealth and political power can be strongly territorial. Canada, United Kingdom since the 1990s, Spain, and Belgium are examples. In such cases, gains and losses of market integration, jurisdictional unification (suppression of subnational unit specificity or heterogeneity), political integration, and redistribution within the national polity will be distributed unevenly, both across and within units. Regional inequality and prevailing power balances among regions give rise to divergent preferences.

Figure 7.1 represents these differences schematically. This figure returns to Chapter 5's two-dimensional typology of regional actors (persistent electoral blocs) as either politically advantaged, economically advantaged, advantaged on both dimensions, or disadvantaged on both. Cell 1 represents what was identified in Chapter 5 as a persistent electoral bloc that arises in an economically leading region, and that is aligned with the regime in power. Leading regions that are aligned with the regime in power may expect to reap a disproportionate share of the benefits of centralization, market integration, and jurisdictional unification. This is not only because market forces of agglomeration will tend to favor already developed regions, but also because political advantage can be used to check the redistributive demands of lagging regions. Bayart (2013) called such regions "drivers of national unity."

Cell 3 describes economically strong regions that do not control the central government. The prediction here is that leading actors in such regions will seek to shelter their wealth and prerogatives from central control. Examples are Katanga in the DRC, ex-Biafra in Nigeria, and the other "wealthy opposition-leaning zones" that were identified in Chapter 5.

The preferences of regions that lack resources will also depend on their position in the national distribution of power. Cell 2 denotes lagging regions that

7.4 State Structure/National Design

control the central government; the suggestion here is that they are likely to push centralization as a way to enforce taxation on the wealthier regions and to weaken local centers of possible resistance. Ghana from the mid-1950s to 1966 is an example of this: Nkrumah drove strong state centralization "in order to enforce a distributionally-favorable property rights regime and system of fiscal redistribution" (Firmin-Sellers 1996: 92). Nyerere in Tanzania from the 1960s to the 1980s, and Kaunda in Zambia from the 1960s to 1980s are also examples.

Cell 4 is economically lagging regions that do not control the central government. They often see devolution as a way to redistribute resources from rich to poor regions and protect local prerogatives. In Kenya, demands for devolution have traditionally been associated with minorities and regions that lack power and resources. Majimboism, called for by KADU in the 1960s, by the Moi government in the 1980s,[55] and by the Rift Valley persistent electoral bloc in the 1990s and 2000s, favored a regional form of government to distribute resources to the periphery, avoid domination by the center, and maintain (and indeed, extend) a protectionist land tenure regime in the Rift Valley.

Opposed regional preferences regarding state structure feature strongly in the cases considered in Chapters 5 and 6. Kenya has been strained for 60 years by the centralization–devolution struggle that has pitted the Central bloc and Central Province–Nairobi against the Rift Valley bloc, which first coalesced politically in the late 1950s around demands for "Majimboism" or regional devolution. Central Province was the only region to vote against Kenya's new devolution constitution in 2010. In Zambia, demands for autonomy for Western region, represented in the electoral arena in Zambia's poorest and most peripheral electoral bloc, are in strong tension with the centralizing, nationalizing drive of incumbents and Copperbelt North bloc (and urban interests) (Englebert 2005). In Malawi, Banda's state-building was explicitly territorial. He sponsored the buildup of Lilongwe as a capital to rival the colonial-era economic and administrative capital of Blantyre–Limbe. Banda simultaneously restructured the national political economy to build up his own power base in the Central Region. In Côte d'Ivoire, when the Houphouët-Boigny government (a regime that would fit into Figure 7.1's Cell 1) lost power in the late 1990s to actors anchored in the Western Region (Cell 4), the centralizing thrust of state-building pursued since Independence was thrown into reverse gear as the Gbagbo government championed decentralization in favor of the West. Gbagbo's agenda was shelved when the Western electoral bloc was excluded from national power in 2010 (Boone 2018).

Meanwhile, Mali, Cameroon, and Nigeria have all faced chronic and overweening struggles around national design that have gone far in determining the fate of these nations. Strains have degenerated into war against regional groups in Mali, Cameroon, and Nigeria, as well as in Uganda, Côte d'Ivoire, Kenya, and Zimbabwe, all countries that figure in the 12-country study presented above.

---

[55] Under the "District Focus" program. See Kanyinga 2016: 158.

These dynamics resonate strongly with findings of the OECD-focused literature on the economic logics that shape regional preferences for political and fiscal centralization and redistribution (Keating 2003: 260–261). They are also consistent with findings in the conflict literature, which stress the centrality of state redesign – in the form of devolution, local autonomy, protectionism, etc. – in concessions to would-be secessionist regions and as a peace-building strategy.

Federalism, weaker forms of devolution, and decentralization are founded upon the logic of territorial redistribution of power and resources away from the political center and to lower scales of government. They arise in response to demands for redistribution framed in terms of regional (spatial) forms of inequality.

Subnational unit creation modifies state structure and, like many other instances of state redesign, can be interpreted as a form of distributive politics. Its declared beneficiary is obviously the population within a *territorial unit*, rather than the individual, family, or functional group, and it is justified as a response to grievances arising from territorial inequalities.[56] Museveni famously increased the number of districts in Uganda from 34 to 112 between 1990 and 2010.[57] Creating new districts and electoral constituencies induces a downward flow of state resources to new districts. It also transfers powers over territory, often empowering new actors to allocate land and other state-controlled natural resources (e.g., forest or water access) within the new jurisdiction. A political science literature on the electoral logic of subnational unit creation in African countries underscores the electoral and regime-strengthening logics of such moves. Where there is a strong push for this form of decentralization, it often comes from lagging regions demanding local autonomy and land-rights protections. These dynamics underscore the salience of local units defined by the state's territorial grid as units of resource allocation, and thus the tight link between state territorial structure, mobilization of local constituencies, and the politics of electoral clientelism. These geographic and institutional factors are often not evident when polling station logics are examined on their own.

Some analysts have seen the high salience of the politics of national design in African countries – struggles over constitutional design – as the consequence of centrifugal pulls that naturally occur in societies with high social or

---

[56] On subnational unit creation in Africa, see Green 2008, Grossman and Lewis 2014, Hassan 2016, Hassan and Sheely 2017, and Resnick 2017.

[57] Nsamba et al. (2009) and Nsamba (2013) argue that Museveni's subnational unit creation has aimed at weakening regional collectivities (such as Karamoja) rather than offering them representation or gaining their electoral support. In African countries, executive action is the driver of district and constituency creation. It is therefore a good bet that it strengthens the position of incumbent and ruling party. Resnick (2017) found that in Ghana, incumbents of the two main parties create new districts by splitting safe constituencies, thereby building the strength of the ruling party in the national parliament.

Conclusion

ethnic diversity (Dickovick 2014). The present study offers a theory of spatial inequality and territorial institutions that helps explain great spatial unevenness in where, how, and why this plays out in national political arenas. How spatial inequalities are framed within the institutional matrix of colonial-era regions goes far in accounting for the *spatial scale* of collective actors likely to emerge as protagonists in such political competition (i.e., at the national level, it is very often the scale of colonial-era Admin1 – it is not *tous azimuts*). This reasoning also helps to explain *which regions* are likely to have the cohesive interests and collective action capacity to advance claims in the national arena (i.e., producer regions deeply incorporated into the national economy). Spatial inequalities and regions' relative standing in the national political economy also help predict *preferences* regarding institutional structure.

If sectional competition shapes state structure, then state structure is endogenous to politics. The outcome of competition around state design at a given moment in time affects subsequent rounds of sectional competition. This is a mechanism by which spatial inequality shapes state structure itself, and may work to lock-in both regional inequalities and the territorial character of state institutions over time (see Wibbels 2005; Rodden 2009; Tillin 2013).

CONCLUSION

Much existing research on distributive politics in African countries in the era of multiparty elections has focused on the retail politics of clientelism. There is much attention to the supply side at the retail level, where individual candidates (usually MPs) strategize in targeting voters.[58] At the national scale, we have less theory to go on, other than urban bias theory (which depicts the rural areas as remote, deprived, and disempowered) and ethnic bias theory, which depicts politics as a divide-the-dollar struggle among ethnic groups for state resources, or as a "capture the flag" contest to win office.

In this chapter, I show that at the national level, policies that are regionally targeted, that are designed in response to regional tensions, and/or that have highly uneven impact across regions, are highly salient in national politics in many African countries. The high visibility and salience of regional issues and the supply of regionally targeted policies at Time 1 shapes party and coalition formation at Time 2. This works to reproduce the salience of regionalism over time.

On the demand side, we should expect that in countries with high regional inequality, there will be high demand for interregional redistribution. Territorial institutions that make spatial inequality salient, and define citizens' political opportunity structures in territorial terms, should channel these demands into

---

[58] Targeting logic may accentuate or militate against the determinacy of ethnicity as a driver of MP and voter behavior, since ethnic outsiders living in a given locality, such as a small town, will also benefit from roads and electrification (Ichino & Nathan 2013; Harris & Posner 2019).

the political arena. This is in fact what we see at all scales. At the retail local level and constituency level, strong localism is the outcome we would predict for much of rural Africa even without ethnicity, given land and labor market imperfections, the inherent nonmobility of land assets, place-specific skills, and locality- and constituency-specific entitlements. In the multi-tier political systems that exist in African countries, the effects can also be anticipated at the electoral bloc or regional level in demands for sectorally specific policies, regionally tailored land policies, local market protectionism, and constitutional arrangements that enhance regional clout.

Distinctive dynamics arise from territorial unevenness of the system as a whole. At the national level, strong regionalism is likely to work in the domain of redistributive social policy as it does in non-African countries. It is likely to create impediments to universal redistributive policies. Regional inequalities may elicit conflicts of interest around such policies directly, as when advantaged regions resist subsidizing poorer ones. Such tensions may be mediated through institutional structures that accentuate regional interests, bring these to the fore, and impede mobilization of nonregional interests. Counterfactually, there is a close association between programmatic and universalistic (centralized) social policy in countries with *non*territorial representation and industrialized economies. In these settings, institutional and social-structural factors create conditions propitious for centralized social policy. In the Republic of South Africa, the most industrialized, urbanized, proletarianized, unionized economy of the continent, the predicted effects are visible. South Africa has the strongest investment in universal/programmatic social policy. Land policy debates in South Africa are also cast at the national level in the way that this theory would predict. Also as expected, demands for constitutional redesign of the distribution of central and local powers are low in South Africa, except in the outlier case of IFP demands for more local autonomy (advanced in the name of Zulu nationalism).

High salience of regionally targeted policies in national politics is an effect predicted by uneven economic development and strong institutions of regional governance. Potential for a highly fragmented policy space at the national level is a corollary of this, as Rogers (2016) argues, and this can perhaps be considered a default expectation for many African countries, especially given generally low levels of party nationalization. It is thus all the more striking that, in many countries featured in the 12-country study, a single axis of territorial cleavage predominates at the national level. Consistency in the shape of sectional cleavage *between two predominantly rural regions* – the same cleavage line defining competition in multiple policy areas over several decades – is one of the major findings of this book, as argued in Chapter 6. This is evidence of the strong pull of uneven economic development on cleavage structure at the national level.

8

Conclusion

Inequality and Political Cleavage in African Politics

> [M]ost people's perceptions of their prosperity and quality of life depends crucially not only on the productivity of the region in which they live and work but also on their awareness of the experiences of other regions .... Indeed, within an individual country, the geography of inequality is at least as important as interpersonal inequality as the source of political shocks because our democratic political systems are fundamentally geographical in nature .... Moreover, it is interregional inequality that is now fundamentally challenging many of our national institutional and governance systems
>
> McCann, 2020: 257

Sub-Saharan African countries evidence some of the highest levels of economic inequality in the world. Even so, much existing work in social science tells us that economic inequalities do not structure interests or political competition in Africa or do so only at the margins. Scholars have directed our attention to other drivers of politics – to ethnic identity, weak institutions, or politicians' own ambitions. Here, I have taken the opposite position, arguing that economic inequalities do structure politics in African countries and do so in persistent, systematic, and consequential ways. Earlier scholars have looked for politics structured along the *class divide* and often not found strong signs of this, but in doing so they have tended to overlook the politics of *region*. This book argues that high levels of spatial inequality, combined with strongly territorial institutions, produce strong *regional cleavages* that structure [mold] competitive politics in most African countries. What classic works in social cleavage theory call the "spatial–territorial dimension of politics" is a critical but largely unobserved driver of competitive politics in African countries.[1]

---

[1] Lipset and Rokkan 1967; Rokkan 1971; Caramani 2004.

The main argument is that national political life in many, perhaps most, African countries is strongly structured around geographic cleavages arising out of spatial economic inequalities and sectoral differentiation across predominantly rural regions. As Lipset and Rokkan (1967: 44) wrote of state- and market-building struggles in predominantly agrarian countries in other parts of the world, these often have to do with "the economics of nation-building." Historical and empirical analyses in the chapters have shown that hitherto largely unexplored patterns of geographic competition in politics overlay stark patterns of regional inequality.

This study has proposed new sets of concepts, explanatory typologies, methodological strategies, and theoretical claims about regions and regionalism in African countries, pushing beyond data constraints that have limited the reach of earlier work on the political economy of electoral politics. Subnational data have come from many different sources, varying by geographic scale, time period, measurement approaches, and quality. We adapted electoral geography methods to detect volatility and persistence over the course of a series of presidential elections in each country. Chapters situated these arguments about regions and regionalism in adjacent literatures and concepts having to do with party systems, elections, ethnicity, clientelism, and policy salience in African countries.

Understanding dynamics of space and scale opens the door to significant revisions and advances in scholarly analysis of politics in Africa. By linking the study of politics in Africa to classic works on social cleavage and political economy, the book creates a larger, more general, theoretical and conceptual map for analyzing constancy and change over time in African countries. For comparative political economy, it offers a new theorization of the structural forces and mechanisms that link spatial inequality to political and economic development. For policy, analysis of electoral and issue cleavages in African countries underscores the need to bring geographic and territorial balancing priorities back into policy and planning. This chapter summarizes my main arguments and then turns to these extensions.

8.1 SUMMARY: UNEVEN ECONOMIC DEVELOPMENT AND NATIONAL POLITICS

Spatial inequality arises mainly from the heterogeneity of the subnational components that make up the national economy. Its contours and configurations are shaped by natural endowment and location, as well as by market and agglomeration effects, and the regulatory, administrative, and investment policies of government. In African countries, highly uneven patterns of economic development arise from the uneven distribution of the natural endowments that are the basis for primary-product-producing sectors of the economy, geographically segmented markets for land and labor, and uneven connectivity. Regional economic heterogeneity often follows the contours of regional "divisions of labor"

8.1 Uneven Economic Development and National Politics

deliberately fostered by colonial (and postcolonial) state-led economic development strategies. Institutional factors impede population and capital mobility, constraining forces that would, in a perfectly neoclassical world, smooth out regional differences in individual incomes. Spatial inequalities often align with territorial institutions of administration and political representation. This sets the stage for political cleavages that form along geographic lines.

Comparative politics theory predicts that where high spatial inequalities and strongly territorial institutions structure the national political economy, regional interests are likely to come to the fore. National politics is likely to revolve around issues of interregional distribution of power and resources (Rogers 2016). Differentiated economic positions of regions within the national political economy will give rise to regionally distinctive ideologies and policy preferences (Rickard 2018) and, in some cases, to divergent priorities and preferences for the organization and goals of the system as a whole (Lipset & Rokkan 1967: 10). The comparative literature also suggests that, given high regional inequalities and strongly territorial institutions, we should expect to see low levels of party nationalization, localism and pork-barrelism in distributive politics, and the prominence in national politics of regionally targeted policy (as distinct from universal or state-wide policies). Devolution is expected to both emerge from and reinforce regionalizing forces at the national level (Beramendi 2012; Rogers 2016). We see all these effects in the African countries examined here.

I take persistent multiethnic bloc voting in national electorates as a political expression of, and indeed evidence of, *socioeconomic cleavage* in national electorates. The electoral blocs, including the opposition-leaning zones, are the expression of a form of politics that has developed since the late colonial period *at a particular political scale* – that is, the regional scale. This form of politics predominates at the national level in many African countries.

Persistent regional electoral blocs and oppositional zones map onto the uneven geography of producer regions, reflecting uneven integration of regions into the national economy. Patterns of bloc persistence and coalescing in presidential elections arise from the enduring salience of sectional political institutions and agendas, sectoral economic organization and interests, and ideologies of regional advantage and disadvantage in national politics. Economic and political dominance usually coincide, but in exceptional cases, including Uganda where an insurgent movement took control of the central state apparatus by force, they do not (Chapters 5 and 6). There are also strong patterns of similarity in the types of politically salient issues that animate national politics (Chapter 7).

Almost all the blocs and opposition-leaning regions exhibit strong overlap with provincial units (Admin1 units) delimited in the colonial era (some of which were subsequently subdivided). Electoral constituencies themselves overlap with districts (Admin2 units) that were delimited in the colonial era. Such overlaps suggest that territorial grids established by the colonial state play a strong role in structuring both political and economic space in almost all of the countries considered here. What Esping-Anderson (190:20) called "historical

226 *Inequality and Political Cleavage in African Politics*

legacies of regime institutionalization" have shaped the coalescing of interests and patterns of political mobilization in the national arena, producing effects that have been sustained more than a half-century after independence.

This analysis suggests new interpretations of the results of earlier studies, new questions about African politics, and policy prescriptions that are different from those that have emerged from earlier studies that have often focused strongly on ethnicity as a master cleavage. It also helps bring Africa into wider comparative politics and comparative political economy studies of economic inequality and territorial politics.

8.2 NEW TAKES ON EARLIER ARGUMENTS

Shin and Agnew (2007: 300) suggested that a spatial analytical framework yields an account of electoral processes that can change interpretations of empirical results derived from behavioral (individual-level) and nationally aggregated data. This holds true for the material considered here. The foregoing analysis proposes alternative takes on concepts and arguments that have been influential in political science work on African politics. In doing so, it opens the door to new understandings of the relationship between economic structure, state building and nation building, and development.

Economic Cleavage

Scholars have been too quick to dismiss economic understandings of social–structural cleavages in African politics. Politically salient cleavage in African settings often runs along the lines of economically advantaged versus economically disadvantaged regions, with the relative wealth and educational assets of the leading regions often highly correlated with, and parlayed into, advantages in political organization, mobilization, and ability to capture national leadership. In African countries, territorial divisions often align with these socioeconomic distinctions, reinforcing the visibility and political salience of regional economic inequality. This is evident in forms of regional consciousness and identity that form around relative standing in the national economic hierarchy, and the fact that these are often colloquially understood and invoked in national discourse in terms of regional templates and hierarchies inherited from the colonial era. Territorial disparities and differences often form the most striking and persistent lines of political cleavage at the national level, shaping not only competition for national office but also conflict over policy and rival visions of national political integration and growth strategy.

Institutions

Existing literatures have often taken institutions to be of low significance in structuring national political life in African countries. This has been an

8.2 *New Takes on Earlier Arguments*

important source of bias *against* institutional and historical explanation, and in favor of culturalist and time-invariant understandings of politics. I invert this argument, suggesting that much existing work has not focused on the institutions that are the most salient in organizing the citizenry, and structuring incorporation into national political life. For much of sub-Saharan Africa, the colonial territorial grid remains intact, defining the spatial and scalar institutions that construct economic regions and that organize social groups in their interactions with each other and the state.[2]

In the African countries featured in this analysis, institutions of territorial administration have segmented territory, creating "containers" within which state-led strategies of economic development and rule are crafted and implemented in regionally specific ways. This has contributed directly to differences in the economic and sectoral makeup of subnational units and to cross-unit heterogeneity in the composition of populations (in terms of occupational profiles, modes of production in agriculture, ethnic identities, regional identities, and socioeconomic standing relative to other subnational groups) and forms of rule.[3] This goes far in reproducing the high political salience of regional inequality and regional economic heterogeneity in contemporary African countries.

In 80% or so of the farming regions of sub-Saharan Africa today, land access is organized through various types of neocustomary land tenure institutions (Boone 2014). These institutions operate within neocustomary land tenure jurisdictions (territorial units), wherein landholding rights are allocated on the basis of membership in state-recognized ethnic groups. These territories are nested within administrative districts that (1) carry the DNA of the colonial native authorities and ethnic homelands and (2) double as electoral constituencies in most countries. There are obvious and strong connections between ethnic membership, ethnicized territory, and jointness in the demand for and supply of government protection of ethnic land rights. Representative institutions are embedded in ethnically structured property institutions. This helps explain the salience of ethnic identity, the reproduction of this over time, and the substantive connections between ethnic identity and political economy issues of land rights, sectoral policy, agricultural subsidies, taxes, large-scale infrastructural development, etc., that may become salient in elections.

Scalar divisions nested within the administrative grid of the state shape group identities, mobilization, and political aggregation into national-level coalitions. Parties and coalitions form by building alliances at different scales, from the local to the constituency, district, and regional levels. Vote aggregation rules often incentivize this. Where there is heterogeneity in the nature of

---

[2] Leonardi 2020.

[3] As others have argued, persistence in the structuration of space (in terms of spatial hierarchy or territorialization) as well as codifications/classifications of population groups are often *state effects* that are mistaken as cultural features or effects. See Mitchell 1999, for example.

politics at different scales of the polity, multiscalar institutional structures create possibilities for vertical coalition-building strategies that can accommodate these differences (Gibson 2006, 2013; Boone 2014; Mares 2015). As Heller and Evans (2010) have argued for urban India, electoral clientelism itself is partially an effect of political institutional structures that shape politicians' incentives at the constituency level, as well as the resources and powers at their disposal.

Recent works in economic history have underscored the importance of colonial institutions, especially land tenure institutions, in shaping long-term patterns of economic growth (Banerjee & Ayer 2005) and political development (Engerman & Sokoloff 2002). Colonial patterns of spatial inequality linked to export crop production and infrastructure provision have also proven to be enduring (Huillery 2009; Roessler et al. 2022). This strongly resonates with the arguments presented here. I add to this work by economic historians by focusing on *territorial administration*, both as an administrative arm of government and as a regime of boundary, local authority, and property institutions. Territorial administration also produces political effects as an "organizational actor" in national politics (conceptually akin to the military or the civil service) (Branch & Cheeseman 2006; Hassan 2020). It shapes political communities themselves and their strategies for pursuing representation, coalition-building, and political power at the national level.

Electoral Alignments

Previous work has largely eschewed "social cleavages" explanations of party system structure. It has focused on national-level features of African party systems and described party organization and strategy as fluid and opportunistic.[4] Many scholars have indeed observed that, in African elections, cross-ethnic coalitions must form to win national elections because, in most countries, no single ethnic group dominates at the national level. But ethnic coalition formation is modeled as an essentially random, opportunistic, and unpredictable process of patronage allocation, driven only by elite horse-trading and the logic of democratic competition itself.

The analysis here, by contrast, underscores spatial unevenness in the presence and absence of such multiethnic coalitions, the overtime persistence of only some of them, and the institutional and economic factors that differentiate those that do form and persist from those that do not. One-off clientelism is a dynamic that often characterizes the attempts of actors anchored in the leading electoral blocs to incorporate nonbloc constituencies into national electoral coalitions, but the persistent electoral blocs themselves, many of

---

[4] See Erdmann 2004; Erdmann and Basedau 2008: 249; Bleck and van de Walle 2012; Resnick 2014; Riedl 2014.

8.2 New Takes on Earlier Arguments

them multiethnic, cohere around regionally based preferences regarding public goods, policy interests, and positional issues (i.e., position relative to other regions). This contributes to the stability of the persistent electoral blocs (and oppositional zones) over time, even where partisan labels and partisan alignments are unstable.

Policy Interests and Coalitions

Earlier work has insisted on the low salience of policy appeals in national electoral politics in African countries. This work nuances this view with two arguments. First, the effectiveness of policy appeals (as opposed to pure electoral clientelism) varies across space within national units. Policies are expected to have electoral appeal in persistent electoral blocs, where voters are likely to be conscious of sectoral and other regionally specific policy interests, to be more educated and wealthier than voters in nonbloc areas, and to be connected to social networks and organizations with distinct policy interests. Nonbloc areas, by contrast, are characterized (by definition) by low cross-constituency political cohesion. Rural nonbloc constituencies are generally poorer than the average rural constituency and are not specialized producer regions. Most are less integrated into national markets.[5] The general implication is that policy appeals, one-off electoral clientelism, and voter coercion may be substitute means of electoral mobilization that are applied unevenly across space, wherein different mobilizing and control strategies operate in different types of constituencies.

Second, the types of policies that typically mobilize voters in regionally divided, spatially unequal African countries are often *not* those associated with the classic left–right policy dimension in OECD country politics (i.e., regulation of formal sector labor markets and national social protection schemes). Indeed, the generally low electoral salience of left–right policy issues in most African countries is one of the observable implications of the argument advanced here. Yet as Chhibber and Verma (2018) argued for India, the absence of left–right policy debate does not necessarily imply the absence of economic policy debate. Instead, in many and perhaps most African countries, policies that activate voters (albeit in spatially uneven ways) are likely to be the types of policy that aminate electorates in countries where *regionalism* is a strong force in national politics. These have to do with interregional distribution and redistribution, spatially targeted sectoral policy, policies that restrict (or expand) market integration across regions, and collective decisions around the constitutional design (the division of powers between central and regional government) (Chapter 7).

---

[5] Capital-city constituencies also do not vote together as blocs. They lie at the other extreme on these measures: They are extremely heterogeneous socially and in occupational terms, and are found in the dense urban core of national economies.

Opposition Parties and Regional Parties

Scholars have suggested that, in African countries, opposition parties tend to arise in cities and then rally regional support in the up-country ethnic constituency that is home to the opposition party leader. They are often described "niche" parties. A different picture emerges from the analysis here. Many opposition parties and persistently oppositional regions are anchored in relatively wealthy provinces that have repeatedly failed to gain control of national government. In predominantly rural regions that are relatively well-off by national standards, oppositional interests can mobilize the human and economic resources needed to create political organizations that endure over time. The sectoral sources of their relative economic advantage – in export crops, commercial food crop production, and the institutions and organizations linked to these – contribute to regionally specific economic interests, identities, and collective action capacity. Examples are the UNPD in Zambia, Chadema in northern Tanzania, and the opposition parties of western (Anglophone) Cameroon.

This argument provides economic geography foundations for Arriola's (2013: 19) "pecuniary theory" of multiethnic opposition coalitions in national elections. Whereas Arriola focuses on rich businessmen who have the financial wherewithal to build patronage alliances without access to central state resources, the argument here directs attention to what Arriola calls relatively wealthy "exporter constituencies." These are the regional and sectoral bases of the private accumulation that produces individual wealth and helps power civil society associations, political parties, and electoral mobilization. Such constituencies and blocs of constituencies are fertile grounds for both opposition politics and the persistent electoral blocs that back national incumbents.[6]

Regional Advantage and Disadvantage

The literature on electoral patronage and clientelism in African countries often suggests that wealthy regions are rich because their coethnics have captured national office, but the analysis here suggests that the opposite is the case. Almost all the economically leading regions identified in the country case studies trace their advantages to the colonial era. This position of structural economic advantage – the taproot of which is usually the production of export crops – contributes to the political capacity that underwrites

---

[6] Arriola (2013: 79) focuses on wealthy business interests linked to "exporter constituencies." He provides the examples of the "merchants and traders whose livelihoods were tied to the groundnut trade" in Northern Nigeria, who operated in "symbiotic relation with the NPC" which was pitted against other regional parties in competition for national power in Nigeria in the 1950s and 1960s, and the business leaders anchored in the coffee-producing Mt. Kenya region during the 1980–2000 years, when a rival political coalition controlled the presidency. On business interests in politics and policy-making, see also Pitcher 2012 and 2017.

8.2 New Takes on Earlier Arguments

advantage, even dominance, in national politics. Political dominance does have its payoffs, as shown in several vignettes in Chapters 6 and 7, but this is not the source of long-term regional advantage in national politics. The largest regional disparities observed in the 12-country study presented above are between Uganda's wealthy central oppositional zone, centered on Buganda, and Uganda's very poor western persistent electoral bloc. The latter is the home region of Yoweri Museveni, who has been in power in Uganda for the last 25 years. Regional representatives of what is still Uganda's wealthiest region have never controlled the national government. Likewise, Tanzania's economically leading northern region was sidelined under CCM rule for almost three decades, but this did not erase the fundamental sources of its economic advantage. This helps explain how the North has rebounded, politically, in the 2000s.

Identities: Ethnic, Economic, and Regional

Much political science literature has assumed or argued explicitly that ethnic identity is a force in electoral politics that is orthogonal to programmatic economic interests and economic policy interests. In this book, I endogenize ethnic identity in a larger theory of territorial interests that are defined largely in terms of economic interests, and relative economic (dis)advantage within the national unit.

I defined regional identities as distinct from colonially recognized ethnic identities (what Posner [2005] called "tribal" identities) and argued that the theoretical connotations associated with the leading "ethnic determinants" theories in political science (i.e., as-if primordial kinship, supposed precolonial origins, unbargainability of political demands) do not apply to regional identities. Politically relevant *regional* identities are theorized here as *arising from* uneven economic development, consciousness of regional socioeconomic heterogeneity and regional economic specializations, positionality within the national economy (i.e., of regional economic advantage and disadvantage), and the economic and political salience of regions and districts as units of national territorial administration. As such, regional identities generate demands and claims at the national level that are negotiable, and indeed, often have to do with issue domains that are similar to those that arise from regional inequality in territorially divided countries in other parts of the world (Chapter 7). Regional identities coalesce unevenly across space within countries and are visible in the persistent electoral blocs and oppositional zones that feature in Chapters 4–6 of this study.

While some scholars have argued that "ethnic group voting" and regional bloc voting are hard to distinguish in practice, this statement does not hold across most of the countries and persistent electoral blocs and oppositional zones identified here. Most of the blocs are multiethnic. Ethnic theories of voting do not explain why particular non-coethnic constituencies would persistently vote together over many electoral cycles, or which ones are likely to do so. Reciprocally, while most constituencies in many countries have a strong ethnic identity, most constituencies are not members of persistent electoral blocs. Large tracts of six to eight constituencies with the same ethnic majority do not necessarily coalesce as persistent "electoral blocs" (e.g., Somali and Mijikenda in Kenya). Reading across country studies, it is striking how many of the politically salient identities in these cases emerged from regional consciousness and/or regionally specific occupational or sectoral consciousness, not the reverse (Akan, Bemba, Kalenjin, Luo, "northerners," Hausa-Fulani, Bété, Baoulé, Dioula, Biafran, Lomwe, Tumbuka, "anglophone" in Cameroon).

Political and policy interests arising from the sectoral profiles of regional political economies, and the *positionality* of regions in the national political economy, provide the basis for multiethnic regional alliances and the coalescing of supra-local regional identities that express these.[7] In the national political arena, these find expression as mega-ethnic identities that are an *effect* of electoral incentives and shared policy interests, rather than of ethnic identities that have no economic geography content. The contouring of economic geography within the gridlines of the state helps explain the scale at which such interests and identities are likely to coalesce, and their persistence over time.

In studies of regionalism in Italy, John Agnew (1997) wrote that political identities are associated with particular representations of scale in politics. This is true in the African countries studied here. Coalitions that form the most persistent cleavage lines in the *national political arena* are regional identities that tend to form along the lines of colonial-era Admin1 units. These are often layered upon more local identities that are activated in more local contests and alignments, but the relationship between regional and local ethnic (what Posner calls "tribal") identity is variable. The two do not arise from the same causal mechanisms or operate the same way in national politics. "Ethnicity" as a generic term (like clientelism) offers little analytic purchase when it comes to distinguishing among the great variety of phenomena and contexts in which these appear. Empirical evidence confined to the micro- or behavioral level biases interpretation in favor of cognitive and psychological explanations. Most such evidence is produced in a way that is designed to "hold constant" (not analyze) the effects of political structure.

An emergent literature on "ethnic inequality" links ethnicity to economic inequality, measuring disparities at the individual level or the level of the areal unit (e.g., ethnic homelands as defined by Alesina et al. 2016). So far, this work has been framed within an ethnic politics paradigm, and the spatial measure is interpreted as the composite effect of the economic standing of individual

---

[7] The same argument was stressed by an earlier generation of Africa scholars. In a study of Zambia, for example, Robert Molteno (1974: 87–93) argued that nested supra- and sub-group ethnic identities may be activated strategically, in response to electoral and policy incentives.

8.2 New Takes on Earlier Arguments

coethnics. This book suggests an alternative way of using such data. Rather than interpreting the findings in a spatial vacuum, these observations can be connected to national economic geography, geographically specific interests, and the ranking of regions in national political economies. Doing so makes it possible to discern the economic profiles of geographic units, see geographic patterns in the data, recognize economic policy correlates of strongly territorialized ethnic identities, and analyze coalitional dynamics among economically differentiated groups.

Urban–Rural

The urban–rural distinction has a long-standing and prominent place in the study of African politics. Influential urban bias theories of the 1980s depicted rural Africa as uniformly repressed and exploited by pro-urban rulers. Yet hypotheses about *rivalry* between rural and urban interests – often drawn from the political history of urbanization and industrialization in Europe and the United States – were often rejected by Africa-focused scholars. They observed that in political competition in general, and electoral politics in particular, the cities did not square off against the countryside. One important explanation for this in the 1980s had to do with "urban–rural straddling." Because the urban poor had one foot in the rural areas (because many of their family members resided there) and the other in the city, the urban poor were inclined to vote with their rural family members. Another argument had to do with the economic interests of the national elite. Where the ruling elite was invested in commercial agriculture, as in countries like Kenya and Côte d'Ivoire, rather than in industry, their policy interests did not diverge so much from those of the peasantry and market-oriented smallholders.

With the returns to multipartyism in the 1990s, rural areas have often been taken to be more or less uniformly under the sway of communalism and traditional rulers (Herbst 2000); linked to central rulers mainly through brokered ties of clientelism and the micro-electoral patronage politics centered on the discretionary distribution of schools, clinics, and roads (Baldwin 2015; Nathan 2019); and largely *supportive* of incumbents (Koter 2013; Harding 2020). Susanne Mueller (2011) showed that, in Kenya, rural electoral "zoning" divided rural constituencies into authoritarian enclaves controlled by either the incumbent or the opposition, where rural voters were intimidated into acquiescing to whichever strongman had gained control of the locality. These arguments contribute to explanations of how and why incumbent rulers are able to win elections, even if rulers do not deliver pro-rural policy or are corrupt. (Harding [2020] flips this argument by defining rural service distribution as pro-rural *policy*, which most rural citizens support.) Major cities are the epicenters of anti-incumbent voting.

Few studies take into account geographic, economic, or socioeconomic variation across the regions and districts that comprise "the rural areas." In survey research that aims for nationally representative results, "rural" has often been taken as an individual-level attribute that is considered to have uniform valence across the national territory. This method generates an average effect for "rural-ness" that washes out the variation across rural districts and regions that is at the center of the present analysis. In experimental work, in a bid for external validity, scholars often describe rural localities as "typical" on the basis of generic features of rurality, defined in terms of poverty, ethnic homogeneity, and low connectivity (and low information), or report an average treatment effect that washes out local variations. The general picture is that the rural poor are a largely homogeneous mass, drawn into electoral politics mostly in pursuit of the state-provided services that everyone wants.

The analysis here develops the altogether different model of "the rural poor" or rural citizens as spatially differentiated by the types of livelihoods that prevail in different rural settings, the median socioeconomic profile of households in that rural setting, the district's or region's position within the national economy, its mode and degree of incorporation into the national economy and history of political mobilization, and local governance structures. As a result of these differences, the kinds of institutions, organizations, and networks that draw individuals and communities into politics vary across space. Differences give rise to distinct and often divergent preferences over substantive policy issues: issues of land policy, agricultural commodity subsidies and prices, the targeting of redistributive policies, growth strategies, and preferences with respect to the autonomy and powers of what Mamdani (1996) called "the local state." These issues may mobilize voters and influential local leaders in elections.

From this perspective, rural populations are situated within a policy space that can be conceptualized as fractured, polarized along the lines of a single axis of "territorial opposition," or indeed both, if regions that are not opposed along a dominant axis of competition are variably positioned within a residual, more fractured, policy space (Chapters 6 and 7). Heterogeneity of rural interests can be a cause or an effect of regionally targeted growth policies. It may be as important in explaining the regime persistence or incumbent longevity, or policy inconsistency, as the presumed rural homogeneity that has been emphasized by earlier scholars. This model does not generate a default hypothesis on the relation between urban and rural voters, or the urban poor versus the rural poor. It does, however, focus on policy interests that can underpin regional electoral coalitions, and thus suggests how new coalitions may be built in the future.

These urban–rural and regional dynamics have important implications of the overall character of national politics. In African countries, capital cities have rarely captured and held power, and governed in their own right. They are often treated as volatile hot-spots of opposition. Most countries have been ruled by national parties and politicians with provincial, predominantly *rural*, bases of political support. This shapes the thrust of national politics in policy

8.2 New Takes on Earlier Arguments

areas from land tenure reform, to redistributive policy, to sectoral growth strategies, to questions of constitutional and electoral system design.[8]

Class Politics

Bienen and Herbst (1996) underscored the absence of stable, class-based electoral alignments in most African countries at the national level, and rightly so. Yet class cleavages and class politics are visible within subnational regions in many of the countries considered in this book: central Kenya, Zambia's Copperbelt, southern Malawi, and Uganda's central region. This is also true of Ghana's central region, anchored in Ashanti (Allman 1993), and western Nigeria. Within countries deeply cleaved by spatial inequalities, class inequalities and class politics are often visible within the most highly developed subnational regions.

Writing of Central Province of Kenya, Lonsdale argued that the development of Kikuyu ethnic consciousness was driven in part by efforts to knit together into one political community a people increasingly divided by class and threatened by rival class-based political alignments.[9] The politics of agrarian colonization of adjacent farming districts in the Rift Valley (experienced as postcolonial "internal colonialism" by those who lost out) has been one strategy for managing the class tensions within central Kenya, but it has been very costly in terms of inflaming the regional tensions that bedevil national politics. Scholars have been writing of an overt class divide in the electoral politics of Kenya's Central Province more than a decade. Class-based politics in Central Province erupted into the national presidential election in 2022 when coethnic voters turned against the incumbent president in his presumptive ethnic stronghold, throwing the election to the rival candidate, William Ruto, who is rooted in the Rift Valley electoral bloc.[10] The long-standing axis of territorial opposition that divides the Central electoral bloc from Western also contributed to this outcome (Chapter 6).

As suggested by historian David Sabean (1998, 2006) in his studies of class formation in early modern Europe, it may well be that the national scale is not the proper *scale* for seeing class politics in most African countries. Spatially uneven patterns of economic development are associated with not only differentiated patterns of associational life, but also different social relations of production and, indeed, class formation. And as Agnew (1996, 1997: 104–105)

---

[8] South Africa is an exception that helps to prove the rule: the ruling ANC came to power with deep roots in city and municipal structures.

[9] About half of Kenya's counties register Gini coefficients above 0.4 (based on DHS consumption data), for example (Burbidge 2019: 130). This line of analysis is echoed widely in the literature on Kenyan politics. See Berman and Lonsdale (1992), Kanyinga (2000), Peterson (2012), D'Arcy and Cornell (2016), and Pitcher (2017).

[10] See also LeVan (2019) and Obe (2019) on Nigeria.

236 Inequality and Political Cleavage in African Politics

argues in analyses of Italian politics, the high salience of class politics within particular regional political arenas does not necessarily mean that this will predominate at the national level.

8.3 NEW MAPS, NEW CLEAVAGES? THEORIZING CHANGE OVER TIME

Agglomeration forces can work to intensify regional disparities along core–periphery lines over time. Lagging regions can be expected to fall further and further behind.[11] Yet a logical implication of the theory advanced here is that when fundamental restructurings of economic geography do happen, they will impact political alignments and territorial cleavages in African countries. Such shifts could result over time from incremental change arising from diseconomies of agglomeration (e.g., pollution, overcrowding, declining soil fertility, rising land prices) or new super profits to be had in once economically marginal regions (perhaps through discoveries of new sources of mineral rent). Urbanization can pass a tipping point at which elections can no longer be won the basis of rural votes. Rural class formation or population growth could produce widespread landlessness in predominantly rural regions.

Some examples of decisive shifts over time in economic geography emerge in the country case studies featured above. In Côte d'Ivoire and Ghana, the geographic expansion of smallholder cocoa production in the 1970s and 1980s brought the southwestern reaches of both countries into play politically as major regional players, even disrupting the old balance of power in Côte d'Ivoire and propelling the rise of the Western persistent electoral bloc (Chapter 4).

In Nigeria, the rise of the East as an oil producer in the mid-1960s fatefully disrupted the geopolitical balance between the regions. In some countries, the electoral data used in Chapter 4 hinted at the possible emergence in the 2000s and 2010s of new electoral blocs in regions with strengthening producer profiles due to economic liberalization and rising commodity prices. One such case was the Mbeya region of Tanzania. Long marginalized under CCM rule, the Mbeya region began to reemerge as a dynamic producer region under Tanzania's turn to more market-oriented policies in the 1990s. It evinced potential as an opposition-leaning zone in 2010 and 2015.[12]

New infrastructural mega-projects – featuring railroads, pipelines, dams, ports, and highways – may jump-start new patterns of market integration, bringing old regions into play in national politics in novel ways. New connectivity may "awaken" sleepy regions by deepening their market integration, stimulating the scaling-up of commercially oriented food crop production, and

---

[11] Judith Heyer wrote in 1987 that "[i]t is becoming increasingly obvious to those familiar with Kenya that not only are some areas [of smallholder farming] very much worse off than others, but some are deteriorating" (1987: 553).

[12] See Chapter 4.

8.3 New Maps, New Cleavages? Theorizing Change over Time 237

triggering new waves of population mobility. Big infrastructural projects of the 2010s and 2020s promise to rewire the economies of transnational regions. In East Africa, the largest of these in the early 2020s was the LAPSSET corridor linking Kenya's Lamu Port to South Sudan.[13] Agricultural development corridors in east and southern Africa aim to connect landlocked production areas to global markets, envisioning new geographies of regional development and market-making on a scale reminiscent of spatial planning strategies of the late 1940s through the mid-1980s.[14] Investments in mineral extraction promise less in terms of region-making but are also accompanied by development of transport infrastructure and new demand for land, labor, and agricultural produce. Such massive undertakings generate intense political churn around the apportionment of costs and benefits, both at the local and at the national level. Simultaneously, they are vectors for territorial strategies of state formation. These are shaped, in the national political arena, by regionalism – that is, by competition among regional political blocs for policies and position, regional consciousness of historical patterns of uneven (often adverse) incorporation into national political economies, and territorial logics of political party-building at the regional scale.[15]

Change in government spending patterns can play some role in altering regional economic trajectories and the regional balance of power at the national level. Through sheer force of will, governments of Côte d'Ivoire, Nigeria, Tanzania, and Malawi erected new capital cities in regions of middling rank in the national economic hierarchy (Yamoussoukro, Abuja, Dodoma, and Lilongwe, respectively). "New capitals" became growth poles that supported new development in surrounding regions, at least to some extent. In the cases of Yamoussoukro, Dodoma, and Lilongwe, the new capitals were located in the regional strongholds of the national incumbent, elevating these regions in national significance and giving them additional political weight. In Nigeria, the development of Abuja as a new national capital city in the 1970s and 1980s created a new government-spending-led growth pole in the country's Middle Belt. Cutbacks in state spending can have the reverse effect. Those introduced in the context of Structural Adjustment Programs in the 1990s dealt an especially heavy blow to the cotton- and parastatal-dependent economies of northern Nigeria and northern Côte d'Ivoire, which were already burdened by cost and locational disadvantages.

---

[13] Lamu Port, South Sudan, Ethiopian Transport Corridor (LAPSSET). See Browne (2015); Gambino (2020); Mkutu, Müller-Koné, and Atieno (2021).

[14] The SAGCOT corridor project (Southern Agricultural Growth Corridor of Tanzania) aimed to link southern Tanzania to coastal ports and southern Africa (Tups and Dannenberg 2021). Tanzania's Central Corridor project connects the Great Lakes countries to Tanzania's Indian Ocean ports, running through the CCM heartland of central Tanzania (Enns and Bersaglio 2019). On the reemregence of spatial planning strategies, see Schindler and Kanai 2021

[15] See Burr et al., 2019 on the multiscalar politics of investments in extractives in three African countries.

These examples do, however, reinforce a sobering theme in the regional economic geography literature: Forces of agglomeration (path dependency of regional economic growth trajectories) are driven by the gravitational pull of markets. They may be amplified or accelerated by targeted state spending, but they are hard to neutralize or offset by purely policy-led growth measures targeted at lagging regions.[16] The persistent advantage of leading regions is especially visible in the case of those that are integrated into the global economy as export commodity producers, many of which have persisted as relatively advantaged regions over many decades. This tendency is reinforced by policy advantages that accrue from the important role many such sectors play as foreign exchange earners. By the same reasoning, lagging regions may be supported somewhat by spatially targeted growth policies, but these rarely overturn provincial economic hierarchies that are rooted in the production profiles of regions.

Internal migration, climate change, and demographic growth have spatially uneven effects. Changing agrarian economies and trade flows may work incrementally – especially in conjunction with factors just mentioned – to change regional production profiles, and to disrupt power balances within and between regions.

The theory advanced here also suggests that institutional change can heighten, reduce, or otherwise alter the political salience of regional economic inequality, and indeed, affect the interaction of spatial inequalities and ethnic identities. The jury is still out on post-2000 processes of devolution and new subnational unit creation that have been tracked by political scientists (Nsamba 2013; Grossman & Lewis 2014; Kanyinga 2016; Resnick 2017). While the creation of smaller units often appears to further entrench the overlap between territorial jurisdiction and the distinctive economic profile of "state segments," this may erode the cohesion of larger regions if the new units escape the old forms of region-based administrative control and political coalition-building. This may be the case in Uganda, where Museveni has been able to draw Eastern Region constituencies toward Uganda's regional growth centers and into the political orbit of the ruling party. In Kenya, devolution reinforced the salience of interregional redistribution regimes and the alignment of spatial inequalities with institutions of administration and political representation, with the expected political effect of fueling territorial politics.

More decisive in the long run could be institutional changes that contribute to the building of national land markets in Kenya, Côte d'Ivoire, and elsewhere. The opening of land markets is designed to induce inflows of capital and new land buyers into high-potential agricultural regions. This may fuel a Polanyian (Polanyi 1944) "double movement" consisting of rural class formation and counterreaction to this. Counterreaction can be expected to take the form of demands for social protection from those dependent on the customary

---

[16] Storper 2018: 260; Rodriguez-Posé 2018: 202–204; Iammarino et al., 2019.

8.4 CONTRIBUTIONS TO POLITICAL SCIENCE

or neocustomary land rights that most African states have, until now, guaranteed to large swaths of the rural population. Governments may be pulled ever more strongly in opposite directions by such moves to deepen national market integration.

8.4 CONTRIBUTIONS TO POLITICAL SCIENCE

The study makes three contributions to political science. First, it contributes to a growing CPE literature on the political effects of spatial inequality. An older tradition in CPE focused mostly on income (interpersonal) inequality in the OECD countries. It treated territorial cleavages as a separate, and largely retrograde, dimension of national cleavage that was orthogonal to socioeconomic cleavage.

In developing countries, with lower levels of industrialization and urbanization than those at the center of the CPE literature on inequality, the geographic dimension has clearly been politically salient over much of the last century. In Latin American studies, there is a contemporary stream of work on the political economy of spatial inequality and uneven state formation (Hagopian 1996; Gibson 2013; Eaton 2017, 2019; Mazzuca 2021).[17] There is also a strong body of work on spatial inequalities in South Asia, especially within India (Sinha 2005; Naseemullah 2022). African countries are among the clearest examples of such national configurations in the developing world. They are characterized by highly uneven economic geographies, spatially dispersed, predominantly rural populations, and strong unevenness in the incorporation of regions into national markets. The African cases highlight in particular the kinds of market imperfections and market failures emphasized in the New Economic Geography (including impediments to labor market mobility, poverty traps, and the high spatial concentration of leading-sector activity). Since the 1980s, these same forces have become increasingly salient in the postindustrial economies of the United Kingdom, United States, and France, where politically divisive patterns of regional inequality now appear to be entrenched.

This study suggests a theoretical approach, conceptual repertoire, and methodological strategies for harnessing electoral data to the study of spatial inequality's political effects in developing countries. At a theoretical level, it joins with Rogers (2016) and others in arguing that uneven development across subnational regions shapes national trajectories, and does so in particular ways, depending on systems of political representation, sectoral differentiation and regional heterogeneity of interests among both masses and elites, and the extent and modes of population mobility. The pace and direction of economic development are affected by often predictable sectoral and core–periphery policy struggles, as is the character of the state formation process as a whole.

---

[17] See also Giraudy, Moncada, and Snyder, eds., 2019; Soifer 2019; and before that, Cardoso and Faletto 1979.

Second, analysis of African countries helps reinforce the argument that inequality politics cannot be understood without taking into account both the structure of economic inequality in a particular polity and the institutions that structure the political arenas in which inequality politics plays out. Theories of inequality politics and distributive politics – class, median voter, identity-based, politician-driven – need to be linked more tightly to analysis of spatial dimensions of inequality, taking account of specific institutional and incentive structures that condition the political expression of inequality. This is necessary not only for theory but also for policy. The preeminent challenge for both developing and developed countries today is to design and deliver policy choices (and institutional arrangements) that promote both national cohesion and sustainable growth.

Third, endogenizing ethnicity and embedding it in explicitly scalar and spatial theories of politics in African countries has repercussions for political science theories of ethnicity in other world contexts. Work on Africa has often provided a benchmark for comparative politics and International Relations theories that hold ethnic politics to be uniquely disruptive, categorically different from interest group politics, and generative of violence. Yet much scholarship on Africa has been highly stylized in this regard. It has often looked away from institutions, paid little attention to the heterogeneity of politics across different scales of multitiered political systems, screened out analysis of economic and class interests, treated geographical features of both ethnicity and inequality in ad hoc and unsystematic ways, and paid scant attention to policy issues that animate national politics. New research on African countries that focused on inequalities, institutions, uneven development, and the social cleavages that drive national political trajectories could make it possible to draw richer inferences from existing work and, in doing so, bring new depth to studies of ethnic politics in countries in other world regions.

An implication of the present study is that "ethnicity" may be overstretched as a catch-all explanatory concept in studies of other world regions, just as it has often been in African studies. More nuanced analyses often reveal that economic inequalities can carry much of the explanatory burden in accounting for identity dynamics, political cleavages, and patterns of political mobilization in largely agrarian societies. This may be especially true of those characterized by the "enclave type" development of export sectors that was typical of nineteenth- and twentieth-century European colonialism. Highly uneven patterns of regional integration into national economies are a generic feature of these countries.

This work helps explain why economic growth based on the export of primary commodities may deepen regional political cleavages. This complicates efforts to build the kinds of truly *national* growth coalitions that contribute to political stability, and indeed, the sustainability of growth and development. Such a diagnosis provides a basis for advocating for trade and investment policies that build cross-regional complementarities within countries, aiming to

8.4 *Contributions to Political Science*

reduce the kinds of regional economic disparities that complicate prospects for political cooperation. At the same time, it helps explain why this is difficult, politically, to accomplish.

The findings here run against the now-outdated free market prescriptions of the World Bank's *World Development Report* 2009, which argued for space-blind economic growth strategies in developing countries. At that time, the Bank argued that the goal of government should be to induce economically active populations to leave lagging regions, and to migrate to regions of opportunity whose growth was fueled by agglomeration. Yet scholars of subnational inequality trends in Latin America, the European Union, and the United Kingdom argued then, and do so now, that traditional market-reliant and job-based measures for tackling spatial inequality do not overturn entrenched spatial hierarchies.[18] Research presented here reinforces such observations by highlighting the long-run persistence of patterns of spatial inequality in African countries that date to the mid-twentieth century, if not before. As the politically divisive and disruptive consequences of regional poverty traps have become much more obvious in OECD countries, there is a convergence with the themes of this study on the political salience of spatial inequality in African countries. Ideologies based on regional consciousness and economic positionality within national political economies can be powerful drivers of political cleavage, conflicting policy priorities across regions, and territorial oppositions over redistributive policy and even questions of national constitutional design. In African countries, there is a strong need for renewed consideration of regionally specific planning (e.g., in the domain of land tenure), for redistributive national cohesion policies, and for growth strategies that diversify and build economic coalitions across regions, even if these are politically difficult to achieve.

---

[18] See, for example, Iammarino et al. 2019: 287–288. Part of the reason is constrained internal labor mobility, which is much lower, even in the United States, than previously thought (Ibid.: 285).

APPENDICES

Appendix A

African Inequalities in Comparative Perspective

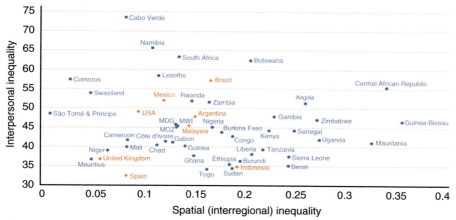

FIGURE A.1 Interpersonal and spatial inequality in African countries using population-weighted CoV
Sources: Milanovic (2014), Lessmann and Seidel (2015, 2017).

While there is a significant negative correlation between the interpersonal income and spatial inequality measures when we use the unweighted spatial inequality measure, the correlation between the two measures loses statistical significance when we use the population-weighted measure in calculating the coefficient of variation (CoV) in regional GDP. Some countries migrate across the cartesian space. Niger and Mali, both large and sparsely populated, flip to the left side of the figure and the apparent significance of territorial inequality drops. South Africa, a large, heavily urbanized country, also moves to the left (i.e., the value on the spatial inequality measure falls). This allows us to refine the inferences we draw from these data. With the population-weighted CoV, we both gain and lose important information about Mali and Niger.

The north of both countries is sparsely populated, and taking this into account results in population-weighted measures of spatial inequality which are lower than the unweighted measures. But this does not necessarily correspond to a decrease in the *political salience* of regional inequality. On the contrary, in Mali and Niger, the political salience of regional inequality is extremely high: Both are racked by regional insurgencies arising from regional grievance. At the same time, for South Africa, the population-weighted measures do offer a better sense of why regional inequality is less salient than income inequality – that is, because the South Africa population is largely urbanized, indicating a level of economic development, including industrialization and its attendant socio-structural changes, that is high for Africa. The more urbanized the country and the greater the geographic dispersion of its urban areas, the more the population-weighted CoV will push down the spatial inequality measure (leaving the income inequality measure unchanged). For the most urbanized countries, the *population-weighted* CoV correlates better with our theoretical expectations about which dimension of inequality is likely to be most salient in national politics: The political salience of spatial inequality vs. class inequality can be expected to decrease as urbanization progresses.

Percentage of national land surface is the second most important predictor (after GNP per capita) of a country's weighted CoV (Lessmann & Seidel 2015: 29, 30, 50.) Large African countries have high population-weighted CoVs and even higher unweighted CoVs.

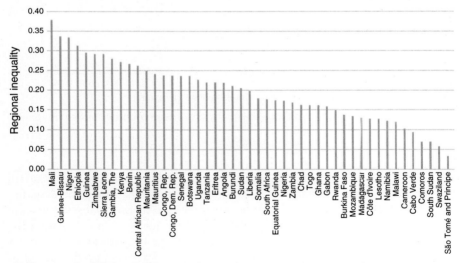

FIGURE A.2 Spatial inequality in African countries (unweighted by population)
Notes: Adjusted nightlight density data (Lessmann & Seidel 2015 [2017]). All African countries, CoV in nightlight density (unweighted by population, as in the figure in the main text).
Source: Lessmann and Seidel 2015 [2017].

Appendices

TABLE A.1 *Spatial inequality averages by world region, 2010*

Region	Spatial inequality: Regional average, 2010
East Asia and Pacific	0.139
Europe and Central Asia	0.080
Latin America and Caribbean	0.110
Middle East and North Africa	0.107
North America	0.059
South Asia	0.108
Sub-Saharan Africa	0.168
World	0.120

Notes: Adjusted GDP proxy, based on nightlight, population-weighted CoV across Admin1 regions, 2010.
Source: Lessmann and Seidel 2017.

Appendix B

Country Cases, Data, and Methods

TABLE B.1 *Overview of twelve countries*

A.

Country	Gini	Spatial inequality, unweighted	Spatial inequality (weighted)	GDP per K, 2010 (current US$)	Polity score YR 1990	Polity score YR 2010
Cameroon	41.68	0.102	0.085	651.61	−3	−4
Côte d'Ivoire	41.34	0.112	0.122	652.93	−7	0
Ghana	37.64	0.16	0.15	258.47	−7	8
Kenya	44.14	0.272	0.223	397.48	−7	8
Malawi	45.30	0.119	0.134	156.39	−9	6
Mali	39.85	0.379	0.084	270.54	−7	7
Nigeria	44.97	0.173	0.168	567.93	−5	4
South Africa	62.90	0.177	0.135	3032.44	5	9
Tanzania	39.28	0.22	0.218	410.95	−6	−1
Uganda	41.79	0.226	0.273	261.87	−7	−1
Zambia	51.30	0.398	0.168	345.69	−9	7
Zimbabwe	46.93	0.291	0.27	563.06	−6	1
Sample average			0.169	630.78		
SSA average		0.219		1594.45		

(*continued*)

TABLE B.1 (continued)

B.

Country	Country size (1000 sq. km)	Total population, 2010 (in thousands)	Rural population, share of total, 1990 (%)	Rural population, share of total, 2000 (%)	Rural population as share of total, 2010 (%)	Urban primacy ratio, 2000
Cameroon	473	19,970	60.34	54.46	48.44	1.10
Côte d'Ivoire	318	20,401	60.65	56.85	52.67	6.41
Ghana	227	24,512	63.56	56.07	49.29	1.41
Kenya	569	41,350	83.25	80.11	76.43	3.24
Malawi	94	15,167	88.44	85.39	84.46	1.11
Mali	1220	15,075	76.68	71.64	64.00	7.63
Nigeria	911	158,578	70.32	65.16	56.52	2.80
South Africa	1213	51,585	47.96	43.11	37.78	1.09
Tanzania	886	46,099	81.12	77.69	71.89	6.65
Uganda	200	33,915	88.92	85.21	80.62	n/a
Zambia	743	13,850	60.59	65.20	60.65	2.96
Zimbabwe	387	14,086	71.01	66.24	66.80	2.08
Sample average		16,571	72.53	68.58	63.85	
SSA average						

Notes: "Urban primacy ratio" is ratio of largest city population to second largest city population.
Sources: GDP from World Development Indicators 2010; Polity scores and regime type from Polity data series; urban/rural and city primacy ratios from UN Population Division, World Urbanization Prospects 2018.

TABLE B.2 *Electoral data and bloc boundaries overview*

		Electoral data used for bloc identification			
Country	Electoral system	Electoral returns[1]	Other sources, incl. maps[2]	Bloc makeup (subunits)	Boundaries used for defining blocs (year)
Cameroon	Mixed, MMD	1992 (Admin1), 2004 (Admin1), 2011 (Admin1 and constituency) [*]		Admin1 (région)	Admin1 boundaries (no change 1992–2011)
Côte d'Ivoire	Mixed (plurality, SMD, MMD)	2010 R1 (Admin3) [*] [**]	1990, 1995,* 2010 R2, 2016	Admin3 (départements)	Admin3 boundaries from GADM shapefile (boundaries 2020)
Ghana	SMD	1996, 2000, 2004, 2008, 2012, 2016 (constituency level)		Constituencies	Constituency boundaries (recoded, based on 1996 boundaries)
Kenya	SMD	1992 [**], 1997, 2002, 2007, 2013 (all at constituency level)		Constituencies	Constituency boundaries (1997–2007)
Malawi	SMD	1999,* 2004,* 2007, 2013 (all at constituency level)		Constituencies	Constituency boundaries (no change 1999–2014)
Mali	Mixed (majority, SMD, MMD)	2002R1, 2007R1, 2013R1, 2013R2 (all at Admin1)	2002, 2013 (constituency)	Admin1 as well as Admin2 and Admin3 (Bamako–Koulikoro bloc and Mopti bloc)	Admin boundaries from GADM shapefile (boundaries 2020)
Nigeria	SMD	2003, 2007, 2011, 2015 (all at Admin1)		Admin1 (states)	Admin1 (state) boundaries (2003–2015)

(continued)

TABLE B.2 *(continued)*

Country	Electoral system	Electoral data used for bloc identification		Bloc makeup (subunits)	Boundaries used for defining blocs (year)
		Electoral returns[1]	Other sources, incl. maps[2]		
South Africa	PR list (president elected by Parliament)	1999, 2004, 2009, 2014 (district level)		Admin2 (district council) and subdistrict level (KwaZulu-Natal bloc)	Shapefile downloaded from GADM (boundaries 2020)
Tanzania	SMD	1995 [**] (constituency), 2005 (Admin1), 2010 (constituency)		Constituencies	Constituency boundaries (2010)
Uganda	SMD	2001 [**], 2006 [**], 2011, 2016 (Admin2)		Admin2 (districts)	District boundaries (2010)
Zambia	SMD	1991, 1996, 2001, 2006, 2011, 2016 (all at constituency level) [3]		Constituencies	Constituency boundaries (1991–2011)
Zimbabwe	SMD	2002 [**], 2008, 2013 (first round, constituency) [*]		Constituencies	Constituency boundaries (2008–2013)

Notes: Electoral data used, aggregation of electoral data (constituency or otherwise), and additional information on the electoral blocs.

[1] Electoral returns were available as data to use in statistical analysis and mapping.

[2] Electoral data were available in processed form (i.e., maps or secondary analysis).

* indicates that we used parliamentary results instead of presidential results.

** indicates that the data quality is poor or that mapping the electoral results was imperfect due to missing shapefiles.

[3] We do not consider electoral results from the two Zambian presidential by-elections (2008 and 2015).

Appendices

SECTION B.2 DATA USED TO DESCRIBE BLOC CHARACTERISTICS

For African countries, taxation and spending, census, and other SES data are very limited in general, and at subnational levels in particular (even for large units like Admin1s, Admin2s, and electoral constituencies). It is especially hard to find data that are comparable cross-nationally and over time.

Colonial-era producer regions. Atlases published from the 1950s to the early 1970s identify colonial-era regions of export crop production, nationally traded food crops (maize, wheat, rice), and mining regions. We used a tracing method to create colonial-era producer region shapefiles in GIS. See References list.

Crop production in 2010. Data from the International Food Policy Research Institute's (IFPRI's) *Spatial Production Allocation Model* that models harvested area and output for Africa's twenty leading agricultural commodities in 2010 (released in 2017) were used to assess the production profile of electoral blocs and non-bloc regions. We are interested in "crop specialization" and consider a bloc to be strongly specialized in the production of a crop when it produces either more than 50% of national output of that crop or 1.5 times as much of the crop than would be expected under a uniform spatial distribution of the crop. This measure, the "specialization ratio," is the ratio of the bloc's share of national output of that crop in 2010, divided by the bloc's share of total national area. The measure controls for bloc size (IFPRI, Global Spatially-Disaggregated Crop Production Statistics Data 2010 v.2, Spatial Production Allocation Model, https://mapspam.info).

Education and ethnicity. DHS data available online at https://dhsprogram .com/ were used to describe the characteristics of the population who reside in blocs and in bloc subunits. DHS survey clusters were matched to blocs and bloc subunits using the GPS coordinates of the DHS clusters. There is a trade-off between pooling data waves, which should lower sampling biases by increasing the number of observations available, and not doing so, which allows the evolution of variables to be tracked over time. To study education, we pool data waves in order to have more precise estimates (even though we lose the ability to track changes over time). This is possible because the education questions do not vary across survey waves. To study the ethnic makeup of blocs, we use only one survey wave per country because the ethnic identity variable is not collected in a time-invariant manner.

Education variables. We use information on individuals' highest education attainment and on the number of years of education to build population-level variables: the percentage of the population that has completed secondary school and the average number of years of education. The data are pooled across the geolocalized DHS survey waves. For most countries, the data span from the late 1990s or early 2000s to the late 2010s. Following DHS's recommendation, each observation is reweighted so that the weighted number of surveyed women and men corresponded to the population of the country (women and

252   *Appendices*

men) in the corresponding year (using population data from the World Bank). Each wave is thus weighted by the survey weights and by population weights.

Ethnicity variables. We use information on respondents' declared ethnic identity to build population-level variables: the share of the population that belongs to each group that is part of the DHS classification. We use only the most recent survey wave for which the ethnicity of respondents was collected. We cannot pool the data when the ethnic categories that are available as possible survey responses vary across waves. In a few cases, there is no survey cluster in a bloc subunit (see discussion in Chapter 4) and no variables are available for this subunit. We use survey weights as described above. Ethnicity data are unavailable for South Africa (only racial categories are available), Tanzania, and Zimbabwe.

Table B.3 reports the DHS waves used for education variables and for ethnicity variables.

Nighttime luminosity as a subnational GDP proxy. Luminosity data were used to create the subnational GDP proxy measure (Chen & Nordhaus 2011; Pinkovskiy & Sala-i-Martin 2016; and Lessmann & Seidel 2017). Nighttime lights series data from the National Oceanic and Atmospheric Administration (NOAA) were used to compute the level of luminosity in each unit of analysis (electoral blocs and Admin1 units) for the years 1992, 2000, and 2013 [Version 4 DMSP-OLS Nighttime Lights Time Series, NOAA, National Geophysical Data Center, E/GC 325 Broadway, Boulder, Colorado USA 80305–3328]. There is no top coding problem. No areal unit – even of the metropolitan capital city units – reaches the maximum value in 2013. To correct for flaring when computing total luminosity in Nigeria's Eastern bloc, we used shapefiles

TABLE B.3 *Demographic and health surveys*

Country	DHS waves (education)				DHS wave (ethnicity)
Cameroon	2004	2011	2018		2018
Côte d'Ivoire	1994	1998	2012		2012
Ghana	2003	2008	2014		2014
Kenya	2003	2008	2014		2014
Malawi	2004	2010	2015		2015
Mali	2001	2006	2012	2018	2018
Nigeria	2003	2008	2013	2018	2018
South Africa	2016				No data
Tanzania	1999	2010	2015		No data
Uganda	2000	2006	2011	2016	2016
Zambia	2007	2013	2018		2007
Zimbabwe	1999	2005	2010	2015	No data

Notes: Demographic and health survey waves used to analyze bloc and bloc subunit characteristics.

Appendices 253

provided by the NOAA to identify areas with flaring. We removed this area from the bloc area and then added to the total luminosity of the nonflaring area the percentage of this total corresponding to the percentage of the Eastern bloc that was removed.

Population and population density. To compute population numbers and population density in electoral blocs and non-bloc regions, the analysis uses population data at 250m resolution from Schiavina, Freire, and MacManus 2019.

Constituency and administrative unit boundaries. Constituency-level shapefiles were used when these were available. We relied on administrative unit shapefiles from the GADM project (https://gadm.org/) to map electoral results when constituency-level shapefiles were not available. To make the colonial-era Admin1 shapefiles, we also used the contemporary GADM files and reamalgamated those that had been split over time to recreate the colonial units. The standard projection used is WTC (produces area in degrees). Electoral bloc shapefiles were reprojected in the relevant UTM zone to obtain areas in km².

Colonial provincial (Admin1) boundaries. The colonial-era Admin1 shapefiles were made using contemporary GADM files. We reamalgamated those that had been split over time to recreate the colonial units. Most of the twelve countries' provincial grids are inherited directly from the colonial period and persist into the 2000s. In some cases, colonial-era provincial units (Admin1) have been subdivided. The original boundaries are almost always left in place: New units are subunits of the original units. Examples are Ghana's Cape Colony unit, which was divided into Eastern and Western Regions in 1957 (retaining intact the Admin2s and NA contained within each of the new regions), and Côte d'Ivoire Admin1s, which have been progressively subdivided, starting in 1969, again without splitting up the lower-level administrative units and cantons. Cameroon's Eastern Region was hived off from Central in 1983. Tanzania has progressively subdivided Admin1 units. The Kenyan case is nuanced by the fact that provincial units were adjusted in 1962, on the eve of independence, when Meru and Embu districts were assigned to Eastern Region, and the border between Central and Rift Regions was moved to the west, expanding the old Central Province. In Nigeria, recrafting of the federal structure preserved the colonial-era divisions between Nigeria's three main regions and left the old NAs intact. Creation of thirty-six states also preserved both the original (1948) regional boundaries and the NA units defined within them. The six geopolitical zones declared under the Abacha regime largely preserve the old structure.

SECTION B.3 IDENTIFYING THE ELECTORAL BLOCS: GLOBAL AND LOCAL MORAN'S I

The Global and Local Moran's I are measures of spatial autocorrelation and are used as exploratory tools. See Anselin 1995, 2005; O'Loughlin 1993. See also Harbers 2017, Harbers and Ingram 2019: 73–76, and Boone, Wahman, Kyburz, and Linke, 2022, Appendices.

Global Moran's I. The Global Moran's I is a spatial autocorrelation coefficient that is used to identify geographic clustering in party-level results (vote shares). It is a single value, ranging from -1.0 to 1.0, that is calculated for each party and election for the A-list countries and for some elections (i.e., where possible) for the other countries. Positive and significant values mean that geographic support for the leading parties in each election is not dispersed uniformly or randomly (i.e., not distributed with uniform heterogeneity). Large and positive Global Moran's I values indicate a high degree of spatial autocorrelation and thus considerable geographic clustering of high vote shares for a given party.

Local Moran's I. The Global Moran's I summarizes the Local Moran's I, which is a value calculated for each areal unit. We calculated a Local Moran's I for each party's vote share in each constituency in all countries and elections where such calculation was possible. The Local Moran's I statistic is then standardized to z-scores, which are used to identify statistically significant clustering (using 5% significance level as a cutoff) across constituencies. The p-value is a pseudo p-value calculated on the basis of 999 permutations (this is the program's default value). In using the Local Moran's I to define electoral blocs, we include "neighbors" when constituencies on the border of the cluster that is identified by the Local Moran's I vote along with the bloc, with the same high vote shares for the same candidate. On neighbors, see Anselin (1995), Habers and Ingram (2019), and Boone, Wahman, Kyburz, and Linke (2022), Appendix A2.

SECTION B.4 IDENTIFYING THE ELECTORAL BLOCS: COUNTRY BY COUNTRY

List A countries: Kenya, Malawi, Zambia, and Ghana. For these countries, we used constituency-level electoral data supplied by national electoral commissions (or similar) for all the elections listed in Table B.2 in Appendix B. The exception to this rule is noted for the case of Malawi, below.

We matched the electoral data to constituency-level shapefiles. Three countries – Ghana, Kenya, and Zambia – experienced changes in constituency boundaries during the study period. Malawi did not experience any changes between 1999 and 2014 (193 constituencies). In Ghana, there were 201 constituencies during the period 1992–2000, 230 in 2004–2008, and 275 in 2012–2016. In Kenya, there were 210 constituencies during the period 1997–2007 and 295 in 2013 (last election considered). In Zambia, there were 150 constituencies during the period 1991–2014 and 156 in 2016 (last election considered).

For Kenya, Malawi, and Zambia, the first step in identifying the electoral bloc was computing the Local Moran's I for each party's vote share in a given election, using the shapefile corresponding to that electoral year. Groups of constituencies that form a cluster of significantly correlated high vote shares constitute an electoral cluster (if there are more than three such constituencies).

Appendices   255

Next, we added "neighbors" to the cluster (constituencies that are adjacent to the cluster and in which the same party wins as in the electoral cluster). Finally, we tracked the persistence over time of these clusters (Local Moran's I cluster plus neighbors).

Over time tracking was straightforward in the case of Malawi, as there were no changes in boundaries during the study period. In the case of Kenya and Zambia, we tracked constituencies as follows. If a constituency kept the same name from one election to the next, it was treated as the same constituency. For constituencies that split into two (or more) constituencies, we held constant the constituency shapefile used to depict persistent electoral blocs and examined each split constituency. A split constituency is included in the persistent electoral bloc if both of the new units cross the relevant thresholds of the Local Moran's I and the plurality vote. If a constituency splits in two, and one new unit crosses the threshold for bloc inclusion while the other does not, we included the original constituency in the bloc if the larger of the new units (in terms of voters) voted along with the electoral bloc. If not, both of the new units are excluded from the persistent bloc count. (An alternative would be to count the original constituency as in or out of the bloc based on Local Moran's I and the plurality vote of all voters in the combined new units – that is, ignore the split and average across the two new units.) See Boone, Wahman, Kyburz, and Linke (2022).

For Ghana, given the high number of boundary changes, an alternative method to work with changes in constituency boundaries was employed. We used the constituency boundaries of 1996 and 2000 and matched constituency boundaries in use in subsequent years to this shapefile. We created a "reference shapefile" containing 200 constituencies (some constituencies from 1996 were merged in order to allow for better tracking over time) and matched electoral data to this reference shapefile. Where constituencies split in years not covered by this shapefile, electoral results were pooled for the parent and child unit. The analysis was based on the pooled result for the parent unit. This procedure was followed for all elections.

Kenya: In addition to notes above, we note that there is a poor match between the 1997 shapefile and the 1992 electoral results.

Malawi: For Malawi electoral data for 1999 and 2004, we rely on the work of Michael Wahman, who used parliamentary election data to approximate presidential election data. For 1999, Wahman merged the parties Malawi Congress Party (MCP) and AFORD, because they ran together as a coalition in the presidential election. For 2004, he merged the parties MDP, MGD, NUP, PPM, PTP, and the Republican party that ran as a coalition in the presidential election. See Boone, Wahman, Kyburz, and Linke, 2022.

Zambia: We did not consider the results of the two by-elections 2008 and 2015. For the Western bloc, see notes to Figure 4.1(a) in Chapter 4. For the Eastern bloc, the result is sensitive to inclusion of estimations made in place of missing data and in consideration of UNIP's boycott of the 1996 election.

Zambia's Eastern region is distinctive – it does not follow the same voting pattern as any of Zambia's other electoral blocs.

Ghana: In addition to notes above, see notes under "Coding capital cities" for Accra.

List B countries: Cameroon, Côte d'Ivoire, Mali, Nigeria, South Africa, Tanzania, Uganda, and Zimbabwe. Where possible, we used spatial autocorrelation measures for one or more years to refine or verify the clustering that we identified by manually mapping winners' vote shares. Overall, changes in unit boundaries were not an issue because we did not have multiple shapefiles per country.

Cameroon. [GIS mapping, three elections; Local Moran's I, one election] Bloc definition was based on GIS mapping of three elections, 1992 and 2004 results at Admin1 level, and 2011 results at both the constituency and Admin1 levels. Blocs were drawn using Admin1 boundaries. For Cameroon 2011, the only year for which we had constituency-level data, the Local Moran's I does not pick up much geographic clustering in the ruling party vote share, as expected given its large hegemony over most of the national space. It is clear that the ruling party's hold on the Centre-Sud regions has been much more consistent than it has been across the other Admin1 regions since 1999. This is why the Centre-Sud region was identified as a persistent electoral bloc. The Western bloc is characterized by high (above 30% in most elections) vote shares for the opposition parties. Additional source: Morse (2018).

Côte d'Ivoire: [GIS mapping, one election] There is imperfect matching of results at the Admin3 (département) level and at Admin1 (Région) level. There is direct election of the president at national level; presidential results are not reported at constituency level. The blocs were conservatively identified by counting contiguous Admin3 units corresponding to constituencies that were members of either the Eastern (PDCI), Western (FPI), and/or Northern bloc in 3/3 elections since 1990 or 1995 (some units were members of Western at the >30% of the vote threshold from 1990), Additional sources: for 2010 Pres. R1 and R2, Bassett 2011, ElectoralGeography.com, Abidjan.net; for 2011 and 2016 parliamentary (Admin2), pesphos.adam-carr.ne [last consulted March 2, 2021]; for 2002, *Elections 2.0.* For 1990 and 1995 legislatives, reported at Admin2 (Crook 1997).

Mali: [GIS mapping, three elections] Blocs drawn using Admin1, Admin2, and Admin3 boundaries. We used Admin1-level presidential results for 2002, 2007 (margins only, no absolute vote counts), and 2013. We identified spatial concentrations of units returning the highest vote shares for each of the two main presidential candidates in each election. Winning shares were often over 70%, but we counted shares in the 50–60% range as strong wins in units in which votes were spread across a large number (often five or more) candidates. Since none of these would-be blocs mimicked one of the others across the elections for which information on electoral returns were available, we concluded that there are three distinctive electoral blocs (or electorally distinctive

Appendices 257

regions) and a large non-bloc area that consists of the far North (Gao and Kidal) and parts of the South (Kayes and the northern half of Koulikoro). In the Timboctou region, the southernmost constituencies tend to vote with the Mopti bloc, as depicted on the Mali map in Figure 4.3. Sources: for Presidential 2002, ElectoralGeography.com (for Admin1, +/- 70% for ATT and S. Cissé); Presidential 2013 (R1, provisoires), constituency level from ElectoralGeography2.0; for Presidential 2018 (R2), Wikipedia (choropleth map) for constituencies returns reported as vote shares for Kieta and Cissé at 10% intervals; additional sources: Legislatives 2002 (R1), République Mali, Min. de l'Admin.Territoriale (by constituency).

Nigeria: [GIS mapping, four elections] Blocs drawn using Admin1 (state) boundaries. State-level electoral results were used for all elections from 1999 to 2015 to identify geographically contiguous blocs of states that returned high vote shares for one of the three leading parties in three of the four elections for which we had data. For Northern Nigeria, the threshold for "high vote share" was set at 60%, and for Western Nigeria, at greater than 55%. Winners' vote shares in the Eastern electoral bloc are much higher. Lagos State was included in the Western bloc. Olanrewaju Lawal's (2019) spatial analysis of state-level clustering in the 2011 and 2015 presidential election results provided confirmation for our definition of electoral blocs in state-level results for those years.

South Africa: [GIS mapping, five elections] We used the General Election results aggregated at the district council level as presented and mapped by Adrian Firth at https://elections.adrianfrith.com/npe2019/nat/muni/lead ing#5/-28.5/25.5. To draw boundaries of KwaZulu-Natal bloc, we used published maps of vote shares within district council subunits.

Tanzania: [GIS mapping, three elections; Local Moran's I, one election] Blocs were drawn using constituency boundaries. For Tanzania, which had constituency-level data for 1995 (with much missing data) and 2010, and Admin1 level data for 2005, we used the party vote shares at either the constituency or Admin1 level to approximate geographic clusters of Chama Cha Mapinduzi (CCM) and opposition-leaning constituencies. This was supplemented by analyses of particular election years in the secondary literature, including Myers 2000, Brewin 2015, Ewald 2011: 261 inter alia, and Mmuya 1995: 45. Results from parliamentary elections helped reconstruct voting patterns for the 2005 election.

Uganda: [GIS mapping, four elections] Blocs drawn using Admin2 (district) boundaries. For Uganda, constituency-level electoral data are available since 1999, but mappable only at the Admin2 level due to frequent, poorly documented constituency boundary changes since 2008. For Uganda, because the ruling party is "hegemonic," the bloc of constituencies in the North returning anti-incumbent vote shares of over 50% in 3/4 elections between 2001 and 2016 was counted as an electoral bloc rather than an "oppositional zone," but as noted in the main text, this distinction is not salient in our analysis.

258 Appendices

Zimbabwe: [GIS mapping, three elections; Local Moran's I for two of these] Blocs drawn using constituency boundaries. For Zimbabwe, we used constituency-level data for 2002, 2008, and 2013, and published maps of constituency-level results for 2002. Results for R1 were used for 2008. Some constituencies are missing from the 2008 election results. Following the 2013 constituency shapefile and Lewanika (2019), the Victoria and Hwange National Parks are included in the Southern bloc (Southern opposition bloc). Most of Bulawayo is also in the Southern bloc. Additional sources: Lewanika (2019); presidential and parliamentary results at ElectoralGeography.com.

SECTION B.5 CODING CAPITAL CITIES

Cities that were considered to be "capital cities" are listed below. The list includes both de jure capital cities and those serving "capital-city functions" (de facto capital cities). Most fall into the non-bloc part of their country. The three exceptions are noted at the bottom of the list below. Where capital cities are part of non-bloc regions, they are excluded from the computation of all indicators for the non-bloc regions in these countries, including the population density indicators. Where capital cities are part of persistent electoral blocs (i.e., Cameroon Centre-Sud, Bamako–Koulikoro bloc, the Uganda Central Oppositional bloc), we *do* include them in our bloc-level computations. Because capital cities make up a very small portion *of the area* of each country, removing them from nighttime luminosity and population density computations does not change the estimates much. For the spatial analyses, we use the urban municipal Admin1 unit shapefiles to define the capital city constituencies.

Côte d'Ivoire (Abidjan, de facto capital)	non-bloc
Ghana (Metropolitan Accra)	non-bloc
Kenya (Nairobi)	non-bloc
Malawi (Lilongwe)	non-bloc
Nigeria (Abuja)	non-bloc
South Africa (Pretoria)	non-bloc
Zambia (Lusaka)	non-bloc
Zimbabwe (Harare)	non-bloc
TZ (Dar es Salaam, de facto capital)	non-bloc
Cameroon (Yaounde)	bloc
Mali (Bamako)	bloc
Uganda (Kampala)	bloc [oppositional zone]

For Ghana, three (predominantly rural) constituencies that are part of Greater Accra are part of the Eastern bloc. For Malawi, a few constituencies that are part of Greater Lilongwe are part of the Central bloc. For Tanzania, the de jure capital city of Dodoma is part of the CCM bloc. For Nigeria, Lagos is part of the Western bloc.

Appendix C

Summaries of Bloc Attributes

TABLE C.1 *"Colonial Admin1" corresponding units*

Country	Electoral bloc	Colonial Admin1 name	Postcolonial Admin1 units that correspond to colonial Admin1 (GADM units)	Postcolonial Admin1 that corresponds most closely to the electoral bloc
Cameroon	Centre-Sud bloc	Centre: Nyong-Sanaga and Mbam, Sud: Ntem	Centre and Sud	Centre and Sud
	Western opposition bloc	British Cameroon	NW and SW	NW, SW, and W
Côte d'Ivoire	Eastern bloc	Eastern	Eastern and Central	Eastern and Central
	Northern bloc	Northern	Nord (Savanes and Denguele)	Nord (Savanes and Denguele)
	Western bloc	Western	Centre-Ouest (Sassandra, Marahoue, Goh and Djiboua)	Centre-Ouest (Sassandra, Marahoue, Goh-Djiboua)
Ghana	Central bloc	Ashanti	Ashanti and Eastern	Ashanti and Eastern
	Eastern bloc	Volta Region	Volta	Volta
	NW bloc	Northern	Northern	Northern
Kenya	Central bloc	Central (1960)	Central Province	Central Province
	Eastern bloc	Eastern	Eastern	Eastern
	Rift Valley bloc	Rift	Rift	Rift
	Western bloc	Western	Nyanza, Western	Nyanza, Western
Malawi	Central bloc	Central	Central	Central
	Eastern bloc	Southern	Southern	Southern
	Northern bloc	Northern	Northern	Northern
	Southern bloc	Southern	Southern	Southern
Mali	Bamako–Koulikoro bloc	Koulikoro	Koulikoro	Koulikoro
	Mopti bloc	Mopti	Mopti	Mopti
	Sikasso bloc	Sikasso	Sikasso	Sikasso

Country				
Nigeria	Eastern bloc	Eastern	SE and half of SS	SE
	Northern bloc	Northern	NW and NE	NW and NE
	Western bloc	Western	SW and half of SS	SW
South Africa	Center bloc	Transvaal and Orange	NW and Gauteng	NW and Gauteng
	KwaZulu bloc	Natal	KwaZulu-Natal	KwaZulu-Natal
	West Cape bloc	Cape	W., N., and E. Cape	Western Cape
Tanzania	CCM bloc	Central	Central	Central
	N'rn opposition bloc	Northern and Lake	Northern, E. and W. Lake	Northern, E. and W. Lake
Uganda	Central opposition bloc	Central	Central	Central
	Northern bloc	Northern	Northern	Northern
	Western bloc	Western	Western	Western
Zambia	Copperbelt-Northern bloc	Copperbelt and Northern	Copperbelt and Northern	Copperbelt and Northern
	Eastern bloc	Eastern	Eastern	Eastern
	Southern bloc	Southern	Southern	Southern
	Western bloc	Western	Western	Western
Zimbabwe	Northern bloc	Mashonaland	Mashonaland	Mashonaland
	Southern bloc	Matabeleland	Matabeleland	Matabeleland

Notes: This table associates colonial-era Adminrs with contemporary electoral blocs and postcolonial Adminrs.

TABLE C.2 *Global Moran's I (vote shares)*

Cameroon	Election year				
	2011				
RDPC	0.09***				
SDF	0.02				
UDC	0.26***				

Ghana+	Election year				
	1996	2000	2008	2012	2016
NDC	0.05	−0.07	−0.08	−0.07	−0.11**
NPP	0.01	−0.08*	−0.04	−0.12**	−0.11**

Kenya	Election year				
	1992	1997	2002	2007	2013
DP	0.74***	0.8***			
FORD	0.63***	0.69***			
FORD-A	0.73***				
KANU	0.68***	0.64***	0.60***		
NDPK		0.65***			
FORD-P			0.64***		
NARC			0.61***		
SDP			0.12***		
KPTP				0.41***	
ODM				0.70***	
ODM-K				0.72***	
PNU				0.69***	
(KNC/POA)					0.20***
(TNA/Jubilee)					0.81***
(UDF/KANU/NFK)					0.76***
(ODM/CORD)					0.79***

Malawi	Election year			
	1999	2004	2009	2014
CONU	0.03***			
MCP-AFORD	0.9***			
MDP	−0.05***			
UDF	0.8***	0.54***		0.91***
MCP		0.87***	0.90***	c.94***
MGWIRIZANO		0.66***		
NDA		0.56***		
DPP			0.89***	0.91***
PETRA			0.48***	
PR			0.13***	
PP				0.85***

(continued)

Appendices

TABLE C.2 *(continued)*

	Election year	
Tanzania		2010
CCM		0.78***
CHADEMA		0.69***
CUF		0.94***
NCCR		0.51***

	Election year					
Zambia	1991	1996	2001	2006	2011	2016
MMD	0.79***	0.47***	0.70***	0.71***	0.72***	
UNIP	0.79***	0.17***	0.74***			
ZDC		0.38***				
NP		0.69***				
FDD			0.64***			
UPND			0.86***		0.91***	0.93***
HP				0.31***		
PF				0.78***	0.81***	0.93***
UDA				0.85***		

	Election year	
Zimbabwe	2008	2013
Mavambo Kusile Dawn	0.74***	
MDC	0.59***	0.23***
ZANU PF	0.64***	0.72***
MDC-Tsvangirai		0.66***

Notes: Results are reported for the largest parties in each country in terms of national vote share. Parties are sorted by year and alphabetically. *** denotes significance at the 1% level, ** at the 5% level, * at the 1% level (based on 9999 randomization permutations). For Malawi 1999 and 2004, we use the work of Michael Wahman, who used parliamentary election data to proxy the presidential results (see Boone, Wahman, Kyburz, & Linke, 2022). For discussion of the method, see Section B.3 in Appendix B identifying the electoral blocs: Global and Local Moran's I.

TABLE C.3 *Area of all blocs, combined, as percentage of national area (sq. km)*

Country	% bloc area	% non-bloc area
Cameroon	41	59
Côte d'Ivoire	32	68
Ghana	37	63
Kenya	21	79
Malawi	63	37
Mali	17	83
Nigeria	59	41
South Africa	55	45
Tanzania	50	50
Uganda	39	61
Zambia	62	38
Zimbabwe	43	57

Source: Authors' calculations.

TABLE C.4 *Bloc population density in 1990, 2000, and 2015, compared to national averages (w/o capital city)*

Country	Electoral bloc/ country average	Population density in 1990 (millions inhabitants/ km²)	Population density in 2000 (millions inhabitants/ km²)	Population density in 2015 (millions inhabitants/ km²)
Cameroon	Centre-Sud bloc	20.3	28.3	46.2
Cameroon	Western bloc	70.4	88.6	121.3
Cameroon	Non-bloc	15.7	21.2	31.5
Cameroon	Country (w/o capital city)	23.4	30.4	43.0
Côte d'Ivoire	Eastern bloc	9.9	13.2	17.5
Côte d'Ivoire	Northern bloc	3.1	4.4	6.4
Côte d'Ivoire	Western bloc	15.4	20.8	28.5
Côte d'Ivoire	Non-bloc	7.3	9.9	13.6
Côte d'Ivoire	Country (w/o capital city)	7.6	10.3	14.2
Ghana	Central bloc	10.1	12.5	18.1
Ghana	Eastern bloc	4.4	5.8	8.5
Ghana	NW bloc	5.2	6.5	8.4
Ghana	Non-bloc	4.2	5.4	7.7
Ghana	Country (w/o capital city)	5.3	6.8	9.7

(continued)

Appendices

TABLE C.4 *(continued)*

Country	Electoral bloc/ country average	Population density in 1990 (millions inhabitants/ km^2)	Population density in 2000 (millions inhabitants/ km^2)	Population density in 2015 (millions inhabitants/ km^2)
Kenya	Central bloc	178.9	224.3	298.2
Kenya	Eastern bloc	49.4	60.7	77.2
Kenya	Rift Valley bloc	61.0	87.3	139.8
Kenya	Western bloc	263.0	330.6	435.8
Kenya	Non-bloc	19.5	26.8	43.4
Kenya	Country (w/o capital city)	38.4	50.8	75.0
Malawi	Central bloc	129.6	159.3	254.1
Malawi	Eastern bloc	99.6	120.5	185.3
Malawi	Northern bloc	46.4	57.9	94.5
Malawi	Southern bloc	211.0	241.2	345.8
Malawi	Non-bloc	113.0	131.5	194.5
Malawi	Country (w/o capital city)	110.0	130.6	198.5
Mali	Bamako– Koulikoro bloc	37.9	54.1	104.8
Mali	Mopti bloc	16.1	19.8	28.0
Mali	Sikasso bloc	21.7	28.3	44.1
Mali	Non-bloc	3.4	4.4	6.6
Mali	Country (w/o capital city)	6.1	7.8	12.0
Nigeria	Eastern bloc	233.0	296.1	429.6
Nigeria	Northern bloc	84.3	108.9	161.8
Nigeria	Western bloc	263.2	340.8	508.2
Nigeria	Non-bloc	61.5	78.1	113.1
Nigeria	Country (w/o capital city)	105.4	135.0	198.3
South Africa	Center bloc	30.3	34.9	38.8
South Africa	KwaZulu bloc	54.1	60.5	63.2
South Africa	West Cape bloc	34.8	48.4	69.5
South Africa	Non-bloc	15.9	18.6	21.1
South Africa	Country (w/o capital city)	24.9	29.4	33.8
Tanzania	CCM bloc	19.2	24.9	36.8
Tanzania	N'rn opposition bloc	46.6	62.5	97.7
Tanzania	Non-bloc	21.9	28.3	41.6
Tanzania	Country (w/o capital city)	26.8	35.1	53.1

(continued)

TABLE C.4 (*continued*)

Country	Electoral bloc/ country average	Population density in 1990 (millions inhabitants/ km²)	Population density in 2000 (millions inhabitants/ km²)	Population density in 2015 (millions inhabitants/ km²)
Uganda	Central opposition bloc	174.7	246.0	441.3
Uganda	Northern bloc	46.2	62.2	101.4
Uganda	Western bloc	65.1	90.7	153.1
Uganda	Non-bloc	68.0	91.8	147.1
Uganda	Country (w/o capital city)	68.2	93.8	155.9
Zambia	Copperbelt-Northern bloc	16.2	19.7	29.2
Zambia	Eastern bloc	12.8	16.0	22.9
Zambia	Southern bloc	12.2	16.1	24.5
Zambia	Western bloc	5.5	6.8	9.0
Zambia	Non-bloc	5.9	7.9	11.9
Zambia	Country (w/o capital city)	9.8	12.5	18.4
Zimbabwe	Northern bloc	25.3	31.2	41.6
Zimbabwe	Southern bloc	18.1	19.7	21.5
Zimbabwe	Non-bloc	25.1	30.3	38.3
Zimbabwe	Country (w/o capital city)	23.2	27.7	34.7

Notes: Country average excludes capital city
Source: Authors' calculations from Schiavina, Freire, and MacManus. 2019. GHS population grid multitemporal (1975, 1990, 2000, 2015) R2019A. European Commission, Joint Research Centre (JRC).

TABLE C.5 *Summary of electoral bloc characteristics, with stability of regional inequalities over time and consistency across indicators*

Country	Electoral Bloc	Mean pixel luminosity (1992)	Mean pixel luminosity (2000)	Mean pixel luminosity (2013)	Average number of years of education	Share of adults who attended secondary school	Producer profile (overlap & specialization)	70% of bloc in colonial admin 1	Bloc is multiethnic
Cameroon	Capital city	21.91	24.43	38.28	9.8	24.3			
	Western bloc	0.19	0.22	0.34	8.2	12.7	Type 1	No	Yes
	Centre-Sud bloc*	0.09	0.11	0.19	8.8	16.9	Type 1	Yes	Yes
	Non-bloc	0.02	0.03	0.05	3.3	2.8			
Côte d'Ivoire	Capital city	10.65	13.51	18.13	6.1	16.9			
	Eastern bloc	0.21	0.75	1.06	3.6	6.2	Type 1	Yes	Yes
	Western bloc	0.10	0.51	1.42	3.5	4.9	Type 1	Yes	Yes
	Non-bloc	0.06	0.28	0.43	3.2	5.0			
	Northern bloc	0.03	0.17	0.32	2.0	4.0	Type 2	Yes	Yes
Ghana	Capital city	48.74	54.11	60.76	10.3	45.3			
	Central bloc	0.51	0.78	1.50	8.3	25.3	Type 1	Yes	Yes
	Non-bloc	0.20	0.40	0.78	6.4	22.3			
	Eastern bloc	0.20	0.33	0.71	6.8	18.3	Type 2	No	Yes
	NW bloc	0.07	0.11	0.35	4.6	16.5	Type 5	Yes	No
Kenya	Capital city	27.54	27.12	39.90	11.0	57.2			
	Central bloc	0.51	0.87	2.01	9.3	36.3	Type 1	Yes	Yes
	Western bloc	0.22	0.22	0.60	8.1	21.5	Type 1	Yes	Yes
	Rift Valley bloc	0.05	0.07	0.19	8.2	27.8	Type 1	Yes	No
	Non-bloc	0.04	0.05	0.10	7.5	24.3			
	Eastern bloc	0.03	0.10	0.26	8.2	23.0	Type 4	Yes	No

(continued)

TABLE C.5 *(continued)*

Country	Electoral Bloc	Mean pixel luminosity (1992)	Mean pixel luminosity (2000)	Mean pixel luminosity (2013)	Average number of years of education	Share of adults who attended secondary school	Producer profile (overlap & specialization)	70% of bloc in colonial admin 1	Bloc is multiethnic
Malawi	Capital city	19.75	22.46	32.57	8.3	30.6			
	Southern bloc	0.76	0.76	0.91	5.2	8.8	Type 1	Yes	Yes
	Non-bloc	0.24	0.29	0.47	5.5	8.4		Yes	
	Central bloc	0.14	0.21	0.42	4.5	6.8	Type 1	Yes	No
	Northern bloc	0.06	0.10	0.21	7.1	10.5	Type 4	Yes	Yes
	Eastern bloc	0.06	0.14	0.14	3.6	3.5	Type 3	Yes	Yes
Mali	Capital city	23.17	28.81	51.90	5.8	14.1			
	Bamako–Koulikoro bloc*	0.15	0.23	0.57	4.1	9.1	Type 1	Yes	Yes
	Sikasso bloc	0.01	0.04	0.08	1.5	2.0	Type 1	Yes	Yes
	Mopti bloc	0.00	0.01	0.03	0.8	0.5	Type 1	Yes	Yes
	Non-bloc	0.00	0.00	0.01	1.3	1.4			
Nigeria	Capital city	1.83	2.75	6.25	9.9	56.3			
	Eastern bloc	1.83	1.34	2.95	9.5	45.6	Type 1	No	Yes
	Western bloc	1.66	1.23	3.12	9.9	54.2	Type 1	Yes	No
	Northern bloc	0.24	0.24	0.40	4.1	18.5	Type 1	Yes	Yes
	Non-bloc	0.15	0.13	0.33	5.8	25.0			
South Africa	Capital city	20.01	19.70	24.74	10.8	50.0			
	West Cape bloc	1.59	1.73	2.21	10.9	47.7	Type 1	Yes	
	Center bloc	0.85	1.16	1.89	9.8	32.2	Type 3	Yes	
	KwaZulu bloc	0.76	1.16	1.80	9.5	36.9	Type 3	Yes	[No]
	Non-bloc	0.49	0.59	0.77	10.2	41.0			

Tanzania	Capital city	7.09	9.07	16.27	8.4	23.5			
	N'rn opposition bloc	0.03	0.08	0.15	5.8	6.6	Type 1	No	[Yes]
	Non-bloc	0.02	0.04	0.07	6.1	7.0			
	CCM bloc	0.02	0.03	0.06	5.7	6.5	Type 2	No	[Yes]
Uganda	Capital city	24.05	33.19	46.89	9.9	30.9			
	Central opposition bloc*	0.72	1.22	2.44	8.8	22.1	Type 1	Yes	Yes
	Non-bloc	0.01	0.03	0.06	5.8	6.2			
	Western bloc	0.00	0.02	0.07	5.5	5.9	Type 3	Yes	Yes
	Northern bloc	0.00	0.03	0.05	6.1	9.9	Type 4	Yes	Yes
Zambia	Capital city	32.03	35.40	48.27	9.2	32.5			
	Copperbelt-North. bloc	0.17	0.18	0.29	7.7	20.3	Type 1	Yes	Yes
	Southern bloc	0.10	0.11	0.24	7.5	14.1	Type 1	Yes	Yes
	Non-bloc	0.04	0.04	0.13	7.0	14.9			
	Eastern bloc	0.02	0.02	0.07	5.4	7.7	Type 1	No	Yes
	Western bloc	0.01	0.01	0.03	5.9	9.8	Type 5	No	Yes
Zimbabwe	Capital city	30.92	32.48	32.24	10.6	29.3			
	Southern bloc	0.19	0.20	0.18	9.2	19.5	Type 5	Yes	[No]
	Non-bloc	0.18	0.24	0.25	8.8	13.3			
	Northern bloc	0.10	0.16	0.21	8.2	8.3	Type 1	Yes	[No]

Notes: Luminosity values from NOAA. Education variables from DHS. In the first five columns containing figures, top-ranked electoral blocs (most advantaged blocs) are shaded in blue. Bottom-ranked blocs (least advantaged of the blocs) are shaded in red. The shading highlights the stability of the rankings. In the last three columns, the blocs that conform to our hypotheses and the dominant tendency in the data are in blue. The producer profile typology is laid out in Table 4.3. On the multiethnicity of the electoral blocs, see Table 4.5.

* indicates that the capital city is part of the bloc (values for the capital city itself are still reported for reference).

The use of brackets in the last column indicates that the result is an estimate based on the secondary literature, rather than on the authors' computations.

Appendix D

Producer Profiles of the Non-bloc Regions

Country	Non-bloc area (as % of country area)	Colonial-era producer region [1]	Non-bloc overlaps with producer region? [2]	% of non-bloc in colonial-era producer region	% of colonial-era producer region in non-bloc	Non-bloc is specialized? [3]	Non-bloc, % of national output 2010	Specialization ratio: % output in 2010/ % national area
Cameroon	58.8	Cotton	Yes	32.3	100.0	Yes	78.9	1.34
Côte d'Ivoire	67.8	Cocoa +*	No	13.8	46.5	Yes	57.7	0.85
Côte d'Ivoire	67.8	Coffee +*	No	13.8	46.5	Yes	57.1	0.84
Ghana	62.9	Palm oil	Yes	4.0	59.4	No	36.7	0.58
Kenya	78.7	Sisal	Yes	0.3	52.6	No	12	0.15
Malawi	37.1	Tobacco*	No	23.8	37.2	No	30.6	0.82
Mali	82.9	Groundnuts*	Yes	5.8	66.4	Yes	53.1	0.64
Nigeria	41.3	Groundnuts*	No	23.2	47.7	No	36.1	0.87
South Africa	45.4	Grain	No	21.7	46.5	No	28.7	0.63
Tanzania	49.8	Cashew	Yes	8.7	99.1	n.d.	n.d.	n.d.
Uganda	60.5	Cotton	Yes	24.4	87.4	Yes	58.7	0.97
Zambia	38.2	S'rn maize*	No	4.1	18.1	No	38.7	1.01
Zimbabwe	56.8	Tobacco*	No	14.7	46.1	No	48.5	0.86

Notes: Data on colonial-era producer regions from Atlases. Current production from IFPRI 2010. n.d. = no data.

[1] The "best match" between the non-bloc and the colonial-era producer region is the pair with the highest overlap as percentage of each country's non-bloc area. * indicates that the colonial-era producer region is also associated with an electoral bloc (see Table 4.3). + indicates that cocoa and coffee are part of the same colonial-era producer region.

[2] The non-bloc is considered as overlapping with colonial-era producer region if their overlap makes up either more than 50% of the colonial-era producer region or more than 50% of the non-bloc.

[3] The non-bloc is specialized if it either produces more than 50% of the total production of the crop associated with the colonial-era producer region or if its specialization ratio in this crop is higher than 1.5.

Appendix Table D.1 reports the "best match" between a colonial-era producer zone and the *non-bloc area* of each country (i.e., highest overlap as % of non-bloc area). Our theory predicts that values in the sixth column will be low, not high, so there are potential anomalies here. Cameroon, Côte d'Ivoire, and Uganda are discussed in the main text. For Ghana and Kenya, it is not surprising that these colonial-era producer regions did not give rise to persistent electoral blocs. In Ghana, palm oil was grown in an archipelago of enclaves close to the Atlantic coast. Sisal in Kenya was and is grown in plantation enclaves. Tanzania's cashew-producing southern coastal zone is not an electoral bloc, but since the 2000s, it shows some potential of becoming one. For most of the other countries, the overlaps reported in the sixth column are limited, as expected. The groundnut-producing region of colonial Mali now corresponds to *both* the Bamako–Koulikoro bloc and the non-bloc area of Mali (as denoted by the asterisk). While Bamako–Koulikoro bloc is the heart of the producer region (the specialization ratio is above 4), the non-bloc area is not specialized in this crop (by our measure).

Table 4.2 identifies six other colonial-era producer regions that are not associated with electoral blocs. They are part of Côte d'Ivoire coffee (the Far West forest zone), the Mali Segou rice zone, Malawi coffee, Nigeria tobacco, Nigeria mining, and Zimbabwe sugar. They retain their specialization, if weakly, but did not "give rise" to blocs.

Appendix E

Maps of Overlap between Electoral Blocs and Colonial-Era Producer Zones

274	*Appendices*

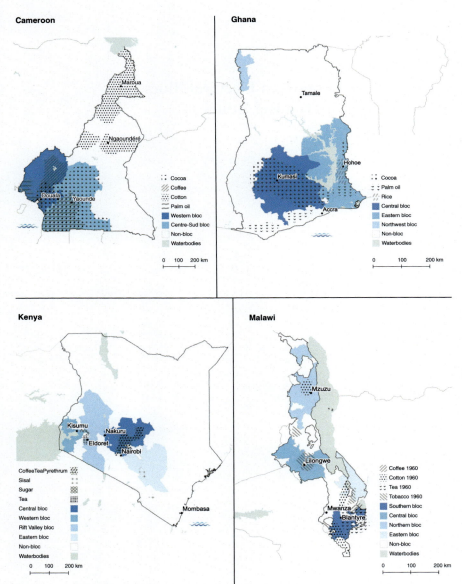

FIGURE E.1 Overlap of electoral blocs and colonial-era producer zones: Cameroon, Ghana, Kenya, and Malawi (For Côte d'Ivoire, see Figure 4.6)
Notes: From Authors' data. See Appendix B, Section B.2.

Appendices

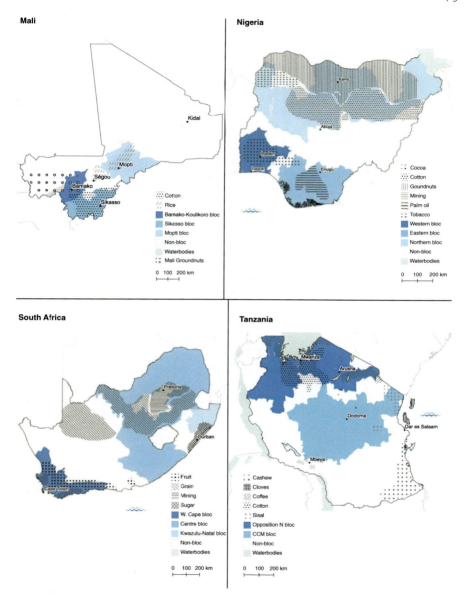

FIGURE E.2 Overlap of electoral blocs and colonial-era producer zones: Mali, Nigeria, South Africa, and Tanzania
Notes: From Authors' data. See Appendix B, Section B.2.

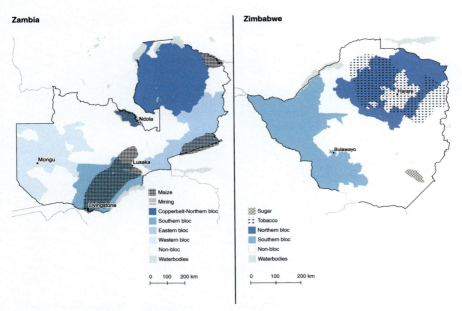

FIGURE E.3 Overlap of electoral blocs and colonial-era producer zones: Zambia and Zimbabwe (For Uganda, see Figure 4.6)
Notes: From Authors' data. See Appendix B, Section B.2.

Appendix F

Bloc Political Dominance and Gap Magnitude

TABLE F.1 *Bloc political dominance*

Country	Electoral bloc	% elections in which winner at national level is the same as winner at bloc level	Rank of bloc (avg. pixel luminosity in 2013)	Number of elections
Cameroon	Centre-Sud bloc	100	2	3
Cameroon	Non-bloc	100	3	3
Cameroon	Western bloc	67	1	3
Ghana	Central bloc	50	1	6
Ghana	Eastern bloc	50	3	6
Ghana	NW bloc	50	4	6
Ghana	Non-bloc	100	2	6
Kenya	Central bloc	60	1	5
Kenya	Eastern bloc	40	3	5
Kenya	Non-bloc	80	5	5
Kenya	Rift Valley bloc	60	4	5
Kenya	Western bloc	20	2	5
Malawi	Central bloc	0	3	4
Malawi	Eastern bloc	50	5	4
Malawi	Non-bloc	100	2	4
Malawi	Northern bloc	25	4	4
Malawi	Southern bloc	100	1	4
Nigeria	Eastern bloc	75	2	4
Nigeria	Non-bloc	100	4	4
Nigeria	Northern bloc	50	3	4
Nigeria	Western bloc	100	1	4

(continued)

278 Appendices

TABLE F.1 (*continued*)

Country	Electoral bloc	% elections in which winner at national level is the same as winner at bloc level	Rank of bloc (avg. pixel luminosity in 2013)	Number of elections
Tanzania	CCM bloc	100	3	1
Tanzania	N'rn opposition bloc	100	1	1
Tanzania	Non-bloc	100	2	1
Uganda	Central opposition bloc	100	1	2
Uganda	Non-bloc	100	3	2
Uganda	Northern bloc	100	4	2
Uganda	Western bloc	100	2	2
Zambia	Copperbelt-N'rn bloc	83	1	6
Zambia	Eastern bloc	50	4	6
Zambia	Non-bloc	83	3	6
Zambia	Southern bloc	33	2	6
Zambia	Western bloc	50	5	6
Zimbabwe	Non-bloc	100	1	2
Zimbabwe	Northern bloc	50	2	2
Zimbabwe	Southern bloc	50	3	2

Notes: Results on bloc political dominance computed using the post-1990 available electoral data, as described in Table B.2 in Appendix B. See Table 5.1.

TABLE F.2 *Gap magnitude: Relative luminosity gap between the bloc ranked first and the bloc ranked second in 1992, 2000, and 2013*

Country	Year	Ratio bloc 1:bloc 2	Bloc 1 name	Bloc 2 name
Nigeria	1992	1.10	Eastern bloc	Western bloc
Tanzania	1992	1.50	N'rn opposition bloc	CCM bloc
Zambia	1992	1.80	Copperbelt-Northern bloc	Southern bloc
South Africa	1992	1.87	W. Cape bloc	Center bloc
Zimbabwe	1992	1.89	Southern bloc	Northern bloc
Côte d'Ivoire	1992	2.17	Eastern bloc	Western bloc
Cameroon	1992	2.21	Western bloc	Centre-Sud bloc
Kenya	1992	2.34	Central bloc	Western bloc
Ghana	1992	2.62	Central bloc	Eastern bloc
Malawi	1992	5.57	Southern bloc	Central bloc
Mali	1992	26.01	Bamako–Koulikoro bloc	Sikasso bloc
Uganda	1992	166.39	Central opposition bloc	Western bloc

(*continued*)

Appendices

TABLE F.2 (*continued*)

Country	Year	Ratio bloc 1:bloc 2	Bloc 1 name	Bloc 2 name
Nigeria	2000	1.09	Eastern bloc	Western bloc
Zimbabwe	2000	1.25	Southern bloc	Northern bloc
Côte d'Ivoire	2000	1.45	Eastern bloc	Western bloc
South Africa	2000	1.49	W. Cape bloc	Center bloc
Zambia	2000	1.70	Copperbelt-Northern bloc	Southern bloc
Cameroon	2000	2.07	Western bloc	Centre-Sud bloc
Ghana	2000	2.40	Central bloc	Eastern bloc
Tanzania	2000	2.64	N'rn opposition bloc	CCM bloc
Malawi	2000	3.65	Southern bloc	Central bloc
Kenya	2000	3.92	Central bloc	Western bloc
Mali	2000	6.40	Bamako–Koulikoro bloc	Sikasso bloc
Uganda	2000	60.95	Central opposition bloc	Western bloc
Côte d'Ivoire	2013	0.75	Eastern bloc	Western bloc
Zimbabwe	2013	0.85	Southern bloc	Northern bloc
Nigeria	2013	0.94	Eastern bloc	Western bloc
South Africa	2013	1.17	W. Cape bloc	Center bloc
Zambia	2013	1.19	Copperbelt-Northern bloc	Southern bloc
Cameroon	2013	1.80	Western bloc	Centre-Sud bloc
Ghana	2013	2.12	Central bloc	Eastern bloc
Malawi	2013	2.15	Southern bloc	Central bloc
Tanzania	2013	2.38	N'rn opposition bloc	CCM bloc
Kenya	2013	3.32	Central bloc	Western bloc
Mali	2013	7.00	Bamako–Koulikoro bloc	Sikasso bloc
Uganda	2013	34.02	Central opposition bloc	Western bloc

Notes: This table reports the ratio of mean pixel luminosity in 1992, 2000, and 2013 in the bloc ranked first in 1992 to mean pixel luminosity in the bloc ranked second in 1992. Using rankings as of 1992 for reporting the luminosity values allows us to pick up cases in which the ranking changes. These are Côte d'Ivoire, Nigeria, and Zimbabwe. A ratio lower than 1 indicates that the bloc ranked second in 1992 overtook the bloc that was ranked first in 1992. Overall, the relative gap decreases.

References

Abdulai, Abdul-Gafaru. 2017. Rethinking Spatial Inequality in Development: The Primacy of Power Relations. *Journal of International Development* 29(3): 386–403.

Acemoglu, Daron and James Robinson. 2006. *Economic Origins of Dictatorship and Democracy*. Cambridge and New York: Cambridge University Press.

Adam, Christopher, David Bevan, and Douglas Gollin. 2018. Rural-Urban Linkages, Public Investment, and Transport Costs: The Case of Tanzania. *World Development* 109: 497–510.

Agnew, John. 1996. Mapping Politics: How Context Counts in Electoral Geography. *Political Geography* 15(2): 129–146.

Agnew, John. 1997. The Dramaturgy of Horizons: Geographic Scale in the "Reconstruction of Italy" by the New Italian Political Parties, 1992–95. *Political Geography* 16(2): 99–121.

Ahlerup, Pelle, Thushyanthan Baskara, and Arne Bigsten. 2016. Regional Development and National Identity in Sub-Saharan Africa. *Journal of Comparative Economics* 45(3): 622–643. Doi: 10.1016/j.jce.2016.02.001

Aker, Jenny C., Michael W. Klein, Stephen A. O'Connell, and Muzhe Yang. 2010. *Borders, Ethnicity, and Trade*. SSRN. https://ssrn.com/abstract=1601711

Albaugh, Ericka A. 2011. An Autocrat's Tool Kit: Adaptation and Manipulation in "democratic" Cameroon. *Democratization* 18(2): 388–414.

Alesina, Alberto, Stelios Michalopoulous, and Elias Papaioannou. 2016. Ethnic Inequality. *Journal of Political Economy* 124(2): 428–488.

Allen, Tim. 1996. Making the Madi: The invention of a Ugandan Tribe. In Louise de la Gorgendière, Kenneth King, and Sarah Vaughan, eds., *Ethnicity in Africa: Roots, Meanings and Implications*. Edinburgh: University of Edinburgh Press, pp. 91–116.

Allman, Jean Marie. 1993. *Quills of the Porcupine: Asante Nationalism in an Emergent Ghana*. Madison: University of Wisconsin Press.

Alvaredo, Facundo, Lucas Chancel, Thomas Piketty, Emmanuel Saez, and Gabriel Zucman. 2017. *World Inequality Report 2018*. World Inequality Lab.

Amin, Samir. 1972. Underdevelopment and Dependence in Black Africa: Origins and Contemporary Forms. *Journal of Modern African Studies*, 10(4): 503–524.

References

Amundsen, Inge. 2015. Playing the Ethnic Card? The Political Game in Malawi, CMI Field Notes, February 4, 2015. Bergen, Norway: Chr. Michelsen Institute.

Anselin, Luc. 1995. Local Indicators of Spatial Association – LISA. *Geographical Analysis* 27(2): 93–115.

Anselin, Luc. 2005. Exploring Spatial Data with GeoDA: A Workbook. Center for Spatially Integrated Social Science. March 6. www.geos.ed.ac.uk/~gisteac/fspat/geo daworkbook.pdf Accessed July 29, 2020.

Archibong, Belinda. 2018. Historical Origins of Persistent Inequality in Nigeria. *Oxford Development Studies* 46(3): 325–347.

Arriola, Leonardo. 2013. *Multiethnic Coalitions in Africa: Business Financing of Opposition Elections*. New York and Cambridge: Cambridge University Press.

Asingo, Patrick. 2020. Nyanza: The Odinga Dynasty and Beyond. In Nic Cheeseman, Karuti Kanyinga, and Gabrielle Lynch, eds., *The Oxford Handbook of Kenyan Politics*. Oxford: Oxford University Press, pp. 617–631.

Atkinson, Anthony B. 2015a. Top Incomes in East Africa before and after Independence. WID.world Working Paper, 2015/2.

Atkinson, Anthony B. 2015b. The Distribution of Top Incomes in Former British West Africa. WID.world Working Paper, 2015/3.

Atzili, Boaz and Burak Kadercan. 2017. Territorial Designs and International Politics: Diverging Constitution of Space and Boundaries. *Territory, Politics, Governance* 5(2): 115–130.

Ayeko-Kümmeth, Jane and Klaus Schlichte. 2021. The State on the Countryside: Food Security as Social Policy in Uganda. SOCIUM SFB 1342 Working Papers, 18, University of Bremen Research Center on Inequality and Social Policy.

Azam, Jean Paul. 2001. The Redistributive State and Conflicts in Africa. *Journal of Peace Research* 38(4): 429–444.

Azam, Jean Paul. 2006. *Trade, Exchange Rates, and Growth in Sub-Saharan Africa*. New York and Cambridge: Cambridge University Press.

Azam, Jean Paul. 2008. The Political Geography of Redistribution. In B. Ndulu et al., eds., *The Political Economy of Economic Growth in Africa, 1960–2000*. Cambridge and New York: Cambridge University Press, pp. 225–248.

Bakke, Kristin M. and Erik Wibbles. 2006. Diversity, Disparity, and Civil Conflict in Federal States. *World Politics* 59(1): 1–50.

Bakwesegha, C. J. 1974. Patterns and Processes of Spatial Development: The Case of Uganda. *East African Geographical Review* 12 (April): 46–64.

Balans, Jean Louis, Christian Coulon, and Jean-Marc Gasellu. 1975. *Autonomie Locale et Intégration Nationale au Sénégal*. Paris: A. Pedone.

Baldwin, Kate. 2015. *The Paradox of Traditional Chiefs in Democratic Africa*. Cambridge and New York: Cambridge University Press.

Baleyte, Jules, Amory Gethin, Yajna Govind, and Thomas Piketty. 2020. Social Inequalities and the Politicization of Ethnic Cleavages in Botswana, Ghana, Nigeria, and Senegal, 1999–2019. WID.world Working Paper N. 2020/18. World Inequality Database. Sept.

Bandyopadhyay, Sanghamitra and Elliott Green. 2016. Precolonial Political Centralization and Contemporary Development in Uganda. *Economic Development and Cultural Change* 64(3): 471–508.

Banégas, Richard and Camille Popineau. 2021. The 2020 Ivoirian Election and the "Third Term" Debate: A Crisis of "Korocracy"? *African Affairs*, 210(480): 461–477.

References 283

Banerjee, Abhijit and Lakshmi Ayer. 2005. History, institutions, and Economic Performance: The Legacy of Colonial Land Tenure Systems in India. *American Economic Review* 95 (4): 1190–1213.

Barkan, Joel and Michael Chege. 1989. Decentralising the State: District Focus and the Politics of Reallocation in Kenya. *The Journal of Modern African Studies* 27(3): 431–453.

Barkan, Joel, Paul J. Densham, and Gerard Rushton. 2006. Space Matters: Designing Better Electoral Systems for Emerging Democracies. *American Journal of Political Science* 50(4): 926–939.

Barkey, Karen. 2008. *Empire of Difference: The Ottomans in Comparative Perspective.* New York and Cambridge: Cambridge University Press.

Bartolini, Stephano and Peter Mair. 1990. *Identity, Competition, and Electoral Availability: The Stabilization of European Electorates, 1885–1985.* New York: Cambridge University Press.

Bartolinli, Stephano. 2005. The Formation of Cleavages. *Revue Internationale de politique comparée* 12(1): 9–34.

Basedau, Matthais. 2019. Party Systems in Africa. Oxford Research Encyclopedias, Politics. Online. Doi: 10.1093/acrefore/9780190228637.013.891

Bassett, Ellen M. 2015. The Challenge of Reforming Land Governance in Kenya. A paper presented at the 2015 annual meetings of the African Studies Association, San Diego, California, November 27.

Bassett, Thomas. 2001. *The Peasant Cotton Revolution in West Africa: Côte d'Ivoire, 1880–1995.* Cambridge: Cambridge University Press.

Bassett, Thomas. 2011. Briefing: Winning Coalition, Sore Loser. Côte d'Ivoire's 2010 Presidential Elections. *African Affairs* 110(440) (July): 469–479.

Bassett, Thomas J. 2014. Capturing the Margins: World Market Prices and Cotton Farmer Incomes in West Africa. *World Development* 59 (July): 408–421.

Bates, Robert H. 1976. *Rural Responses to Industrialization: A Study of Village Zambia.* New Haven: Yale University Press.

Bates, Robert H. 1981. *Markets and States in Tropical Africa: The Political Basis of Agricultural Policies.* Berkeley, CA: University of California Press.

Bates, Robert H. 1983 [2010]. Commercialization of Agriculture and Rural Political Protest. In Robert H. Bates, ed., *Essays on the Political Economy of Rural Africa.* Cambridge: Cambridge University Press, pp. 92–104.

Bates, Robert H. 1983. Modernization, Ethnic Competition, and the Rationality of Politics in Contemporary Africa. In Donald Rothchild and Victor A. Olorunsola, eds., *State versus Ethnic Claims: African Policy Dilemmas.* New York: Routledge, pp. 152–171.

Bates, Robert H. 1989. *Beyond the Miracle of the Market.* Cambridge: Cambridge University Press.

Bates, Robert H. 2017. *The Development Dilemma: Security, Prosperity, and a Return to History.* Princeton, NJ: Princeton University Press.

Bates, Robert H. and Steven A. Block. 2013. Revisiting African Agriculture: Institutional Change and Productivity Growth. *Journal of Politics* 75(2): 372–384.

Bayart, Jean François. 1985. *L'Etat au Cameroun.* Paris: Presses de la Fondation Nationale des Sciences Politiques.

Bayart, Jean François. 2013. Another Look at the Arab Springs. *Sociétés Politiques Comparées* 35 (trans. Andrew Brown): 1–34.

Bayart, Jean-François. 2014. Revisiting the Arab Spring. *Politique Africaine* 133(1): 153–175.

Baylies, Carolyn and Morris Szeftel. 1992. The Fall and Rise of Multi-Party Politics in Zambia. *Review of African Political Economy* 54: 75–91.

Becker, Felicitas. 2019. *The Politics of Poverty: Policy-Making and Rural Development in Tanzania*. Cambridge: Cambridge University Press.

Beegle, Kathleen, Luc Christiaensen, Andrew Dabalen, and Isis Gaddis. 2016. *Poverty in a Rising Africa*. Washington, DC: World Bank.

Behrend, Jacqueline and Laurence Whitehead. 2016. Setting the Comparative Agenda: Territorially Uneven Democratization Processes in Large Federations. In J. Behrend and L. Whitehead, eds., *Illiberal Practices: Territorial Variance within Large Federal Democracies*. Baltimore, MD: Johns Hopkins University Press, pp. 3–22.

Behrendt, Claudia. 2006. The Cotton Sector in Mali: Realizing Its Growth Potential. *OECD Development Centre, Policy Insights* 30 (October).

Behrens, Kristian and Alain Pholo Bala. 2011. Do Rent-seeking and Interregional Transfers Contribute to Urban Primacy in Sub-Saharan Africa? *Papers in Regional Science* 2011: 166. Doi: 10.1111/j.1435-5957.2011.00400.x

Beiser-McGraph, Janina, Carl Müeller-Crepon, and Yannick I. Pengl. 2021. Who Benefits? How Local Ethnic Demography Shapes Political Favoritism in Africa. *British Journal of Political Science* 51(4): 1582–1600.

Bensel, Richard. 1984. *Sectionalism and American Political Development*. Madison: University of Wisconsin Press.

Benton, Lauren. 2009. *A Search for Sovereignty: Law and Geography in European Empires, 1400–1900*. Cambridge and New York: Cambridge University Press.

Beramendi, Pablo. 2007. Inequality and the Territorial Fragmentation of Solidarity. *International Organization* 61(Fall): 783–820.

Beramendi, Pablo. 2012. *The Political Geography of Inequality: Regions and Redistribution*. Cambridge and New York: Cambridge University Press.

Beramendi, Pablo, Silja Häusermann, Herbert Kitschelt, and Hanspeter Kriesi. 2015. *The Politics of Advanced Capitalism*. Cambridge and New York: Cambridge University Press.

Beramendi, Pablo and Melissa Rogers. 2022. *Geography, Capacity, and Inequality: Spatial Inequality*. *Cambridge Elements in Political Economy*. Cambridge and New York: Cambridge University Press.

Bergen, Geoffrey. 2007. Trade Unions, Democracy, and Development in Senegal. In Jon Kraus, ed. *Trade Unions and the Coming of Democracy in Africa*. New York: Palgrave Macmillan, pp. 35–60.

Berman, Bruce J. 1990. *Control and Crisis in Colonial Kenya: The Dialectic of Domination*. London, Nairobi, and Athens: James Currey, Heinemann Kenya, and Ohio University Press.

Berman, Bruce J. 1992. Structure and Process in the Bureaucratic States of Colonial Africa. In Bruce J. Berman and John Lonsdale, eds., *Unhappy Valley: Conflict in Kenya and Africa. Book One: State and Class*. London, Nairobi, and Athens: James Currey, Heinemann Kenya, and Ohio University Press, pp. 140–167.

Berman, Bruce J. 1998. Ethnicity, Patronage and the African State: The Politics of Uncivil Nationalism. *African Affairs* 97(388): 305–341.

Berman, Bruce J. 2014. Ethnic Politics, Economic Reform, Democratisation. In Hiroyuki Hino et al., eds., *Ethnic Diversity and Economic Instability in Africa*. Cambridge: Cambridge University Press, pp. 169–201.

References

Berman, Bruce J. and John Lonsdale. 1992. *Unhappy Valley: Conflict in Kenya and Africa. Book One: State and Class.* Athens: Ohio University Press.

Berry, Sara. 1993. *No Condition Is Permanent: The Social Dynamics of Agrarian Change in Africa.* Madison: University of Wisconsin Press.

Bienen, Henry. 1974. *Kenya: The Politics of Participation and Control.* Princeton, NJ: Princeton University Press.

Bienen, Henry and Jeffrey Herbst. 1996. The Relationship between Political and Economic Reform in Africa. *Comparative Politics* 29(1): 23–42.

Bigsten, Arne. 1977. *Regional Inequality in Kenya.* Nairobi: University of Nairobi, Institute of Development Studies.

Binswanger, Hans P. and Klaus Deininger. 1997. Explaining Agricultural and Agrarian Policies in Developing Countries. *Journal of Economic Literature* 35 (December): 1958–2005.

Bleck, Jaimie and Nicolas van de Walle. 2012. Valence Issues in African Elections: Navigating Uncertainty and the Weight of the Past. *Comparative Political Studies* 4(11): 1394–1421.

Bleck, Jamie and Nicolas van de Walle. 2018. *Electoral Politics in Africa since 1990: Continuity and Change.* New York: Cambridge University Press.

Bloom, David E, Jeffrey D. Sachs, Paul Collier, and Christopher Udry. 1988. Geography, Demography, and Economic Growth in Africa. *Brookings Papers on Economic Activity* 1988(2): 207–295.

Bodea, Cristina and Christian Houle. 2021. Ethnic Inequality and Coups d'Etat. *Oxford Research Encyclopedia: Politics.* March 25, pp. 1–21. Doi: 10.1093/acre fore/9780190228637.013.1906

Boix, Carles. 2003. *Democracy and Redistribution.* Cambridge and New York: Cambridge University Press.

Bolton, Laura. 2019. Economic Impact of Farming Cooperatives in East Africa. K4D Helpdesk report 535. Brighton: Institute of Development Studies. February.

Bolton, Patrick and Gérard Rowland. 1997. The Breakup of Nations: A Political Economy Analysis. *Quarterly Journal of Economics* 112(4): 1058–1090.

Boone, Catherine. 2003. *Political Topographies of the African State: Territorial Authority and Institutional Choice.* Cambridge and New York: Cambridge University Press.

Boone, Catherine. 2007. Africa's New Territorial Politics: Regionalism and the Open Economy in Côte d'Ivoire. *African Studies Review* 50(1) (April): 59–81.

Boone, Catherine. 2012. Territorial Politics and the Reach of the State: Unevenness by Design. *Revista de Ciencia Política* 32(3): 623–642.

Boone, Catherine. 2014. *Property and Political Order in Africa: Land Rights and the Structure of Politics.* Cambridge and New York: Cambridge University Press.

Boone, Catherine. 2018. Shifting Visions of Property under Competing Political Regimes: Changing Uses of Côte d'Ivoire's 1998 Land Law. *Journal of Modern African Studies* 56(2): 189–216.

Boone, Catherine. 2019. Legal Empowerment of the Poor through Property Rights Reform: Tensions and Trade-offs of Land Registration and Titling in Sub-Saharan Africa. *Journal of Development Studies* 55(3) (March): 384–400.

Boone, Catherine. 2019. Internal Borders and the Building-Blocs of Territorialized Representation in African Countries. A paper presented at the 2019 Annual Meetings of the American Political Science Association, Washington, DC, August 30.

References

Boone, Catherine and Lydia Nyeme. 2015. Land Regimes and the Creation of Ethnicity: Evidence from Tanzania. *Comparative Politics* 48(1): 67–84.

Boone, Catherine and Michael Wahman. 2015. Rural Bias in African Electoral Systems: Legacies of Unequal Representation in African Democracies. *Electoral Studies* 40(December): 335–346.

Boone, Catherine and Kostadis Papaiouannou. 2017. Night Light Density and Wealth in Africa. LSE, unpub. ms., April.

Boone, Catherine and Rebecca Simson. 2019. Regional Inequalities in African Political Economy: Theory, Conceptualization and Measurement, and Political Effects. LSE Department of International Development Working Paper #194, March.

Boone, Catherine, Juliette Crespin-Boucaud, and Eun Kyung Kim. 2021. Sectoral Interests and Persistent Electoral Blocs in African Countries. A paper presented at the 2021 Annual Meetings of the American Political Science Association, Seattle and Virtual, September 2021.

Boone, Catherine, Fibian Lukalo, and Sandra Joireman. 2021. Promised Land: Settlement Schemes in Kenya: 1960 to 2016. *Political Geography* 89: 1–13.

Boone, Catherine, Michael Wahman, Stephan Kyburz, and Andrew Linke. 2022. Regional Cleavages in African Politics: Persistent Electoral Blocs and Territorial Oppositions. *Political Geography* 99 (October): 1–24.

Bornschier, Simon. 2009. Cleavage Politics in Old and New Democracies. *Living Reviews in Democracy* 6, on line. At www.livingreviews.org/lrd-2009-6.

Bourmaud, Daniel. 2000. *Histoire Politique du Kenya*. Paris: Karthala.

Bowden, Sue, Blessing Chiripanhura, and Paul Mosley. 2008. Measuring and Explaining Poverty in Six African Countries: A Long-period Approach. *Journal of International Development: The Journal of the Development Studies Association* 20(8): 1049–1079.

Brancati, Dawn. 2009. *Peace by Design: Managing Intrastate Conflict through Decentralization*. New York: Oxford University Press.

Branch, Daniel and Nicolas Cheeseman. 2006. The Politics of Control in Kenya: Understanding the Bureaucratic-Executive State, 1952–1978. *Review of African Political Economy* 33(107): 11–31.

Bratton, Michael. 1980. *The Local Politics of Rural Development: Peasant and Party-State in Zambia*. Hanover, NH and London: University Press of New England.

Bratton, Michael and Mwangi S. Kimenyi. 2008. Voting in Kenya: Putting Ethnicity in Perspective. *Journal of Eastern African Studies* 2(2): 272–289.

Bratton, Michael, Ravi Bhavani, and Tse-Hsin Chen. 2012. Voting Intentions in Africa: Ethnic, Economic or Partisan. *Commonwealth and Comparative Politics* 50(1): 27–52.

Breton, Roland. 1991. Un modèle indien du démultiplication de l'Etat. In Hervé Théry, ed., *L'Etat et les Stratégies du Territoire*. Paris: Editions du CNRS, pp. 79–86.

Brenner, Robert. 1976. Agrarian Class Structure and Economic Development in Pre-Industrial Europe. *Past & Present* 70(1): 30–75.

Brewin, David. 2015. Elections and Results. *Tanzanian Affairs* 113: 1–2.

Brittain, Victoria. 1986. The Liberation of Kampala. *New Left Review* I (156): 51–61.

Brown, Graham and Arnim Langer. 2009. Spatial and Ethnic Inequalities and Development: Country Experiences, Draft Report. Geneva: UNRISD (April).

Browne, Adrian J. 2015. *LAPSSET: The History and Politics of an Eastern African Megaproject*. Nairobi: Rift Valley Institute.

References 287

Borz, J. Lawrence, Jeffry Frieden, and Stephen Weymouth. 2021. Populism in Place: The Economic Geography of the Globalization Backlash. *International Organization* 75(2): 464–494.

Bruederle, Anna and Roland Holder. 2018. Nighttime Lights as a Proxy for Human Development at the Local Level. *PLOS One* 13(9): e0202231. Doi: 10.1371/journal .pone.0202231

Brunori, Paolo, Flaviana Palmisano, and Vito Peragine. 2016. Inequality of Opportunity in Sub-Saharan Africa. World Bank Group, Africa Region, Policy Research Working Paper 7782, August.

Brustein, William. 1996. Mapping Politics: How Mode of Production Counts in Electoral Geography. *Political Geography* 15(2): 153–158.

Bryceson, Deborah Fahy. 2006. Growing Out of Spatial Poverty: Growth, Sub-national Equity and Poverty Reduction Policies – A Five-country Comparison. A synthesis paper prepared for DFID Rural-Urban Change Team. Brighton: The Policy Practice. March (63 pages).

Bundervoet, Tom Laban Maiyo and Apurva Sanghi. 2015. Bright Lights, Big Cities: Measuring National and Subnational Economic Growth in Africa from Outer Space, with an Application to Kenya and Rwanda. World Bank Policy Research Working Paper 7461.

Burbidge, D. 2019. *An Experiment in Devolution: National Unity and the Deconstruction of the Kenyan State*. Nairobi: Strathmore University Press.

Burgoon, Brian, Sam van Noort, Matthjis Roodukun, and Geoffrey Underhill. 2019. Positional Deprivation and Support for Radical Right and Radical Left Parties. *Economic Policy* 34(97): 49–93.

Burrs, Lars, Rasmus H. Pedersen, Malin J. Nystrand, and José Jaime Macuane. 2019. Understanding the Three Key Relationships in Natural Resource Investment in Africa: An Analytical Framework. *The Extractive Industries and Society* 6: 1195–1204.

Cali, Massimiliano. 2014. Trade and Wage Inequality in Uganda. *Journal of Economic Geography* 14: 1141–1174.

Cammett, Malani and Lauren M. McLean. 2011. Introduction: The Political Consequences of Non-state Social Welfare in the Global South. *Studies in Comparative International Development* 46(1): 1–21.

Caramani, Daniele. 2004. *The Nationalization of Politics: The Formation of National Electorates and Party Systems in Western Europe*. Cambridge and New York: Cambridge University Press.

Cardoso, Fernando Henrique and Enzo Faletto. 1979. *Dependency and Development in Latin America*. Berkeley and Los Angeles: University of California Press.

Cell, John. 1982. *Segregation: The Highest Stage of White Supremacy*. Cambridge: Cambridge University Press.

Chandra, Kanchan. 2006. What Is Ethnic Identity and Does It Matter? *Annual Review of Political Science* 9: 397–424.

Chandra, Kanchan, ed. 2012. *Constructivist Theories of Ethnic Politics*. Oxford: Oxford University Press.

Chauveau, Jean-Pierre. 2000. Question foncière et construction nationale en Côte d'Ivoire. *Politique Africaine* 78: 94–125.

Chauveau, Jean-Pierre. 2011. A l'ombre des acquisitions foncières par des intérêts étrangers... les enjeux nationaux de l'appropriation foncière. *Transcontinentales* 10(11): 1–12.

Cheeseman, Nicholas. 2008. The Kenyan Elections of 2007: An Introduction. *Journal of Eastern African Studies* 2(2): 166–184.

Cheeseman, Nicholas and Robert Ford. 2007. Ethnicity as Political Cleavage. AfroBarometer Working Paper No. 83. Detroit: Michigan State University (November).

Cheeseman, Nicholas and Marja Hinfelaar. 2009. Parties, Platforms, and Political Mobilization: The Zambian Presidential Election of 2008. *African Affairs* 109: 51–76.

Cheeseman, Nicholas, Karuti Kanyinga, and Gabrielle Lynch. 2020. *Oxford Handbook of Kenyan Politics*. Oxford: Oxford University Press.

Chen, Xi and William Nordhaus. 2011. Using Luminosity Data as a Proxy for Economic Statistics. *Proceedings of the National Academy of Sciences* 108(21): 8589–8594.

Chen, Xi and William Nordhaus. 2015. A Sharper Image? Estimates of the Precision of Nighttime Lights as a Proxy for Economic Statistics. *Journal of Economic Geography* 15: 217–246.

Chernina, Eugenia, P. Dower, and A. Markevich. 2014. Property Rights, Land Liquidity, and Internal Migration. *Journal of Development Economics* 110: 191–215.

Chhibber, Pradeep and Ken Kollman. 2004. *The Formation of National Party Systems: Federalism and Party Competition*. Princeton, NJ: Princeton University Press.

Chhibber, Pradeep K. and Rahul Verma. 2018. *Ideology and Identity: The Changing Party System of India*. Oxford: Oxford University Press.

Chinigò, D. 2016. Rural Radicalism and the Historical Land Conflict in the Malawian Tea Economy. *Journal of Southern African Studies* 42(2): 283–297.

Chipeta, Mapopa Obryne Japhet. 1986. Labor in Colonial Malawi: A Study of the Growth and Development of the Malawian Working Class, c. 1891–1961. PhD dissertation, Dalhousie University, Department of History. Halifax, Nova Scotia.

Chome, Ngala. 2020. Land, Livelihoods and Belonging: Negotiating Change and Anticipating LAPSSET in Kenya's Lamu County. *Journal of Eastern African Studies* 14(2): 310–331.

Clem, Ralph S. 2006. Russia's Electoral Geography: A Review. *Eurasian Geography and Economics* 47(4): 381–406.

Cliffe, Lionel. 1973. The policy of Ujamaa Vijijini and the class struggle in Tanzania. In Lionel Cliffe and John S. Saul, eds., *Socialism in Tanzania, Volume 2: Policies*. Nairobi and Dar es Salaam: East African Publishing House, pp. 195–215.

Cogneau, Denis and Yannich Dupraz. 2015. Institutions historiques et développement économique en Afrique. *Histoire et Mesure* 30(1): 103–134.

Collier, David and Stephen Levitsky. 1997. Democracy with Adjectives: Conceptual Innovation in Comparative Politics. *World Politics* 49(3): 430–451.

Collier, Paul and Stephen A. O'Connell. 2008. Opportunities and Choices. In Benno J. Ndulu, Stephen O'Connell, Robert H. Bates, Paul Collier, and Chukwuma C. Soludo, eds., *The Political Economy of Economic Growth in Africa, 1960–2000*. Cambridge: Cambridge University Press, pp. 76–136.

Collord, Michaela. 2024. *Wealth, Power, and Authoritarian Institutions: Comparing Dominant Parties and Parliaments in Tanzania and Uganda*. Oxford: Oxford University Press.

Conroy-Krutz, Jeffrey. 2006. African Cities and Incumbent Hostility: Explaining Opposition Success in Urban Areas. Presented at the African Studies Association Annual Meeting, San Francisco, November.

References 289

Conroy-Krutz, Jeffrey. 2012. Information and Ethnic Politics in Africa. *British Journal of Political Science* 43: 345–373.

Cooke, Philip and Loet Leydesdorff. 2006. Regional Development in the Knowledge-Based Economy: The Construction of Advantage. *Journal of Technology Transfer* 31(1): 5–15.

Cordell, Dennis D., John W. Gregory, and Victor Piché. 1996. *Hoe and Wage: A Social History of a Circular Migration System in West Africa (Migration of Burkinabé)*. Boulder, CO: Westview.

Cramer, Katherine J. 2016. *Politics of Resentment: Rural Consciousness in Wisconsin and the Rise of Scott Walker*. Chicago, IL: University of Chicago Press.

Crescenzi, Riccardo, Fabrizio De Filippis, and Fabio Pierangeli. 2015. In Tandem for Cohesion? Synergies and Conflict between Regional and Agricultural Policies of the European Union. *Regional Studies* 49(4): 681–704.

Cresswall, Tim. 2012. *Geographic Thought: A Critical Introduction*, Ch. 4, "Thinking about Regions." Wiley-Blackwell, pp. 65–70.

Crook, Richard C. 1997. Winning Coalitions and Ethno-Regional Politics: The Failure of the Opposition in the 1990 and 1995 elections in Côte d'Ivoire. *African Affairs* 96(383): 215–242.

Crowder, Michael. 1968. *West Africa Under Colonial Rule*. London: Hutchinson.

Cruise O'Brien, Donal B. 1984. Les bienfaits de l'inégalité: Etat et l'économie rural au Sénégal. *Politique Africaine* 14: 34–38.

Cruise O'Brien, Donal B. 1998. The Shadow Politics of Wolofisation. *Journal of Modern African Studies* 36(1): 25–46.

Czuba, Karol. 2019. Karamojan Politics: Extension of State Power and Political Elite in Northeastern Uganda. *Third World Quarterly* 40(3): 558–577.

Czuba, Karol. 2023. Political Mobilization of Layered Ethnic Identities: Evidence from Northern Kenya. *Ethnic and Racial Studies* 46(10): 2138–2162.

D'Arcy, Michelle and Agnes Cornell. 2016. Devolution and Corruption in Kenya: Everyone's Turn to Eat? *African Affairs* 115(459): 246–273.

David, Philippe. 1980. *Les Navétanes: Histoire des Migrants Saisonniers de l'Arachide en Sénégambie, des Origines à Nos Jours*. Dakar and Abidjan: Les Nouvelles Editions Africaines.

Davies, D. Hywel, ed. 1971. *Zambia in Maps*. London: University of London Press.

Davies, Harold Richard John. 1973. *Tropical Africa: An Atlas for Rural Development*. Cardiff: University of Wales Press.

de Brauw, Alan, Valerie Mueller, and Hak Lim Lee. 2014. The Role of Rural-urban Migration in the Structural Transformation of Sub-Saharan Arica. *World Development* 63: 33–42.

De Swaan, Abram. 1973. *Coalition Theories and Government Formation*. Amsterdam: Elsevier Scientific Publishing Company.

De Vries, Lotje, Pierre Englebert, and Marieke Schomerus, eds. 2019. *Secessionism in African Politics*. London: Palgrave Macmillan.

Deaton, Angus. 2005. Measuring Poverty in a Growing World (or Measuring Growth in a Poor World). *Review of Economics and Statistics* 87(1): 1–19.

Deininger, Klaus, Sara Savastano, and Fang Xia. 2017. Land Access in Sub-Saharan Africa: A New Landscape? *Food Policy* 67: 78–92.

Dercon, Stefan, and Douglas Gollin. 2014. Agriculture in African Development: Theories and Strategies. *Annual Review of Resource Economics* 6: 471–492.

Diamond, Larry. 1988. Nigeria: Pluralism, Statism, and the Struggle for Democracy. In Larry Diamond, Juan Linz, and Seymour Martin Lipset, eds. *Democracy in Developing Countries*, Vol. II: Africa. Boulder, CO: Lynne Rienner Publisher, pp. 33–92.

Diao, Xinshen, Peter Hazell, Danielle Resnick and James Thurlow. 2007. The Role of Agriculture in Development: Implications for Africa. *IFPRI Research Report* 153: 20.

Diaz-Cayeros, Alberto. 2006 [2016]. *Federalism, Fiscal Authority, and Centralization in Latin America*. Cambridge and New York: Cambridge University Press.

Dickovick, J. Tyler. 2014. Federalism in Africa: Origins, Operation, and (In)Significance. *Regional & Federal Studies* 24(5): 553–570.

Di Matteo, Francesca, 2022. Imagining the Kenyan Commons: The Stakes of State Control Over Land in the Formulation of the Community Land Act (2011–2016). *The Journal of Development Studies* 58(8): 1550–1568.

Dionne, Kim Yi and Jeremy Horowitz. The Political Effects of Agricultural Subsidies in Africa: Evidence from Malawi. *World Development* 87: 215–226.

Doornbos, Martin. 1988. The Uganda Crisis and the National Question. In Holger Bernt Hansen and Michael Twaddle, eds., *Uganda Now: Between Decay and Development*. London: James Currey, pp. 254–266.

Doro, Elijah and Sandra Swart. 2022. Beyond Agency: The African Peasantry, the State, and Tobacco in Southern Rhodesia (Colonial Zimbabwe), 1900–80. *Journal of African History* 63(1): 55–74.

Dozon, Jean-Pierre. 1985. *La société Bété: Histories d'une ethnie de Côte- d'Ivoire*. Paris: ORSTOM et Karthala.

Dozon, Jean-Pierre. 2008. *L'Afrique à Dieu et à Diable*. Paris: Ellipses.

Dyzenhaus, Alex. 2022. The Price of Redistribution: Local Markets and Agriculture in South Africa's Land Reform Program. PhD dissertation, Cornell University, Department of Political Science.

Easterly, William and Ross Levine. 1997. Africa's Growth Tragedy: Policies and Ethnic Divisions. *Quarterly Journal of Economics* 112(4) (November): 1203–1250.

Eaton, Kent. 2001. Decentralization, Democratization, and Liberalization: The History of Revenue Sharing in Argentina, 1934–1999. *Journal of Latin American Studies* 33(1): 1–28.

Eaton, Kent. 2016. Challenges of Party-Building in the Bolivian East. In Levitsky, Steven, James Loxton, Brandon Van Dyck, and Jorge I. Dominguez, eds., *Challenges of Party-Building in Latin America*. New York: Cambridge University Press, pp. 383–411.

Eaton, Kent. 2017. *Territory and Ideology in Latin America: Policy Conflicts between National and Subnational Governments*. Oxford: Oxford University Press.

Eaton, Kent. 2019. Politics across Territory in Latin America. *Latin America Research Review* 54(2): 532–539.

Ebener, Steeve, Christopher Murray, Ajay Tandon, and Christopher C. Elvidge. 2005. From Wealth to Health: Modelling the Distribution of Income per capita at the Sub-national Level Using Night-time Light Imagery. *International Journal of Health Geographics* 4(1): 1–17.

Eck, Jan. 2014. Federalism and Decentralization in Sub-Saharan Africa: Five Patterns of Evolution. *Regional & Federal Studies* 24(5): 535–552.

Ejdemyr, Simon, Eric Kramon, and Amanda Lee Robinson. 2018. Segregation, Ethnic Favoritism, and the Strategic Targeting of Local Public Goods. *Comparative Political Studies* 51(9): 1111–1143.

References

Elischer, Sebastian. 2013. *Party Politics in Africa*. Cambridge: Cambridge University Press.

Elischer, Sebastian. 2019. "Partisan Politics Was Making People Angry": The Rise and Fall of Political Salafism in Kenya. *Journal of the Middle East and Africa* 10(2): 121–136.

Elvidge, Christopher, Kimberley Baugh, Sharolyn Anderson, Paul Sutton, and Tilottama Ghosh. 2012. The Night Light Development Index (nldi): A Spatially Explicit Measure of Human Development from Satellite Data. *Social Geography* 7(1): 23–35.

Engerman, Stanley L. and Kenneth L. Sokoloff. 2002. Factor Endowments, Inequality, and Paths of Development among New World Economies. Cambridge, MA: National Bureau of Economic Research, NBER Working Paper 9259.

Englebert, Pierre. 2003. Why Congo Persists: Sovereignty, Globalization and the Violent Reproduction of a Weak State. Queen Elizabeth House (QEH) Working Paper Series 95 (QEHWP95), February.

Englebert, Pierre. 2005. Compliance and Defiance to National Integration in Barotseland and Casamance. *Afrika Spectrum* 40(1): 29–59.

Enns, Charis and Brock Bersaglio. 2019. On the Coloniality of "New" Mega-Infrastructure Projects in East Africa. *Antipode* 52(1): 101–123.

Ensminger, Jean. 1992. *Making a Market: The Institutional Transformation of an African Society*. New York: Cambridge University Press.

Erdmann, Gero. 2004. Party Research: Western European Bias and the "African labyrinth." *Democratization* 11(3): 63–87.

Erdmann, Gero. 2007. The Cleavage Model, Ethnicity, and Voter Alignment in Africa: Conceptual and Methodological Problems Revisited. GIGA Research Programme: Legitimacy and Efficiency of Political Systems, Working Paper 63. Hamburg: German Institute of Global and Area Studies (December).

Erdmann, Gero and Matthias Basedau. 2008. Party Systems in Africa: Problems of Categorizing and Explaining Party Systems. *Journal of Contemporary African Studies* 26(3): 241–258.

Erickson, Lennart and Dietrich Vollrath. 2004. Dimensions of Land Inequality and Economic Development, IMF Working paper WP/04/158. Washington DC: International Monetary Fund (Land-holding Ginis, pp. 4, 15.)

Esping-Anderson, Gosta. 1990. *The Three Worlds of Welfare Capitalism*. Princeton, NJ: Princeton University Press.

Essletzbichler, Jergen, Mathias Moser, Judith Derndorfer, Petra Staufer-Steinnocher. 2021. Spatial Variation in Populist Right Voting in Austria, 2013–2017. *Political Geography* 90: 1–11.

Ewald, J. 2011. *Challenges for the Democratisation Process in Tanzania*. Gothenburg: University of Gothenburg.

Fabre, Elodie and Wilfried Swenden. 2013. Territorial Politics and the Statewide Party. *Regional Studies* 47(3): 342–355.

Ferree, Karen E. 2006. Explaining South Africa's Racial Census. *The Journal of Politics* 68(4): 803–815.

Ferree, Karen. 2010. *Framing the Race in South Africa: The Political Origins of Racial Census Elections in South Africa*. Cambridge and New York: Cambridge University Press.

Ferree, Karen. 2012. How Fluid Is Fluid? The Mutability of Ethnic Identities and Electoral Volatility in Africa. In Kanchan Chandra, ed., *Constructivist Theories of Ethnic Politics*. Oxford: Oxford University Press, pp. 312–340.

Ferree, Karen. 2018. Electoral Systems in Context: South Africa. In Erik S. Herron, Robert J. Pekkanen, and Matthew S. Shugart, eds., *The Oxford Handbook of Electoral Systems*. Oxford: Oxford University Press [online], pp. 1–32.

Ferree, Karen. 2022. Choice and Choice Set in African Elections. *The Journal of Politics* 84(4): 2261–2265.

Ferree, Karen and Jeremy Horowitz. 2010. Ties that Bind? The Rise and Decline of Ethno-regional Partisanship in Malawi, 1994–2009. *Democratization* 17(3): 534–563.

Fessha, Yonathan and Coel Kirby. 2008. A Critical Survey of Subnational Autonomy in African States. *Publius* 38(2): 248–271.

Feyissa, Dereje, ed. 2015. *Borders and Borderlands as Resources in the Horn of Africa*. Oxford: James Currey.

Fiorina, Morris P. and David W. Rohde, eds. 1989. *Home Style and Washington Work: Studies of Congressional Politics*. E. Lansing, MI: University of Michigan Press.

Firmin-Sellers, Kathryn. 1996. *The Transformation of Property Rights in the Gold Coast*. Cambridge and New York: Cambridge University Press.

Flint, Colin. 1998. Forming Electorates, Forging Spaces: The Nazi Party Vote and the Social Construction of Space. *American Behavioral Scientist* 4(9): 1282–1303.

Forrest, Joshua. 2004. *Subnationalism in Africa: Ethnicity, Alliances, and Politics*. Boulder, CO: Lynne Rienner Press.

Fotini, Christia. 2012. *Alliance Formation in Civil Wars*. Cambridge and New York: Cambridge University Press.

Fouéré, Marie-Aude. 2011. Chronique des élections de 2010 à Zanzibar. *Politique Africaine* 1(121): 127–145.

Fox, Louise and Tom Jayne. 2020. Unpacking the Misconceptions about Africa's Food Imports. *Africa in Focus*. New York: The Brookings Institution. 14 December.

Franck, Raphaël and Ilia Rainer. 2012. Does the Leader's Ethnicity Matter: Favoritism, Education, and Health in Sub-Saharan Africa. *American Political Science Review* 106(2): 294–325.

Fraser, Alastair. 2017. Post-populism in Zambia: Michael Sata's Rise, Demise, and Legacy. *International Political Science Review* 38(4): 456–472.

Fridy, Kevin S. 2007. The Elephant, Umbrella, and Quarrelling Cocks: Disaggregating Partisanship in Ghana's Forth Republic. *African Affairs* 106(423): 281–305.

Gambino, Elisa. 2020. La Participation Chinoise dans le Développment des Infrastructures de Transport au Kenya: Une Transformations des Géométres du Pouvoir? (traduit de l'anglais part Miriam Périer). *Critique Internationale* 89 (4): 95–114.

Garay, Candelaria, Brian Palmer-Rubin, and Mathias Poertner. 2020. Organization and Partisan Brokerage of Social Benefits: Social Policy Linkages in Mexico. *World Development* 136: 1–12.

Gardner, Leigh. 2012. *Taxing Colonial Africa: The Political Economy of British Imperialism*. Oxford: Oxford University Press.

Garmendia Madariaga, Amuitz. 2014. Units versus Units: Disentangling the Institutional Effects of Asymmetric Autonomy. PhD dissertation, Department of Political Science, State University of New York, Binghamton.

Gay, Laurianne. 2016. A la recherche de l'hégemonie: La fabrique très politique des politiques publiques fonicères en Ouganda sous le régime du National Resistance Movement (NRM). Entre changement et inertie. Thèse de doctorat en droit et Science politique, Université de Montpellier.

References

Gennaioli, Nicola and Ilia Rainer. 2007. The Modern Impact of Precolonial Centralization in Africa. *Journal of Economic Growth* 12(3): 185–234.

Gennaioli, Nicola, Rafael La Porta, Florencio De Silanes and Andrei Shleifer. 2014. Growth in Regions. *Journal of Economic Growth* 19: 259–309.

Gertzel, Cherry. 1970. *The Politics of Independent Kenya*. Nairobi, London, and Ibadan: East African Publishing House and Heinemann.

Geschiere, Peter. 1985. Imposing Capitalist Dominance through the State: The Multifarious Role of the Colonial State in Africa. In Wim van Binsbergen and Peter Geschiere, eds., *Old Modes of Production and Capitalist Encroachment: Anthropological Explorations in Africa*. London: Routledge and Kegan Paul, pp. 94–143.

Geschiere, Peter. 1993. Chiefs and Colonial Rule in Cameroon: Inventing Chieftaincy, French and British. *Africa: Journal of the International African Institute* 68(3): 309–319.

Gethin, Amory. 2020. Extreme Inequality and the Structure of Socio-economic Cleavages in South Africa, 1994–2019. World Inequality Lab, WID.world Working Paper 2020/13 (July).

Gibson, Edward, ed. 2004. *Federalism and Democracy in Latin America*. Baltimore, MD: Johns Hopkins University Press.

Gibson, Edward. 2006. Boundary Control: Subnational Authoritarianism in Democratic Countries. *World Politics* 58: 101–132.

Gibson, Edward. 2013. *Boundary Control: Subnational Authoritarianism in Federal Democracies*. Cambridge and New York: Cambridge University Press.

Gibson, Edward and Ernesto Calvo. 2000. Federalism in Low-Maintenance Constituencies: Territorial Dimensions of Economic Reform in Argentina. *Studies in Comparative International Development* 35(3): 32–55.

Giraudy, Agustina., Eduardo Moncada, and Richard Snyder, eds. 2019. *Inside Countries: Subnational Research in Comparative Politics*. Cambridge and New York: Cambridge University Press.

Githuku, Nicolas. 2013. Votes that Bind: Ethnic Politics and the Tyranny of Numbers, Columbia University Institute of African Studies blog, 17 March 2013. At www.ias .columbia.edu/blog/votes-bind-ethnic-politics-and-tyranny-numbers Accessed 4 June 2022.

Golaz, Valérie and Claire Médard. 2014. Election Results and Public Contestation of the Vote: An Overview of the Uganda 2011 General Elections. In Sandrine Perrot, Sabiti Makara, Jerome Lafargue, and Marie-Aude Fouéré, eds., *Elections in a Hybrid Regime: Revisiting the 2011 Ugandan Polls*. Kampala, Uganda: Fountain Publishers, pp. 54–109.

Golaz, Valérie and Claire Médard. 2016. Agricultural Frontier, Land Tenure Changes and Conflicts along the Gucha-Trans Mara Boundary in Kenya. *Journal of Eastern African Studies* 10(2): 229–246.

González, Lucas and Marcelo Nazareno. 2022. Resisting Equality: Subnational State Capture and the Unequal Territorial Distribution of Inequality. *Comparative Politics* 54(2): 303–325.

Gould, Jeremy. 2010. *Left Behind: Rural Zambia in the Third Republic*. Lusaka: The Lembani Trust.

Gourevitch, Peter. 1979. The Reemergence of "Peripheral Nationalisms": Some Comparative Speculations on the Spatial Distribution of Political Leadership and Economic Growth. *Comparative Studies in Society and History* 21(3): 303–322.

Gourevitch, Peter. 1980. *Paris and the Provinces: The Politics of Local Government Reform in France*. Berkeley: University of California Press.

Granovetter, Mark. 1985. Economic Action and Social Structure: The Problem of Embeddedness. *American Journal of Sociology* 91(3): 481–510.

Gray, Christopher. 2004. The Disappearing District? Territorial Transformation in Southern Gabon 1850–1950. In Allen Howard and Richard Shain, eds., *The Spatial Factor in African History: The Relationship of the Social, Material, and Perceptual*. Leiden and Boston: Brill, pp. 221–245.

Green, Elliott. 2006. Ethnicity and the Politics of Land Tenure Reform in Central Uganda. *Commonwealth & Comparative Politics* 44(3): 370–388.

Green, Elliott. 2008. District Creation and Decentralization in Uganda. Crisis States Research Group, Working Paper Series 2, Working Paper 24. London: London School of Economics.

Green, Elliott D. 2008. Understanding the Limits to Ethnic Change: Lessons from Uganda's "Lost Counties." *Perspectives on Politics* 6(3): 473–485.

Green, Elliott D. 2010. Patronage, District Creation, and Reform in Uganda. *Studies in Comparative International Development* 45(1): 83–103.

Green, Elliott. 2020. Ethnicity, National Identity and the State: Evidence from Sub-Saharan Africa. *British Journal of Political Science* 50(2): 757–779.

Green, Elliott D. 2022. *Industrialization and Assimilation: Understanding the Process of Ethnic Change in the Modern World*. Cambridge and New York: Cambridge University Press.

Green, Eric. 2011. Agrarian Populism in Colonial and Postcolonial Malawi. *African Studies Review* 54(3): 143–164.

Grossman, Guy and Janet I. Lewis. 2014. Administrative Unit Proliferation. *American Political Science Review* 108(1): 196–217.

Grumbach, Jacob M., Jacob S. Hacker, and Paul Pierson. 2021. The Political Economies of Red States. In Jacob S. Hacker, Alexander Hertel-Fernandez, Paul Pierson, and Kathleen Thelen, eds., *The American Political Economy: Politics, Markets, and Power*. Cambridge and New York: Cambridge University Press, pp. 209–244.

Habib, Adam and Sanusha Naidu. 2006. Race, Class, and Voting in South Africa's Electoral System: Ten Years of Democracy. *African Development* 31(3): 81–92.

Habyarimana, James, Macartan Humphreys, Daniel Posner, and Jeremy Weinstein. 2007. Why Does Ethnic Diversity Undermine Public Good Provision? *American Political Science Review* 101(4): 709–725.

Haggard, Stephan and Robert R. Kaufman. 2009. *Development, Democracy, and Welfare States: Latin America, East Asia, and Eastern Europe*. Princeton, NJ: Princeton University Press.

Hagopian, Frances. 1996. *Traditional Politics and Regime Change in Brazil*. Cambridge: Cambridge University Press.

Hakura, Dalia and Christine Deitrich. 2015. Regional Economic Outlook: Sub-Saharan Africa, Dealing with the Gathering Clouds, Ch. 3: Inequality and Economic Outcomes in sub-Saharan Africa. Washington, DC: International Monetary Fund.

Hallink, Courtney and Hangala Siachiwena. 2023. Political Party Ideology in Zambia: Comparing the Ruling PF and the Opposition UPND on Social Welfare. *Journal of Modern African Studies*, First View, pp. 1–20.

Hamaguchi, Nobuaki. 2014. Evidence from Spatial Correlation of Poverty and Income in Kenya. In Hiroyuki Hino et al., eds., *Ethnic Diversity and Economic Instability in Africa*. Cambridge: Cambridge University Press, pp. 202–223.

References

Handley, Antoinette. 2020. *Business and Social Crisis in Africa*. New York: Cambridge University Press.

Harbers, Imke. 2017. Spatial Effects and Party Nationalization: The Geography of Partisan Support in Mexico. *Electoral Studies* 27(June): 55–66.

Harbers, Imke and Matthew C. Ingram. 2019. Politics in Space: Methodological Considerations for Taking Space Seriously in Subnational Research. In Augustina Giraudy, Eduardo Moncada, and Richard Snyder, eds., *Inside Countries: Subnational Research in Comparative Politics*. Cambridge and New York: Cambridge University Press, pp. 57–91.

Harding, Robin. 2020. *Rural Democracy*. Oxford: Oxford University Press.

Harnishfeger, Johannes. 2018. Biafra and Secessionism in Nigeria: An Instrument of Political Bargaining. In Lotje De Vries, Pierre Englebert, and Marieke Schomerus, eds. 2019. *Secessionism in African Politics*. London: Palgrave Macmillan, pp. 329–361.

Harris, Andrew and Daniel Posner. 2019. (Under what conditions) Do Politicians Reward Their Supporters? Evidence from Kenya's CDF. *American Political Science Review* 113(1): 123–139.

Harvey, David. 2006. *Spaces of Global Capitalism*. London: Verso.

Hassan, Mai. 2016. A State of Change: District Creation in Kenya after the Beginning of Multi-Party Elections. *Political Research Quarterly* 69(3): 510–512.

Hassan, Mai. 2020. *Regime Threats and State Solutions: Bureaucratic Loyalty and Embeddedness in Kenya*. Cambridge and New York: Cambridge University Press.

Hassan, Mai and Ryan Sheely. 2016. Legislative-Executive Relations, Party Defections, and Lower-Level Administrative Unit Proliferation: Evidence from Kenya. *Comparative Political Studies* 50(12): 1595–1631.

Hechter, Michael. 2007. *Internal Colonialism: Celtic Fringe in British National Politics*. London: Routledge.

Heller, Patrick and Peter Evans. 2010. Taking Tilly South: Durable Inequalities, Democratic Contestation, and Citizenship in the Southern Metropolis. *Theory and Society* 39: 433–450.

Henderson, Ailsa, Charlie Jeffery, Daniel Wincott, and Richard Win Jones. 2013. Reflections on the "Devolution Paradox": A Comparative Examination of Multilevel Citizenship. *Regional Studies* 47(3): 303–322.

Henderson, Vernon, Adam Storeygard, and David Weil. 2012. Measuring Growth from Outer Space. *American Economic Review* 102(2): 994–1028.

Henderson, Vernon, Adam Storeygard, and David N. Weil. 2011. A Bright Idea for Measuring Economic Growth. *American Economic Review* 101(3): 194–199.

Herbst, Jeffrey. 2000. *States and Power in Africa*. Princeton, NJ: Princeton University Press.

Hern, Erin Accampo. 2020. Infrastructure and Perceptions of Democracy in Zambia: Democracy Off the Rails. *African Affairs* 119(477): 604–632.

Hesseling, Gerti and Han van Dijk. 2005. Administrative Decentralization and Political Conflict in Mali. In Patrick Chabal and Ulf Engel, eds., *Is Violence Inevitable in Africa?* Leiden: Brill, pp. 171–192.

Heyer, Judith. 1987. Sub-Saharan Rural Economies. In Christopher Fyfe et al., eds. *African Futures: 25th Anniversary Conference, Centre of African Studies*. Edinburgh: University of Edinburgh, pp. 547–595.

Hickey, Sam, Tom Lavers, Jeremy Seekings, and Miguel Niño-Zarazúa, eds. 2019. *The Politics of Social Protection in Eastern and Southern Africa*. Oxford: Oxford University Press.

Hien, Pierre Claver. 2003. La dénomination de l'espace dans la construction du Burkina Faso (1919–2001). In Richard Kuba, Carola Lentz, and Claude Nurukyor Somda, eds., *Historie du Peuplement et Relations Interethniques du Burkina Faso*. Paris: Editions Karthala, pp. 23–40.

Higashijima, Masaaki and Christian Houle. 2018. Ethnic Inequality and the Strength of Ethnic Identities in Sub-Saharan Africa. *Political Behavior* 40 (2): 909–932.

Hino, Hiroyuki, John Lonsdale, Gustav Ranis, and Frances Stewart, eds. 2014. *Ethnic Diversity and Economic Instability in Africa*. Cambridge: Cambridge University Press.

Hiribarren, Vincent. 2015. L'Héritage spatial de l'Indirect Rule au Nigeria. *Hérodote* 159(4): 13–26.

Hiribarren, Vincent. 2017. *A History of Borno. Trans-Saharan African Empire to Failing Nigerian State*. London: Hurst.

Hiscox, Michael J. 2002. *International Trade and Political Conflict: Commerce, Coalitions, and Mobility*. Princeton, NJ: Princeton University Press.

Hodder-Williams, Richard. 1974. Dr. Banda's Malawi. *Journal of Commonwealth and Comparative Politics* 12(1): 91–114.

Hodler, Roland and Paul A. Raschky. 2014. Regional Favoritism. *The Quarterly Journal of Economics* 129(2): 995–1033.

Holland, Aisha. 2017. *Forbearance as Redistribution: The Politics of Informal Welfare in Latin America*. Cambridge and New York: Cambridge University Press.

Holmes, Carolin E. 2020. *The Black and White Rainbow: Reconciliation, Opposition, and Nation-Building in Democratic South Africa*. Ann Arbor: University of Michigan Press.

Holmes, Carolyn. 2020. Fighting Back: Rural Issues, Federalism, and Opposition Parties in the 2019 South Africa Elections. A paper presented at the 2020 annual meetings of the American Political Science Association, Seattle and Virtual, Sept. 10–13.

Hooghe, Liesbet, Marks, Gary, and Schakel, Arjan. 2010. *The Rise of Regional Authority*. London: Routledge.

Horowitz, Donald. 1985. *Ethnic Groups in Conflict*. Berkeley: University of California Press.

Horowitz, Jeremy. 2019. Ethnicity and the Swing Vote in Africa's Emerging Democracies: Evidence from Kenya. *British Journal of Political Science* 49(3): 901–921.

Horowitz, Jeremy and James Long. 2016. Strategic Voting, Information, and Ethnicity in Emerging Democracies: Evidence from Kenya. *Electoral Studies* 44: 351–361.

Houle, Christian, Chuncho Park, and Paul D. Kenny. 2019. The Structure of Ethnic Inequality and Ethnic Voting. *Journal of Politics* 81(1): 187–200.

Howard, Allen and Richard Shain, eds. 2005. *The Spatial Factor in African History: The Relationship of the Social, Material, and Perceptual*. Leiden and Boston: Brill.

Hughes, Lotte. 2010. Les racines historiques des conflits sociopolitiques en pays maasai, Kenya: Justice, injustices et réciprocité. In Jean-Pierre Jacob and Pierre-Yves Le Meur, eds., *Politique de la terre et de l'appartenance*. Paris: Editions Karthala. 279–318.

Huillery, Elise. 2009. History Matters: The Long-Term Impact of Colonial Public Investment in French West Arica. *American Economic Journal: Applied Economics* 1(2): 176–215.

Hujo, Katja. 2013. Linking Social Policy, Migration, and Development in a Regional Context: The Case of sub-Saharan Africa. *Regions & Cohesion* 3(3): 30–55.

References

Iammarino, Simona, Andrés Rodriguez-Pose, and Michael Storper. 2019. Regional Inequality in Europe: Evidence, Theory, and Policy Implications. *Journal of Economic Geography* 19(2): 273–298.

Ichino, Nahomi and Noah Nathan. 2013. Crossing the Line: Local Ethnic Geography and Voting in Ghana. *American Political Science Review* 107(2): 344–361.

Iddawela, Yohan, Neil Lee, and Andrés Rodriquez-Pose. 2021. Quality of Sub-national Government and Regional Development in Africa. CEPR Discussion Paper 15651, Centre for Economic Policy Research, 33 Great Sutton Street, London EC1V oDX.

Ihonvbere, Julius O. 1996. *Economic Crisis, Civil Society, and Democratization: The Case of Zambia.* Trenton, NJ, and Asmara, Eritrea: Africa World Press.

Iliffe, John. 1979. *A Modern History of Tanganyika.* Cambridge: Cambridge University Press.

International Food Policy Research Institute (IFPRI); International Institute for Applied Systems Analysis (IIASA). 2016. Global Spatially-Disaggregated Crop Production Statistics Data for 2005 Version 3.2. Doi: 10.7910/DVN/DHXBJX, Harvard Dataverse, V9

Isham, Jonathan, Michael Woolcock, Lant Pritchett, and Gwen Busby. 2005. The Varieties of Resource Experience: Natural Resource Export Structures and the Political Economy of Economic Growth. *World Bank Economic Review* 19(2): 141–174.

Ishiyama, John. 2012. Explaining Ethnic Bloc Voting in Africa. *Democratization* 19(4): 761–788.

Issacman, Alan. 2003. *Cotton is the Mother of Poverty: Peasants, Work, and Rural Struggle in Colonial Mozambique, 1938–1961.* London: James Currey.

Iversen, Torben and David Soskice. 2019. *Democracy and Prosperity: Reinventing Capitalism through a Turbulent Century.* Princeton, NJ: Princeton University Press.

Jablonski, Ryan. 2014. How Aid Targets Votes: The Impact of Electoral Incentives on Aid Distribution. *World Politics* 66(2): 293–330.

Jacobs, Ricardo. 2018. An Urban Proletariat with Peasant Characteristics: Land Occupations and Livestock Raising in South Africa. *Journal of Peasant Studies* 45(5–6): 884–903.

Jaffee, Steven. 2003. Malawi's Tobacco Sector: Standing on One Strong Leg is Better Than None. World Bank Africa Region. *World Bank Working Paper Series* n. 55.

Jayne, T. S., Jordan Chamberlin, and Derek D. Headey. 2014. Land Pressures, the Evolution of Farming Systems, and Development Strategies in Africa: A Synthesis. *Food Policy* 48: 1–17.

Jayne, T. S., J. Govereh, A. Mwanaumo, and J. K. Nyoro. 2002. False Promise or False Premise? The Experience of Food and Input Market Reform in Eastern and Southern Africa. *World Development* 30(11): 1967–1985.

Jedwab, R., and A. Moradi. 2016. The Permanent Effects of Transportation Revolutions in Poor Countries: Evidence from Africa. *Review of Economics and Statistics* 98(2): 268–284.

Jepson, Nicholas. 2020. *In China's Wake: How the Commodity Boom Transformed Development Strategies in the Global South.* New York: Columbia University Press.

Jerven, Morten. 2013. *Poor Numbers: How We Are Misled by African Development Statistics and What to Do about It.* Ithaca, NY: Cornell University Press.

Jerven, Morten. 2021. *The Wealth and Poverty of African States: Economic Growth, Living Standards, and Taxation since the Late Nineteenth Century.* Cambridge and New York: Cambridge University Press.

Jirasevetakul, La-Bhus Fah, and Christoph Langer. 2016. The Distribution on Consumption Expenditure in sub-Saharan Africa: The Inequality among All Africans. World Bank Policy Research Working Paper 7557, February.

Johnston, Ron, David Manley, Kelvyn Jones, Ryne Rohla, et al. 2020. The Geographical Polarization of the American Electorate: A Country of Increasing Electoral Landslides? *GeoJournal* 85: 187–204.

Johnson, Willard R. 1970. The Union des Populations du Cameroun in Rebellion: The Integrative Backlash of Insurgency. In Robert I. Rotberg and Ali A. Mazuri, eds., *Protest and Power in Black Africa*. New York: Oxford University Press, pp. 671–694.

Jorgensen, Jan Jelmert. 1981. *Uganda: A Modern History*. London: Croom Helm.

Kadima, Denis. 2014. Special Issue: Understanding the Causes and Consequences of Political Party Alliances and Coalitions in Africa. *Journal of African Elections* 13(1): 242.

Kagwanja, Peter and Roger Southall. 2009. Kenya – A democracy in Retreat? *Journal of Contemporary African Studies* 27(3): 259–277.

Kakwani, Nanak and Fabio Veras Soares. 2005. Conditional Cash Transfers in African Countries, International Poverty Research Center (IPC) and UNDP, Working paper #9, Brazilia, Brazil, IPC and UNDP (November).

Kalipeni, Ezekiel. 1997. Regional Polarisation in Voting Pattern: Malawi 1994 Election. *African Journal of Political Science* 2(1): 152–167.

Kanbur, Ravi and Anthony J. Venables. 2005. Spatial Inequality and Development: Overview of the UNU-WIDER Project. Working Papers 127127, Cornell University, Department of Applied Economics and Management.

Kanduza, Ackson. 1992. *Socio-Economic Change in Eastern Zambia*. Lusaka: Historical Association of Zambia.

Kanyeihamba, George. 1988. Power that Rode Naked through Uganda under the Muzzle of a Gun. In Holger Bernt Hansen and Michael Twaddle, eds., *Uganda Now: Between Decay and Development*. London: James Currey, pp. 70–82.

Kanyinga, Karuti. 1994. Ethnicity, Patronage, and Class in a Local Arena: "High" and "Low" Politics in Kiambu, Kenya, 1982–1992. In Karuti Kanyinga, Andrew S. Z. Kiondo, and Per Tidemand, eds., *The New Local Politics in East Africa: Studies on Uganda, Tanzania, and Kenya*. Research Report no. 95. Uppsala: Nordiska Afrikainstitutet, pp. 66–86.

Kanyinga, Karuti. 2000. *Redistribution from above: The Politics of Land Rights and Squatting in Coastal Kenya*. Uppsala: Nordic Africa Institute.

Kanyinga, Karuti. 2016. Devolution and the New Politics of Development in Kenya. *African Studies Review* 51(3): 155–167.

Kanyinga, Karuti and Colin Poulton. 2014. The Politics of Revitalising Agriculture in Kenya. *Development Policy Review* 32(S2): S151–S172.

Kasara, Kimuli. 2007. Tax Me If You Can: Ethnic Geography, Demography, and the Taxation of Agriculture in Africa. *American Political Science Review* 101(1): 159–172.

Kasara, Kimuli. 2017. Does Local Ethnic Segregation Lead to Violence?: Evidence from Kenya. *Quarterly Journal of Political Science* 11(4): 441–470.

Kasfir, Nelson. 1988. Land and Peasants in Western Uganda: Bushenyi and Mbarara Districts. In Holger Bernt Hansen and Michael Twaddle, eds., *Uganda Now: Between Decay and Development*. London: James Currey, pp. 158–174.

References

Kasfir, Nelson. 2005. Guerrillas and Civilian Participation: The National Resistance Army in Uganda, 1981–86. *The Journal of Modern African Studies* 43(2): 271–296.

Kaspin, Deborah. 1995. The Politics of Ethnicity in Malawi's Democratic Transition. *Journal of Modern African Studies* 33(4): 592–620.

Keating, Michael. 2009. Social Citizenship, Solidarity, and Welfare in Regionalized and Plurinational States. *Citizenship Studies* 13(5): 501–513.

Keating, Michael. 2003 [1997]. The Invention of Regions: Political Restructuring and Territorial Government in Western Europe. *Environment and Planning C: Government and Policy* 15: 383–398. Reprinted in Neil Brenner, Bob Jessop, Martin Jones, and Gordon MacLeod, eds. *State/Space: A Reader*. Chichester: John Wiley & Sons, pp. 256–277.

Keefer, Philip and Razvan Vlaicu. 2008. Democracy, Credibility, and Clientelism. *The Journal of Law, Economics, and Organization* 24(406): 371–406.

Kenya Institute for Education in Democracy (IED). 1998. Understanding Elections in Kenya: A Constitutional Profile Approach, Nairobi.

Kenya National Bureau of Statistics (KNBS). 2014. *Socio-Economic Atlas of Kenya*, Section 2:11. Nairobi: Herufi House.

Kenya National Bureau of Statistics (KNBS). 2019. *KNBS Economic Survey 2019*. Nairobi: Herufi House.

Kerosi, Geoffrey. 2018. PesaCheck, 23 Nov. 2018. Does the Mt. Kenya Region contribute 60% of Kenya's GDP?, at https//pesacheck/org/does-the-mt-Kenya-region Accessed 15 March 2021

Key, V. O. 1964. *Politics, Parties, and Pressure Groups*. New York: Knopf.

Khadiagala, Gilbert. 2010. Boundaries in East Africa. *Journal of Eastern Africa Studies* 4(2): 266–278.

Kim, Eun Kyung. 2017. Party Strategy in Multidimensional Competition in Africa: The example of Zambia. *Comparative Politics* 50(1): 21–43.

Kim, Eun Kyung. 2018. Sector-based Vote Choice: A New Approach to Explaining Core and Swing Voters in Africa. *International Area Studies Review* 21(1): 28–50.

Kim, Eun Kyung. 2019. Issue Ownership and Strategic Policy Choice in Multiparty Africa. *Politics and Policy* 47(5): 956–983.

Kim, Eun Kyung. 2020. Economic Signals of Ethnic Voting in Africa: Analysis of Correlation between Agricultural Subsectors and Ethnicity in Kenya. *Journal of Modern African Studies* 58(3): 361–395.

Kim, Sukkoo. 2008. Spatial Inequality and Economic Development: Theories, Facts, and Policies. Commission on Growth and Development, Working Paper No. 16. Washington, DC: World Bank.

Kimenyi, Mwangi S. and Njuguna S. Ngung'u. 2005. Sporadic Ethnic Violence: Why Has Kenya Not Experienced a Full-blown Civil War? In Paul Collier and Nicolas Sambanis, eds., *Understanding Civil War: Evidence and Analysis, Vol. 1: Africa*. Washington, DC: World Bank, pp. 123–156.

King, Elizabeth and Cyrus Samii. 2020. *Diversity, Violence, and Recognition: How Recognizing Ethnic Identity Promotes Peace*. Oxford: Oxford University Press.

Kishindo, Paul and Peter Mvula. 2017. Malawi's Land Problem and Potential for Rural Conflict. *Journal of Contemporary African Studies* 35(3): 370–382.

Kitschelt, Herbert. 1992. The Formation of Party Systems in East Central Europe. *Politics and Society* 20(1): 7–50.

Kitschelt, Herbert and Steven Wilkinson, eds. 2007. *Patrons, Clients, and Policies*. Cambridge: Cambridge University Press.

Kjaer, Anne Mette. 2015. Political Settlements and Productive Sector Policies: Understanding Sector Differences in Uganda. *World Development* 68: 230–241.

Knight, Jack. 1992. *Institutions and Social Conflict*. Cambridge: Cambridge University Press.

Kofele-Kale, Ndiva. 1986. Ethnicity, Regionalism, and Political Power: A post-mortem of Adhijo's Cameroon. In M. Schatsburg and Wm. Zartman eds., *The Political Economy of Cameroon*. New York: Praeger, pp. 53–82.

Kohler, Jennifer and Leigh Gardner. 2018. Preliminary Boundary Persistence Results. Unpub. ms., LSE, 23 August (updated November 2021).

Kopper, Sarah A. and Thomas S. Jayne. 2019. Market Access, Agro-ecological Conditions, and Boserupian Agricultural Intensification Patterns in Kenya: Implications for Agricultural Programs and Research. *World Development* 124: 1–11.

Koter, Dominika. 2013. Urban and Rural Voting Patterns in Senegal: The Spatial Aspects of Incumbency, 1978–2012. *Journal of Modern African Studies* 51(4): 653–679.

Kpressa, Michael, Daniel Béland, and André Lecours. 2011. Nationalism, Development, and Social Policy: The Politics of Nation-building in Sub-Saharan Africa. *Ethnic and Racial Studies* 34(12): 2115–2133.

Kraus, Jon, ed. 2007. *Trade Unions and the Coming of Democracy in Africa*. New York: Palgrave Macmillan.

Kraxberger, Brennan. 2005. Strangers, Indigenes and Settlers: Contested Geographies of Citizenship in Nigeria. *Space and Polity* 9(1): 9–27.

Krugman, Paul. 1991. Increasing Returns and Economic Geography. *Journal of Political Economy* 99: 483–499.

Krugman, Paul. 1998. What's New About the New Economic Geography? *Oxford Review of Economic Policy* 14(2): 7–17.

Kuba, Richard and Carola Lentz. 2003. Introduction. In Richard Kuba, Carola Lentz, and Claude Nurukyor Somda, eds., *Histoire du Peuplement et Relations Interethnique au Burkina Faso*. Paris: Editions Karthala, pp. 5–20.

Kuenzi, Michelle and Gina Lambright. 2001. Party System Institutionalization in 30 African Countries. *Party Politics* 7(4): 437–468.

Kuété, Martin. 2008. Café, café culture et vie politique dans les hautes terres de l'Ouest-Cameroun. *Cahiers d'Outre Mer* 243(juillet): 285–302.

Kurtz, Markus. 2013. *Latin American State Building in Comparative Perspective*. Cambridge and New York: Cambridge University Press.

Kuznets, S. 1955. Economic Growth and Income Inequality. *American Economic Review* 45(1): 1–28.

Kuznets, Simon. 1963. Quantitative Aspects of the Economic Growth of Nations, VIII: The Distribution of Income by Size. *Economic Development and Cultural Change* 11: 1–92.

Kyriacou, Andres P. and Oriol Roca-Sogalés. 2014. Regional Disparities and Government Quality: Redistributive Conflict Crowds Out Good Government. *Spatial Economic Analysis* 9(2): 183–201.

Ladouceur, Paul André. 1979. *Chiefs and Politicians: The Politics of Regionalism in Northern Ghana*. London: Longman.

References

Ladouceur, Paul André. 1984. Review of Benjamin Amonoo, Ghana, 1957–1966: Politics of Institutional Dualism (1981). *International Journal of African Historical Studies* 17(1): 150–152.

Lahoti, Rahul, Arjun Jayadev, and Sanjay Reddy. 2016. The Global Consumption and Income Project (GCIP): An Overview. *Journal of Globalization and Development* 7(1).

Laji, Adoyo. 2019. Regional Development Inequalities in Kenya: Can Devolution Succeed Where Other Strategies Have Failed? *International Journal of Regional Development* 6(1): 39–56.

Lane, Charles. 1996. *Pastures Lost: Barabaig Economy, Resource Tenure, and the Alienation of their Land in Tanzania*. Nairobi: Initiatives Publishers.

Larmer, Miles. 2006. "The hour has come at the Pit": The Mineworkers' Union of Zambia and the Movement for Multi-Party Democracy, 1982–1991. *Journal of Southern African Studies* 32(2): 293–312.

Larmer, Miles and Alistair Fraser. 2007. Of Cabbages and King Cobra: Populist Politics and Zambia's 2006 Election. *African Affairs* 106: 611–637.

Laver, Michael J. and Kenneth A. Shepsle. 1996. *Making and Breaking Governments*. Cambridge and New York: Cambridge University Press.

Lavers, Tom. 2013. Food Security and Social Protection in Highland Ethiopia: Linking the Productive Safety Net to the Land question. *Journal of Modern African Studies* 51(3): 459–485.

Lavers, Tom. 2019. Understanding Elite Commitment to Social Protection: Rwanda's Vision 2020 Umurenge Programme. In Hickey, Sam, Tom Lavers, Jeremy Seekings, and Miguel Niño-Zarazúa, eds., *The Politics of Social Protection in Eastern and Southern Africa*. Oxford: Oxford University Press, pp. 73–99.

Lavers, Tom. 2023. *Ethiopia's Developmental State: Political Order and Distributive Crisis*. Cambridge and New York: Cambridge University Press.

Lavigne Delville, Philippe. 2011. Vers une socio-anthropologie des interventions de développement comme action publique. Anthropologie sociale et ethnologie. Université Lumière Lyon II. HAL Id: tel-00683177.

Lavigne Delville, Philippe. 2017. Pour une socio-anthropologie de l'action publique dans les pays sous régime d'aide. *Anthropologie & Développement (APAD)* 45: 33–64.

Lavigne Delville, Philippe and Anne-Claire Moalic. 2019. Territorialities, Spatial Inequalities and the Formalization of Land Rights in Central Benin. *Africa: The Journal of the International African Institute* 89(2): 329–352.

Lawal, Olanrewaju. 2019. Geographical Pattern and Structure of the 2011 and 2015 Nigeria Presidential Election. *African Geographical Review* 38(1): 1–18.

Lawler, Nancy. 1990. Reform and Repression under the Free French: Economic and Political Transformation in the Côte d'Ivoire, 1942–45. *Africa: Journal of the International African Institute* 60 (1): 88–110.

Le Roy, Etienne. 2011. *La terre de l'autre: Une anthropologie des régimes d'appropriation foncière*. Paris: LGDJ Lextenso Editions, Série anthropologique.

LeBas, Adrienne. 2011. *From Protest to Parties: Party-Building and Democratization in Africa*. Oxford: Oxford University Press.

Lee, Dong-wook and Melissa Rogers. Measuring Regional Inequality for Political Research. Claremont Institute for Economic Policy Studies. unpublished manuscript.

Lemarchand, René. 1962. The Limits of Self-determination: The Case of the Katanga Secession. *American Political Science Review* 56(2): 404–416.

Lemarchand, René. 2000. Exclusion, Marginalization, and Political Mobilization: The Road to Hell in the Great Lakes. University of Copenhagen, Centre of African Studies, Occasional Paper. March. Accessed 2 January 2022 at https://teol.ku.dk/cas/publications/publications/occ._papers/lemarchand2001 2.pdf

Lentz, Carola. 2013. *Land, Mobility, and Belonging in West Africa*. Bloomington: Indiana University Press.

Leonardi, Cherry. 2013. South Sudanese Arabic and the Negotiation of the Local State, c.1840–2011. *Journal of African History* 54(3): 351–372.

Leonardi, Cherry. 2020. Patchwork States: The Localisation of State Territoriality on the South Sudan-Uganda Border, 1914–2014. *Past & Present* 248(1): 209–258.

Lessmann, Christian. 2013. Regional Inequality and Internal Conflict. CESIFO Working Paper N. 4112. Category 6: Fiscal Policy, Macroeconomies, and Growth. Munich: LMU: Center for Economic Studies and Ifo Institute. February.

Lessmann, Christian and André Seidel. 2015. Regional Inequality, Convergence, and Its Determinants: A View from Outer Space. CESifo Working Paper No. 5322.

Lessmann, Christian, and André Seidel. 2017. Regional Inequality, Convergence, and Its Determinants: A View from Outer Space. *European Economic Review* 92: 110–132.

LeVan, Carl. 2015. *Dictators and Democracy in African Development: The Political Economy of Good Governance in Nigeria*. New York: Cambridge University Press.

LeVan, Carl. 2019. *Contemporary Nigerian Politics*. New York: Cambridge University Press.

Levitsky, Steven, James Loxton, Brandon Van Dyck, and Jorge I. Dominquez, eds. 2016. *Challenges of Party-Building in Latin America*. Cambridge and New York: Cambridge University Press.

Lewanika, McDonald. 2019. Campaigning, Coercion, and Clientelism: ZANU-PF's Strategies in Zimbabwe's Presidential Elections, 2008–2013. A PhD thesis submitted to the London School of Economics and Political Science, Department of Government, December.

Lieberman, Evan. 2003. *Race and Regionalism in the Politics of Taxation in Brazil and South Africa*. Cambridge and New York: Cambridge University Press.

Lieberman, Evan and Gwyneth H. McClendon. 2012. The Ethnicity-Policy Preference Link in Sub-Saharan Africa. *Comparative Political Studies* 46(5): 574–602.

Lindemann, Stefan. 2011. The Ethnic Politics of Coup Avoidance: Evidence from Zambia and Uganda. *Africa Spectrum* 46(2): 3–11.

Linke, Andrew. 2013. The Aftermath of an Election Crisis: Kenyan Attitudes and the Influence of Individual-level and Locality Violence. *Political Geography* 37: 5–17.

Linke, Andrew, John O'Laughlin, et al. 2015. Rainfall Variability and Violence in Rural Kenya: Investigating Drought and the Role of Local Institutions with Survey Data. *Global Environmental Change* 34: 35–47.

Lipset, Seymour Martin and Stein Rokkan. 1967. Cleavages, Structures and Voter Alignments: An Introduction. In Seymour Martin Lipset and Stein Rokkan, eds., *Party Systems and Voter Alignments*. New York: Free Press, pp. 1–64.

Locke, Richard M. 1995. *Remaking the Italian Economy*. Ithaca, NY: Cornell University Press.

Lockwood, Sarah J., Matthias Krönke, and Robert Mattes. 2022. Party Structures and Organization Building in Africa. *Party Politics* 82(2): 203–207.

References

303

Lonsdale, John. 1969. Local Origins of Nationalist Politics in Western Kenya. In *Autonomy & Dependence in Parochial Politics* (London: Institute of Commonwealth Studies, Collected Seminar Papers No.7), pp. 76–91.

Lonsdale, John. 1971. Rural Resistance and Mass Political Mobilisation amongst the Luo. In Ernest Labrousse et al., eds., *Commission Internationale d'Histoire des Movements Sociaux et des structures sociales, Mouvements Nationaux d'Indépendance et classes populaires aux XIXe et XXe siecles en Occident et en Orient, Tome II*. Paris: Librarie Armand Colin, pp. 459–478.

Lonsdale, John. 1981. States & Social Processes in Africa: An Historiographical Survey. *African Studies Review* 24: 139–225.

Lonsdale, John. 1986. Explanations of the Mau Mau Revolt, Kenya, 1952–1956. In Tom Lodge, ed., *Resistance and Ideology in Settler Societies*. Johannesburg: Raven Press, pp. 168–178.

Lonsdale, John. 2012. Ethnic Patriotism and Markets in African History. In H. Hino et al., eds., *Ethnic Diversity and Economic Instability in Africa*. Cambridge and New York: Cambridge University Press, pp. 19–55.

Lonsdale, John. 2015. Have Tropical Africa's Nationalisms Continued Imperialism's World Revolution by Other Means? *Nations and Nationalism* 21(4): 609–629.

Looney, Kristin. 2018. *Mobilizing for Development: The Modernization of Rural East Asia*. Ithaca, NY: Cornell University Press.

Low, D. Anthony. 1988. The Dislocated Polity. In Holger Bernt Hansen and Michael Twaddle, eds., *Uganda Now: Between Decay and Development*. London: James Currey, pp. 36–53.

Luebbert, Gregory M. 1991. *Liberalism, Fascism, or Social Democracy: Social Classes and the Origins of Regimes in Interwar Europe*. New York: Oxford University Press.

Lund, Christian. 2008. *Local Politics and the Dynamics of Property in Africa*. New York and Cambridge: Cambridge University Press.

Lynch, Gabrielle. 2011. *I Say to You: Ethnic Politics and the Kalenjin in Kenya*. Chicago, IL: University of Chicago Press.

Maas, William, ed. 2013. *Multilevel Citizenship*. Philadelphia: University of Pennsylvania Press.

MacArthur, Julie. 2016. *Cartography and the Political Imagination: Mapping Community in Colonial Kenya*. Athens: Ohio University Press.

Macharia, Peter M., Emanuele Giorgi, Pamela N. Thurania, Noel K. Joseph, Benn Sartorius, Robert W. Snow, and Emelda A. Okiro. 2019. Sub National Variation and Inequalities in Under-five Mortality in Kenya since 1965. *BMC Public Health* 19(146): 1–12.

Macola, Giacoma. 2010. *Liberal Nationalism in Central Africa: A Biography of Harry Mwaanga Nkumbula*. London: Palgrave Macmillan.

Mafeje, Archie. 1971. The Ideology of "Tribalism." *Journal of Modern African Studies* 9(2): 253–261.

Maguire, Andrew. 1970. The Emergence of the Tanganika African National Union in the Lake Province. In Robert I. Rotberg and Ali A. Mazrui, eds., *Protest and Power in Black Africa*. New York and Oxford: Oxford University Press, pp. 639–671.

Mambo, Robert M. 1987. Nascent Political Activities among the Mijikenda of Kenya's Coast During the Colonial Era. *Transafrican Journal of History* 16: 92–120.

Mamdani, Mahmood. 1976. *Politics and Class Formation in Uganda*. New York: Monthly Review Press.

Mamdani, Mahmood. 1996. *Citizen and Subject: Contemporary Africa and the Legacy of Late Colonialism.* Princeton, NJ: Princeton University Press.

Mamdani, Mahmood. 2001. *When Victims Become Killers: Colonialism, Nativism, and the Genocide in Rwanda.* Princeton, NJ: Princeton University Press.

Manji, Ambreena. 2006. *The Politics of Land Reform in Africa: From Communal Tenure to Free Markets.* New York and London: Zed Books.

Marchand, Yannick, Jean Dubé, and Sébastien Breau. 2020. Exploring the Causes and Consequences of Regional Income Inequality in Canada. *Economic Geography* 96(2): 83–107. Doi: 10.1080/00130095.2020.1715793

Mares, Isabela. 2015. *From Open Secrets to Secret Voting: Democratic Electoral Reforms and Voter Autonomy.* Cambridge and New York: Cambridge University Press.

Markakis, John. 2011. *Ethiopia: The Last Two Frontiers.* Oxford: James Currey.

Martin, Terry. 2001. *Affirmative Action Empire: Nations and Nationalism in the Soviet Union, 1923–1939.* Ithaca, NY: Cornell University Press.

Massetti, Emanuele and Arjan H. Schakel. 2015. From Class to Region: How Regionalist Parties Link (and Subsume) Left-right into Centre-periphery Politics. *Party Politics* 21(6): 866–886.

Matthijs, Matthias and Craig Parsons. 2019. Muscles in Brussels: The EU's Economic Authority in Comparative and Theoretical Perspective. A talk presented at the LSE CP/CPE seminar series, 28 Feb.

Maurel, Marie-Claude. 1984. Pour une géopolitique du territorire, le maillage politico-administratif. *Hérodote* 33–34(2e et 3e trimestres): 131–144.

Mavungu, Eddy Mazembo. 2016. Frontiers of Power and Prosperity. *African Studies Review* 59(2): 183–208.

Mazrui, Ali. 1988. Is Africa Decaying? The View from Uganda. In Holger Bernt Hansen and Michael Twaddle, eds., *Uganda Now: Between Decay and Development.* London: James Currey, pp. 336–358.

Mazzuca, Sebastian. 2021. *Latecomer State Formation: Political Geography and Capacity Failure in Latin America.* New Haven: Yale University Press.

McCann, Philip. 2020. Perceptions of Regional Inequality and the Geography of Dissent: Insights from the UK. *Regional Studies* 54(2): 256–267.

McCracken, John. 1968. African Politics in Twentieth Century Malawi. In T. O. Ranger, ed., *Aspects of Central African History.* London, p. 207.

McDoom, Omar S. 2020. *The Path to Genocide in Rwanda: Security, Opportunity, and Authority in an Ethnocratic State.* Cambridge and New York: Cambridge University Press.

Meadwell, Hudson. 1991. A Rational Choice Approach to Political Regionalism. *Comparative Politics* 23(4): 401–421.

Médard, Claire. 1999. Territoires de l'ethnicité: Encadrement, revendications, et conflits territoriaux au Kenya. Doctoral thesis, UFR de Géographie, University de Paris I Panthéon-Sorbonne (Juin).

Médard, Claire and Stephanie Duvail. 2020. Accaparement foncier et officialisation de la propriété privée au Kenya. *Hérodote: Revue de géographie et de géopolitique* 179: 165–180.

Mellander, Charlotta, José Lobo, Kevin Stolarick, and Zara Matheson. 2015. Night-time Light Data: A Good Proxy Measure for Economic Activity? *PloS One* 10(10): e0139779.

References

Mertha, Andrew C. 2005. China's "Soft" Centralization: Shifting *Tiao/Kuai* Authority Relations. *China Quarterly* 184(December): 791–810.

Michalopoulous, Stelios. 2012. The Origins of Ethnic Diversity. *American Economic Review* 102(4): 1508–1539 (see on land inequality).

Michalopoulos, Stelios and Elias Papaioannou. 2013. Precolonial Ethnic Institutions and Contemporary African Development. *Econometrica* 81(1): 113–152.

Michalopoulos, Stelios and Elias Papaioannou. 2017. Spatial Patterns of Development: A Meso Approach. NBER Working paper 24088, November.

Milanovic, Branko. 2003. The Two Faces of Globalization: Against Globalization as We Know It. *World Development* 31(4): 667–683.

Milanovic, Branko. 2014. *Description of All the Ginis Dataset*. Washington, DC: World Bank. https://stonecenter.gc.cuny.edu/research/all-the-ginis-alg-data set-version-february-2019/

Mitchell, Timothy. 1999. Society, Economy, and the State Effect. In George Steinmetz, ed., *State/Culture: State-Formation after the Cultural Turn*. Ithaca and London: Cornell University Press, pp. 76–97.

Molteno, Robert. 1974. Cleavage and Conflict in Zambian Politics: A Study in Sectionalism. In William Tordoff, ed., *Politics in Zambia*. Berkeley and Los Angeles: University of California Press, pp. 87–93.

Morse, Yonathan. 2014. Party Matters: The Institutional Origins of Competitive Hegemony in Tanzania. *Democratization* 21(4): 655–677.

Moss, Sigrun Marie and Kjetil Tronvoll. 2015. We Are All Zanzibari! Identity Formation and Political Reconciliation in Zanzibar. *Journal of Eastern African Studies* 9(1): 91–109.

Mozaffar, Shaheen, James Scarritt, and Glen Galaich. 2003. Electoral Institutions, Ethnopolitical Cleavages, and Party Systems in Africa's Emerging Democracies. *American Political Science Review* 97(3): 379–391.

Mkandawire, T. 1999. Agriculture, Employment, and Poverty in Malawi. ILO/SAMAT Policy Paper No. 9. Harare: International Labor Organization and SRN Africa Multidisciplinary Advisory Team (ILO/SAMAT).

Mkandawire, T. 2016. Colonial Legacies and Social Welfare Regimes in Africa: An Empirical Exercise. Working paper 2016-4. Geneva: United Nations Research Institute for Social Development (UNRISD), May.

Mkutu, Kennedy, Marie Müller-Koné, and Evelyne Atieno Owino. 2021. Future Visions, Present Conflicts: The Ethnicized Politics of Anticipation Surrounding an Infrastructure Corridor in Northern Kenya. *Journal of Eastern African Studies* 15(4): 707–727.

Mmuya, Maximillian. 1995. *Government and Political Parties in Tanzania: After the 1995 General Elections, Facts and Figures*. Dar es Salaam: Friedrich Ebert Stiftung.

Momba, Jotham C. 1985. Peasant Differentiation and Rural Party Politics in Colonial Zambia. *Journal of Southern African Studies* 11(2): 281–294.

Moore, Mick. 1997. Leading the Left to the Right: Populist Coalitions and Economic Reform. *World Development* 25(7): 1009–1028.

Morse, Yonatan. 2014. Party Matters: The Institutional Origins of Competitive Hegemony in Tanzania. *Party Politics* 21(4): 655–677.

Morse, Yonatan L. 2018. Electoral Authoritarianism and Weak States in Africa: The Role of Parties versus Presidents in Tanzania and Cameroon. *International Political Science Review* 38(1): 114–129.

Moyo, Sam. 2014. *Land Ownership Patterns and Income Inequality in Southern Africa*. World Economic and Social Survey Papers 2014. New York: United Nations, Department of Social and Economic Affairs, 59 pages.

Mozaffar, Shaheen, James R. Scarritt, and Glen Galaich. 2003. Electoral Institutions, Ethnopolitical Cleavages, and Party Systems in Africa's Emerging Democracies. *American Political Science Review* 97(3): 379–390.

Mueller, Susanne. 1981. The Historical Origins of Tanzania's Ruling Class. *Canadian Journal of African Studies* 15(3): 459–497.

Mueller, Susanne D. 1984. Government and Opposition in Kenya, 1966–9. *Journal of Modern African Studies* 22(3): 399–427.

Mueller, Susanne D. 2011. Dying to Win: Elections, Political Violence, and Institutional Decay in Kenya. *Journal of Contemporary African Studies* 29(1): 99–117.

Mueller, Susanne. 2022. Why Did Kenyans Elect Ruto as President? Monkey Cage. *The Washington Post*, 25 August.

Mugizi, Francisco M. P. and Parestico Pastory. 2022. Do Hegemonic-party Regimes Reward or Punish Voters? A Tale of Distributive Politics in Tanzania. *Africa Spectrum* 57(3): 235–263.

Müller-Crepon, Carl. 2023. Building Tribes: How Administrative Units Shaped Ethnic Groups in Africa. *American Journal of Political Science,* in press.

Müller-Crepon, Carl, Guy Schvitz, and Lars-Erik Cederman. 2023. Shaping States into Nations: The Effects of Ethnic Geography on State Borders. *American Journal of Political Science*.

Munro, William. 2001. The Political Consequences of Local Electoral Systems: Democratic Change and the Politics of Differential Citizenship in South Africa. *Comparative Politics* 33(3): 295–313.

Mutibwa, Phares. 1992. *Uganda since Independence: A Story of Unfulfilled Hopes*. London: Hurst.

Mveyange, Anthony. 2015. Night Lights and Regional Income Inequality in Africa. United Nations University WIDER Working Paper Series 2015/85.

Mwakubo, Sambili Kwale, E. C. Sambili, and H. K. Mariim. 1996. A Historical Perspective of the Socio-economic Impediments to Agricultural Development in the Coast Province of Kenya, with Reference to Kwale District. *Journal of East African Research and Development* 26: 32–53.

Myers, G. A. 2000. Tanzania's New Political Regionalism. *South African Geographical Journal* 82(1) (2000): 64–74.

Naseemullah, Adnan. 2022. *Patchwork States: The Historical Roots of Subnational Competition and Conflict in South Asia*. Cambridge and New York: Cambridge University Press.

Nathan, Noah. 2019. *Electoral Politics and Africa's Urban Transition*. Cambridge and New York: Cambridge University Press.

Nattrass, Nicoli and Jeremy Seekings. 2001. Democracy and Distribution in Highly Unequal Economies: The Case of South Africa. *Journal of Modern African Studies* 39(3): 471–498.

Naudé, W. A. and W. F. Krugell. 2006. Sub-national Growth Rate Differentials in South Africa: An Econometric Analysis. *Papers in Regional Science* 85(3): 443–457.

Ndegwa, Stephen. 2002. Decentralization in Africa: A Stocktaking Survey. World Bank Africa Regional Working Paper No. 40, Washington, D.C.

References

307

Ndiaye, Sambou. 2022. Récits et matérialités du passé du développement : traces et empreintes des projets fonciers dans la commune de Gandon (Sénégal). *Anthropologie et développement, APAD* 53: 39–52.

Ndlovu-Gatsheni, Sabelo J. 2009. Mapping Cultural and Colonial Encounters, 1880–1930s. In Brian Raftopolous and Alois Mlambo, eds., *Becoming Zimbabwe: A History from the Pre-colonial Period to 2008*. Harare: Weaver Press, pp. 39–74.

Ndulu, Benno J. and Stephen A. O'Connell. 2008. Policy Plus: African Growth Performance, 1960–2000. In Benno J. Ndulu, Stephen O'Connell, Robert H. Bates, Paul Collier, and Chukwuma C. Soludo, eds., *The Political Economy of Economic Growth in Africa, 1960–2000*. Cambridge: Cambridge University Press, pp. 3–75.

Ndulu, Benno J., Stephen O'Connell, Robert H. Bates, Paul Collier, and Chukwuma C. Soludo, eds. 2008. *The Political Economy of Economic Growth in Africa, 1960–2000*. Cambridge: Cambridge University Press.

Ngaruko, Floribert and Janvier D. Nkurunziza. 2000. An Economic Interpretation of Conflict in Burundi. *Journal of African Economies* 9(3): 370–409.

Ngigi, Samuel and Doreen Busolo. 2019. Devolution in Kenya: The Good, the Bad, and the Ugly. *Public Policy and Administration Research* 9(6): 9–21.

Nin-Pratt, Alejandro and Linden McBride. 2014. Agricultural Intensification in Ghana. Evaluating the Optimist's Case for a Green Revolution. *Food Policy* 48: 153–167.

Novotny, Josef. 2007. On the Measurement of Regional Inequality: Does the Spatial Dimension of Income Inequality Matter? *Annals of Regional Science* 41(3): 563–580.

Nsamba, Morris Adam. 2013. Decentralization and Territorial Politics: The Dilemma of Constructing and Managing Identities in Uganda. *Critical African Studies* 5(1): 48–60.

Nsamba, Morris A., Bernard Kasozi Okot, Stephen Oola, and Winnie Agabo. 2009. Breeding Fragmentation? Issues in the Policies and Practice of Decentralization in Uganda. Faculty of Law, Makerere University, Refugee Law Project and Human Rights & Peace Centre, Issue paper n. 1, June.

Nugent, Paul. 2019. *Boundaries, Communities and State-Making in West Africa: The Centrality of the Margins*. Cambridge and New York: Cambridge University Press.

Nugent, Paul and A. I. Asiwaju, eds. 1996. *African Boundaries: Barriers, Conduits, and Opportunities*. London: Cassell/ Pinter.

Nyenhuis, Robert and Matthias Krönke. 2021. The Effects of the Economic Freedom Fighters on Black South Africans' Political Behavior. A paper presented at the Political Parties in Africa online conference, 18 February 2021.

Nzau, Mumo. 2020. Eastern: The Dynamics of "Bridesmaid Politics." In Nic Cheeseman, Karuti Kanyinga, and Gabrielle Lynch eds., *The Oxford Handbook on Kenyan Politics*. Oxford: Oxford University Press, pp. 702–714.

Obe, Ayo. 2019. Aspirations and Realities in Africa: Nigeria's Emerging Two-Party System. *Journal of Democracy* 30(3): 109–123.

O'Connor, Anthony. 1988. Uganda: The Spatial Dimension. In Holger Bernt Hansen and Michael Twaddle, eds., *Uganda Now: Between Decay and Development*. London: James Currey, pp. 83–94.

O'Donnell, Guillermo. 1993. On the State, Development, and Some Conceptual Problems: A Latin American View with Some Glances at some Post-Communist Countries. *World Development* 21: 1355–1369.

Okafor, Stanley. 2013. Nigeria's Electoral Geography since 1999. In J. J. Ayoade et al., eds., *Nigeria's Critical Election 2011*. Lanham: Lexington: 1–16.

Okojie, Christiana and Adebe Shimeles. 2006. Inequality in Sub-Saharan Africa: A Synthesis of Recent Research. Overseas Development Institute (ODI). February.

O'Loughlin, John. 1993. Spatial Analysis in Political Geography. In John Agnew, Katharyne Mitchell, and Gerard Toal, eds., *A Companion to Political Geography*. Oxford: Basil Blackwell.

O'Loughlin, John. 2002. The Electoral Geography of Weimar Germany: Exploratory Spatial Analyses of Protestant Support for the Nazi Party. *Political Analysis* 10(3): 217–243.

Onoma, Ato Kwamena. 2013. *The Politics of Property Rights Institutions in Africa*. Cambridge and New York: Cambridge University Press.

Openshaw, S. and Taylor, P. 1979. A million or So Correlation Coefficients: Three Experiments on the Modifiable Areal Unit Problem. In N. Wrigley, ed. *Statistical Applications in the Spatial Sciences*. London: Pion, pp. 127–144.

Organization for Economic Cooperation and Development (OECD). 2016. *OECD Regions at a Glance 2016*, 16 June 2016, posted at www.oecd.org/regional/oecd-regions-at-a-glance-19990057.htm

Osei-Hwedie, Betha. 1998. The Role of Ethnicity in Multi-Party Politics in Malawi and Zambia. *Journal of Contemporary African Studies* 16(2): 227–247.

Osei-Kwame, Peter and Peter J. Taylor. 1984. A Politics of Failure: The Political Geography of Ghanaian Elections, 1954–1979. *Annals of the Association of American Geographers* 74(4): 574–589.

Ostby, G., R. Nordas, and J. K. Rod. 2009. Regional Inequalities and Civil Conflict in Sub-Saharan Africa. *International Studies Quarterly* 53(21): 301–324.

Ottaviano, Gianmarco. 2003. Regional Policy in the Global Economy: Insights from New Economic Geography. *Regional Studies* 37(6–7): 665–673.

Oucho, John O. 2002. *Undercurrents of Ethnic Conflict in Kenya*. Leiden: Brill Publishers.

Paller, Jeffrey. 2019. *Democracy in Ghana: Everyday Politics in Urban Africa*. Cambridge and New York: Cambridge University Press.

Palmer, Robin H. 1973. European Resistance to African Majority Rule: The Settlers' and Residents' Association of Nyasaland, 1960–63. *African Affairs* 72(288): 256–272.

Paget, Dan. 2019. The Authoritarian Origins of Well-organized Opposition Parties: The Rise of CHADEMA in Tanzania. *African Affairs* 184(473): 692–711.

Paget, Dan. 2022. A People Power Philosophy: Republican Ideology in Opposition in Tanzania. *Democratization* 30(3): 398–418.

Papaioannou, Elias. 2013. National Institutions and Subnational Development in Africa. *The Quarterly Journal of Economics* 129(1): 151–213.

Paret, Marcel. 2018. Beyond Post-Apartheid Politics? *Journal of Modern African Studies* 56(3): 471–496.

Parsons, Timothy. 2012. Being Kikuyu in Meru: Challenging the Tribal Geography of Colonial Kenya. *Journal of African History* 53: 65–86.

Patel, Nadini and Michael Wahman. 2015. The Presidential, Parliamentary and Local Elections in Malawi, May 2014. *Africa Spectrum* 50(1): 79–92.

Pengl, Yannick I., Philip Roessler, and Valeria Rueda. 2021. Cash Crops, Print Technologies, and the Politicization of Ethnicity in Africa. *American Political Science Review* 116(1): 1–19.

Perrot, Sandrine. 2014. An NRM Recapture of Teso in 2011? What Voting Means in a Hybrid Regime. In Sandrine Perrot, Sabiti Makara, Jerome Lafargue, and Marie-Aude

References

Fouere, eds., *Elections in a Hybrid Regime: Revisiting the 2011 Ugandan Polls.* Kampala, Uganda: Fountain Publishers, pp. 372–415.

Persson, Torsten and Guido Tabellino. 1996. Federal Fiscal Constitutions: Risk Sharing and Redistribution. *Journal of Political Economy* 104(5): 979–1009.

Petersen, Derek. 2012. *Ethnic Patriotism and the East African Revival.* Cambridge and New York: Cambridge University Press.

Pierson, Paul. 1993. When Effect Becomes Cause: Policy Feedback and Political Change. *World Politics* 45(4): 595–628.

Pinkovskiy, M. and Sala-i-Martin, X. 2016. Lights, Camera … Income! Illuminating the National Accounts-Household Surveys Debate. *The Quarterly Journal of Economics* 131(2): 579–631.

Piombo, Jessica. 2005. Political Institutions, Social Demographics and the Decline of Ethnic Mobilization in South Africa, 1994–1999. *Party Politics* 11 (4): 447–470.

Pitcher, Anne. 2012. *Party Politics and Economic Reform in Africa's Democracies.* Cambridge and New York: Cambridge University Press.

Pitcher, Anne. 2016. Party System Competition and Private Sector Development in Africa. *Journal of Development Studies* 53(1): 1–17.

Pitcher, Anne. 2017. Varieties of Residential Capitalism in Africa: A Comparison of Urban Housing Provision in Angola and Kenya. *African Affairs* 116(464) (July): 365–390.

Poertner, Mathias. 2021. The Organizational Voter: Support for New Parties in Young Democracies. *American Journal of Political Science* 65(3): 634–651.

Polanyi, Karl. 1944 [2001]. *The Great Transformation.* Boston: Beacon Press.

Pop-Eleches, Grigore. 2009. *From Economic Crisis to Reform: IMF Programs in Latin America and Eastern Europe.* Princeton, NJ: Princeton University Press.

Porter, Michael E. 2003. The Economic Performance of Regions. *Regional Studies* 37(6–7): 549–578.

Posner, Daniel. 2004a. Measuring Ethnic Fractionalization in Africa. *American Journal of Political Science* 48(4): 849–863.

Posner, Daniel. 2004b. The Political Salience of Cultural Difference: Why Chewas and Tumbukas Are Allies in Zambia and Adversaries in Malawi. *American Political Science Review* 98(4): 529–545.

Posner, Daniel. 2005. *Institutions and Ethnic Politics in Africa.* Cambridge: Cambridge University Press.

Poteete, Amy. 2009. Defining Political Community and Rights to Natural Resources in Botswana. *Development and Change* 40(2): 281–305.

Potts, David, ed. 2019. *Tanzanian Development: A Comparative Perspective.* Cambridge and New York: Cambridge University Press.

Potts, Deborah. 2006. Rural Mobility as a Response to Land Shortages: The Case of Malawi. *Population, Space and Place* 12: 291–311.

Poulton, Colin. 2012. Democratisation and the Political Economy of Agricultural Policy in Africa. Future Agricultures, Working paper 043. Sussex, Brighton: Future Agricultures Consortium. Available at www.future-agricultures.org.

Poulton, Colin. 2014. Democratisation and the Political Incentives for Agricultural Policy in Africa. *Development Policy Review* 32(2): s101–s122.

Poulton, Colin and Karuti Kanyinga. 2013. The Politics of Revitalizing Agriculture in Kenya. Future Agricultures Working paper 059. Brighton, UK: Future Agricultures Consortium.

Pourtier, Roland. 1980. La crise de l'agriculture dans un État minier: Le Gabon. *Études Rurales* 77: 39–62.

Pourtier, Roland. 1989. Les Etats et le contrôle territoriale en Afrique centrale: principes et partitiques. *Annales de Géographie* 98(547): 286–301.

Putnam, Robert. 1993. *Making Democracy Work: Civic Traditions in Modern Italy* (with Robert Leonardi and Raffaella Nanetti). Princeton: Princeton University Press.

Rabinowitz, Beth. 2018. *Coups, Rivals and the Modern State: Why Rural Coalitions Matter in Sub-Saharan Africa*. Cambridge and New York: Cambridge University Press.

Rabut, E. 1979. Le mythe Parisien de la Mise en Valeur. *Journal of African History* 20(2): 271–287.

Rafa, Mickey, Jonathan Moyer, Xuantong Wang, and Paul Sutton. 2017. Estimating District GDP in Uganda, University of Denver, Korbel School Working Paper for USAID.

Rajagopalan, Swarna. 1999. Internal Unit Demarcation and National Identity: India, Pakistan, Sri Lanka. *Nationalism and Ethnic Politics* 53–54: 191–211.

Rakner, Lise, Lars Svåsand, and Nixon Khembo. 2007. Fission and Fusion, Foes, and Friends: Party System Restructuring in Malawi in the 2004 General Election. *Comparative Political Studies* 40(9): 1112–1137.

Rambanapasi, C. O. 1989. Regional Development Policy and Its Impact on Regional Planning Practice in Zimbabwe. *Planning Perspective* 4(3): 271–294.

Ramírez, Juan Carlos and Johan Manuel de Aguas. 2017. Configuración territorial de las provincias de Colombia: Ruralidad y redes. Commissión Económca para América Latina y el Caribe (UNECLAC), Bogata, June.

Ranger, Terence. 1968. Nationality and Nationalism: The Case of Barotseland. *Journal of the Historical Society of Nigeria* 4(2) (June): 227–246.

Ranger, Terence. 1983. The Invention of Tradition in Colonial Africa. In Eric Hobsbawm and Terence Ranger, eds., *The Invention of Tradition*. Cambridge: Cambridge University Press, pp. 211–262.

Rathbone, Richard. 1996. Defining Akyemfo: The Construction of Citizenship in Akyem Abuakwa, Ghana, 1700–1939. *Africa: Journal of the International African Institute* 66(4): 506–525.

Reich, Michael R, et al. 2016. Moving Towards Universal Health Coverage: Lessons from 11 Countries. *The Lancet* 387(10020): 811–816.

Reno, William. 2008. *Corruption and State Politics in Sierra Leone*. Cambridge and New York: Cambridge University Press.

République de la Côte d'Ivoire. 2011. Decret n. 2011-262 du 28 Septembre 2011 portant détermination des circonscriptions électorales pour la législature 2011–2016.

Resnick, Danielle. 2014. *Urban Poverty and Party Populism in African Democracies*. Cambridge and New York: Cambridge University Press.

Resnick, Danielle. 2017. Democracy, Decentralization, and District Proliferation: The Case of Ghana. *Political Geography* 59 (July): 47–60.

Ricart-Huguet, Joan. 2022. The Origins of Colonial Investments in British and French Africa. *British Journal of Political Science* 52(2): 736–757.

Ricart-Huguet, Joan and Elliott Green. 2018. Taking it Personally: The Effect of Ethnic Attachment on Preferences for Regionalism. *Studies in Comparative International Development* 53(1): 67–89.

Rickard, Stephanie. 2018. *Spending to Win: Political Institutions, Economy Geography, and Government Subsidies*. Cambridge and New York: Cambridge University Press.

References

Riedl, Rachel. 2014. *Authoritarian Origins of Democratic Party Systems in Africa.* New York: Cambridge University Press.

Riker, William. 1964. *Federalism: Origin, Operation, Significance.* Boston: Little Brown.

Rodden, Jonathan. 2004. Comparative Federalism and Decentralization: On Meaning and Measurement. *Comparative Politics* 36(4): 481–500.

Rodden, Jonathan. 2010. The Geographic Distribution of Political Preferences. *Annual Review of Political Science* 13: 321–340.

Rodden, Jonathan. 2019. *Why Cities Lose: The Deep Roots of the Urban-Rural Political Divide.* New York: Basic Books.

Rodriguez-Pose, Andrés. 2018. The Revenge of the Places that do not Matter (and What to do about It). *Cambridge Journal of Regions, Economy, and Society* 11(1): 189–209.

Rodriguez-Pose, Andrés and Enrique Garcilazo. 2015. Quality of Government and the Returns of Investment: Examining the Impact of Cohesion Expenditure in European Regions. *Regional Studies* 49(8): 1274–1290.

Rodríguez-Silveira, Rodrigo. 2013. The Subnational Method and Social Policy Provision: Socioeconomic Context, Political Institutions, and Spatial Inequality. Working paper n. 36. desiguALdades.net, Berlin, Germany.

Roessler, Philip, Yannick I. Pengl, Robert Marty, Kyle Sorlie Titlow, and Nicolas van de Walle. 2022. The Cash Crop Revolution, Colonialism and Economic Reorganization in Africa. *World Development* 158: 1–17. Article 105934.

Rogers, Melissa Ziegler. 2016. *The Politics of Place and the Limits to Redistribution.* Milton Park, Abingdon: Routledge.

Rogowski, Ronald. 1989. *Commerce and Coalitions: How Trade Affects Domestic Political Alignments.* Princeton, NJ: Princeton University Press.

Rokkan, Stein. 1971. Nation-Building: A Review of Models and Approaches. *Current Sociology* 19(3): 7–38.

Rovny, Jan. 2015. Riker and Rokkan: Remarks on the Strategy and Structure of Party Competition. *Party Politics* 21(6): 912–918.

Roy, Alexis. 2010. Peasant Struggles in Mali: From Defending Cotton Producers' Interests to Becoming Part of the Malian Power Structures. *Review of African Political Economy* 37(125): 299–314.

Rubin, Jeffrey. 1997. *Decentering the Regime: Ethnicity, Radicalism, and Democracy in Juchitán, Mexico.* Durham: Duke University Press.

Rudra, Nita. 2015. Social Protection in the Developing World: Challenges, Continuity, and Change. *Politics and Society* 43(4): 463–470.

Rutten, Marchel. M. E. 1992. *Selling Wealth to Buy Poverty: The Process of Individualization of Landownership among the Maasai Pastoralists of Kajiado District, 1890–1990.* Saarbrücken: Breitenbach.

Sabean, David Warren. 1998. *Kinship in Neckarhausen, 1700–1870.* Cambridge: Cambridge University Press.

Sabean, David Warren. 2006. Reflections on Microhistory. In Gunilla Budde, Sebastian Conrad, and Oliver Janz, eds., *Transnationale Geschiechte: Themen, Tendenzen, und Theorien.* Geburtstag: Vandenhoeck and Ruprecht, pp. 275–290.

Sack, Robert David. 1986. *Human Territoriality: Its Theory and History.* Cambridge: Cambridge University Press.

Sahn, David E. and David C. Stifel. 2000. Poverty Comparisons over Time and Across Countries in Africa. *World Development* 28(12): 2123–2155.

Sahn, David E. and David C. Stifel. 2003. Urban-Rural Inequality and Living Standards in Africa. *Journal of African Economies* 12(4): 564–597.

Sartori, Giovanni. 1976. *Parties and Party Systems: A Framework for Analysis*. Cambridge: Cambridge University Press.

Saylor, Ryan. 2014. *State Building in Boom Times: Commodities and Coalitions in Latin America and Africa*. Cambridge and New York: Cambridge University Press.

Scarritt, James R. and Shaheen Mozaffar. 1999. The Specification of Ethnic Cleavages and Ethnopolitical Groups for the Analysis of Democratic Competition in Contemporary Africa. *Nationalism and Ethnic Politics* 5(1): 82–117.

Schakel, Arjan H. 2011. Congruence between Regional and National Elections. *Comparative Political Studies* 46(5) (2011): 631–662.

Schakel, Arjan H. and Charlie Jeffrey. 2013. Are Regional Elections really "Second Order" Elections? *Regional Studies* 47(3): 323–341.

Schensal, Jean J., et al. 1999. *Mapping Social Networks, Spatial Data, and Hidden Populations: Ethnographer's Toolkit, Vol. 4*. Walnut Creek, London, New Delhi: Sage.

Scheve, Kenneth F. and Matthew J. Slaughter. 2001. What Determines Individual Trade Policy Preferences? *Journal of International Economics* 54(2): 267–292.

Schiavina, Marcello, Sergio Freire, and Kytt MacManus. 2019. GHS Population Grid Multitemporal (1975, 1990, 2000, 2015) R2019A. European Commission, Joint Research Centre (JRC).

Schindler, Seth, and J. Miguel Kanai. 2021. Getting the Territory Right: Infrastructure-led Development and the Re-emergence of Spatial Planning Strategies. *Regional Studies* 55(1): 40–51.

Schlee, Günther and Abdullahi A. Shongolo. 2012. *Pastoralism and Politics in Northern Kenya and Southern Ethiopia*. Oxford: Boydell & Brewer and James Currey.

Schneider, Geoffrey E. 2018. The Post-Apartheid Development Debacle in South Africa: How Mainstream Economics and Vested Interests Preserved Apartheid Economic Structures. *Journal of Economic Issues* 52(2): 306–322.

Schulz, Daniel Nicolai. 2020. *Power of the Masses – Group Size, Attribution, and the Politics of Export Bans in Africa*. A PhD thesis submitted to the London School of Economics and Political Science, Department of International Development, February.

Scott, Allen J. and Michael Storper. 2003. Regions, Globalization, Development. *Regional Studies* 37(6–7): 579–593.

Seekings, J. 2008. Welfare Regimes and Redistribution in the South. In I. Shapiro, P. A. Swenson, and D. Donno, eds., *Divide and Deal: The Politics of Distribution in Democracies*. New York and London: New York University Press, pp. 19–42.

Seekings, Jeremy. 2017. Affordability and the Political Economy of Social Protection in Contemporary Africa, WIDER Working paper 2017/43 (February).

Seekings, Jeremy. 2019. Building a Conservative Welfare State in Botswana. In Sam Hickey, Tom Lavers, Jeremy Seekings, and Miguel Niño-Zarazúa, eds., *The Politics of Social Protection in Eastern and Southern Africa*. Oxford: Oxford University Press, pp. 46–72.

Seekings, Jeremy and Nicoli Nattrass. 2005. *Class, Race, and Inequality in South Africa*. New Haven and London: Yale University Press.

Seely, Jennifer C. 2001. A Political Analysis of Decentralization: Coopting the Tuareg Threat in Mali. *Journal of Modern African Studies* 39(3): 499–524.

References

Selanius, Victor. 2017. Notes on the *rédécoupage* of Ivoirian administrative boundaries. Unpub. paper, LSE Department of Government, August.

Selway, Joel Sawat. 2015. *Coalitions of the Well-being: How Electoral Rules Shape Health Policy in Developing Countries*. Cambridge and New York: Cambridge University Press.

Serra, Renata. 2014. Cotton Sector Reform in Mali: Explaining the Puzzles. *Journal of Modern African Studies* 52(3): 379–402.

Shimeles, Adebe and Tiguene Nabassaga. 2017. Why Is Inequality High in Africa? ADB Office of the Chief Economist, African Development Bank Working Paper No. 246. January.

Shimeles, Abebe, and Tiguene Nabassaga. 2018. Why Is Inequality High in Africa? *Journal of African Economies* 27(1): 108–126.

Shin, Michael and John Agnew. 2007. The Geographical Dynamics of Italian Elections, 1987–2001. *Electoral Studies* 26: 287–302.

Sichinava, David. 2018. Cleavages, Electoral Geography, and the Territorialization of Political Parties in the Republic of Georgia. *Eurasian Geography and Economics* 58(6): 670–690.

Simson, Rebecca. 2018. Mapping Recent Inequality Trends in Developing Countries, LSE International Inequalities Institute Working Paper no.24.

Sinha, Assema. 2005. *The Regional Roots of Developmental Politics in India: A Divided Leviathan*. Bloomington, IN: Indiana University Press.

Sitko, Nicholas J. and T. S. Jayne. 2014. Structural Transformation or Elite Land Capture? The Growth of "emergent" Farmers in Zambia. *Food Policy* 48: 194–202.

Sjögren, Anders. 2015. Battles over Boundaries: The Politics of Territorial Identity and Authority in Three Ugandan Regions. *Journal of Contemporary African Studies* 33(2): 268–284.

Sjögren, Anders and Henrik Angerbradt. 2019. Accommodating, Opposing, or Dismissing? Ethno-Regional Mobilization, (De)Centralization, and State-Wide Party Strategies in Nigeria and Kenya. *Nationalism and Ethnic Politics* 25(4): 343–362.

Sklar, Richard. 1979. The Nature of Class Domination in Africa. *The Journal of Modern African Studies* 17(4): 531–552.

Skocpol, Theda. 1995. *Protecting Soldiers and Mothers: The Political Origins of Social Policy in the United States*. Cambridge, MA: Harvard University Press.

Smith, Daniel A. 2002. Consolidating Democracy? The Structural Underpinnings of Ghana's 2000 Elections. *Journal of Modern African Studies* 40(4): 621–650.

Snyder, Richard. 2001. Scaling Down: The Subnational Comparative Method. *Studies in Comparative International Development* 36(1): 93–110.

Soifer, Hilel David. 2019. Units of Analysis in Subnational Research. In A. Giraudy, E. Moncada, and R. Snyder, eds., *Inside Countries: Subnational Research in Comparative Politics*. Cambridge and New York: Cambridge University Press, pp. 92–112.

Solt, Frederick. 2014. The Standardized World Income Inequality Database, v.14. Washington, DC: IMF. http://hdl.handle.net/1902.1/11992.

Solt, Frederik. 2015. On the Assessment and Use of Cross-national Inequality Datasets. *Journal of Economic Inequality* 13: 683–691.

Southhall, Aidan. 1988. The Recent Political Economy of Uganda. In H. B. Hansen and M. Twaddle, eds., *Uganda Now: Between Development and Decay*. London: Currey, pp. 54–69.

Stacey, Paul. 2016. Rethinking the Making and Breaking of Traditional and Statutory Institutions in Post-Nkrumah Ghana. *African Studies Review* 59(2): 209–230.

Staniland, Martin. 1970. Colonial Government and Populist Reform: The Case of the Ivory Coast. Part I. *Journal of Administration Overseas* 9(1): 33–43, and Part II, 9(4): 113–127.

Statistics South Africa. 2011. Gross Domestic Product: Annual Estimates 2002–2010; Regional Estimates 2002–2010. Statistical Release P0441.

Stewart, Frances. 2000. Crisis Prevention: Tackling Horizontal Inequalities. *Oxford Development Studies* 28(3): 245–262.

Stewart, Frances, Graham Brown, and Luca Mancini. 2005. Why Horizontal Inequalities Matter: Some Implications for Measurement, Oxford University, Centre for Research on Inequality, Human Security and Ethnicity (CRISE), CRISE Working Paper No. 19, June.

Stokes, Susan C., Thad Dunning, Marcelo Nazareno, and Valeria Brusco. 2013. *Brokers, Voters, and Clientelism: The Puzzle of Distributive Politics.* Cambridge and New York: Cambridge University Press.

Storeygard, Adam, Vernon Henderson, and David N. Weil. 2012. Measuring Economic Growth from Outer Space. *American Economic Review* 102(2): 994–1028.

Storper, Michael. 2018. Separate Worlds? Explaining the Current Wave of Regional Economic Polarization. *Journal of Economic Geography* 18(5): 247–270.

Svolik, Milan W. 2012b. *The Politics of Authoritarian Rule.* Cambridge and New York: Cambridge University Press.

Taggart, Karen. 1995. How People Vote Around the World: Electoral Rules in Africa. Electoral Systems Survey. At http://archive.fairvote.org/reports/1995/chp7/taggart .html. Accessed 26 March 2023.

Thomson, Henry. 2018. Grievances, Mobilization and Mass Opposition to Authoritarian Regimes: A Subnational Analysis of East Germany's 1953 Abbreviated Revolution. *Comparative Political Studies* 51(12): 1594–1627.

Thorold, Alan. 2000. Regionalism, Tribalism and Multiparty Democracy: The Case of Malawi. *South African Journal of International Affairs* 7(2): 135–139.

Throup, David and Charles Hornsby. 1998. *Multi-Party Politics in Kenya.* Athens, OH: Ohio University Press.

Tilly, Charles. 2003. Inequality, Democratization, and De-democratization. *Sociological Theory* 21(1): 37–43.

Tice, Matthew. 2020. Beyond the Neoliberal-Statist Divide on the Drivers of Innovation: A Political Settlements Reading of Kenya's M-Pesa Success Story. *World Development* 125 (January): 1–14.

Tillin, Louise. 2013. *Remapping India: New States and their Political Origins.* London: Hurst.

Tilly, Helen. 2011. *Africa as a Living Laboratory: Empire, Development, and the Problem of Scientific Knowledge, 1870–1950.* Chicago, IL: University of Chicago Press.

Tordoff, William. 1965. Regional Administration in Tanzania. *Journal of Modern African Studies* 3(1): 63–89.

Tordoff, William. 1968a. Provincial and District Government in Zambia, Part I: Provincial Level. *Public Administration and Development* 7(3): 415–486.

Tordoff, William. 1968b. Provincial and District Government in Zambia, Part II. *Public Administration and Development* 7(4): 487–545.

References   315

Tordoff, William and Ian Scott. 1974. Political Parties: Structures and Policies. In William Tordoff, ed., *Politics in Zambia*. Manchester: Manchester University Press.

Treakle, Jordan. 2016. Agricultural Cooperatives and the Social Economy in Kenya's changing governance landscape. International Master of Science in Rural Development from Ghent University (Belgium) and others, defended at Wageningen University, unpublished.

Trotter, Philipp A. 2016. Rural Electrification, Electrification Inequality, and Democratic Institutions in Sub-Saharan Africa. *Energy for Sustainable Development* 34 (October): 111–129.

Trubowitz, Peter. 1998. *Defining the National Interest*. Chicago, IL: University of Chicago Press.

Tups, Gideon and Peter Dannenberg. 2021. Emptying the Future, Claiming Space: The Southern Agricultural Growth Corridor of Tanzania as a Spatial Imaginary for Strategic Coupling Processes. *Geoforum* 123: 23–35.

UNRISD, United Nations Research Institute for Social Development. 2010. Flagship Report: *Combating Poverty and Inequality*, UNRISD: Geneva.

Vail, Leroy. 1981. Ethnicity, Language, and National Unity: The Case of Malawi. In Phillip Bonner, ed., *Working Papers in Southern African Studies, Volume 2*. Johannesburg: Ravan, pp. 121–163.

Vail, Leroy. 1989. Tribalism in the Political History of Malawi. In Leroy Vail, ed., *The Creation of Tribalism in Southern Africa*. Berkeley and Los Angeles: University of California Press, pp. 151–192.

Van de Walle, Nicolas. 2003. Presidentialism and Clientelism in Africa's Emerging Party Systems. *Journal of Modern African Studies* 41(2): 297–321.

Van de Walle, Nicolas. 2009. The Institutional Origins of Inequality in Sub-Saharan Africa. *Annual Review of Political Science* 12: 307–327.

Van Waijenburg, Marlous. 2018. Financing the African Colonial State: The Revenue Imperative and Forced Labor. *Journal of Economic History* 78(1): 40–80.

Vandergeest, Peter and Nancy L. Peluso. 1995. Territorialization and State Power in Thailand. *Theory and Society* 24(3): 385–426.

Vansina, Jan. 1990. *Paths in the Rainforests*. Madison, WI: University of Wisconsin Press.

Venables, Anthony. 2010. Economic Geography and African Development. *Papers in Regional Science* 89(3): 469–483.

Von Oppen, Achim. 2006. Village as Territory: Enclosing Locality in Northwest Zambia, 1950s–1990s. *Journal of African History* 47(1): 57–75.

Wahman, Michael. 2011. Offices and Policies: Why do Oppositional Parties form Pre-electoral Coalitions in Competitive Authoritarian Regimes? *Electoral Studies* 30(4): 642–657.

Wahman, Michael. 2017. Nationalized Incumbents and Regionalized Challengers: Opposition- and Incumbent-Party Nationalization in Africa. *Party Politics* 23(3): 309–322.

Wahman, Michael. 2024. *Controlling Territory, Controlling Voters: The Electoral Geography of African Campaign Violence*. Oxford: Oxford University Press.

Wahman, Michael and Catherine Boone. 2018. Captured Countryside? Stability and Change in Sub-National Support for African Incumbent Parties. *Comparative Politics* 50(2): 189–209.

References

Wallerstein, Immanuel. 1967. Class, Tribe, and Party in West African Politics. In Seymour Martin Lipset and Stein Rokkan, eds., *Party Systems and Voter Alignments*. New York: Free Press, pp. 497–518.

Wang, Xuantong, Mickey Rafa, et al. 2019. Estimation and Mapping of Sub-National Uganda using NPP-VIIRS Imagery. *Remote Sensing* 11(163): 1–14.

Wankuru, Peter Chacha. 2019. For the First Time, the Relative Economic Size of Kenya's Counties Is Clear, World Bank Blog. 2 May.

Wantchekon, Leonard. 2003. Clientelism and Voting Behavior: Evidence from a Field Experiment in Benin. *World Politics* 55 (April), 399–422.

Wayama, Fredrick O., Patrick Develterre, and Ignace Pollet. 2009. Reinventing the Wheel? African Cooperatives in a Liberalized Economic Environment. *Annals of Public and Cooperative Economics* 80(3): 361–392.

Wedig, Karin and Jörg Wiegratz. 2018. Neoliberalism and the Revival of Agricultural Cooperatives: The Case of the Coffee Sector in Uganda. *Journal of Agrarian Change* 18(2): 348–369.

Weghorst, Keith R. and Michael Bernhard. 2014. From Formlessness to Structure? The Institutionalization of Competitive Party Systems in Africa. *Comparative Political Studies* 47(12): 1707–1737.

Weghorst, Keith R. and Staffan I. Lindberg. 2013. What Drives the Swing Voter in Africa. *American Journal of Political Science* 57(3): 717–734.

Weingast, Barry R. 1995. The Economic Role of Political Institutions: Market-Preserving Federalism and Economic Development. *Journal of Law, Economics, and Organization* 11(1): 2–31.

Weinstein, Jeremy. 2007. *Inside Rebellion: The Politics of Insurgent Violence*. Cambridge and New York: Cambridge University Press.

Weiss, Herbert. 1967. *Political Protest in the Congo: The Parti Solidaire Africain*. Princeton, NJ: Princeton University Press.

Weidmann, Nils B. and Sebastian Schutte. 2017. Using Night Light Emission for the Prediction of Local Wealth. *Journal of Peace Research* 54(2): 125–140.

West, W. Jefferson II. 2005. Regional Cleavages in Turkish Politics: An Electoral Geography of the 1999 and 2002 National Elections. *Political Geography* 24(4): 499–523.

Whitehead, Laurence and Jacqueline Behrend. 2016. Uneven Processes and Multiple Pathways. In Jacqueline Behrend and Laurence Whitehead, eds., *Illiberal Practices: Territorial Variance within Large Federal Democracies*. Baltimore: Johns Hopkins University Press, pp. 291–314.

Whitfield, Lindsay, Ole Therkildsen, Lars Burr, and Anne Mette Kjaer. 2015. *The Politics of African Industrial Policy: A Comparative Perspective*. Cambridge and New York: Cambridge University Press.

Wibbles, Erik. 2005. *Federalism and the Market: Intergovernmental Conflict and Economic Reform in Developing Countries*. Cambridge and New York: Cambridge University Press.

Widner, Jennifer. 1992. *The Rise of the Party State in Kenya*. Los Angeles: University of California Press.

Wilfahrt, Martha. 2018. Precolonial Legacies and Institutional Congruence in Public Goods Delivery: Evidence from Decentralized West Africa. *World Politics* 70(2): 239–274.

References

317

Wilfahrt, Martha. 2021. *Precolonial Legacies and Postcolonial Politics: Representation and Redistribution in Decentralized West Africa*. Cambridge and New York: Cambridge University Press.

Williamson, J. G. 1965. Regional Inequality and the Process of National Development: A Description of Patterns. *Economic Development and Cultural Change* 13: 3–47.

Willis, Justin and Ngala Chome. 2014. Marginalization and Participation on the Kenya Coast: The 2013 Elections. *Journal of Eastern African Studies* 8(1): 115–134.

Wily, Liz Alden. 2001. Reconstructing the African Commons. *Africa Today*, 48(1): 77–99.

Wimmer, Andreas. 2009. Herder's Heritage and the Boundary-Making Approach: Studying Ethnicity in Immigrant Societies. *Sociological Theory* 27(3): 244–270.

Woods, Dwayne. 1990. Ethno-regional Demands, Symbolic and Redistributive Politics: Sugar Complexes in the North of the Ivory Coast. *Journal of Ethnic and Racial Studies* 2: 469–489.

World Bank. 2009. *World Development Report 2009: Reshaping Economic Geography*. Washington, DC: The World Bank.

World Bank. 2010. *World Development Indicators 2010*. Washington, DC: The World Bank.

World Bank. 2015. *The State of Social Safety Nets*. Washington, DC: The World Bank. (ASPIRE data).

World Bank. 2016. Poverty in a Rising Africa. *Africa Research Newsletter*, n. 103358, February, pp. 1–5.

Young, Alden. 2017. *Transforming Sudan: Decolonization, Economic Development, and State Formation*. Cambridge and New York: Cambridge University Press.

Young, Crawford. 1970. Rebellion in the Congo. In Robert I. Rotberg and Ali A. Mazuri, eds., *Protest and Power in Black Africa*. New York: Oxford University Press, pp. 969–1011.

Young, Alden. 2018. *Transforming Sudan: Decolonization, Economic Deveopment, and State Formation*. Cambridge and New York: Cambridge University Press.

Young, Crawford. 2012. *The Postcolonial State in Africa*. Madison, WI: University of Wisconsin Press.

Ziblatt, Daniel. 2006. *Structuring the State: The Formation of Italy and Germany and the Puzzle of Federalism*. Princeton: Princeton University Press.

ATLASES

Cameroon

Ady, Peter H., and Arthur Hazlewood. 1965. *Oxford Regional Atlas of Africa*. Oxford: Clarendon Press.

Davies, H. R. J. 1973. *Tropical Africa: An Atlas for Rural Development*. Cardiff.

Côte d'Ivoire

Atlas de Côte d'Ivoire. Ivory Coast. Ministère du Plan.; O.R.S.T.O.M. (Agency: France); Université d'Abidjan. Institut de géographie tropicale.

References

Iloeje, Nwadilibe P. 1972. *A New Geography of West Africa*. London: Longman.
UNFAO [Juan Papadakis]. 1966. Crop ecologic survey in West Africa: Liberia, Ivory Coast, Ghana, Togo, Dahomey, Nigeria. Rome: UNFAO.

Ghana

Atlas of the Gold Coast. Survey Department. Accra: Survey Department 1949 5th ed.
Ghana National Atlas Project. Accra, Survey Department. 1976.
Iloeje, Nwadilibe P. 1972. *A New Geography of West Africa*. London: Longman.

Kenya

Ady, Peter H. and Arthur Hazlewood. 1965. *Oxford regional economic atlas of Africa*.
Ady, Peter H. and Arthur Hazlewood. 1970. National Atlas of Kenya.
The Atlas of Kenya. Nairobi: The Survey of Kenya, 1959.

Malawi

The National Atlas of Malaŵi, National Atlas Coordinating Committee (Malawi). 1983. Malawi Department of Surveys. Lilongwe : National Atlas Coordinating Committee, for "Agricultural Economy During the Colonial Period, 1890–1964."
Fraym Report, "Insights into the Current Tobacco Farming Landscape for Malawi," January 2019, Report for Tobacco Areas, c. 2015.

Mali

Iloeje, Nwadilibe P. 1972. *A New Geography of West Africa*. London: Longman.
Traoré, Mamadou, Yves Monnier, and Georges Laclavère. 1980. *Atlas du Mali*. Paris: Éditions Jeune Afrique.

Nigeria

Ady, Peter A. and Arthur Hazelwood. 1965. *Oxford Regional Economic Atlas of Africa*. Oxford: Clarendon Press.
Davies, H. R. J. [Harold Richard John]. 1973. *Tropical Africa: An Atlas for Rural Development*. Cardiff: University of Wales Press.
Iloeje, Nwadilibe P. 1972. *A New Geography of West Africa*. London: Longman.

South Africa

Christopher, Anthony John. 2000. *Atlas of a Changing South Africa*. Second Edition. London: Routledge.
Waldner, Francois, Matthew Hanse, and Peter V. Potapov. 2017. National-scale Cropland Mapping Based on Spectral-Temporal Features and Outdated Land Cover Information. August 2017. *PLoS ONE* 12(8): e0181911. https://doi.org/10.1371/journal.pone.0181911. Downloaded from ResearchGate, 15 March 2021.

References

Zietsman, H. L. and Izak J. Van Der Merwe. 1981. *Economic Atlas of South Africa.* Stellenbosch: University of Stellenbosch.

Tanzania

Atlas of the Tanganika Territory. 1942. Survey Division, Dept. of Lands and Mines, Dar es Salaam. Government Press, 1942.

Atlas of East Africa: Tanganika, Third Edition. 1956. Survey Division, Department and Lands and Surveys, Dar es Salaam.

Atlas of Tanzania, Survey and Mapping Division, Ministry of Lands, Settlement, and Water Development, Dar es Salaam, Tanzania. 1967.

Republic of Tanzania. Atlas of Tanzania. Tanzania. 1976. Wizara ya Ardhi, Nyumba na Maendeleo Mijini. Dar-es-Salaam: Surveys and Mapping Division, Ministry of Lands, Housing and Urban Development (based on 1971 data).

Uganda

Atlas of Uganda. 1967. Uganda Department of Lands and Surveys, 2nd edition (data from 1962/63). Entebbe.

O'Connor, A. M. 1965. *Railways and Development in Uganda.* Makerere/ East African Institute of Social Research. East African Series 18. Nairobi: Oxford University Press.

Zambia

Borland, Kim, Almaz Naizghi, and Steve Longabaugh. 2009. Mapping Zambian Regions of Staple Food Net Consumption, Geo 425: GIS Project, 17 April 2009 (with the Food Security Group, Department of Food, Agriculture, and Resource Economics, Michigan State University).

Davies, Hywel D. 1971. *Zambia in Maps.* London: University of London Press.

United States Department of Agriculture (USDA), Foreign Agricultural Service (FAS). 2014. Zambia Livelihoods 2014. Famine Early Warning Service (FEWS), Final Report. Washington, DC: USDA.

Zimbabwe

Rhodesia and Nyasaland, Federal Department of Topographic Surveys. 1962. Agricultural Production Map of the Federation of Rhodesia and Nyasaland. Salisbury, Federal Government Printer.

Chemura, Abel. 2013. Assessing the impact of climate change on the suitability of rainfed flue-cured tobacco production in Zimbabwe. First climate science symposium of Zimbabwe, UNDP, UNOCA, Cresta Lodge, Harare, 12 June 2013.

Mhiribidi, Delight et al., 2018. Optimal Water Resource Allocation Modelling in the Lowveld of Zimbabwe. *OpenAccess PIAHS* 378: 67–72.

Zimbabwe, Central Statistical Office, Cartography Section. 1989. *Zimbabwe in Maps: A Census Atlas.* Harare, Zimbabwe: Central Statistical Office.

Index

Admin1 units
  boundary persistence, 129
  colonial, 65
  definition, 17
  and electoral blocs, 129
Admin2 units (districts), 31, 225
  colonial, 65
Afrobarometer data, 27, 209
agglomeration, 149, 236
  theory, 14
Agnew, John, 96, 226
agrarian welfare regimes, 204
agricultural export economies
  colonial, 56
  post 2000, 206
agriculture, labor relations, 117
agriculture, plantation, 117, 181
  colonial, 56
agriculture, settler, 117, 178
  colonial, 57
agriculture, smallholder, 32, 36
  colonial, 56
  and colonial export crops, 66
  producer regions, 117
  and sectoral interests, 141
Arriola, Leonardo, 81, 92, 230
associational ties, 67, 142

Bates, Robert, 67, 78, 90, 142, 176
Bensel, Richard, 40, 169
Beramendi, Pablo, 16, 198
Bolivia, 155
borders, internal, 216

AOF, 74
  change, 83
  colonial, 55, 62
  unit persistence, 72–74
Botswana, 10, 199
boundaries, internal
  unit persistence, 129

Cameroon, 67, 107, 129, 151, 164–165, 192, 217, 256
  Northern, 126
  regional bloc voting, 106
  Western, 106
capital cities
  coding, 258
capital markets, 37
Caramani, Daniele, 9, 12, 168
cash crops. *See* agriculture, smallholder; export-producing regions
Cercles and *cantons*, 60. *See also* Native Authorities
China
  branch-and-bloc system, 82
  hukou system, 58
cities, capital
  coding, 110
  and economic advantage, 15
  as growth poles, 182
  voting patterns, 107, 233
cities, secondary, 109
civil war, 203
  and regionalism, 29
class analysis, Africa, 2, 26

321

Index

class cleavage
  South Africa, 91
class formation, rural, 236, 238. *See also* Land
  tenure reform
class identities, 172
class politics, 12, 18, 213, 235–236
cleavage, territorial. *See* core–periphery
  politics; regionalism
cleavages. *See also* regional cleavages
  regional, 4
closed districts, 58
coalition-building, electoral, 43, 81
  policy-based, 229
  and sectoral policy, 206
collective action, 141
colonial conquest, 53
colonial producer regions, 116–119,
  273–276
colonial states in Africa, 52–54
comparative political economy (CPE)
  and national integration, 39–41
  and redistribution, 195–196
  and regional policy issues, 40
  and spatial inequality, 16–17, 239
  and territorial politics, 8, 225, 239
Congo, Katanga, 87, 215
connectivity, 128, 143
convergence, economic, 14, 34
cooperatives, agricultural, 13, 78, 142
  colonial, 64
  and nationalist mobilization, 67
core–periphery politics, 15, 169, 174
Côte d'Ivoire, 161, 166, 192
  Agni kingdoms, 63
  Baoulé identity, 68
  devolution, 219
  Northern, 156
  producer regions, 124
  regional balancing, 85
  regional bloc voting, 100
cotton regions, 59, 68, 110, 127

Democratization, Third Wave, 88, 202
devolution, 225, 238
  politics of, 217–220
district creation, 80, 190, 220

economic geography
  theory, 14, 15, 239
economic planning. *See also*
    growth strategies
  colonial, 53

economic specialization
  colonial, 56
  non-persistence, 127
  and policy interests, 46, 141
  versus diversification, 124, 143
educational achievement
  measure, 109
  wealth in, 182
electoral authoritarian regimes, 163
electoral clientelism, 86, 92, 196, 228
  and non-bloc regions, 229
electoral coalitions. *See also* coalition-building,
    electoral
  asymmetric, 161
  and inequality structure, 161
  regional scale, 83
electoral constituencies
  boundary persistence, 73
  competitiveness, 207
  origins, 70, 74
electoral data quality, 95, 99
electoral geography methods, 98. *See also*
    Moran's I
electoral malapportionment, 145, 157, 162
electoral rules, 76
  and PR, 9, 17, 41, 146
  and SMD, 17, 76, 145, 146
  in the 12 countries, 94, 248–250
endowment, natural, 35, 108, 132, 224
ethnic arithmetic, 13
ethnic boundary persistence, 72
ethnic groups
  as amalgams, 61–62, 134
  politically relevant (PREGs), 68, 139
  and spatial clustering, 27
ethnic homelands
  and electoral blocs, 138
ethnic identity
  economic correlates, 133
  political scale, 63
ethnic inequality, 29, 147
ethnic land units
  persistence, 79
ethnic politics, 84
  as institutional effect, 74
ethnic territories. *See also* ethnic homelands;
    ethnic land units
  colonial, 61
ethnicity
  DHS categories, 134
  as endogenous, 11, 147, 231
  mega-ethnicities, 84, 147

Index

and neocustomary land tenure, 84
and regional bloc voting, 107
and social cleavage, 26
and spatial clustering, 3
and super-ethnicities, 28, 139, 185
ethnicity, language groups, 62, 147. *See also*
Posner, Daniel
ethno-linguistic fractionalization, 143
ethno-regionalism, 27
Europe
territorial cleavages, 12, 39, 150
European Union, "territorial cohesion"
policy, 204
export-producing regions, 36, 88, 116–118.
See also colonial producer regions
colonial, 56
economic advantage, 116–118

federal contract, 216
federal systems, 43, 82, 85, 201
bids for, 215
and spatial inequality, 216
food crops, nationally traded, 116, 177. *See
also* maize
France, 17, 170

Gabon, 10
Ghana
internal boundary persistence, 72
regional bloc voting, 100
spatial inequality, 7
Ghana, Ashanti, 63
Gibson, Edward, 162
Gini index, 6, 199
Gourevitch, Peter, 150, 169
growth poles. *See* cities, capital
growth strategies, 174, 179, 190,
194, 241

Harding, Robin, 233
Harvey, David, 50
Herbst, Jeffrey, 4, 42, 233
hometown associations, 67

ideology, 146
ideology, regional, 46, 85–88, 175, 179
indirect rule, 51, 63
inequality, ethnic. *See* ethnic inequality
inequality, horizontal, 29. *See also* ethnic
inequality
inequality, interpersonal income
global comparisons, 5–7

inequality, spatial, 2, 8, 18–20, 108,
223–225, 244
global comparisons, 5, 32, 196, 239
inequality measures, 108–110, 243
institutions, 227. *See also* land tenure regimes;
territorial grid
African countries, presumed weakness,
42, 226
and inequality, 8
nationalizing, 17, 200
representative, and territorial politics, 41
territorial, 17
internal colonialism, 175, 235

Kenya, 170–175
2010 Constitution, 204
district Focus, 78
majimboism, 174, 219
regional bloc voting, 100, 171
spatial inequality, 7, 170
Rift Valley, 85, 173
Western, 126, 171–173
"White Highlands", 57, 175
Kim, Eun Kyung, 162, 174, 208
Kuznets curve, 6

labor mobility. *See* labor-exporting regions;
migrant labor; mobility of population
labor reserves. *See* labor-exporting regions
labor unions, 142–143
labor-exporting regions, 110, 120, 126, 141,
175, 183–184
colonial, 57
land expropriation, 62
land policy
as distributive policy, 209
state activism, 210–211
land tenure reform, 212–214, 238
land titling, 212–213
Malawi, 183
land tenure regimes
colonial, 58
neocustomary, 38, 84, 205, 210, 227
and population mobility, 38, 66
as social policy, 205
landslide vote, 97
LAPSSET corridor, 237
Latin America, 150, 157
inequality, 6
studies, 239
League of Nations mandate
territories, 132

Index

Lipset and Rokkan (1967), 12, 39, 96, 168–169, 224
Lonsdale, John, 133, 146, 172
low-income coalition, 186. *See also* revisionist coalition

maize, 116, 121, 143, 178, 179, 185
Malawi, 157, 180–185
  economic regions, colonial, 59
  internal boundary persistence, 72
  regional bloc voting, 100
  Shire Highlands, 181
Mali, 194, 243, 256
  Office du Niger, 77
  regional inequality, 113–115
  regional politics, 161
  regional voting patterns, 106
  Sikasso region, 106
marketing boards, 81, 143
migrant labor
  colonial, 57
migration, internal, 37, 238
  colonial, 58
  of labor, 172
  low rates, 37
  state-organized, 62
migration of labor, circular, 180
  colonial, 58, 183
military recruitment, 65
mining regions, 117, 176
  colonial, 57
mobility of population, 16
  colonial impediments, 66
Moran's I, 98–99

Namibia, 200
nation building, 154
national integration, 79
  economic, 15, 34, 35, 83, 224, 237
  land markets, 212
  market, 168
  and regionalism, 40
national market. *See* national integration, economic
nationalist era, 142
native authorities (NA), 51, 60
  boundary persistence, 72
  and neocustomary tenure, 227
  postcolonial persistence, 79
neoliberal reforms, 142. *See also* Structural Adjustment Programs
New Economic Geography. *See* economic geography

Nigeria
  3 region structure, 85
  Biafra, 87
  internal border change, 83
  internal boundary persistence, 72
  Middle Belt, 60
  Northern, 70, 156, 217
  regional inequality, 113–115
  regional voting blocs, 104, 163
  Sokoto, 63
nighttime luminosity
  as a measure, 6, 95
  as a regional GDP proxy, 108
"non-bloc" regions, 97, 106, 143
  and economic diversification, 124
  economic profile, 128
  urban, 143

O'Donnell, Guillermo, 162
oppositional zones. *See* persistent electoral blocs, oppositional zones
organizations, 142–143
Ottoman Empire, 50, 63, 82

party systems
  hegemonic, 91, 97, 99
  nationalized, 202
  one-party, 88
  regionalized, 18, 43
pastoral regions, 58, 110
patrimonialism, theory, 27
persistent electoral blocs, 44, 91. *See also* non-bloc regions
  attributes, 22
  causal mechanisms, 23, 45, 140
  causes, 92
  erosion of, 156, 236
  hierarchies, 23
  multiethnicity, 133
  and non-bloc regions, 92
  and oppositional zones, 91, 97
  political dominance, 154
  rural character, 110
  swing, 156, 163
Polanyian double movement, 238
policy, programmatic
  and spatial bias, 13, 197
policy, regionally-targeted, 36, 198
policy coalitions, 162, 229
policy issue ownership, 208
political agency, 46, 139–147, 207
political *alternance*, 164

Index

political parties, 143, 217. *See also* regional
  parties
  opposition parties, 81, 230
political representation, 132
political scale, 140, 221, 227
  and class politics, 235
  and coalition-building, 83
  and political identity, 225
population density
  and collective action, 144
  increase, 113
  as an inequality measure, 110
population density, rural, 35
Posner, Daniel, 51, 83–85, 147, 231
poverty data, mapping, 35
poverty traps, 115
precolonial polities, 63, 132, 180, 186, 188
provincial administration. *See* territorial
  administration

racial identities, 201
redistribution, 198–200
redistribution, regional. *See* Regional
  redistribution policies
redistributive politics, 202, 205
region, definition, 31
  admin. unit, 31
  functional unit, 31
regional autonomy bids, 215
regional balancing, 85
regional balancing policies, 78
regional bloc hierarchy
  stability, 115
regional capitals, 109
regional cleavages, 84, 90, 191
  persistence, 93
  as socioeconomic cleavages, 225, 226
regional economic structure
  description of, 36, 39, 45, 93
regional identities, 68, 84, 85, 146, 185, 204
  political scale, 85, 225
  versus "tribal" identity, 231
regional interests, 86
  in land policy, 211–214
  and policy, 39, 205–210
regional parties, 145, 202, 207, 230
  in Europe, 40
regional redistribution policies, 38, 78, 198,
  203–204
regionalism, 3, 192
  and electoral rules, 9
  intensity of, 196
  salient issue areas, 196

Regionalism by Design, 18, 48
regionalization, 48, 236–237
  colonial, 55
regionalization of politics, 79
remittances, 109
remote regions, 35, 37
remoteness, 143
revisionist coalition, 156
revisionist regime, 169, 194
  Uganda, 186
Rickard, Stephanie, 14, 18, 46
Rogers, Melissa, 7, 16, 18, 157, 195–196
rural development policy, 81, 205
  spatial targeting, 77
rural political mobilization, 93, 144, 181,
  208–209
  colonial era, 67

secessionist regions, 87, 132, 165
sectoral interests, 140
sectoral policy, 206–209
segregation, racial, 57
Senegal
  navétanes, 57
  Terres Neuves, 62
Sierra Leone, internal boundary
  persistence, 72
social policy, 198–200, 204
social safety nets, 35
South Africa, 200–203
  ANC, 103, 202
  apartheid, 201
  electoral rules, 103
  inequality in, 7, 200
  inequality structure, 9
  regional parties, 202
  regional voting, 100, 194
South Asia, 239
spatial inequality, 239
  and clientelism, 196
  and political coalitions, 158
specialization. *See* economic specialization
state structure, 42. *See also* district creation;
  federal systems; territorial grid
  divergent regional preferences, 217–220
  struggles over, 217
state-building, 168, 239
  and economic integration, 224
  and regionalism, 40
State-led development, 79
Structural Adjustment Programs, 38, 78, 206
structural transformation, African economies,
  14, 151, 236–238

subnational unit proliferation. *See* district creation

Sudan
regional division, 58
Nuba Mountains, 61

Tanzania, 193–194
growth policy, 115
land tenure regime, 79
mainland
inequality structure, 10
Mbeya region, 106, 128, 236
Northern, 79, 115, 193
colonial, 68
regional bloc voting, 106
regional inequality, 113–115
spatial inequality, 7
suppression of NAs, 79–80
Ujamaa, 82–83, 193, 212
uniformization, 79
Zanzibar, 106
territorial administration, 17, 50
colonial, 54, 65
and resource allocation, 77
territorial grid, 52, 220
and coalition-building, 144
colonial, 54
and electoral blocs, 129
and precolonial polities, 63, 132
territorial strategies of rule, 50
territorially-divided states, 195
trade theory, 11, 36

Uganda, 186–191, 220
Karamoja, 61
Northern, 126
NRM, 189
producer regions, 124
regional bloc voting, 103, 191
spatial inequalities, 187, 231
uneven development, 15, 50, 108, 194, 196.
See also inequality, spatial
colonial, 53
and regionalism, 30
United States, sectionalism, 40
urban bias, 15
urban bias theory, 7
urban primacy ratio, 180
urbanization, 200, 233, 244
urban-rural cleavage, 32, 176
urban-rural straddling, 233

valence issues, 206

Wahman, Michael, 94, 98,
161, 171

Zambia, 175–180
Barotseland, 63, 180
Copperbelt, 126, 175
regional bloc voting, 100
spatial inequalities, 177
Zimbabwe, 98, 194
regional voting, 103

Cambridge Studies in Comparative Politics

Adam Michael Auerbach, *Demanding Development: The Politics of Public Goods Provision in India's Urban Slums*

David Austen-Smith, Jeffry A. Frieden, Miriam A. Golden, Karl Ove Moene, and **Adam Przeworski,** eds., *Selected Works of Michael Wallerstein: The Political Economy of Inequality, Unions, and Social Democracy*

S. Erdem Aytaç and **Susan C. Stokes,** *Why Bother? Rethinking Participation in Elections and Protests*

Andy Baker, *The Market and the Masses in Latin America: Policy Reform and Consumption in Liberalizing Economies*

Laia Balcells, *Rivalry and Revenge: The Politics of Violence during Civil War*

Lisa Baldez, *Why Women Protest? Women's Movements in Chile*

Kate Baldwin, *The Paradox of Traditional Chiefs in Democratic Africa*

Stefano Bartolini, *The Political Mobilization of the European Left, 1860–1980: The Class Cleavage*

Robert H. Bates, *The Political Economy of Development: A Game Theoretic Approach*

Robert H. Bates, *When Things Fell Apart: State Failure in Late-Century Africa*

Mark Beissinger, *Nationalist Mobilization and the Collapse of the Soviet State*

Pablo Beramendi, *The Political Geography of Inequality: Regions and Redistribution*

Nancy Bermeo, ed., *Unemployment in the New Europe*

Carles Boix, *Democracy and Redistribution*

Carles Boix, *Political Order and Inequality: Their Foundations and their Consequences for Human Welfare*

Carles Boix, *Political Parties, Growth, and Equality: Conservative and Social Democratic Economic Strategies in the World Economy*

Catherine Boone, *Inequality and Political Cleavage in Africa: Regionalism by Design*

Catherine Boone, *Merchant Capital and the Roots of State Power in Senegal, 1930–1985*

Catherine Boone, *Political Topographies of the African State: Territorial Authority and Institutional Change*

Catherine Boone, *Property and Political Order in Africa: Land Rights and the Structure of Politics*

Michael Bratton and **Nicolas van de Walle,** *Democratic Experiments in Africa: Regime Transitions in Comparative Perspective*

Michael Bratton, Robert Mattes, and **E. Gyimah-Boadi,** *Public Opinion, Democracy, and Market Reform in Africa*

Valerie Bunce, *Leaving Socialism and Leaving the State: The End of Yugoslavia, the Soviet Union, and Czechoslovakia*

Daniele Caramani, *The Nationalization of Politics: The Formation of National Electorates and Party Systems in Europe*

John M. Carey, *Legislative Voting and Accountability*

Kanchan Chandra, *Why Ethnic Parties Succeed: Patronage and Ethnic Headcounts in India*

Eric C. C. Chang, Mark Andreas Kayser, Drew A. Linzer, and Ronald Rogowski, *Electoral Systems and the Balance of Consumer-Producer Power*

José Antonio Cheibub, *Presidentialism, Parliamentarism, and Democracy*

Ruth Berins Collier, *Paths toward Democracy: The Working Class and Elites in Western Europe and South America*

Daniel Corstange, *The Price of a Vote in the Middle East: Clientelism and Communal Politics in Lebanon and Yemen*

Pepper D. Culpepper, *Quiet Politics and Business Power: Corporate Control in Europe and Japan*

Sarah Zukerman Daly, *Organized Violence after Civil War: The Geography of Recruitment in Latin America*

Christian Davenport, *State Repression and the Domestic Democratic Peace*

Donatella della Porta, *Social Movements, Political Violence, and the State*

Alberto Diaz-Cayeros, *Federalism, Fiscal Authority, and Centralization in Latin America*

Alberto Diaz-Cayeros, Federico Estévez, and Beatriz Magaloni, *The Political Logic of Poverty Relief: Electoral Strategies and Social Policy in Mexico*

Jesse Driscoll, *Warlords and Coalition Politics in Post-Soviet States*

Thad Dunning, *Crude Democracy: Natural Resource Wealth and Political Regimes*

Thad Dunning et al., *Information, Accountability, and Cumulative Learning: Lessons from Metaketa I*

Gerald Easter, *Reconstructing the State: Personal Networks and Elite Identity*

Antje Ellerman, *The Comparative Politics of Immigration: Policy Choices in Germany, Canada, Switzerland, and the United States*

Margarita Estevez-Abe, *Welfare and Capitalism in Postwar Japan: Party, Bureaucracy, and Business*

Henry Farrell, *The Political Economy of Trust: Institutions, Interests, and Inter-Firm Cooperation in Italy and Germany*

Karen E. Ferree, *Framing the Race in South Africa: The Political Origins of Racial Census Elections*

M. Steven Fish, *Democracy Derailed in Russia: The Failure of Open Politics*

Lorenza B. Fontana, *Recognition Politics: Indigenous Rights and Ethnic Conflict in the Andes*

Robert F. Franzese, *Macroeconomic Policies of Developed Democracies*

Roberto Franzosi, *The Puzzle of Strikes: Class and State Strategies in Postwar Italy*

Timothy Frye, *Building States and Markets After Communism: The Perils of Polarized Democracy*

Mary E. Gallagher, *Authoritarian Legality in China: Law, Workers, and the State*

Geoffrey Garrett, *Partisan Politics in the Global Economy*

Scott Gehlbach, *Representation through Taxation: Revenue, Politics, and Development in Postcommunist States*

Edward L. Gibson, *Boundary Control: Subnational Authoritarianism in Federal Democracies*

Jane R. Gingrich, *Making Markets in the Welfare State: The Politics of Varying Market Reforms*

Miriam Golden, *Heroic Defeats: The Politics of Job Loss*

Yanilda María González, *Authoritarian Police in Democracy: Contested Security in Latin America*

Jeff Goodwin, *No Other Way Out: States and Revolutionary Movements*

Merilee Serrill Grindle, *Changing the State*

Anna Grzymala-Busse, *Rebuilding Leviathan: Party Competition and State Exploitation in Post-Communist Democracies*

Anna Grzymala-Busse, *Redeeming the Communist Past: The Regeneration of Communist Parties in East Central Europe*

Frances Hagopian, *Traditional Politics and Regime Change in Brazil*

Mark Hallerberg, Rolf Ranier Strauch, and **Jürgen von Hagen,** *Fiscal Governance in Europe*

Henry E. Hale, *The Foundations of Ethnic Politics: Separatism of States and Nations in Eurasia and the World*

Stephen E. Hanson, *Post-Imperial Democracies: Ideology and Party Formation in Third Republic France, Weimar Germany, and Post-Soviet Russia*

Mai Hassan, *Regime Threats and State Solutions: Bureaucratic Loyalty and Embeddedness in Kenya*

Michael Hechter, *Alien Rule*

Timothy Hellwig, *Globalization and Mass Politics: Retaining the Room to Maneuver*

Gretchen Helmke, *Institutions on the Edge: The Origins and Consequences of Inter-Branch Crises in Latin America*

Gretchen Helmke, *Courts Under Constraints: Judges, Generals, and Presidents in Argentina*

Yoshiko Herrera, *Imagined Economies: The Sources of Russian Regionalism*

Alisha C. Holland, *Forbearance as Redistribution: The Politics of Informal Welfare in Latin America*

J. Rogers Hollingsworth and **Robert Boyer,** eds., *Contemporary Capitalism: The Embeddedness of Institutions*

Yue Hou, *The Private Sector in Public Office: Selective Property Rights in China*

John D. Huber, *Exclusion by Elections: Inequality, Ethnic Identity, and Democracy*

John D. Huber and **Charles R. Shipan,** *Deliberate Discretion? The Institutional Foundations of Bureaucratic Autonomy*

Ellen Immergut, *Health Politics: Interests and Institutions in Western Europe*

Torben Iversen, *Capitalism, Democracy, and Welfare*

Torben Iversen, *Contested Economic Institutions*

Torben Iversen, Jonas Pontussen, and **David Soskice,** eds., *Unions, Employers, and Central Banks: Macroeconomic Coordination and Institutional Change in Social Market Economics*

Torben Iversen and **Philipp Rehm,** *Big Data and the Welfare State: How the Information Revolution Threatens Social Solidarity*

Thomas Janoski and **Alexander M. Hicks,** eds., *The Comparative Political Economy of the Welfare State*

Joseph Jupille, *Procedural Politics: Issues, Influence, and Institutional Choice in the European Union*

Karen Jusko, *Who Speaks for the Poor? Electoral Geography, Party Entry, and Representation*

Stathis Kalyvas, *The Logic of Violence in Civil War*

Stephen B. Kaplan, *Globalization and Austerity Politics in Latin America*

David C. Kang, *Crony Capitalism: Corruption and Capitalism in South Korea and the Philippines*

Junko Kato, *Regressive Taxation and the Welfare State*

Orit Kedar, *Voting for Policy, Not Parties: How Voters Compensate for Power Sharing*

Robert O. Keohane and Helen B. Milner, eds., *Internationalization and Domestic Politics*

Herbert Kitschelt, *The Transformation of European Social Democracy*

Herbert Kitschelt, Kirk A. Hawkins, Juan Pablo Luna, Guillermo Rosas, and Elizabeth J. Zechmeister, *Latin American Party Systems*

Herbert Kitschelt, Peter Lange, Gary Marks, and John D. Stephens, eds., *Continuity and Change in Contemporary Capitalism*

Herbert Kitschelt, Zdenka Mansfeldova, Radek Markowski, and Gabor Toka, *Post-Communist Party Systems*

David Knoke, Franz Urban Pappi, Jeffrey Broadbent, and Yutaka Tsujinaka, eds., *Comparing Policy Networks*

Ken Kollman, *Perils of Centralization: Lessons from Church, State, and Corporation*

Allan Kornberg and Harold D. Clarke, *Citizens and Community: Political Support in a Representative Democracy*

Amie Kreppel, *The European Parliament and the Supranational Party System*

David D. Laitin, *Language Repertoires and State Construction in Africa*

Egor Lazarev, *State-Building as Lawfare: Custom, Sharia, and State Law in Postwar Chechnya*

Fabrice E. Lehoucq and Ivan Molina, *Stuffing the Ballot Box: Fraud, Electoral Reform, and Democratization in Costa Rica*

Benjamin Lessing, *Making Peace in Drug Wars: Crackdowns and Cartels in Latin America*

Janet I. Lewis, *How Insurgency Begins: Rebel Group Formation in Uganda and Beyond*

Mark Irving Lichbach and Alan S. Zuckerman, eds., *Comparative Politics: Rationality, Culture, and Structure, 2nd edition*

Evan Lieberman, *Race and Regionalism in the Politics of Taxation in Brazil and South Africa*

Richard M. Locke, *The Promise and Limits of Private Power: Promoting Labor Standards in a Global Economy*

Julia Lynch, *Age in the Welfare State: The Origins of Social Spending on Pensioners, Workers, and Children*

Pauline Jones Luong, *Institutional Change and Political Continuity in Post-Soviet Central Asia*

Pauline Jones Luong and Erika Weinthal, *Oil is Not a Curse: Ownership Structure and Institutions in Soviet Successor States*

Doug McAdam, John McCarthy, and Mayer Zald, eds., *Comparative Perspectives on Social Movements*

Gwyneth H. McClendon and Rachel Beatty Riedl, *From Pews to Politics in Africa: Religious Sermons and Political Behavior*

Lauren M. MacLean, *Informal Institutions and Citizenship in Rural Africa: Risk and Reciprocity in Ghana and Côte d'Ivoire*

Beatriz Magaloni, *Voting for Autocracy: Hegemonic Party Survival and its Demise in Mexico*

James Mahoney, *Colonialism and Postcolonial Development: Spanish America in Comparative Perspective*

James Mahoney and **Dietrich Rueschemeyer,** eds., *Historical Analysis and the Social Sciences*

Scott Mainwaring and **Matthew Soberg Shugart,** eds., *Presidentialism and Democracy in Latin America*

Melanie Manion, *Information for Autocrats: Representation in Chinese Local Congresses*

Scott de Marchi and **Michael Laver,** *The Governance Cycle in Parliamentary Democracies: A Computational Social Science Approach*

Isabela Mares, *From Open Secrets to Secret Voting: Democratic Electoral Reforms and Voter Autonomy*

Isabela Mares, *The Politics of Social Risk: Business and Welfare State Development*

Isabela Mares, *Taxation, Wage Bargaining, and Unemployment*

Cathie Jo Martin and **Duane Swank,** *The Political Construction of Business Interests: Coordination, Growth, and Equality*

Anthony W. Marx, *Making Race, Making Nations: A Comparison of South Africa, the United States, and Brazil*

Daniel C. Mattingly, *The Art of Political Control in China*

Kevin Mazur, *Revolution in Syria: Identity, Networks, and Repression*

Bonnie M. Meguid, *Party Competition between Unequals: Strategies and Electoral Fortunes in Western Europe*

Joel S. Migdal, *State in Society: Studying How States and Societies Constitute One Another*

Joel S. Migdal, Atul Kohli, and **Vivienne Shue,** eds., *State Power and Social Forces: Domination and Transformation in the Third World*

Eduardo Moncada, *Resisting Extortion: Victims, Criminals and States in Latin America*

Scott Morgenstern and **Benito Nacif,** eds., *Legislative Politics in Latin America*

Kevin M. Morrison, *Nontaxation and Representation: The Fiscal Foundations of Political Stability*

Layna Mosley, *Global Capital and National Governments*

Layna Mosley, *Labor Rights and Multinational Production*

Wolfgang C. Müller and **Kaare Strøm,** *Policy, Office, or Votes?*

Maria Victoria Murillo, *Political Competition, Partisanship, and Policy Making in Latin American Public Utilities*

Maria Victoria Murillo, *Labor Unions, Partisan Coalitions, and Market Reforms in Latin America*

Monika Nalepa, *Skeletons in the Closet: Transitional Justice in Post-Communist Europe*

Noah L. Nathan, *Electoral Politics and Africa's Urban Transition: Class and Ethnicity in Ghana*

Ton Notermans, *Money, Markets, and the State: Social Democratic Economic Policies since 1918*

Simeon Nichter, *Votes for Survival: Relational Clientelism in Latin America*

Richard A. Nielsen, *Deadly Clerics: Blocked Ambition and the Paths to Jihad*

Aníbal Pérez-Liñán, *Presidential Impeachment and the New Political Instability in Latin America*

Roger D. Petersen, *Understanding Ethnic Violence: Fear, Hatred, and Resentment in Twentieth-Century Eastern Europe*

Roger D. Petersen, *Western Intervention in the Balkans: The Strategic Use of Emotion in Conflict*

Simona Piattoni, ed., *Clientelism, Interests, and Democratic Representation*

Paul Pierson, *Dismantling the Welfare State? Reagan, Thatcher, and the Politics of Retrenchment*

Marino Regini, *Uncertain Boundaries: The Social and Political Construction of European Economies*

Philipp Rehm, *Risk Inequality and Welfare States: Social Policy Preferences, Development, and Dynamics*

Kenneth M. Roberts, *Changing Course in Latin America: Party Systems in the Neoliberal Era*

Marc Howard Ross, *Cultural Contestation in Ethnic Conflict*

David Rueda and **Daniel Stegmueller,** *Who Wants What? Redistribution Preferences in Comparative Perspective*

Ignacio Sánchez-Cuenca, *The Historical Roots of Political Violence: Revolutionary Terrorism in Affluent Countries*

Ben Ross Schneider, *Hierarchical Capitalism in Latin America: Business, Labor, and the Challenges of Equitable Development*

Roger Schoenman, *Networks and Institutions in Europe's Emerging Markets*

Lyle Scruggs, *Sustaining Abundance: Environmental Performance in Industrial Democracies*

Jefferey M. Sellers, *Governing from Below: Urban Regions and the Global Economy*

Yossi Shain and **Juan Linz,** eds., *Interim Governments and Democratic Transitions*

Victor C. Shih, *Coalitions of the Weak: Elite Politics in China from Mao's Stratagem to the Rise of Xi*

Beverly Silver, *Forces of Labor: Workers' Movements and Globalization since 1870*

Prerna Singh, *How Solidarity Works for Welfare: Subnationalism and Social Development in India*

Theda Skocpol, *Social Revolutions in the Modern World*

Dan Slater, *Ordering Power: Contentious Politics and Authoritarian Leviathans in Southeast Asia*

Austin Smith et al, *Selected Works of Michael Wallerstein*

Regina Smyth, *Candidate Strategies and Electoral Competition in the Russian Federation: Democracy without Foundation*

Richard Snyder, *Politics after Neoliberalism: Reregulation in Mexico*

David Stark and **László Bruszt,** *Postsocialist Pathways: Transforming Politics and Property in East Central Europe*

Sven Steinmo, *The Evolution of Modern States: Sweden, Japan, and the United States*

Sven Steinmo, Kathleen Thelen, and **Frank Longstreth,** eds., *Structuring Politics: Historical Institutionalism in Comparative Analysis*

Susan C. Stokes, *Mandates and Democracy: Neoliberalism by Surprise in Latin America*

Susan C. Stokes, ed., *Public Support for Market Reforms in New Democracies*

Susan C. Stokes, Thad Dunning, Marcelo Nazareno, and **Valeria Brusco,** *Brokers, Voters, and Clientelism: The Puzzle of Distributive Politics*

Milan W. Svolik, *The Politics of Authoritarian Rule*

Duane Swank, *Global Capital, Political Institutions, and Policy Change in Developed Welfare States*

David Szakonyi *Politics for Profit: Business, Elections, and Policymaking in Russia*

Sidney Tarrow, *Power in Movement: Social Movements and Contentious Politics*

Sidney Tarrow, *Power in Movement: Social Movements and Contentious Politics, Revised and Updated Third Edition*

Sidney Tarrow, *Power in Movement: Social Movements and Contentious Politics, Revised and Updated Fourth Edition*

Tariq Thachil, *Elite Parties, Poor Voters: How Social Services Win Votes in India*

Kathleen Thelen, *How Institutions Evolve: The Political Economy of Skills in Germany, Britain, the United States, and Japan*

Kathleen Thelen, *Varieties of Liberalization and the New Politics of Social Solidarity*

Charles Tilly, *Trust and Rule*

Daniel Treisman, *The Architecture of Government: Rethinking Political Decentralization*

Guillermo Trejo, *Popular Movements in Autocracies: Religion, Repression, and Indigenous Collective Action in Mexico*

Guillermo Trejo and Sandra Ley, *Votes, Drugs, and Violence: The Political Logic of Criminal Wars in Mexico*

Rory Truex, *Making Autocracy Work: Representation and Responsiveness in Modern China*

Lily L. Tsai, *Accountability without Democracy: How Solidary Groups Provide Public Goods in Rural China*

Lily L. Tsai, *When People Want Punishment: Retributive Justice and the Puzzle of Authoritarian Popularity*

Joshua Tucker, *Regional Economic Voting: Russia, Poland, Hungary, Slovakia and the Czech Republic, 1990–1999*

Ashutosh Varshney, *Democracy, Development, and the Countryside*

Yuhua Wang, *Tying the Autocrat's Hand: The Rise of the Rule of Law in China*

Jeremy M. Weinstein, *Inside Rebellion: The Politics of Insurgent Violence*

Andreas Wiedemann, *Indebted Societies: Credit and Welfare in Rich Democracies*

Martha Wilfahrt, *Precolonial Legacies in Postcolonial Politics: Representation and Redistribution in Decentralized West Africa*

Stephen I. Wilkinson, *Votes and Violence: Electoral Competition and Ethnic Riots in India*

Andreas Wimmer, *Waves of War: Nationalism, State Formation, and Ethnic Exclusion in the Modern World*

Jason Wittenberg, *Crucibles of Political Loyalty: Church Institutions and Electoral Continuity in Hungary*

Elisabeth J. Wood, *Forging Democracy from Below: Insurgent Transitions in South Africa and El Salvador*

Elisabeth J. Wood, *Insurgent Collective Action and Civil War in El Salvador*

Deborah J. Yashar, *Homicidal Ecologies: Illicit Economies and Complicit States in Latin America*

Daniel Ziblatt, *Conservative Parties and the Birth of Democracy*

Printed in the United States
by Baker & Taylor Publisher Services